Perspectives on Ethnicity

World Anthropology

General Editor

SOL TAX

Patrons

CLAUDE LÉVI-STRAUSS
MARGARET MEAD
LAILA SHUKRY EL HAMAMSY
M. N. SRINIVAS

MOUTON PUBLISHERS · THE HAGUE · PARIS

Perspectives on Ethnicity

Editors

REGINA E. HOLLOMAN
SERGHEI A. ARUTIUNOV

MOUTON PUBLISHERS · THE HAGUE · PARIS

General Editor's Preface

The usual translation of anthropology as "the study of man" refers to the genus itself. But at least since the Middle Paleolithic *Homo* has probably been subdivided into self-conscious groups, and *Homo sapiens* from its beginning has probably been characterized by social groups each of which named itself at least as "we." The term ethnology took account not only of anthropologically recognized "races," but also of national, linguistic, and cultural subdivisions of all kinds, including these smallest self-conscious communities. "Populations" and "peoples" are terms often used for any or all of them. In recent years Soviet anthropologists have adopted technical terms (e.g. *ethnoses, ethnogenesis*) systematically to study their evolution and history as well as the processes of boundary maintenance as culturally distinct peoples and communities are integrated into modern politico-economic structures. This book thus breaks boundaries of anthropological ethnoses, embodying a variety of perspectives on ethnicity, resulting from a Congress organized precisely to encourage the meeting of differences.

Like most contemporary sciences, anthropology is a product of the European tradition. Some argue that it is a product of colonialism, with one small and self-interested part of the species dominating the study of the whole. If we are to understand the species, our science needs substantial input from scholars who represent a variety of the world's cultures. It was a deliberate purpose of the IXth International Congress of Anthropological and Ethnological Sciences to provide impetus in this direction. The *World Anthropology* volumes, therefore, offer a first glimpse of a human science in which members from all societies have played an active role. Each of the books is designed to be self-contained; each is an attempt to update its particular sector of scientific knowledge and is written by specialists from all parts of the world. Each volume should be read and reviewed individually as a separate volume on its own given subject. The set as a whole will indicate what changes are in store for anthropology as scholars from the developing countries join in studying the species of which we are all a part.

The IXth Congress was planned from the beginning not only to include as many of the scholars from every part of the world as possible, but also with a view toward the eventual publication of the papers in high-quality volumes. At previous Congresses scholars were invited to bring papers which were then read out loud. They were necessarily limited in length; many were only summarized; there was little time for discussion; and the sparse discussion could only be in one language. The IXth Congress was an experiment aimed at changing this. Papers were written with the intention of exchanging them before the Congress, particularly in extensive pre-Congress sessions; they were not intended to be read aloud at the Congress, that time being devoted to discussions — discussions which were simultaneously and professionally translated into five languages. The method for eliciting the papers was structured to make as representative a sample as was allowable when scholarly creativity — hence self-selection — was critically important. Scholars were asked both to propose papers of their own and to suggest topics for sessions of the Congress which they might edit into volumes. All were then informed of the suggestions and encouraged to rethink their own papers and the topics. The process, therefore, was a continuous one of feedback and exchange and it has continued to be so even after the Congress. The some two thousand papers comprising *World Anthropology* certainly then offer a substantial sample of world anthropology. It has been said that anthropology is at a turning point; if this is so, these volumes will be the historical direction-markers.

As might have been foreseen in the first post-colonial generation, the large majority of the Congress papers (82 percent) are the work of scholars identified with the industrialized world which fathered our traditional discipline and the institution of the Congress itself: Eastern Europe (15 percent); Western Europe (16 percent); North America (47 percent); Japan, South Africa, Australia, and New Zealand (4 percent). Only 18 percent of the papers are from developing areas: Africa (4 percent); Asia-Oceania (9 percent); Latin America (5 percent). Aside from the substantial representation from the USSR and the nations of Eastern Europe, a significant difference between this corpus of written material and that of other Congresses is the addition of the large proportion of contributions from Africa, Asia, and Latin America. "Only 18 percent" is two to four times as great a proportion as that of other Congresses; moreover, 18 percent of 2,000 papers is

360 papers, 10 times the number of "Third World" papers presented at previous Congresses. In fact, these 360 papers are more than the total of *all* papers published after the last International Congress of Anthropological and Ethnological Sciences which was held in the United States (Philadelphia, 1956).

The significance of the increase is not simply quantitative. The input of scholars from areas which have until recently been no more than subject matter for anthropology represents both feedback and also long-awaited theoretical contributions from the perspectives of very different cultural, social, and historical traditions. Many who attended the IXth Congress were convinced that anthropology would not be the same in the future. The fact that the next Congress (India, 1978) will be our first in the "Third World" may be symbolic of the change. Meanwhile, sober consideration of the present set of books will show how much, and just where and how, our discipline is being revolutionized.

This series on *World Anthropology* brings to us many specialized volumes on ethnicity and on interfaces, migrations, and processes of urbanization of ethnic groups; and on more general problems of the origins, characteristics, and continental distributions of populations and cultures.

Chicago, Illinois   SOL TAX
July 26, 1978

Table of Contents

SECTION ONE

Theoretical Issues in the Study of Ethnicity

The Study of Ethnicity: An Overview

REGINA E. HOLLOMAN

Anthropology is a field science. The result of intimate contact with life-in-progress is that our work very quickly reflects the impact on people of large-scale political, economic, and ideational change. It is no accident that many of the most interesting papers presented to the IXth International Congress dealt with interethnic relations and ethnic identification. The major social-historical facts of our time — the spread of urbanism, accelerated industrial development and related resource shortages, detribalization and nationbuilding, migration and other demographic shifts — all have disrupted old balances between groups and have brought formerly separate worlds of thought into contact and conflict. Much of the response to change has been organized along ethnic lines. There is every reason to believe that it has always been so. Indeed, Fredrick Barth (1969) has defined ethnicity as "the social organization of cultural difference.' An understanding of ethnic processes is basic to an understanding of human history.

One of the most influential books published in the United States in this generation was Thomas Kuhn's *The structure of scientific revolutions* (1962). Kuhn's book made researchers acutely aware of the degree to which the direction and nature of their work is governed by the theoretical constructs they have adopted. The influence of contrasting paradigmatic assumptions was immediately apparent in the Congress papers on ethnicity. The papers from the Soviet Union and Eastern Europe are written from a theoretical perspective (*ethnos* theory) which will be unfamiliar to scholars who do not follow the Soviet and Eastern European journals. At the same time, the Soviet Union is itself one of the most important examples of multiethnic states. From these circumstances grew a major purpose of this book: the decision to make available in English a selected group of papers dealing with ethnos theory and fieldwork based upon it and to provide the necessary background information to assure its diffusion. Arutiunov (cochairman of the session and coeditor of this volume) and Bromley (Director of the Institute of Ethnography of the USSR) have prepared an introductory article on the publications and fieldwork program of the Institute. Bromley has also contributed a major article on ethnic community types. The papers of Kozlov, Maretin, Porshnev, and others give additional insight into the Soviet approach.

Soviet ethnos theory fits within a Marxist framework. Ethnic processes are viewed within an evolutionary-historical framework in which the determinants are political-economic. Hence, the concern with questions of the relationship between particularistic ethnic process and more general processes governing societal evolution in a dialectical sense. This perspective directs research priority to the establishment of types and stages. Field methods are adapted to the identification of units and the assessment of their stage of development in terms of the model. The long-range outcome of the interplay of processes is predicted by the model: ethnicity as an organizing factor is subject to evolutionary laws and is characteristic of stages up to and including the formation of national units (the nation being the most complex ethnos, in the broad sense).

Unlike the situation with ethnos theory, there is no single theoretical model underlying the other papers, but the influence of several seminal thinkers is clear. (Typically, these are *not* strictly theories of ethnicity; they are more general theories of society which have been applied to problems of ethnicity.) The earliest of these is Robert Redfield, whose work on rural-urban contacts and acculturation is still influential. Furnivall's (1944) and M. G. Smith's work on structural and cultural pluralism continue to be used and discussed, particularly *The plural society in the British West Indies* (Smith 1965). Also important are Lewis Coser's *The functions of social conflict* (1956), which views intergroup conflict as the major fomentor of positive social change; and Ralf Dahrendorf's *Class and class conflict in industrial society* (1959) in the same tradition. George Beckford's *Persistent poverty: underdevelopment in plantation economies of the Third World* (1972) and Eric Wolf's *Peasants* (1966) are two sources of Marxist-derived theory which are used by anthropologists interested in interethnic conflict. The most recent attempt at a comprehensive treatment of ethnicity as a principle of social organization is Fredrik Barth's introductory essay in *Ethnic groups and boundaries: the social organization of culture difference* (1969). As the subtitle implies, Barth regards ethnicity as a general social status which, like class, age, and sex can be used to organize interaction in many contexts. In that essay Barth raised all or most of the issues dealt with in these papers. (For specific uses of Barth see the paper by Tweddell and the *World Anthro-*

pology volume *Ethnicity and resource competition in plural societies*, edited by Leo Despres.)

Although differences in paradigmatic assumptions account for much of the contrast among the papers, influences of sociopolitical realities are also important. The USSR is committed simultaneously to national integration and encouragement of the development of its major ethnic groups (nationalities). Socioeconomic transformations are, at least in theory, subjects for planning. Interethnic conflict appears to be structurally muted. Anthropological fieldwork is government-funded, and is coordinated for the nation as a whole through a central scientific institute. All this contrasts with the situation in most other parts of the world. Third World nations such as Nigeria and India present examples of minimally controlled interethnic conflict as a major aspect of the nationbuilding process. The push for equal participation by subgroups which are relatively powerless politically and economically is a fact of social life in the United States and most of Latin America. In many parts of the world such groups have discovered that ethnic identity is a powerful rallying symbol and boundary marker. Dominant groups have often applied ethnic labels to subgroups in a manner which cannot be supported on the basis of cultural history, but which has a social-psychological reality. This process of labeling a "they" on the basis of presumed ethnic traits has often been a factor in the formation of a new "we." Examples in the United States are the politico-social movements which stress black ethnicity and pan-Indian ethnicity. However, the "new ethnic" phenomenon is not limited to the United States.

During the discussions at the Congress the Soviet delegates noted what they considered a tendency on the part of Western colleagues to "mix" the concepts of ethnicity, race, and minority group. On the other hand, some Western researchers contended that ethnos theory was not suited to the treatment of many of the problems in which they were interested. It became apparent that differences in the working situations of the two groups have affected the development of theory.

Because the volume brings the ethnos paradigm into juxtaposition with models used by anthropologists from other culture areas, it is appropriate that the metatheoretical paper of Maruyama has been placed as a keynote to the other papers. Maruyama contends that most work done by researchers trained in the Western tradition (in this sense, including the Soviets) is governed by the assumption that processes are either linear or stochastic. The more recent systems assumptions of mutually interactive and deviation amplifying processes have not yet been incorporated into fieldwork.

The remaining papers deal with ethnic process in many different societies and circumstances. Although the actual situations vary considerably, the analyses focus on a limited range of problems:

1. the disintegration, assimilation, and consolidation of ethnic groups;
2. the emergence of "new ethnics";
3. niching and symbiosis among ethnic groups;
4. causes and forms of interethnic conflict;
5. ethnic identity and identity change;
6. interethnic marriage;
7. the integration of multiethnic nation states;
8. the relationship between social class and ethnic status;
9. the historical and systemic relationships between ethnic processes and societal evolution.

The papers are also important as ethnographic contributions. This is especially true of Gandonu's long and detailed paper which presents a survey and mapping of 250 ethnic groups in Nigeria. It will certainly be a basis for discussion and debate among Nigerianists for many years.

Several papers deal with ethnic niching. Andrásfalvy describes symbiosis between Germans and Hungarians in rural Hungary. In that case prestige-oriented Hungarians who practiced equal-share inheritance provided a market for the crafts produced by the younger brothers of market-oriented German farmers, who transmitted their land under primogeniture. Chow describes the establishment and then the breakdown of a specialized niche among the Chinese population of Canada as a result of changes in the social characteristics of the Chinese immigrant population. Tweddell describes the relationship betwen Tuli and Chinese within a castelike structure, and the functions of Tuli identity under those circumstances. Salovesh examines the impact on the interethnic situation of the actual behavior of two cultural brokers in Mexico. Zenner presents data on Jewish communities in several places and times and suggests that we have been too rigid in denying ethnic group status to these dispersed populations.

The paper of Berdichewsky complements the papers by Maretin and Kulichenko which are concerned with general relationships between cultural and social processes, in that it is a case study of the relationship between ethnic and class consciousness among the Mapuche of Chile.

Several of the Soviet papers deal with intermarriage and/or changes in family structure in the USSR. Bondarchik and Sobolenko relate reduced family size in Belorussia to urbanization, increased mobility, and "reformation of the villages along socialist lines." Naulko compares 1920 baseline data for the Ukrainian Republic with 1969 field data, finding a significant decline in uninational marriages among Ukrainians, Russians, and Jews over the period. Busygin and Zorin, and Gantskaja and Terent'eva make interesting use of the fact that when a Soviet citizen becomes sixteen he must declare his nationality and that of his parents in obtaining a domestic passport. Using these data they analyze rates of ethnic intermarriage and the relationship between ethnicity of parents and the child's self-identification. Roberts' data on Negro-white intermarriage in Chicago complements the Soviet cases in an interesting manner.

A poignant example of what can happen when a way of life is interrupted without the provision of new alternatives is provided by Siverts' study of the Jívaro. The suppression of headhunting has simultaneously affected the process of alliance formation and removed the basis for validation of adult male status. The impact on group élan is similar to that caused by the suppression of warfare among Plains Indians in the United States. A highly contrastive situation is provided by Arens. The Waswahili are "new ethnics." In this case, they are individuals from many tribal backgrounds who have moved into a new locality and who are, in fact, participating in the formation of a national culture in Tanzania. The local level process seen here was strongly affected by shifts in the valuation placed on this new ethnicity when the British were replaced by native national administration.

The papers of Apte and Gupta deal with two different cases of the relationship between language, social class, and ethnicity in India. Apte describes the acculturation in Tamilnadu of Marathi-speaking migrants from two castes. He found that the Marathi-speaking Brahmans tended to share elite status with the local Brahmans and to identify as a common class despite language differences. Marathi-speaking tailors, on the other hand, had no directly equivalent *varṇa* group in Tamilnadu and continued to identify in terms of religious ties to their place of origin. Despite shared language, the interactional barrier between the two Marathi-speaking caste groups in Tamilnadu remained sharp.

The channeling effect of Indian national language policy is clearly reflected in Gupta's paper concerning the extreme complexity of language use in Rajasthan. He describes a transitional situation involving a struggle to establish the demotic as the official language of the state. Although Hindi was the official language of schools, courts, and other institutions in the area where Rajasthani was demotic, English (the "temporary" language) was more widely used. Aspirations and discontents of the mass of the Rajasthani population were expressed in attempts to raise the official status of their language. These aspirations were not, however, shared by the local elite which had been educated in Hindi and had access to jobs and other prerequisites open to those with a command of Hindi. It is interesting to juxtapose Gurvich's data on consolidation of tribal groups in Siberia with the Indian data. There, several oral languages were given a written form in the years following the 1918 revolution, for example, Yakut in 1922 and Tuvinian in 1930. Language, together with consolidation of political administration and the setting up of large-scale collective farms for cattlebreeding have all been factors in the consolidation of closely related but isolated tribal units into relatively cohesive Yakut and Tuvinian ethnic regions. Gurvich does not mention the degree to which bilingualism in Russia has kept pace with this development but presumably the two processes — regional ethnic consolidation and national integration — are proceeding in tandem.

It was suggested earlier that the difference between the major positions represented here are partly traceable to differences in the historical situations which form the major portion of the data for each group of theorists. This is not to downplay the very real differences between ethnos theory and the other positions represented here, but simply to suggest that they focus on somewhat different problems. Ethnic politics and especially the formation of "new ethnic" groups in relation to the mobilization of people for political participation have set problems of description and analysis which are clearly reflected in Western ethnic theory. The tight definitions of ethnos theory often seem not to apply in these situations. Yet, since the rhetoric of ethnicity is involved, and at least some ethnic processes are set in motion over time, most Western theorists want to treat such cases within the framework of ethnic studies. However, it is clear that this has resulted in a neglect of the study of the cultural processes themselves. For example, "black ethnicity" has been an aspect of life in the United States for a generation. Is it, today, simply an ideology, or are important ethnic (in the Soviet sense) processes observable? The answer is not obvious. On the other hand, Maretin's paper, by stressing that many ethnic situations are transitional, and that ethnic processes are often responsive to processes of state formation, national level politics, and the position of the state with regard to ethnic groups, calls attention to the need for a clearer specification of how ethnos theory articulates with (especially) sociological theory. By presenting these papers in a single volume we hope to impact theoretical and fieldwork in both traditions.

REFERENCES

BARTH, FREDRIK
  1969   *Ethnic groups and boundaries: the social organization of culture differ-ence.* Boston: Little, Brown.
BECKFORD, GEORGE
  1972   *Persistent poverty: underdevelopment in plantation economies of the Third World.* New York: Oxford University Press.
COSER, LEWIS
  1956   *The functions of social conflict.* Glencoe, Ill.: The Free Press.
DAHRENDORF, RALF
  1959   *Class and class conflict in industrial society.* Standford, Ca.: Stanford University Press.

DESPRES, LEO A., *editor*
  1975 *Ethnicity and resource competition in plural societies.* World Anthropology. The Hague: Mouton.
FURNIVALL, JOHN
  1944 *Netherlands India: a study of plural economy.* Cambridge: Cambridge University Press.
KUHN, THOMAS
  1962 *The structure of scientific revolutions.* Chicago: University of Chicago Press.
REDFIELD, ROBERT
  1965 *The primitive world and its transformations.* Ithaca, N.Y.: Cornell University Press.
SMITH, MICHAEL
  1965 *The plural society in the British West Indies.* Berkeley: University of California Press.
WOLF, ERIC
  1966 *Peasants.* Englewood Cliffs: Prentice-Hall.

Problems of Ethnicity in Soviet Ethnographic Studies

S. A. ARUTIUNOV and YU. V. BROMLEY

The very word, ethnography, implies the focus of its studies — the *ethnos*. In Soviet science we understand the following by this term: stable human communities, tied together by unity of territory and history of their formation, and by a common language and culture — all of which are manifested in a certain self-consciousness or self-identification based on ethnicity.

The concept of ethnic entity is hierarchic. For example, Ukrainians as a nation are an ethnic entity, as are their subdivision, the *Gutsuls*, and their secondary subdivisions, e.g., *Lemki* and *Boiki*. On the other hand, a certain ethnic unity is constituted by the totality of Slavonic peoples. It is characteristic of Soviet anthropology that it pays equal attention to the study of small ethnic entities and subdivisions and to the largest ethnic formations, including nations with many millions in population. The processes of their integration or differentiation, of cultural rapproachment and interaction, and the evolution of their characteristic variables constitute the general complex of problems in the study of ethnic processes.

Another characteristic of work in the Soviet Union is our historical approach to the phenomenon of ethnos, especially the specification of those forms which are characteristic for specific historical socioeconomic formations. These categories include the tribe or group of related tribes in the primitive-communal era, nationality (*narodnost*) in pre-capitalist social formations, and nation (*natsia*) in the era of developed capitalism and later socialism. Almost all of our scholars agree that such categories should be considered in an analysis, although, obviously, there are certain differences of opinion in the exact understanding and application of each.

This category system provides the framework for the dynamic/historical study of ethnic process. Various subfields of ethnology are devoted to the study of the several aspects of culture and of regularities in the existence and development of ethnic entities, such as material culture (dwelling, costume, food, working tools); spiritual culture (oral art, ornament, rituals and customs, customary law, value systems) and kinship systems. But all these objects of study exist not as a final aim but are subordinated to the master task of providing a general, dynamic picture of an ethnos in its historical development.

Therefore, elaboration of the theory of ethnic entities has fundamental significance for all areas of ethnography. One of the main tasks of such studies is a reconstruction of *ethnogenesis*, i.e., of the components that constituted a certain ethnos, their balance and mode of integration, the subsequent ethnic history of the given unit, inclusion into it of new groups, transformation of its culture, etc., and finally of modern ethnic process — mutual relations of this entity with others, the ways and perspectives of its modern development.

These are the main directions taken by basic studies of the Institute of Ethnography, Academy of Sciences of the USSR, and the numerous regional ethnographic institutions throughout the USSR. Many of these studies have been brought together in the fundamental series, *Peoples of the world*, in thirteen volumes, where one may find a bibliography of studies on various peoples. For a bibliography on theoretical works, see the footnotes in *Ethnos and ethnography* by Yu. V. Bromley. The Institute of Ethnography generates studies based on fieldwork combined with other sources (written, museum, etc.) on practically every people of the USSR and many abroad, with the final aim of possibly embracing the whole population of the globe. Many general monographs are already available for various ethnoses.

Contrary to the formerly widespread concept that ethnography should deal mainly with primitive, nonliterate ethnoses and should embrace all aspects of the life of such peoples, modern ethnography studies any and all ethnoses, including the most highly developed. These latter studies are focused mainly on those sides of life which function in ethnic integration (i.e., in maintaining the stability of the ethnos) and of ethnic differentiation (i.e., delimitation of one ethnos from others). But the tasks of such studies are not just to define the peculiar aspects of life in a given ethnos, but also the common aspects that are postulated by its inclusion in a given socioeconomic formation, cultural-economic type, historico-cultural, or historico-ethnographic province.

As long as mankind exists in numerous ethnoses, the science of ethnography will exist as a discipline to study the historical aspects of that ethnicity and its living reality. There is a certain shift in our studies which corresponds to a shift in the nature of ethnos-specific traits from the area of material culture and production to that of spiritual life, value orientations and self-consciousness. At the same time the recording of vanishing ethnos-specific cultural traits is an urgent task. To this end a large amount of fieldwork is devoted, with subsequent publication of historico-ethnographic atlases. We have already published atlases on the peoples of Siberia and on Russians in the European part of the USSR. Nearly completed are atlases for the Baltic Sea area, Belorussia, Ukraine, and Moldavia. Being planned are first issues on the Caucasus, Middle Asia, and Kasakhstan.

Recent studies and debates on problems in ethnic theory and praxis are regularly published in the bi-monthly *Sovetskaya ethnographia*, the annual *Rassy i Narody*, and other periodicals. Fieldwork is carried on every year by a large number of expeditions in almost every region of the USSR. The main method of study remains the traditional one of direct observation and interviewing of informants, preceded by a thorough examination of administrative documentation and archival data for the locality; demographic data; consideration of family-kin structure; and so on. Paralleling this, ethnosociological studies are encouraged with broad use of mass questionnaire data to clarify ethnic stereotypes and value orientations, with subsequent data processing by computer.

In the contemporary era, when social, scientific, and technological progress is accompanied by an unprecedented widening of ties and contact between various peoples, the study of ethnic entities and processes has acquired an especially important role. Contacts between people on a basis of equality demand a deeper study of the cultural traits of all peoples. This fact urges ethnographers to play a more important part in strengthening mutual trust and understanding among ethnoses, in the definition of possibilities and perspectives on their cultural cooperation, and mutual enrichment for the benefit of all mankind.

On the Typology of Ethnic Communities

YU. V. BROMLEY

Among the multitude of human unions, the community termed "narod" in Russian, "das Volk" in German, "a people" in English is of great importance for the ethnographers-ethnologists. It is this community that is ultimately the principal object of their investigations. However, the common, everyday name of such a community is polysemantic in all European languages.[1] In view of this fact, it is quite justifiable to introduce in science the term "ethnos" to denote the object of ethnographic-ethnological investigations. In addition, use of this term in such a context fully accords with the name of these branches of science. The prospects of international unification of the basic nomenclature in the field of ethnographic-ethnological investigations will become more tangible with the introduction of the term "ethnos," another weighty argument in its favor. It is to be hoped that such a unification of terminology may facilitate the process of bringing the notions closer together with the subject of investigations of this kind.

It is true that until now there has been insufficient unanimity in interpreting both the term "ethnos" and its basic analogues — "ethnic community" and "ethnie." Existing interpretations of these terms can generally be divided into two basic groups. On the one hand is the notion that "ethnos" is a comparatively small community, with a predominantly archaic character (see Naroll 1964; Barth 1969). On the other hand, this term is understood to be an equivalent of the word "a people," including not only those that are "small" but also those with millions of members, and embracing not only backward peoples but also those in highly developed states (see for example, Mühlmann 1964).

---

[1] For instance, in Russian the word *narod* often means the "working masses," or simply "a group of people." In German *das Volk* is used to denote not only "people" but also "the common people", this is also true of English (people) French (*peuple*), Spanish (*pueblo*).

From the very beginning of Russian ethnography the term "ethnos" denoted "people" (Mogilianskiĭ 1909). This interpretation survives in Soviet ethnography, where it has become especially widespread in the last few decades (Kushner 1949, 1951; Tokarev 1964; Kozlov 1969; Bromley 1971; Chistov 1972). Recently, the term "ethnos" has become more frequently used in Western ethnological literature, due in part to certain works by the Russian ethnographer, Shirokogorov (1922, 1923, 1937; see also Mühlmann 1964:58).

In our view, there are ample grounds for using the term "ethnos" to define the object of ethnographic-ethnological investigations as an equivalent of the word "a people" in its broad meaning, even moreso because it would hardly be correct to limit the scope of this object "only" to small backward communities. They are not only the Hopi, the Aztecs, the Aimara, and other comparatively small communities, but also such large ethnoses — the Russians, the English, the Japanese, the French — which are formed of many millions. Using the word "a people" as a general equivalent in interpreting "ethnos" does not completely predetermine its content. In particular, this has been vividly revealed in the distinctions of its definitions in Soviet ethnographic literature in recent years. Proceeding from the general notion that ethnos is a people, some authors mention language and culture as the main distinctions of ethnos (Kushner 1951); others add to this territory and ethnic self-identification (Cheboksarov 1967); others include common origin and state affiliation (Tokarev 1964); still others believe that ethnos is a biological unit — population (Gumilev 1967).

In defining these common characteristic features of ethnoses-peoples which distinguish them from other human communities it seems necessary, above all, to take into account that they are communities that emerge as a result of the natural-historical process and not as a result of the given peoples' will. At the same time, it should be borne in mind that ethnoses are complex formations; each possesses not only a certain internal unity but also specific features that distinguish it from all other formations of the same type. A special role in this is played by self-identification among ethnos members both through mutual identification and also by general distinctiveness as a whole from other similar communities with a "we" — "they" antithesis. And when, for instance, we speak about the French ethnos-people, it always implies that it possesses definite features that distinguish it from all other peoples, and that this distinction is registered through everyday self-consciousness. True, distinctions between ethnoses sometimes can be viewed as a matter of secondary importance when the essense of ethnic communities is investigated. However, it should not be forgotten that ethnic community without conscious delimitation from other such communities is a fiction.

At the same time, it would be an oversimplification to reduce the essence of ethnos to the self-identification of its representatives. Behind this self-identification are real distinctions which express definite inner integrity. The characteristic of stability of ethnos should be taken into consideration, first and foremost, because ethnoses-peoples themselves, as a rule, have a continued existence over many centuries.

But what are the concrete spheres of objective existence of these characteristics?

It may seem at first sight that above all these are predominantly the external distinctions of people's physical type, that is racial distinctions. In reality, however, racial distinctions do not as a rule play any essential ethno-distinctive role. This can be explained not so much by the fact that there are no "pure," racially unmixed people as by the absence of clearcut anthropological boundaries between contiguous peoples-ethnoses belonging to one of the major races. It is because of this that the attempts in everyday life to determine people's ethnic identity solely on the basis of the external physical anthropological distinctions are usually of a rather approximate character. This can also explain the fact that cases in which racial distinctions are the main ethnic determinant are extremely rare. These cases are related predominantly to ethnoses whose neighbors belong to other major or small races.

Among distinctive features inherent in people, group specific features of culture in the broadest sense, i.e., when it is regarded as the sum total of specifically human activity and its results, are of a far greater importance for ethnic delimitation than physical appearance. It is in this sphere of culture interpreted in this way that all the basic distinctive features of ethnoses-peoples are concentrated. It is not accidental that in daily practice, when they are differentiated, special mention is made, as a rule, of such stable and outwardly more pronounced components of culture as language, religion, folk art, folklore, customs, rites, norms of behavior, habits, etc. True, it has long been established that not a single component of culture is an indispensable ethno-differentiating feature (Tokarev 1964:43–46). It would be wrong, however, to claim on this basis that culture has no ethnic functions (Gumilev 1967:5). We have evidence that not only a separate component of culture determines the character of ethnos but the sum of the specific features of culture inherent in it. If language and ethnos, language division and ethnic division always coincided, differentiation of these notion's would lose all meaning.

Ethnoses also differ from one another in certain specific psychic features mainly in the nuances and style of displaying psychic traits common to all mankind (Bagramov 1964). This is precisely the so-called ethnic (national) character.

An indispensable distinction of ethnos, as we have already seen, is ethnic self-identification — the realization by ethnos members of their affiliation to it, connected with its delimitation from any other ethnos and expressed, above all, in the use of a common name which the ethnos gives to itself (an ethnonym). An important component of ethnic self-identification is the belief in a common origin. Its reality is derived from common historical destinies of ethnos members and their ancestors throughout their existence.

Common specific features of culture and psychology, self-identification and self-nomination (an ethnonym), in our view, can be defined as ethnic feature proper. Members of each ethnos necessarily possess them, to a greater or lesser extent, regardless of whether they live within a compact territory or are dispersed (as is the case of the Armenians in the USSR, Syria, the United States, and elsewhere).

Accordingly, an ethnic community proper, or ethnos in the narrow sense of the word, may be defined as a historically formed aggregate of people who share common, relatively stable specific features of culture (including language) and psychology, realization of their unity and distinctiveness from other similar aggregates of people as well as the self-nomination. We propose to use the term "ethnikos" to denote the ethnos in this narrow sense. But ethnikos is not an isolated phenomenon. In objective reality it does not exist apart from the social institutions proper[2] at various levels from family to state. The combination of ethnic properties with social properties as such depends, to a certain extent, on the spatial parameters of ethnikos, on a compact or scattered distribution of the bearers of ethnic properties themselves.

Among compact ethnic formations, a special place is occupied by those that are connected with the so-called social organisms. The latter are taken as separate societies, independent macro-units of social development (clan and tribal in primitive society and sociopolitical in class society). This connection may take various forms. In some cases ethnikos and social organism coincide in the main, and only separate representatives or small groups of the given ethnikos (for example, the Dutch in the Netherlands and outside the country) are left outside the boundaries of the latter. In others, one and the same ethnikos can be "divided" among several socio-political formations (Arab ethnikos can serve as an example). There are also cases where the main parts of several large ethnikoses (for instance, the Ukrainians, Poles, Armenians, Lithuanians, and other peoples as parts of the Russian Empire) can be found within the framework of one sociopolitical formation.

In any case, it is evident that mutual intersection of ethnikoses and social organisms is a widespread phenomenon. Special formations attending it are, in many cases, relatively independent, which ensures especially

---

[2] One should note the conditional nature of the differentiation of ethnic and social phenomena, where the latter are understood, above all, as the class and labor relations and institutions corresponding to them. For the social in the broad sense include the ethnic, consequently, ethnoses themselves are social institutions.

favorable conditions for stability of ethnikos and its reproduction. These "synthetic" formations which are a most important form of the existence of ethnos can, in our opinion, be termed ethnosocial organisms (ESO).

Organisms of this kind, together with ethnic (cultural) unity also have territorial, economic, social, and political unity (this is so to say a maximal variant). But the main components of the ethnosocial organism are undoubtedly ethnic factors, on the one hand, and socioeconomic factors, on the other. Forming the basis of all social phenomena, ethnic included, the socioeconomic factors are considerably more flexible than the ethnic ones. It is this relative conservatism, and also certain independence of purely ethnic properties, that determines the possibility of preserving an ethnikos with the same ethnic parameters throughout several socioeconomic structures. For instance, Ukrainian ethnikos has existed during feudalism and capitalism, and it exists now, under socialism.

But an ethno-social organism is another thing. Its belonging to a definite socioeconomic formation inevitably lends it a specific character. This fact underlies the principle accepted in Soviet sociological literature of singling out such historical-phasic types of ethnic communities as tribe, nationality, bourgeois, and socialist nation. The first of these types of communities is usually regarded as the principal one for the primitive society epoch; the second for the slave-owning and feudal epochs, whereas the term "nation" is used only in denoting ESO capitalist and socialist societies. In contrast to ESO-nations, ethnikoses of capitalist and socialist societies (and sometimes also pre-capitalist class societies) are usually termed "nationalities" (Bromley 1970).

Ethnikoses and ethno-social organisms are the basic kinds of ethnic communities. But they do not exhaust the ethnic structure of humanity. It is hierarchical, and along with the basic ethnic units, it has communities at other levels, too. Thus, one person can be a member of several ethnic communities at various levels at one and the same time. For example, a man can be a Don Cossack, a Russian, an Eastern Slav, and a Slav in general.

It seems possible now to single out the following levels of ethnic hierarchy: (1) "basic ethnic units" — aggregates of people having ethnic properties of the most intensive character (these are ethnikoses and ESOs we already know); (2) "elementary ethnic units," or "micro-ethnic units," the smallest components of the basic ethnic unit, the limit of divisibility of the latter; (3) "macro-ethnic units" — ethnic communities embracing several basic ethnic units; and (4) "intermediate ethnic communities," or "sub-ethnoses" — ethnic groups that are components of basic ethnic units.

All these levels, like the basic ethnic units (ethnikoses and ESOs) can, in their turn, be subdivided into ethnic units proper and ethno-social units. Thus, if a man is a direct bearer of ethnic properties, a proper ethnic micro-unit, then the ethno-social micro-unit in class societies is usually a monogamous family (in pre-class societies it was more often a localized part of a clan). Ethno-linguistic community with self-identification (the Slavs, for one, have been such a community from the Middle Ages up to the present) can serve as an example of the proper ethnic macro-unit. Ethno-social macro-units of class societies are ethno-political social organisms distinguished by a certain cultural unity which are conscious of unity (such communities are being formed in the USSR, Yugoslavia, and India at present). In pre-class societies the role of the basic ethno-social macro-units was played by tribe unions (Bromley 1972).

Soviet scientific literature makes a distinction between ethnic communities and ethnographic formations. Two levels of such formations are usually referred to. The "lowest" level is the so-called ethnographic group, a unit within ethnikos, with certain specific elements of culture. The "highest" level is the so-called historico-ethnographic community embracing several neighboring ethnikoses which, due to common features of socio-economic development and ties of long standing and mutual influence, have developed similar cultural features (Levin, Cheboksarov 1955:4).

So far, there are no generally accepted criteria for differentiating ethnographic units. In our view, the main distinction of ethnographic units (both lowest and highest) is that though they are historically shaped cultural communities, just as all ethnic units, they do not have self-consciousness. Therefore such formations can only be found through special ethnographic investigations, which explains their name "ethnographic." Consequently, if the Pomors, or various groups of Cossacks, having self-consciousness, represent ethnic groups (sub-ethnoses) of the Russian people then the Northern and Southern Great Russians represent its ethnographic groups.

Thus, in typologizing ethnic communities, it is necessary to take into account their hierarchical character, division into purely ethnic and ethno-social units, historical phasic division, as well as the principal distinction of ethnic units from ethnographic ones.

REFERENCES

BAGRAMOV, È. A.
    1964 Burzhuaznaia sotsiologiia i problema "natsional'nogo kharaktera" [Bourgeois sociology and the problem of "national character"]. Voprosy filosofii 6.
BARTH, F.
    1969 Ethnic groups and boundaries: the social organization of culture difference. Boston: Little, Brown.

BROMLEY, YU. V.
1970 Ėtnos i etnosotsial'nyĭ organizm [Ethnos and ethnosocial organism]. *Vestnik Adademii nauk SSSR* 8.
1971 K kharakteristike poniatia "etnos" [Toward a characterization of the concept of "ethnos"]. *Rassy i Narody* vyp. 1. Moscow.
1972 Opyt tipologizatsii ėtnicheskikh obshchnosteĭ [An experiment in typology of ethnic communities]. *Sovetskaya ethnographia* 5.
CHEBOKSAROV, N. N.
1967 Problemy tipologii ėtnicheskikh obshchnosteĭ v trudakh sovetskikh uchenykh [Problems of typology of ethnic communities in the works of Soviet scholars]. *Sovetskaya Ethnographia* 4.
CHISTOV, K. V.
1972 Ėtnicheskaia obshchnost', ėtnicheskoe soznanie i nektorye problemy dukhovnoĭ kul'tury [Ethnic community, ethnic consciousness, and some problems of spiritual culture]. *Sovetskaya Ethnographia* 3.
GUMILEV, L. N.
1967 O termine "ėtnos" [On the term "ethnos"]. *Doklady otdeleniĭ i komissiĭ Geograficheskogo obshchestva SSR* vyp. 3. Leningrad.
KOZLOV, V. I.
1969 *Dinamika chislennosti narodov* [Dynamics of the numerical strength of peoples]. Moscow.
KUSHNER, P. I.
1949 Natsional'noe samosoznanie kak ėtnicheskiĭ opredelitel' [National self-consciousness as an ethnic determinant]. *Kratkie soobshcheniia Instituta ėtnografii* vyp. 8.
1951 *Etnicheskie territorii i etnicheskie granitsy* [Ethnic territories and ethnic boundaries]. Moscow.
LEVIN, M. G., N. N. CHEBOKSAROV
1955 Khoziaistvenno-kul-turnye tipy i istoriko-etnograficheskie oblasti (K postanovke voprosa) [Economico-cultural types and historico-ethnographic regions (toward a formulation of the question)]. *Sovetskaya Ethnographia* 4.
MOGILIANSKĬ, N. M.
1909 Etnografiia i eė zadachi [Ethnography and its tasks]. *Ezhegodnik russkogo antropologicheskogo obshchestva* 3. St. Petersburg.
MÜHLMANN, N.
1964 *Rassen, Ethnien, Kulturen. [Races, ethnic groups, cultures].* Berlin.
NAROLL, R.
1964 On ethnic unit classification. *Current Anthropology* 5 (4).
SHIROKOGOROV, S. M.
1922 *Mesto ėtnografii sredi nauk i klassifikatsiia ėtnosov* [The place of ethnography among sciences and the classification of ethnos]. Vladivostok.
1923 *Ėtnos. Issledovanie osnovnykh printsipov izmeneniia ėtnicheskikh i ėtnograficheskikh iavleniĭ* [Ethnos. A study of the basic principles of change in ethnic and ethnographic phenomena]. Shanghai.
1937 Ethnographie und Ethnologie. *Archiv für Anthropologie und Völkerforschung* 24.
TOKAREV, S. A.
1964 Problemy tipov etnicheskikh obshchnosteĭ [Problems of types of ethnic communities]. *Voprosy filosofii* 2.

Psychotopology and its Application to Cross-Disciplinary, Cross-Professional, and Cross-Cultural Communication

MAGOROH MARUYAMA

INTRODUCTION

The difficulty in cross-disciplinary, cross-professional, and cross-cultural communication lies not so much in the fact that the communicating parties use different vocabularies or languages to talk about the same thing, but rather that they use different *structures of reasoning*. If the communicating parties remain unaware that they are using different structures of reasoning and are aware of their communication difficulties only, each tends to perceive the problem as resulting from the other's illogicality, lack of intelligence, or even deceptiveness and insincerity. One party may also succumb to the illusion of understanding while being unaware of his misunderstandings. "I understand you perfectly, but you don't understand me" is an expression typical of such a situation. Or all communicating parties may fall into a collective illusion of mutual understanding. In such a situation, each party may wonder later why the other parties do not live up to the "agreement" they had reached.

In the fields of social planning, urban and regional planning, and public works the need for communication between fields of specialization, professions, social and cultural groups, as well as between local, regional, and national political divisions is increasing. More and more often, participants must communicate with persons whose structures of reasoning differ from their own. The frustrations are numerous. Social scientists are frustrated by the ethnocentricism of many engineers, technologists, and economists. In turn, engineers, technologists, and economists are frustrated by the social scientists' apparent unwillingness or inability to come up with a uniform prescription for human satisfaction. Many planners are frustrated by the dissatisfaction expressed by community members toward their plans and consider them incapable of appreciating their "beautiful" or "rational" plans. On the other hand, community members are often frustrated because they believe planners either do not try or cannot make their plans relevant to community problems.

The situation most often is not neatly categorical. There are, for example, field engineers who are more sensitive and responsive to community needs than most social scientists. Some social scientists consider themselves to be the ultimate authority and regard community members as incapable of conducting research or formulating theories. Many social scientists regard community people as useful objects for academic research regardless of its relevance to the community. Other social scientists satisfy their psychological needs by being do-gooders to community members they consider to be intellectually inferior. To counteract what would otherwise be one-way exploitation, community people have learned how to foster an illusion of self-appointed relevance in these do-gooders as long as they cannot get rid of them but can counterexploit them.

These difficulties in communication, the frustrations they cause, and the resultant necessity for manipulation run much deeper than differences in relative values or priorities. They stem from what may be called psychotopological differences. This paper will focus on such differences.

Various terminologies have been used to describe psychotopological differences in several disciplines. Systems engineers, operational researchers, and some experimental psychologists have used the term "models." Some philosophers and logicians have used the term "logics." Anthropologists and psycholinguists have used the term cognitive structure and more recently epistemology or epistemologies. Sociologists also have used the last term but more in the sense of the sociology of knowledge than in the sense of experimental study of cognitive structure. More recently sociologists and anthropologists have begun using the term paradigms, mainly because of the inspiration they derive from physics, especially from Thomas Kuhn's work (1962) on paradigms.

In this paper, I define the term psychotopology as a *science of structures of reasoning which vary from discipline to discipline, from profession to profession, from culture to culture, and sometimes even from individual to individual.*

FORERUNNERS OF PSYCHOTOPOLOGY

Awareness of the different structures of reasoning must have come about with the beginnings of philosophy. However, until very recently, philosophical works could be divided into two main types: those in which a philosopher *advocates* his own philosophy; and those in which historians of philosophy *describe* different philosophers' works. Neither type directly posed the problem of communication between different structures of reasoning.

Certain trivialities, for example, the consideration that the quality of perception of color by different individuals cannot be compared, have been discussed since the beginning of philosophy. There were philosophers who went much beyond this. For example, Søren Kierkegaard, Henri Bergson, and Edmund Husserl have discussed in depth the impossibility of communicating certain types of realities.

As far as I know, the first person who systematically studied different structures of reasoning and discussed the problem of communication between them was Karl Mannheim (1929). He was not a philosopher but a sociologist in the Max Weber tradition. He raises several points that are relevant to our discussion: (1) there are several types of logics; (2) the communicating parties, who are unaware that they are using different kinds of logics, accuse one another of being illogical, unintelligent, infantile, insincere, etc; (3) the choice between logics is based on factors which are beyond, and independent of, any logic; (4) in cases involving social classes, the choice is based on goals, interests, purposes, and feelings which are generated under specific sociohistorical conditions and shared among members of each social class but not shared between different social classes.

For the most part, Mannheim's contribution remained unnoticed by the forerunners of psychotopology with the possible exceptions of Karl Pribram and Karl Jaspers. But Jaspers' work *Psychologie der Weltanschauungen* (1919) appeared ten years before the publication of Mannheim's *Ideologie and Utopie* (1929), and could not have benefited from the latter.

Three types of works led to the present development of psychotopology: (1) those which show that there are different types of logics and that the choice between them depends on extralogical factors (factors independent of and beyond any logic); (2) those that deal with the problem of communication between different types of logics; (3) those that discuss individuals' capacity to transcend their present logic and invent new types.

The three groups may be tentatively called: (1) study of epistemologies; (2) study of cross-epistemological communication; and (3) study of trans-epistemological process.

1. The works of the first group have come mainly from five fields of specialization: (a) history; (b) anthropology; (c) psychology and psychiatry; (d) physics; and (e) biology.

a. The historian-philosopher Karl Pribram, the uncle of another Karl Pribram who is a neurophysiologist at Stanford University, discussed the development of three main sociopolitical epistemologies in the Western world (1949). The three are: universalistic (France); organismic (Germany); and nominalistic-democratic (England).

b. Anthropology includes numerous works on the epistemologies (called "belief systems" by anthropologists) of different cultures. The most systematic was Clyde Kluckhohn's work (1949) on the Navajo logic. He demonstrated that Navajo logic is mutualistic, harmonistic, nonhierarchical, and empirical, as compared to the Western unidirectional, competitive, hierarchical, and deductive logic.

c. The contributions from psychology and psychiatry include two types: (cl) those that deal primarily with structures of reasoning; and (c2) those which examine the factors influencing the choice between different paradigms. Among the former, we can count Jaspers' classic *Psychologie der Weltanschauungen* (1919) as well as more recent works by existential psychiatrists, such as Minkowski (1923), Binswanger (1944–1945) and Ellenberger (1958). Among the latter there are Bateson, Kubie, and Feuer. Bateson has shown that schizophrenics (1956) and alcoholics (1971) have logics of their own, that the choice of these logics originates in an adaptive process under specific psychological interaction patterns, and that often behavior based on these logics has a survival value, particularly in the case of schizophrenics. Kubie (1956) and Feuer (1959) have shown that even among scientists and philosophers the choice of logics depends on extra-logical factors.

d. Physics, along with the fields of philosophy of science and the history of science until recently dominated this topic. Thomas Kuhn's *The structure of scientific revolutions* (1962) had an effect of popularizing the topic among nonphysicists, particularly among social scientists and humanists, who have come to realize that the traditional social paradigm is becoming obsolete.

e. Paradigms in biology are as old as paradigms in physics. During certain periods in the history of philosophy, biological paradigms were sources of inspiration. On the whole, however, philosophy tended to rely on physics paradigms, usually after a considerable time lag. Biologists may have tended to fail to appreciate the full philosophical importance of their paradigms. For example, Hans Spemann's pioneering work *Embryonic development and induction* (1938) and, in a slightly different sense, Wright's theory of the speed of evolution (1931) contained the same basic concept that later became theories of negative feedback systems (Wiener 1948) and positive feedback systems (Myrdal 1944; Ulam 1960; Maruyama 1963a; Milsum 1968; Buckley 1968). Spemann's and Wright's works included the principle of growth of complexity and heterogenization, which even the more recent information theory by Shannon and Weaver (1949) failed to consider. But biologists of that time did not fully recognize the philosophical impact of Spemann's and Wright's works. As for philosophers, they operate under a time lag of about fifty years and have not yet caught up with these paradigms. Meanwhile, about a decade ago, biologists began realizing that their recent paradigms involved basic philosophical change and began trying to identify new paradigmatic directions (Waddington 1969–1971; Riedl 1976).

2. The study of cross-epistemological communication has also developed without reference to Mannheim's work. However, many authors have arrived at insights similar to his. (I, myself, had done a considerable amount of work before I discovered, in 1968, that Mannheim had made similar points before I was born.)

The studies of cross-epistemological communication may be divided into those that deal with: (a) communication between members of different cultures; (b) those that deal specifically with research situations in which the researcher is exogenous to the culture under study.

a. One of the earliest systematic works was Mead's study of communication between English people and Americans (1946). Another was Balgooyen's on the communication between Plains Indians and white people (1962). I have analyzed communication between Danes and foreigners (1961b) and between same-culture persons with different logics (1962a, 1963b). On the more theoretical side, I have constructed various mathematical models of misunderstandings (1959, 1960, 1961a, 1962b).

b. Studies based on research situations include: Wax's work (1971) on war-time relocation camps for Japanese-Americans; Burk and Adams' work (1970) on deviant groups; my own work (1968, 1969a, 1975) on San Quentin and Vacaville prisons. There are undoubtedly many others.

3. The study of trans-epistemological process is the youngest of the research related to psychotopology. It is mainly carried out in a field that may be called *cultural futuristics*, by those who see the obsolescence of our traditional social paradigms and are concerned with generating new social paradigms. Examples of works in this new and expanding field include Maruyama (1970).

EXAMPLES OF EPISTEMOLOGIES

Many different epistemologies exist, and undoubtedly many more will be developed in the future.

Let us take the following four epistemologies as examples: (1) non-reciprocal causal epistemology; (2) independent-event epistemology; (3) homeostatic epistemology; (4) morphogenetic epistemology.

These examples are not meant to be exhaustive or mutually exclusive. Any attempt to separate epistemologies into nonoverlapping categories is itself a victim of an epistemology that assumes that the universe consists of nonoverlapping categories. Such an attempt exludes nonclassificational epistemologies and therefore negates itself in the sense of Russell's paradoxes.[1]

In actuality, these four epistemologies mix and overlap with each other as well as with many other epistemologies. Table 1 is a simplified summary of the four "pure" types.

Table 1.   Summary of the four "pure" epistemology types

Homogenistic	Heterogenistic		
Nonreciprocal	Isolationistic	Reciprocally causal	
Hierarchical	Independent-event	Homeostatic	Morphogenetic
PHILOSOPHY			
Universalism: Abstraction has higher reality than concrete things. *Organismic:* The parts are subordinated to the whole.	*Nominalism:* Only the individual elements are real. Society is merely an aggregate of individuals.	*Equilibrium or cycle:* Elements interact in such a way as to maintain equilibrium or go in cycles.	*Heterogenization, symbiotization, and evolution:* Symbiosis thanks to diversity. Generate new diversity and patterns of symbiosis.
CAUSALITY			
Two things cannot cause each other. Cause-effect relations may be deterministic or probabilistic.	Independent events are most natural, each having its own probability. Non-random patterns and structures are improbable, and tend to decay.	*Reciprocal:* Counteracts deviations (negative feedback loops), both probabilistic and deterministic.	*Reciprocal:* Amplifies differentiation (positive feedback loops), both probabilistic and deterministic.
LOGIC			
Deductive, axiomatic. Mutually exclusive categories. Permanence of substance and identity.	Inductive, Statistical.	Complementarity.	Heterogenization, symbiotization, nonpermanence. Irrepeatable and irreversible processes.

(continued)

[1]   Bertrand Russell gave several examples of logical paradoxes. One of them is the statement written on a sheet of paper: "Any statement written on this sheet is false." If this statement is true, then it must be false. But if this statement is false, then in a bi-value logic its negation is true, i.e., the statement must be true; hence, a paradox. Bateson (1956) suggested another paradox. It is a command: "Be self-assertive." If someone becomes self-assertive, he is obeying this command and is therefore not self-assertive. If he refuses to become self-assertive, he is disobeying the command and therefore becomes self-assertive. As pointed out by Bateson, the solution to these paradoxes, including ours, lies in distinguishing the statements from the comments on statements. But if we do this in our own example, we will still be falling into a classificational epistemology.

Table 1 (*continued*)

Homogenistic	Heterogenistic		
Nonreciprocal	Isolationistic	Reciprocally causal	
Hierarchical	Independent-event	Homeostatic	Morphogenetic

PERCEPTION

| Rank-ordering, classifying and categorizing into neat scheme. Find regularity. | Isolating. Each is unique and unrelated to others. | *Contextual*: Look for meaning in context. Look for mutual balance, seek stability. | *Contextual*: Look for new interactions and new patterns. Things change and relations change. Therefore meanings change and new meanings arise. |

KNOWLEDGE

| Belief in existence of one truth. If people are informed, they will agree. There is the "best" way for all persons. Objectivity exists independent of perceiver. Quantitative measurement is basic to knowledge. | Why bother to learn beyond my own interest? | *Polyocular*: Binocular vision enables us to see three-dimensionally, because the *differential* between two images enables the brain to compute the invisible dimension. Cross-subjective analysis enables us to compute invisible dimensions. Diversity in perception enriches our understanding. | |

INFORMATION

| The more specified, the more information. Past and future inferrable from present probabilistically or deterministically. | Information decays and gets lost. Blueprint must contain more information than finished product. Embryo must contain more information than adult. | Loss of information can be counteracted by means of redundancy or by means of feedback devices. | Complex patterns can be generated by means of simple rules of interaction. The amount of information needed to describe the generated pattern may be greater than the amount of information to describe the rules of interaction. Thus amount of information can increase. |

COSMOLOGY

| Causal chains. Hierarchy of categories, | The most probable state is random distribution of events | Equilibrium by means of mutual corrections, or | Generate new patterns by means of mutual interaction. |

Table 1 (*continued*)

Homogenistic	Heterogenistic		
Nonreciprocal	Isolationistic	Reciprocally causal	
Hierarchical	Independent-event	Homeostatic	Morphogenetic
COSMOLOGY (*cont.*) supercategories and subcategories. "Oneness" with the universe. Processes are repeatable if conditions are the same.	with independent probability. Structures decay.	cycles due to mutual balancing. Structures maintain.	Structures grow. Heterogeneity, differentiation, symbiotization and further heterogenization increase.
ETHICS *Competition.* Zero-sum. If not homogeneous, then conflict. Let the "strongest" dominate homogenistically. Majority rule (domination by quantity).	Isolationism. Zerosum or negative sum. Virtue of *self-sufficiency.* If poor, own fault. Do your own thing. Grow your own potatoes.	*Symbiosis: static harmony.* Avoid disturbance. Restore previous harmony. Positive sum.	*Symbiotization:* *evolving harmony.* Positive sum. Look for mutually beneficial relations with new elements and aliens. Regard differences as beneficial. Incorporate new endogenous and exogenous elements.
RELIGION *Monotheism:* Creator and prime mover, omniscient, omnipotent, perfect god. Missionary work to convert others (belief in superiority of own religion).	Individual beliefs.	*Static polytheism:* Maintain established harmony of diverse elements.	*Dynamic polytheism:* Evolving harmony of diverse elements. Look forward to new harmony when new elements are added or new events occur.
RESEARCH RATIONALE Dissimilar results must have been caused by dissimilar conditions. Differences must be traced to corresponding differences in conditions which produced them.	Find out probability distribution and conditional probability.	Dissimilar conditions may lead to similar results due to asymptotic convergence to an equilibrium or cyclic oscillation. Find range of initial conditions which lead to same states. (*Note*: Equilibrium does not mean homogeneity. It	Similar conditions may produce dissimilar results due to differentiation–amplification. Find the amplifying network instead of looking for different initial conditions. (*Note*: Same amplifying network may produce different results: The

Table 1 (*continued*)

Homogenistic	Heterogenistic		
Nonreciprocal	Isolationistic	Reciprocally causal	
Hierarchical	Independent-event	Homeostatic	Morphogenetic

RESEARCH RATIONALE (*cont.*)

		means *maintenance* of heterogeneity.)	difference is due to a disproportionally small initial kick which may be accidental. The amplifying network is more crucial than the initial kick itself.)

In this article, certain terms are used somewhat interchangeably, but with some subtle differences. These terms are: epistemologies; logics; models; and paradigms.

"Epistemologies" is used in the sense of basic structures of thinking underlying not only science and philosophy but also social relations, perception, religions, ethics, planning process, design principles and esthetics. "Logics" is used when the meaning is somewhat narrower, referring to consciously articulated procedure. "Models" refers to theoretical or mathematical structures with which a process is interpreted. "Paradigms" is used for philosophical rationale which underlie the models. But in many occurrences, these terms are interchangeable. "Psychotopology" is the term used to indicate the study of different structures of thinking at these multiple levels.

(1) *Nonreciprocal Causal Epistemology*

This epistemology until recently has been commonly regarded as *the* scientific way of thinking. In this epistemology, influence flows one-way from the cause to the effect. There is nothing in the effect which cannot be traced back to its cause. Therefore, there cannot be less information in the cause than in its effect. If you know the conditions of the cause, you can deduce the conditions of the effect. On the other hand, if you know the conditions of the effect, you can infer the conditions of the cause. The past and future can be inferred from the present if we have a complete knowledge of the present. For the same reason, the present can be inferred from the past or from the future if we have complete information. In essence, the scientific method consists in identifying the cause when the effect is known and in predicting the effect when the cause is known. If there are differences in the effect, there *must* be corresponding differences in the cause. The strategy of scientific research is aimed at discovering these differences in the cause.

PROBABILISTIC NONRECIPROCAL CAUSAL EPISTEMOLOGY. This epistemology became fashionable after the discovery of indeterminism in quantum mechanics. It continues to be fashionable in philosophy of science and sociology, although the physical and biological sciences have already moved on. According to it, influence flows one-way from the cause to the effect. But influence occurs with some probability rather than with certainty. The effect can be predicted from the cause with some probability, and the cause can be inferred from the effect with some probability. Complete information can never be obtained, not even on a present situation, because the information-collecting instrument and the act of collecting information interferes with and disturbs the observed phenomena. Thus, the scientific method consists in discovering the probability distribution in the effect when the cause is hypothetically specified (neither can be completely accurately measured) and in establishing the limits of accuracy of observation. Multivariate statistical analysis, such as factor analysis, correlation analysis, regression analysis, etc., can be used to study phenomena which are not completely amenable to laboratory experiments. Examples of these phenomena are weather, tropospheric scattering of electromagnetic waves, and social revolution. Statistical relations between two variables may be due to one of the following nonreciprocal causal relations: (a) one causes the other with some probability, either directly or through other intermediate variables; or (b) both are influenced by some common cause with some probability. The causal direction cannot be known from statistics alone and must be determined by logical considerations.

(2) *Independent-Event Epistemology*

This epistemology is related to the development of equilibrium thermodynamics in the nineteenth century. It is based on logic similar to that of tossing coins. In the coin-tossing situation, each toss is considered to be independent of other tosses. The outcome of the first toss should not influence the outcome of the second toss. The third toss should not be influenced by the outcome of the two previous tosses, etc. This assumption is considered true even if the coin itself may be "unfair," i.e., heavy on one side. For example, if the coin is unfair and has a probability of thirty to seventy in favor of the head on each toss, the second toss should have the same probability regardless of what came up on the first toss.

Suppose you have 1,000 coins, each similarly unfair, with a head-tail probability of thirty to seventy. Suppose you paint the head sides of all coins blue and the tail sides yellow. Suppose you put the coins in a box, shake them well, and pour them onto a tray. Spread over the tray, most coins will be yellow side up, some will be blue. If you put the tray on the table in your garden, go to the airport, rent a helicopter, and hover over your garden, you will see the tray without being able to distinguish individual coins. The tray will look yellowish-green.

Given the thirty to seventy probability, the chances of getting two heads out of two throws are $0.3 \times 0.3 = 0.09$ or 9 percent. The chances of getting two tails are $0.7 \times 0.7 = 0.49$ or 49 percent. The chances of getting 1,000 heads out of 1,000 throws are very small, even though such a possibility does exist. Therefore, the chances of getting a completely blue-looking or yellow-looking tray are very small. Most of the time you get a green-looking tray, more to the yellow side than to the blue. In addition, the possibility of getting a tray that looks half blue and half yellow exists, but it is very small. Most of the time, both sides of the tray are of about the same hue.

Similar reasoning may be applied to the temperature distribution in equilibrium thermodynamics. Heat is caused by movements of molecules. If a system is left alone for a long time without interference from outside, it is most probable that its temperature distribution will be even.

If an isolated system is found in a state of uneven temperature distribution, the system is in a thermodynamically improbable state. The more uneven the temperature distribution, the more improbable its state. Heat tends to move from warmer zones to colder zones, either by direct transmission through a solid body, carried by the flow of a liquid or gas, or by radiation. The system tends to change from low probability state to a higher probability state. Still there is a low probability that the change might occur in the other direction, just as it does once in a while when a coin-toss produces a very improbable distribution of hues.

This tendency is called the law of increase of entropy. Entropy is defined in such a way that the higher the degree of homogeneity of the temperature distribution, the higher the entropy. The change from a low entropy state to a higher entropy state occurs gradually, not suddenly, because it takes time for the heat to move. Some degree of continuity exists in the sense that the state of the system at a given time is related to the state of the system at a previous time. Therefore, change is not independent in the sense of a coin-toss. In fact, the state at a later time is related to the state at an earlier time by a certain probability distribution. This type of change is called stochastic process.

So, this second epistemology may be called stochastic epistemology instead of independent-event epistemology. But I prefer to call it the latter because entropy is defined on the basis of the system's closeness to the state of random distribution.

Shannon's theory of information (1949) is based on the same epistemology. Working at the Bell Telephone Laboratories, Shannon had to deal with the problem of loss of transmitted information in telephone circuits due to overloading or noise. He also had to develop ways to pack information in compact, coded forms, in order to make maximum use of transmission circuits.

In telephone circuits the human voice is converted into patterns of electric oscillation. At the listener's end, these electric oscillations are reconverted into vibrations of air which correspond to the orginal voice of the talker. In the transmission lines and in the amplifiers inserted along them, there are random movements of electrons caused either by the amplifiers themselves or by external electromagnetic phenomena, such as lightning. These random movements of electrons interfere with the transmitted patterns of electronic oscillations and decrease the amount of information. It was, therefore, natural for Shannon to define the amount of information as the degree of nonrandomness of the patterns. It is not surprising that the mathematical formula for the amount of information thus conceptualized by Shannon (1949) turned out to be exactly the same as the mathematical formula for thermodynamic entropy. The only difference is that thermodynamic entropy, as defined, is greater when the degree of randomness is higher, while the amount of information, as defined, is greater when randomness is lower. Thus, mathematically, the formula for the amount of information has a negative sign, compared to the formula for thermodynamic entropy.

This relationship can be restated in many ways. One way is to say that the amount of information transmitted corresponds to the degree of improbability of the given pattern assuming certain random independent events. For example, a series of footprints on a sand beach is improbable, assuming that the sand is blown randomly by the wind, but conveys the "message" that something other than wind was present. When the footprints are left to the winds or waves, they decay. The more details of the footprints remain, the more information they transmit as to what kind of an animal was there.

Just as in the thermodynamic process in which temperature distribution in an isolated system becomes increasingly homogeneous, in information theory as formulated by Shannon, the amount of information gradually decays if left to random influences. Shannon's information theory was partly aimed at combating this decay and restoring lost information. It cannot, and was not intended to, generate new information. The other part of Shannon's information theory was aimed at coding and compacting information to maximize the total amount transmitted in a given channel. For example, suppose you want to transmit a black-and-white image on a television screen. It is uneconomical to transmit the brightness of all the points of the image. It is more economical to indicate only the places where the brightness changes in the scan. By this means and others, you can pack the information more efficiently.

If you notice, the above procedure ignores the homogeneous parts and pays attention only to the heterogeneous parts. In this sense, homogeneous parts have less information than heterogeneous parts. For the same reason, the repetition of identical elements conveys less information than combinations of different elements. It suffices to transmit information about one element and indicate how many times it is repeated, instead of transmitting the same information several times. It is worth remembering that the amount of Shannonian information is greater when the degree of heterogeneity is greater. We will reconsider this point in the discussion of the morphogenetic epistemology.

The purpose of science based on Shannon's information theory is to identify the amount of information, the type of coding and decoding, and the mode of transmission in living organisms and in man-made control and communication devices. Since noise and overloaded channels result in lost information, and since information can never be increased, the primary concern of this type of science is *economy* and *efficiency* in coding and decoding as well as the maximum use of channel capacity without creating overload.

Examples of specializations which flourished under this epistemology are: the study of so-called genetic codes; neurophysiology; coded data transmission in space technology; data bank and information retrieval.

(3, 4) *Homeostatic and Morphogenetic Epistemologies*

These attained a sophisticated mathematical formulation in Western science during World War II, although they existed in many non-Western philosophies for several thousand years. Their development in Western science occurred in two phases: (a) the deviation-counteracting and equilibrating reciprocal causal epistemology which occurred in the 1940s and the 1950s; (b) the differentiation-amplifying and heterogeneity-increasing reciprocal causal epistemology which extended from the early 1960s to present. A third phase, which may yet be developed, would be characterized by mathematical elaboration of the diversity-symbiotizing reciprocal causal epistemology. (See Maruyama [1963a], Milsum [1968], and Buckley [1968] for history of development of this paradigm.)

Even though intuitive formulations of reciprocal causality in Western science can be traced back to Darwin, Adam Smith, and several others in various fields (Maruyama 1963a; Milsum 1968), it did not become a respectable scientific paradigm until it was formulated with some mathematical sophistication in mid-twentieth century.

The mathematical formulation which marked the beginning of the first phase occurred during World War II, when antiaircraft artillery became equipped with a corrective feedback loop consisting of a radar and a computer (Wiener 1949). The initial mathematical formulation for the second phase occurred in 1960, when mathematician Stanislaw Ulam (1960) developed the theory that complex patterns can be generated by means of simple rules of interaction (Maruyama 1963c).

Deviation-counteracting equilibrating reciprocal causal loops can be found in many self-regulating processes in biology, ecology, and man-made devices. Examples are the self-regulation of body temperature, the prey/predator radio, and the autopilot mechanism. In such a causal loop, the effect of any change in one element returns to itself through others in such a way that any change is counteracted and cancelled out. For example, if for some reason the number of prey decreases, the predators starve and their number decreases. If the predators decrease in number, fewer of the prey are eaten, and as a result their number increases. The opposite is also true. Thus, any change in the number of prey cancels itself by affecting the number of predators. Similarly, any change in the number of predators also cancels itself by affecting the number of prey. There is a reciprocal deviation-counteracting equilibrating causal relationship between the number of prey and predators (Holling 1976).

Differentiation-amplifying heterogenizing reciprocal causal loops can be found in most biological and social processes which increase in complexity, diversity, and structure. For example, in the interaction between a species of moth and a species of bird which feeds on it, camouflaged mutants of the moth will survive better, and the mutants of the bird which are clever at discovering the camouflaged moths will also survive better. As a result, the moth gets more and more camouflaged, generation after generation, and the bird gets more and more skillful at discovering it. Another example is the growth of a city on a homogeneous plain. Suppose that a plain is homogeneous before the arrival of human pioneers. One day someone arrives and settles down in a certain spot. The spot may be selected accidentally because the man is too tired to get any further or his horse is ill, etc. But once the man is settled, someone else may join him, and gradually a village may grow. The attractiveness of the spot to other pioneers grows as its population increases. Gradually industries develop, and a city grows. The plain is no longer homogeneous. Within the city many types of differentiation and heterogenization take place.

Ulam's formulation (1960) has profound implications for these processes. He discovered that when a complex pattern is generated by interaction, a greater "amount of Shannonian information" is often needed to describe the finished pattern than to describe the interaction rules which generated the pattern. In other words, the amount of Shannonian information *grows* in such processes. We remember that in Shannon's formulation, based on the random process paradigm, the amount of information can never increase. In the random process paradigm, structures decay and information decreases. On the other hand, the deviation-counteracting equilibrating reciprocal causal processes can prevent structures and information from decaying, and the differentiation-amplifying heterogenizing reciprocal causal processes can *generate* and *increase* structures and information.

This new formulation solves one of the puzzles of science. Equilibrium thermodynamics, based on the random process paradigm, could not explain how a living organism decreased its entropy (increased temperature differentiation). It simply begged the question by stating that living organisms are not isolated systems. But this explanation was as unsatisfactory as saying that a computer works because it is plugged into a power source. A more satisfactory explanation lies in the recognition that biological processes are reciprocal causal processes, not random processes. Because reciprocal causal processes can maintain and increase heterogeneity, they are sometimes called *anti-entropic processes*. Furthermore, deviation-counteracting equilibrating reciprocal causal processes are sometimes called *morphostatic processes*, and differentiation-amplifying heterogenizing reciprocal causal processes are called *morphogenetic processes*.

Let us recall for a moment the example of the footprints in a sand. As late as 1953, Hans Reichenbach, one of the leading philosophers of science at that time, denied the possibility of reciprocal causal processes (Reichenbach 1956:39) and advanced the following argument: There are several types of time-asymmetrical processes. If you take a movie film of a time-asymmetrical process and run the film backwards, you can tell it is run backwards because the process does not obey the laws of physics.

As an example of one type of time-asymmetrical process, Reichenbach discussed the footprint in sand being blown by winds. He said that the actual event runs in the direction of gradual decay of the footprint. If you take a movie film of this event and run it backwards, you can recognize that the film is being run backwards. His argument was that it is highly improbable, though not completely impossible, that random influences consistently accumulate in such a way as to gradually produce a structure. Faced with the question of how structures came about in the first place, Reichenbach tended to think that they can be created by sudden events such as an explosion but not by a gradual, slow process. His nonreciprocal causal logic could not explain the gradual growth of structure such as the growth of a city on a homogeneous plain. He had to introduce the notion of finality, i.e., of the future determining the present, to account for processes he could not explain with his nonreciprocal causal logic.

Some readers may have noticed the affinity of Reichenbach's explosion theory to LeMaitre's "big bang theory" — one of two current theories in astronomy on how the universe got started. The big bang theory states that the universe began with a big explosion. The other is the "condensation theory" according to which the universe initially consists of homogeneously distributed gases which gradually condensed into astronomical bodies because of mutual gravity. The condensation theory is in a reciprocal causal logic. An interesting question posed by this theory is the following: If we regard the entire universe as an isolated system, then the entropy in it decreases, provided the condensation theory is correct. This is a very interesting epistemological possibility.

At the end of the nineteenth century, Boltzmann (1898) proposed another paradigm. He suggested that there may be other universes in which the direction of time runs opposite to ours. We cannot receive any information from such a universe, because any information leaving it according to its time direction would be seen by us as going toward it. But if it were possible to observe that universe, decay in it would look like growth and growth like decay. In such a case, it would not be easy to talk about decay and growth.

Let us return to the reciprocal causal epistemologies and discuss their third phase. This phase, which is not yet mathematically formulated, will have to deal with the question of symbiotization of diversities at a more sophisticated level than it is now. A great deal of data from ecology and biology are already available on symbiosis and heterogeneity. But in ecology and biology we have so far been studying the symbiotic relations which are already established between diverse species. We do not concern ourselves with the possibility of creating new symbiotic relations between species which are not yet interacting. Yet, this is the kind of concern we need to develop in dealing with the social and cultural change taking place in our world, not only to avoid possible catastrophes but also to explore positive alternatives.

In most cases, ecological and biological thinking proceeds with two assumptions: (a) that the animal and plant species have no alternatives and can live only the way they live; (b) that the ecological relationship established among them should be maintained as much as possible. A change in any of its parts may affect the whole ecosystem and may have disastrous and irreversible consequences. On the other hand, our social thinking proceeds with two different assumptions: (a) that each culture, social group, or individual has its own goal, and there are several alternative ways to attain this goal; (b) that current international, intercultural, and intergroup relations, power structures, etc., are by no means satisfactory. We must find more satisfactory ways of rearranging these relations and structures.

We have not yet produced a mathematical formulation for this kind of thinking. The existing mathematical models of society have many short-comings: (a) they are culture-bound and cannot be applied to different cultures; (b) they are homogenistic, and cannot even deal with the heterogeneity in our own culture; (c) consequently, they do not even conceive the problem of finding possible symbiotic combinations among heterogeneous elements; (d) not many of them consider the existence of alternatives.

The formulation of the third phase of the morphogenetic epistemology may begin with certain considerations. Suppose there are three individuals: A, B, and C. A has a goal which we call Ga. (B's goal is called Gb; C's is Gc.) Suppose A has five different ways to accomplish Ga; B has two different ways to accomplish Gb; C has three different ways to accomplish Gc. Then there are $5 \times 2 \times 3 = 30$ different combinations of alternative ways for all three individuals to attain their different goals. Some of these thirty combinations may produce symbiosis among the three individuals, while others may not. Our problem is to find the combinations which produce symbiosis. We need a formulation that is not only mathematically sophisticated, but also capable of implementation, to deal with symbiotization of a wide range of heterogeneous elements.

In the homogenistic, quantitative, and competitive epistemology, the survival of the fittest was misinterpreted as the survival of the strongest or the most aggressive. But in the reciprocal causal epistemology, the survival of the fittest is interpreted as *the survival of the most symbiotic*. The random process epistemology may be called the decay principle. The morphogenetic epistemology may be called the life principle, or the love principle (the name given it by Elise Boulding).

One of the characteristics of homeostatic processes is that dissimilar conditions are counteracted, and the results converge into similar conditions. On the other hand, the morphogenetic processes have the characteristic that similar initial conditions may produce very dissimilar results. These properties have very profound theoretical consequences:

a. Neither the past nor the future can be inferred from the present; nor can the present be inferred from the past or from the future. This is not because of indeterminism and probabilism, but because of the deviation-counteracting and differentiation-amplifying reciprocal causal loops.

b. In the research method, the existence of a difference in the initial condition cannot be assumed on the basis of a difference in the result. One would be looking for a nonexisting straw-man if one looked for a difference in the initial condition. One must look for the amplification network. For example, the difference between the national characters of the Danes and the Dutch may not be due to differences in climate, geography, racial origin, or other such conditions. Instead, the ways these aspects reinforce one another may be more significant.

Concepts about information also change considerably in the reciprocal causal epistemologies. In Shannon's epistemology, the amount of information can never grow. Therefore, all existing information must have come from somewhere. For example, genes must contain the information necessary to describe the adult body. It must be possible to locate in the genes a unit of information that corresponds to each part of an adult body. Research, therefore, aims at locating these units.

On the other hand, in the morphogenetic epistemology, the amount of information as defined by Shannon may grow by interaction. Therefore, it may be more profitable to discover rules of cellular interaction than to try to locate in the genes the information units corresponding to body parts. Accordingly, experiments in embryonic grafting or embryonic interference may be performed instead of analysis of genes.

PROBABILISTIC INDEPENDENT EVENT EPISTEMOLOGY. As we have seen, even without the introduction of probabilistic indeterminism, the reciprocal causal processes do not conform to the notion that similar conditions produce a similar result. In the *deterministic* reciprocal causal processes, dissimilar conditions may end in similar results due to deviation-counteracting, or similar conditions may produce dissimilar results due to differentiation-amplifying. But when we combine indeterminism with the reciprocal causal processes, we obtain the following: (a) the same conditions may produce different results; (b) different conditions may produce the same results.

a. This is because a very small initial difference, which is within the range of high probability, may be amplified to a degree which would be very improbable in the probabilistic nonreciprocal causal processes.

b. In the deterministic deviation-counteracting process, equilibrium is usually reached asymptotically, but not necessarily completely. The process approaches the ideal equilibrium but does not completely attain it. On the other hand, if small probabilistic fluctuations are allowed, it is possible that the process jumps into the ideal equilibrium state once in a while, even though it may jump out of it as well.

DETERMINISTIC RECIPROCAL AND NONRECIPROCAL CAUSAL PROCESSES. Not all causal relations are reciprocal. There are some nonreciprocal causal relations mixed with reciprocal causal relations.

PROBABILISTIC RECIPROCAL AND NONRECIPROCAL CAUSAL PROCESSES. This is the most flexible combination. It contains the characteristics of all four pure epistemologies.

THE RELATION OF PSYCHOTOPOLOGY TO SOCIAL ORGANIZATION AND PERCEPTION

As we have seen in Table 1, epistemologies affect not only theories in science but also the organization of society and the way in which people perceive and structure their everyday activities. Let us discuss this relationship, again taking the four epistemologies as examples.

Some readers may ask, "Which comes first — scientific theories or everyday life perceptions and social organization?" Such questions are already epistemology-bound, i.e., in this case they are bound by the nonreciprocal causal epistemology. It may as well be that the everyday life perception, social organization, and scientific theories cause and reinforce one another. As Kubie (1956) and Feuer (1959) have pointed out, even the scientist's choice of specific theories is influenced particularly by psychological factors and by other factors which are beyond and independent of logics. On the other hand, scientific theories legitimize and rationalize certain forms of social organization and certain types of everyday perceptions.

Like previous ones, the following examples are not meant to be mutually exclusive or exhaustive.

Relation of the Nonreciprocal Causal Epistemology to Social Organization and Perception

This epistemology is related to hierarchical, classificational, anthropocentric, quantitative, homogenistic, and competitive social organizations and perceptions.

HIERARCHICAL. There are two ways the word hierarchy is used. In the field of social science, it is used in the sense of subordinate-superordinate relationship of political, economic, or social power, as in the channel of command, organizational chart, or exploiter/exploited relationship. On the other hand, in physical and biological sciences, hierarchy is used in the sense of larger or smaller units of organization. For example, atoms combine and make a molecule; molecules combine and make a cell or a crystal; cells combine and make a tissue; tissues combine and make an organ; organs combine and make a body.

Let me first use the word hierarchy in the sense of subordinate-superordinate relationship and return to its other use in the section entitled "Quantitative."

The nonreciprocal causal epistemology is related to hierarchical thinking, such as the notion of god as creator, prime mover, and the only master. In Christian and Islamic cultures, religion is almost always defined as belief in one god. Another aspect of this type of hierarchical thinking is the assumption that everything can be rank-ordered. If there are two different things, one must be superior to the other. If there are many things, one must be the supreme, etc. One of the definitions of god, given by a medieval theologian, is: The being, to which nothing else is superior. This type of thinking generated the notions of perfect, omnipotent, omniscient, etc.

The assumption that all things can be ranked also fosters the notion of the value system. It assumes that in every culture values can be ranked. It does not consider the possibility that in many cultures the universe has structures that cannot be ranked. This type of relativism based on the assumption that all things can be ranked is only pseudorelativism. It is a hierarchical relativism which assumes hierarchy in each culture.

Hierarchical thinking also looks for leadership structure even where there is no hierarchy. Thus, many politicians attributed the ghetto riots of the 1960s to "a small number of agitators from outside," and were unable to see that the widespread dissatisfaction among ghetto residents was the main cause. Similarly, many laws made by white legislators compelled some nonhierarchical American Indian tribes and Eskimos to organize hierarchical structures, such as chiefs and tribal councils. The result was not only a disruption of their cultures but also the legitimation and glorification of cultural deviants who, against their tradition of nonhierarchy, seized the opportunity for careers in the hierarchical system imposed from outside.

CLASSIFICATIONAL. The nonreciprocal epistemology is closely related to classificational thinking. This is because the Aristotelian logic, in which the nonreciprocal causal epistemology originated, was based on the concepts of substance and identity. Let us first review these origins.

Early Greek philosophers entertained the notion of the universe as composed of some basic *substances*, such as air, water, earth, and fire. Then in the sixth century B.C., a Greek scientist, Anaximandros, conceived the notion of infinity as the inexhaustible protosubstance of the universe. Since no material substance knowable by human senses fulfilled his requirements for the infinity-substance, he thought that this substance must be beyond all human experience. Xenophanes applied this concept to religion. Until then the Greeks had many gods who were like humans. Proud of his "discovery" and scornful of the human-like gods, Xenophanes declared that his infinite god was not comparable with humans and was eternal. In the fifth century B.C., a philosopher, Anaxagoras, developed the notion of a power-substance which penetrated into things and caused them to move. He thought that the power-substance must be a soul and must have order and purpose. He ascribed rationality to it.

A little later the sophists taught the principle of identity and the law of contradictions and originated the Western tendency to think in categories. Plato gave abstract ideas higher reality than concrete things and advocated that true reality had no materiality. Plato also formulated the logical subordination of the more particular to the more general. In the fourth century B.C., Aristotle established the logic of deduction of the particular from the general. Circular reasoning became forbidden. Here was the foundation of the nonreciprocal causal epistemology. Despite occasional rebellions within the Western philosophy against this epistemology, it remained the "mainstream" epistemology until recently, when the theory of relativity, quantum mechanics, and cybernetics began questioning the notions of substance, identity, and unidirectional causality.

Thus, the nonreciprocal causal epistemology is very closely related to the notions of substance, identity, and categorizability of the universe. Furthermore, classificational thinking is related to hierarchical thinking: categories are divided into subcategories, and may be combined into supercategories. This subordination-superordination relationship forms a "hierarchy" in the second sense, i.e., in the sense of units of organization.

To people who accept classificational thinking, the universe appears to consist of categories. They live in the classificational universe. These categories are thought to be mutually exclusive and invariable in different situations; they persist in time and space and have a higher reality than things and individuals. This type of thinking causes many people to draw up a list of factors or dimensions which are supposed to be universally valid. It also results in patterns of reasoning, such as, "If someone criticizes our government, he must be a Communist"; or, "If someone is against homogenization and standardization, he must be an Anarchist"; or "If someone does not agree with me, he must be an enemy and must be eliminated."

These are exaggerated examples. But classificational thinking may sneak in at a more sophisticated level, in a more subtle way. For example, the distinction between open system and closed system arises because of the assumption that something can be looked at as a closed system. This assumption may come from classificational thinking. People in the classificational universe tend to perceive all systems as closed unless otherwise stated, while people who are not in the classificational universe perceive exactly the opposite. Or more exactly, people who do not use classificational thinking see the entire universe as a connected whole, and do not even perceive systems as something isolated. In this perception, there is only one system which is the whole universe, which may be called closed, if you wish.

I once had a slight miscommunication when I was discussing steady state with a physicist. Steady state is a situation in which the structure remains the same but the elements in it move. We were talking about a waterfall and evaporation from a lake, as examples. At one point he said that these are two different kinds of systems. I did not quite understand what he meant. Further discussion made it clear to us that he was perceiving the waterfall as water passing through and never coming back and the lake as water evaporating and returning through condensation. In my perception, water passed through the waterfall and returned eventually as rainfall or in some other way. The physicist was thinking of open versus closed systems. I was thinking of the whole earth as a single system.

Classificational thinking can occur also in certain uses of spatial analogies. For example, what some persons in classificational thinking mean by perspective is different from what others not in classificational thinking mean. The former use it in the sense of space divisible into sections or dimensions. There are several versions of this use: (a) as corresponding to different parts, as in the case of blind men touching different parts of an elephant; (b) as corresponding to different dimensions, as in the case of photos of a building taken from different angles; (c) as corresponding to different magnification factors of a microscope or a telescope, often corresponding to the size of unit of organization. On the other hand, for many of the persons who are not in classificational thinking, perspective may mean something like overlays of different color components of the same photograph.

Classificational thinking also makes people perceive science as though it consisted of distinct fields of specialization. However, the reality which science studies is not divided into such categories. This misconception has several consequences:

a. Often reality is not studied as it is.

b. Persons in specialized fields tend to see their views as valid and applicable to any situation regardless of the context. For example, a civil engineer may consider his highway design as desirable in any society; an educator may consider his philosophy of education as applicable to any culture; a physician may consider the American type of treatment as desirable in any country; etc.

c. Experts are given excessive confidence and authority. For example, a city planner may disregard the opinions of grass-roots people on the assumption that he is the expert. He may assume that their disagreement is due to their ignorance. He may not realize that the disagreement may result from his ignorance of the community conditions, goals, and relevance.

Too often sociologists and anthropologists entertain the illusion that they are the experts on the community they study. This occurs in two ways: (a) many an anthropologist talks patronizingly about "my tribe," as if the tribe were his or her property or territory to be guarded against other anthropologists; (b) he (she) considers himself (herself) as a spokesperson for the tribe, as if the tribe members could not speak for themselves. When it is suggested that the tribe members can speak for themselves or can conduct a research from their own point of view, such anthropologists feel threatened and immediately erect an array of defense mechanisms. He or she may claim that the tribe members have no professional training, or are not objective enough.

Still worse, many sociologists and anthropologists are more theory-centered than people-centered: they regard the community from the point of view of its utility for testing theories, without even questioning whether their theories are relevant to the community people. If the community people perceive the irrelevance of the purpose of the research conceptualized by outsiders, they may use many sophisticated ways to feed phony information to the researchers. They can even foster the illusion of relevance in the researchers' minds, and pretend to be stupid and ignorant in order not to arouse suspicion in the researchers (Maruyama 1969). Many researchers are unaware of, or ignore, such possibilities for two reasons: (a) awareness would make them realize that the community people are more intelligent than the researchers; (b) awareness would make them realize that the findings of their research are based on phony data.

Not only many social scientists consider themselves "experts" on the community they study, but also many others consider them to be experts on the community. All this comes from the fallacious notion of "experts" in classificational thinking.

Another consequence of the categorization of science into fields of specialization is the necessity for remedy by such roundabout procedures as interdisciplinary programs, holistic views, and suggestions that generalists should be produced. The concept of interdisciplinary presupposes that there are first disciplines which have to be recombined. Since reality is not divided into disciplines, it is more appropriate to promote nondisciplinary, not interdisciplinary programs. Too often interdisciplinary programs consist in bringing together categorized experts, categorized courses. Holistic thinking often uses similar procedures.

To compound the problem further, some people promote generalists. This idea has two epistemological fallacies: (a) generalists are supposed to be different from specialists and therefore are not required or supposed to have detailed knowledge of anything specific. This concept of generalists, the result of classificational thinking, is a monstrosity. Generalists are armchair speculators whose work does not correspond to reality and is useless to anyone but themselves. They cannot even relate to specialists (Maruyama 1977b).

Interdisciplinary programs, holistic views, and the production of generalists are all patchworks which perpetuate and aggravate the inade-

quacies of classificational thinking. What we need, instead, is nondisciplinary programs, decategorization of science, and transspecialization.
Transspecialization consists in maintaining a contextual view while focus-
ing on specifics and details.

Shannon's information theory is related to classificational thinking and
is extremely useful in tasks requiring classification. The purpose of a
message is to *specify* one alternative, or a small number of alternatives,
among many. Suppose you want to know where a friend of yours has
moved to and write to your friends who might know where he is. An
answer specifying the country of his new residence has some information
value. A letter specifying the city has more information value. A letter
giving you his street number as well as the name of the city has even
more information value. But a letter which does not specify either state,
city, or street number has no more information value than the tossing
of coins. The chance of guessing the right state out of fifty states by
tossing coins is not very high, but higher than the chance of guessing the
right city out of 200 cities. The more specific the guess has to be, the lower
the chance of guessing it right by a random process. Therefore, the
measure of specificity corresponds to the measure of nonrandomness.

ANTHROPOCENTRIC. The nonreciprocal causal epistemology puts *Homo
sapiens* at the top of the subordinate-superordinate hierarchy. It considers animals, plants, and natural elements as inferior to humans and
advocates man's exploitation of them. The same type of argument has
been used in support of white colonialism against nonwhite nations. We
will discuss this aspect under the section entitled competitive.

QUANTITATIVE. The nonreciprocal causal epistemology is related also to
quantitative social organization and perception. The notion of ranking
has already been discussed.

Another quantitative notion is legitimation of domination by quantity,
such as the *majority rule* (so-called democracy). The advocates of majority rule say that it is better than minority rule. This argument is fallacious
because it is based on the assumptions: (a) that somebody must rule; (b)
that society must be ruled homogeneously; (c) that if it is not the majority
that is ruling, it has to be the minority. All three assumptions come from
the nonreciprocal causal epistemology. The first comes from hierarchical
thinking; the second from homogenistic thinking, which will be discussed
next; and the third from classificational thinking. This argument does not
consider a heterogenistic symbiotic system as an alternative to majority
rule.

As mentioned earlier, quantitative thinking manifests itself also in the
second usage of the term "hierarchical," in the sense of larger or smaller
units of organization. It is also related to the third meaning of perspective,

in the sense of different magnification factors. Another consequence is that ethnic, genetic and other differences are assumed to imply superiority/inferiority ranking (Maruyama 1978).

HOMOGENISTIC. The nonreciprocal causal epistemology is closely related to homogenistic thinking: in it, there is only one god. In nonreligious terms, it is assumed that there is one universally valid truth. It also is assumed that there is one logic, one right answer, one right way of doing things, etc. This type of thinking fosters ethnocentrism: whatever is good for Americans — three meals a day, flush toilets, or encounter groups — is the salvation for everybody else in the world. We need not explore the many travesties of ethnocentrism. But let us examine several specific ethnocentric statements. "Mexican-Americans should organize and come up with a leader if they want to be heard"; "Orientals must have made it in this country because they look happy and make no complaints." These two statements are ethnocentric because they are based on the assumptions: (a) that people who are dissatisfied make complaints; (b) that you must make noise in order to be heard. In addition, the first statement is ethnocentric because it further assumes (c) that lack of hierarchical structure is a deficiency.

Let me elaborate on these three assumptions. The American culture is a noise-making, complaint-making culture. Many other cultures are not, but this does not mean that they are inferior. They have different systems of communication. The assumption that everybody does and ought to make noise when dissatisfied is a very ethnocentric assumption. Furthermore, not all cultures are hierarchical. The Chicano (Mexican-American) culture is basically family centered and built on mutual loyalty between friends, not on formal hierarchical structure.

Our ethnic question is: Why should these nonstandard cultures conform to the main society to have their opinions and feelings taken into consideration? After all, Chicanos (called "Mexican-Americans" by white people), Asian Americans (called "Orientals" by white people), and Native Americans (called "American Indians" by white people) are all citizens and taxpayers. Why shouldn't they have the right to be heard by using their own way of communication?

We have already discussed under the section quantitative the fallacious assumption that democracy can be achieved by majority rule. Homogenistic thinking produces a similar fallacy by assuming that equality lies in homogeneity. There are two epistemologically different directions in the concept of "integration." In homogenistic thinking, integration consists in letting a black man move into a white neighborhood and letting him behave like a white man. In heterogenistic thinking, on the other hand, integration consists in having Japanese, Africans, etc., move into a white neighborhood and make Japanese gardens, African gardens, etc., in their front yards. Similarly, the Women's Liberation Movement has two epistemologically different components. One component aims at homogenization of women and men. The other component aims at asserting that women's right to be different from men's.

People in homogenistic thinking look for universals at two levels. The less sophisticated assume that their own system must be the universal for everybody else. These people produce the missionary do-gooders. The more sophisticated assume that the differences are only on the surface. These persons assume that all religions in the world ultimately worship the same god whom they assume to be omnipotent, omniscient, and perfect, the prime-mover and supreme being. They exclude religions which are based on harmony between many gods, none of whom is superior to others. They insist that beyond these many gods there must be one god. Such an insistence is an ethnocentric distortion, which fails to understand its own misinterpretation. This will be discussed further under the heterogenistic thinking related to the reciprocal causal epistemology.

Homogenistic thinking exists even among many sociologists and anthropologists, who insist that they have a universally valid research method and are therefore better qualified to do research than community members.

Another manifestation of homogenistic thinking is an almost philosophical tendency to ignore differences in many aspects of our official activities. A post office is supposed to be open for a fixed number of hours a day, regardless of the seasonal change in the length of daylight. A pregnant secretary is supposed to work as if she is not pregnant. In fact, in most cases an employee is supposed to work like any other employee. Homogenistic liberals compel themselves to be diversity-blind.

COMPETITIVE. The nonreciprocal causal epistemology legitimizes and encourages the exploitation of the less powerful by the more powerful and the exploitation of the less fortunate by the more fortunate. It is considered almost a moral obligation to take advantage of power and of every opportunity for exploitation. The underdog is considered to be of his own making and to deserve to be exploited. In such an epistemology, one must defend oneself from being exploited, and the only way to defend oneself is to exploit before being exploited, or to counterexploit while and after being exploited. Parasitism is justified, legitimized, and admired in such a system. In competitive thinking, differences are supposed to cause conflicts, and one's equals are supposed to be his competitors. There are constant fear, tension, and preventive aggression.

IMPACT ANALYSIS. A currently fashionable activity in many government and planning agencies is impact analysis. This activity is based on the

nonreciprocal causal epistemology. The actual biological and social processes, however, are characterized by many reciprocal causal loops which
cause the effect of an action or an undertaking to come back to itself in
such a way as to cancel or amplify itself. For example a highway, which
was unnecessary when it was built, may cause residential developments
along it. This will make the highway not only necessary, but also overloaded. As a result, more highways must be built. Impact analysis, which
does not take the network of causal loops into consideration, is a fundamentally wrong logical model.

Relation of the Independent-Event Epistemology to Social Organization and Perception

This epistemology is related to egocentric, isolationistic, atomistic, and
capricious social organization and perception.

EGOCENTRIC. "Vote for your own interest" has been the principle of
American democracy. Each person is encouraged to vote for his/her
interest or for the interest of his/her faction or party. Persons voting in this
fashion have accomplished their duty and are considered to be exemplary
citizens. A statistical tabulation is supposed to take care of the rest. This
amounts to domination by quantity, as we have discussed.

ISOLATIONISTIC. The "do your own thing" philosophy, which recently
developed among the youths is nevertheless traditional because it
belongs to the independent-event epistemology. On the other hand, the
communal philosophy, which is practiced by some of the same people, is
closer to the reciprocal causal epistemology.

An extension of the "do your own thing" philosophy can be mutualistic
toward group members but isolationistic toward the outside. I once
talked with the director of an encounter group institute near San Francisco. She was devoted to her program but she hated black people. Often
such activities serve not as a device to relate to others, but as a device to
escape into an enclave. Many of the exclusive clubs and secret societies
serve similar purposes.

The "here and now" philosophy is another version of isolationistic
thinking: it isolates the individual from the past and from the future and
from those who are not in the immediate vicinity.

ATOMISTIC. The atomistic, noncontextual perception is related to the
independent-event as well as to classificational thinking. People with this
type of perception tend to consider each object as separate from other
objects. "Small is beautiful" movement may become atomistic.

A black basketball coach once told me that white coaches drive black basketball players nuts: white coaches tell black players how to react to specific moves of specific opponents step by step, while the black players perceive the flow of the entire floor and move accordingly. Similarly, there are differences in the way Judo is taught in Japan and in the United States. Americans tend to emphasize step-by-step reactions. On the other hand in Japan, the first phase of Judo education consists in cultivating the state of mind while the person is in a sitting or standing position, without being distracted by specific happenings to perceive the entire surroundings. A real test of a samurai is not in his swordsmanship but in his ability to perceive someone approaching from behind or sense a hidden enemy behind a doorway.

Atomistic thinking tends to separate individuals as units first, before making connections between them. The individual in the American culture is considered to be somewhat empty unless efforts for self-fulfillment are made.

NONCONTEXTUAL RELATIVISM. "Anybody may do anything in any which way as long as he does not bother anybody else" is a principle related to the independent-event epistemology. It is a noncontextual relativism. This type of thinking advocates that since Eskimos used to kill their grandfathers, it is all right for anyone to kill his grandfather in American culture, or that since the Japanese practice public nude bathing of mixed sexes, it is all right for an American in Japan to walk in the nude on the street. Persons who think noncontextually do not realize that the appropriateness of behavior is determined by cultural context and in relation to other behaviors.

THE CREATIVITY CONTROVERSY. Much of the controversy over creativity stems from inappropriate epistemologies. There are two common fallacies regarding creativity: (a) the tendency to equate randomness with creativity and spontaneity; (b) the argument that artists do not really create new patterns but make new combinations of old patterns. The first fallacy does not even apply Shannon's information theory where it can be applied.

The first fallacy is particularly common among American grammar school teachers. Let me begin with some examples. Three years ago I taught a workshop of school teachers. For some weeks we concentrated our efforts on developing ways to encourage school children to question traditional assumptions and propose and examine new assumptions. One day a teacher said that a boy in her class came up with the idea of a flying chair, and she thought it was wonderful. What I would like to emphasize here is that she stopped there and did not do anything creative with the boy. She could have explored with him different designs or means of propulsion for a flying chair, or could have conducted various experiments which might have lead to the invention of a real flying chair.

Another teacher mentioned that the children in her class said they see ghosts which grownups do not see. She thought this was a wonderful example of creative thinking. Like the first teacher, she did not do anything creative with the idea. She could have set up various experiments. For example, she could have had each child write a detailed description of the ghost independently of other children. If the descriptions by different children disagreed, then there was very little validity to the ghost. If the descriptions agreed, further experiments could have been conducted. For example, the agreement might have come from the children having read the same ghost story. She could have had one group of children read one ghost story, and another group another ghost story, and seen whether these different stories had different influences on the description of the ghosts they claimed to see. It is also possible that the children did see something which the teacher did not see. Then she could have made various traditional and nontraditional hypotheses including optical illusion, extra sensory perception, the possibility that some animal, more intelligent than humans, was playing a trick, and many others.

A one-shot fantasy may be the beginning of a chain of creative activities. But if one stops after a one-shot fantasy, one is hardly being creative. One simply becomes a capricious, wishful dreamer. The point I would like to make is not that the person is incapable of implementing the dream in a material form, but that he or she is not pursuing imagination further and elaborating.

Symphonies, great paintings, architecture, literature, poetry, etc., are works of creativity. But they are not born by accumulation of random caprice. They require a great deal of elaboration and development. The artist develops new patterns during the laborious process. This process is not a dull routine, though it may take years. The same goes for technological inventions and scientific discoveries. The caprice approach to creativity taken by a considerable percentage of grammar school teachers and others is hardly conducive to creativity. Even Shannon's information theory can show that it is highly unlikely that accumulation of random noises can compose a beautiful symphony.

The second fallacy is the faulty application of Shannon's theory in which information can decrease but never increases. Following this type of reasoning, if you have some information, you could not have created it: it must have come from somewhere. Or if you have an artistic pattern, you could not have created it: it must have come from somewhere.

Those who argue this way do not realize that they are using a faulty causal model. Their argument holds only if the human activities were random processes. Ironically, this argument shares the same epistemology with the random caprice theory of creativity. But thanks to the recent

development of the reciprocal causal models, we now know that reciprocal causal processes can increase differentiation, heterogeneity, structuredness, and nonredundant complexity. Human activities, both interpersonal and intrapsychic, are reciprocal causal processes. Thus, creativity is possible. Where there are interactions, whether among individuals
or within one person's mind, new patterns can be created. New patterns
do not have to come from elsewhere.

Those who applied Shannon's information theory wrongly to human
creativity were faced with the fact that people do create new patterns.
Unable to explain this contradiction, they escaped by begging the question, saying that creative people make new combinations out of old
elements. This explanation was incorrect in two ways: (a) they still did not
explain how new combinations come about; (b) they held that there could
be no new elements.

Now the elements/combinations dichotomy has become unnecessary.
New patterns, whether within an element or between elements, can be
created. The key is the reciprocally amplifying interaction between artists
or between concepts in one person's mind. Creativity does not come from
random caprice. It comes from reciprocally amplifying interactive processes. Therefore, development of creativity in children is not a matter of
developing caprice, but a matter of exploring the opportunities and the
skills for: (a) exchanges of ideas between persons; (b) interaction of
concepts within one person's mind.

Two studies throw new light on this process: Mead's *Continuities in
cultural evolution* (1964) and Wright's classic study on the speed of
evolution (1931). Mead analyzed how the informal networks among
scientists produce innovations. Wright studies how the speed of evolution
is related to the ratio of the mutation rate to the size of interactive
population. When the mutation rate is low and the population size is
large, interbreeding between mutants and normal individuals or between
mutants of opposite directions tend to cancel out the mutations and the
speed of evolution is very slow. When the mutation rate is very high and
the population size is small, the inbreeding effect tends to amplify the
mutations rapidly. Evolution may take place so fast that the newly
evolved species has no time to adapt to the environment, to seek an
appropriate new environment, or to work out new types of relationships
between individuals. And the whole species may become extinct.

When the mutation rate is moderate and the population size is neither
too large nor too small, a mixture of stabilization and change takes place,
and the phenomenon of random drift occurs: a change may be amplified
for a while followed by stabilization, another change in a new direction,
and so on. A faster rate of evolution occurs when the total population is
subdivided into semi-isolated colonies, connected by occasional interbreeding.

Wright's theory holds true when the Mendelian law is operative in the breeding process. Intellectual evolution does not always follow the Mendelian law. For example, in intellectual intercourse between an unusual mind and an ordinary mind, the product would be "pulled down" by the ordinary mind, if the Mendelian law were operative. In fact, this may be the case when an innovator is held back by bureaucracy or by his conservative colleagues. If the percentage of innovators is small and the total population is large and conservative, the situation is analogous to that of a low mutation rate and large population size. But it is quite possible that the others do not hold back the innovators. In this case, Mendelian law does not apply, and evolution may be rapid.

If a number of similar minded innovators get together and seclude themselves from the innovators of different mind as well as from the rest of society, the situation is similar to that of a high mutation rate within a small population. The peculiarities within the group may be amplified so fast that there is no time for working out the details and making them fit together within the new intellectual structure, not to mention time for the adjustment of the new ideology to the rest of the society. On the other hand, small networks of innovators, scattered in many different cultures or different social contexts, may work out their intellectual evolution independently, and exchange ideas between networks, while avoiding excessive mutual imitation which would lead to homogenization. Then perhaps the speed of intellectual evolution might be greater.

Subdivision of a very large population into moderate-size subpopulations has at least two advantages in the biological evolution: (a) it encourages development of heterogeneity between the subpopulations and increases the number of different stocks between which crossbreeding can be made; (b) it allows multibranch evolution, in which the different branches serve as different alternatives for the total species. In case of unexpected disasters, such as a change in climate, the existence of many branches of evolution increases the probability of survival of the species as a whole.

Basically the same may be said about intellectual evolution. However, there are some differences between physical and intellectual breeding: (a) physical breeding depends on two individuals being physically together, while intellectual communication can take place over a great distance, and can bypass individuals who are physically near; (b) one can exercise a great deal of selectivity and filtering in communication; (c) the Mendelian law does not apply to intellectual communication; (d) one person may communicate with many persons at the same time.

Therefore, the subpopulations in intellectual communication do not have to be geographically separated. The communication selectivity among individuals tends to separate individuals who do not select one another and divides the total population into subpopulations. A network may be non geographical: it may include individuals from many countries and many cultures and exclude many individuals within the same geographic location.

Taking these differences into consideration, Wright's theory can be interpreted as follows: a high speed of intellectual evolution can be achieved by allowing international and local networks of innovators to develop. The formation of a network is based mainly on mutual selection among innovators, provided the innovators have sufficient opportunities to meet and get to know one another before making their selections. Different networks work independently in order to allow different directions to develop. Exchanges of ideas between networks are possible but not to promote imitation.

A question naturally arises here: who are innovators and who are not? Here we should not fall into hierarchical and classificational thinking. Being an innovator has nothing to do with having a high intelligence quotient or a doctorate. An innovator is anyone who looks for, experiments with, and implements ideas that are not traditional.

The next question is: is being creative the same as being innovative? There are several opinions on this question. Some say that being creative is being capricious and impulsive, as we discussed. Others say that being creative is making something that goes into history books. Still others say that being creative is experiencing and doing something that is new to yourself, not necessarily new to anybody else. I tend to agree with this third opinion. I think the persons who experience, experiment with, and implement ideas new to themselves are genuine innovators and genuinely not traditional, while persons who primarily aim at accomplishing something that will go into history books may be compulsive and rigid. Those who look for new ideas accept input from others and are delighted to share their ideas. Those who aim at attaining historical fame may be less free in communication, and may be hierarchical, classificational, and competitive.

The caprice school of creativity falls in the random process epistemology. The history-making school of creativity follows the nonreciprocal causal epistemology. The third alternative is a theory of creativity in the morphogenetic epistemology. We must also take the following into consideration: Should the teacher assign children to groups, or should there be some process in which children can form non hierarchical groups themselves without being dominated by bullies? Should children with the same interest get together, or should children of different interest mix together? I think the answer depends on the children's age. But basically it is beneficial for a child to work sometimes in a homogeneous group, and sometimes in a heterogeneous group.

*Relation of the Reciprocal Causal Epistemologies to Social
Organization and Perception*

These epistemologies related to nonhierarchical, heterogenistic, symbiotic, harmonistic, contextual, relational, polyocular, and process-oriented
social organization and perception.

NONHIERARCHICAL. The Navajo culture is an example of nonhierarchical
societies. The Navajo universe is characterized by mutual relations between several types of beings as well as between beings of the same type:
human, animals, supernatural beings, ghosts, and natural forces (Kluckhohn 1949). Humans can manipulate supernatural and natural forces
by using appropriate formulas, and these forces can influence humans;
animals can influence people; and people can influence animals; etc.
There is no hierarchy in terms of the direction of influence. Among
native Americans, there were no hierarchical organizations before the
white government made Navajos organize the tribal council and other
structures. There were no chiefs in the sense of political authority. Old
men and women, as well as people with experience, were sought out as
advisers when the occasion arose, but those who sought their advice did
not have to obey them. They could ignore the advice or change the
advisers. White people often mistook these advisers for chiefs or leaders.
   No one, either human or supernatural, is perfect, omnipotent or
omniscient. In fact, such concepts do not exist in Navajo epistemology.
There are not even the concepts "good" and "evil." The Navajo concept
closest our "good" is "nice." Each of the supernatural beings can be both
beneficial and dangerous to humans, depending on the circumstances and
the way humans behave toward them.
   Epistemologically, Navajos may be considered to resemble the
Nominalists in some ways. Like Swedes and Danes, Navajos judge each
situation according to its specific circumstances and do not think in terms
of general principles or absolutes. Yet Navajos are not atomistic as some
Nominalists were, because Navajos think in terms of harmony, relations
and contexts, not in terms of unrelated individuals.
   The Eskimo culture is also nonhierarchical. Traditionally there are no
chiefs. But often the legal technicalities imposed from outside require
that there be a chief in each village in Alaska. Eskimos get around these
technicalities by letting someone in the village who speaks English function as an interpreter and calling him "chief."
   Not all native American (American Indian) cultures are nonhierarchical. There are many highly hierarchical cultures like Kwakiutl and Hopi.
But most of the people in native American cultures shy away from
competition. Among the Indians and Eskimos who now work in factories,
promotion of someone to a supervisory position makes everybody

uncomfortable, including the promoted person. The usual white procedure, in schools, "those who know the answer raise your hand" is very alien, and incompatible with native American culture.

The proponents of hierarchical systems claim that nonhierarchical systems do now work in a large society. But the Navajo population is 135,000 (1969) on the reservation in addition to the 50,000 or more living and working in urban areas. This is a good-sized society, more than half the size of Dayton, Ohio, which had 243,600 persons at the time of the 1970 census. The size of the society is not a basic obstacle to implementation of nonhierarchical systems, especially if we make nonhierarchical use of computers.

HETEROGENISTIC. Thanks to the mathematical sophistication of reciprocal causal analysis in biological sciences in recent years, it has become clear that the basic principle of biological and social processes is increase of differentiation, diversification, heterogenization, symbiotization, networks, and nonrepetitious complexity. On the other hand, our social philosophy and ideology have been until recently, and in many ways are today, homogenistic. It was commonly believed that standardization would lead to efficiency, social unity, decrease of conflict, and so-called democracy.

Some propose that such a philosophy and ideology was necessary in the industrialization of society, in which humans worked like machines and mass production was promoted for its economic efficiency. It is also said that we are getting out of this type of thinking as we enter the new post-industrial stage, in which material productivity becomes only a minor portion of our concern. We can shift our efforts to destandardization and heterogenization.

There is much truth in this point of view. But it is a mistake to equate standardization with efficiency. In biological sciences, we know that diversification and heterogenization are often more efficient than standardization and homogenization. The tropical rain forest makes maximum use of the solar energy with its heterogeneous vegetation. It consists of many different species of plants: tall trees, short trees, undergrowth, vines. Similarly, the coral reef hosts many species of fish and other animals and plants. This heterogeneity enables a large number of individuals to coexist within a given area by allowing them to feed on different types of food. If all species ate the same food, there would be food shortage, competition, and conflict. If not all species were eaten, there would be waste.

There are many aspects of human life which can be made more efficient by heterogenization. For example, the commuter traffic jam as a result of many people going to and returning from work, at the same time. The jam can be alleviated by diversifying working hours. In fact, the city of

Sacramento, California, has been practicing diversification of office hours for many years, in order to decrease the traffic jam. Sacramento is the state capital of one of the largest states in America, and government office workers are a major percentage of its labor force. Instead of enforcing an 8:00 a.m. to 5:00 p.m. schedule in all agencies, the state government established diversified work schedules: from 7:00 a.m. to 4:00 p.m.; from 7:30 a.m. to 4:30 p.m.

Heterogenization can also increase in efficiency within the life pattern of an individual. Time is not homogeneous within the twenty-four hour cycle. Each individual has certain specific hours of the day in which he/she is more effective at certain activities and to treat all hours of the day and all days of the week homogeneously is a very inefficient practice. There are days or hours in which one's mind is not clear enough for intellectual work, and to force oneself to do intellectual work at such times is not only frustrating but also highly inefficient. The time can be spent more efficiently in routine or miscellaneous work, etc.

Another consideration is that the human mind, unlike the machine, is oriented toward heterogeneity, though there are individual differences in this respect. Some individuals need a high degree of heterogeniety, while others are more comfortable with a high degree of homogeneity. In our discussion of creativity we mentioned the interaction *within* an individual's mind as well as between individuals: nobody is completely single-tracked, and each individual has some degree of heterogeneity of interests, ideas, feelings, etc. Just as the body needs various nutrients, vitamins, and minerals for healthy activity and equilibrium, the mind needs heterogeneous mental food. Monotonous or restricted work or even interesting but single-track work impoverishes and atrophies the mind and makes it less efficient. In such cases efficiency can be increased by heterogenizing the work: an individual can be hired, not for a fixed task, but for as wide a range of tasks as his/her mind requires, but caution must be taken not to overreach the worker's comfort level of heterogeneity. This philosophy of employment may be bewildering to the bureaucracy which equates efficiency with simplicity. But in the long run it can increase workers' efficiency many times.

So far we have discussed heterogenization within the individual's pattern of life. But heterogeneity between individuals or between communities is more commonly discussed. In this respect, there are two ways in which heterogenization can take place: (a) localization; and (b) interweaving. Localization consists in increasing the heterogeneity between groups, while increasing the homogeneity within each group. An example is the establishment of a Chinatown or a black community. The special group becomes distinguished from others, but it becomes homogeneous within itself. Interweaving, on the other hand, increases the heterogeneity in each group but decreases the differences between the groups. An example is the increasing popularity of Judo, Karate, Yoga, etc., among white Americans and of golf in Japan. In this process each person increases his/her inventory of choices and opportunities, regardless of geographical location or group affiliation. Interweaving should not be confused with assimiliation, which decreases each individual's inventory of choices and opportunities.

I mentioned earlier that integration has two opposite meanings depending on which epistemology is used: it may mean homogenization or heterogenization. Now we may say that its second meaning is interweaving.

Similarly, internationalization can mean either homogenization or heterogenization. It is often said that in the future internationalization will increase world communication, understanding, and unity. Behind such a statement there may be a hidden fallacy or an incorrect assumption. First of all, if homogenization is meant, the statement itself is a gross misunderstanding: it fails to understand the basic principle of the increase of heterogeneity in biological and social processes. But there is a second, different assumption which is also fallacious: commonness will increase communication. This notion is fallacious because *it is heterogeneity, not homogeneity, that increases communication*. Even in Shannon's formulation, the amount of information increases with the increase in the nonredundant part of complexity; in other words with the increase of heterogeneity. A message has an information value if it conveys something different from what one already knows or from what one can guess easily. If two persons think exactly in the same way and have exactly the same information, no message between them has any information value, and there is no need to communicate in the first place. Communication becomes interesting, informative, and enlightening because there is heterogeneity in the world.

In closing my discussion on the topic of heterogeneity, let me add that there are even aesthetic principles of heterogeneity. Aesthetic principles vary from culture to culture (Maruyama 1972b). Some of the Islamic designs are characterized by intricate repetitions of minute details. The French and Italian gardens and Gothic architecture achieve their design unity by repetitions of similar elements. On the other hand, the Japanese gardens and flower arrangements avoid repetitions and redundancies and create harmony out of dissimilar elements. Many Japanese designs use a triangle of unequal sides as the basic layout, often with secondary triangles added, which are supposed to be *dissimilar* to the main triangle. In contrast, European architectural design, the subdominant forms are supposed to repeat the main form. In China, however, we find both the principle of repetition and the principle of nonredundancy. Chinese architecture and interior decoration can be highly repetitious and elaborate, and some of the ancient Chinese poems are profuse in extravagant adjectives. But the traditional Chinese paintings as a whole have non-repetitious compositions.

As can be seen from Table 2, it is incorrect to identify the homogenistic epistemology and the independent-event epistemology as "Western" epistemologies. They are predominant in some of the non-Western cultures also. The Islamic religion is more hierarchical and categorical than

Table 2. Epistemological characteristics related to aesthetic principles, architecture and planning procedure

Homogenistic	Heterogenistic		
Nonreciprocal	Isolationistic	Reciprocally causal	
Hierarchical	Independent-event	Homeostatic	Morphogenetic
AESTHETIC PRINCIPLES			
Unity by similarity, repetition and symmetry. Dominant theme is reflected in subdominant themes. *Examples*: Gothic. Islamic. French garden. Japanese Yamato culture.	Random, capricious, haphazard, self-sufficient and unrelated to others.	Static harmony of diverse elements. Balance. Completed equilibrium which cannot be disturbed. Design may be asymmetrical. Avoid repetition of similar elements. Perfectionist. *Example*: Japanese Yayoi culture.	Changing harmony of diverse elements. Avoid repetition and symmetry. Designed for simultaneously multiple as well as changing interpretations. Deliberate incompleteness to enable addition of new elements and changes. *Example*: Japanese Jomon culture.
Some Japanese architecture shows hierarchical principles originating from Korea, homogenistic principles originating from China, and more recently from Europe and USA.		The Japanese garden design and flower arrangement incorporate both homeostatic and morphogenetic principles in varying proportions, depending on whether the Yayoi principle or the Jomon principle is emphasized.	
SPACE			
Defined as between masses, between points, along shafts.	Unrelated units.	Miniature universe. Self-contained internal interaction of heterogeneous elements.	Locality with its characteristics (spirits or feelings) connected to other localities. Often thought of as around something (rock, grove) which is considered to be condensation of spirits permeating the locality.

Table 2 (*continued*)

Homogenistic	Heterogenistic		
Nonreciprocal	Isolationistic	Reciprocally causal	
Hierarchical	Independent-event	Homeostatic	Morphogenetic

OBJECTS

As volume and mass opposing empty space. Often mass represents human; space represents nature.	Each is its own expression.	Represents elements of universe in static harmony.	Represents growing process, vitality, vicissitude. Often the object is a condensation of spirits which permeate locality, and therefore represents space, not mass.

TIME

Building is designed to persist in time. Permanence. Building is also considered to embody eternal principles.	Permanence is unimportant.	The form persists while the building materials may be renewed. (Example: re-building of ISE Shrine every twenty years).	Increasing heterogeneity and symbiotization. Design permits addition of new elements, change in patterns, etc. (Example: KATSURA Villa)

CONCEPTUAL MOVEMENT BETWEEN OBJECTS

Tension. Straight shaft extending beyond object. Straight line spanned between points. Lines radiating from a point or converging to a point. Curves created by physical contour of buildings.	Caprice. Random	Balance. Triangles of unequal sides. Circular loops or oscillation keeps returning to the same points. *Example*: some Japanese gardens.	Flow. Spiral or curve suggested by relative positions of objects, but not by objects themselves. Curves extend and do not return. If returned, some change has occurred such as height. *Example*: some flower arrangements.

PERCEIVER'S MOVEMENT

Sequential. The perceiver maintains his identity as a point which moves in space.	Random.	Perceiver permeates simultaneously in all parts, and feels invisible parts and behind objects. The entire design is perceived simultaneously, not sequentially.	Spiraling in the sense that at each return to the same point, the perceiver has been enriched and changed by intervening experience.

Table 2 (*continued*)

Homogenistic	Heterogenistic		
Nonreciprocal	Isolationistic	Reciprocally causal	
Hierarchical	Independent-event	Homeostatic	Morphogenetic

HOUSE

Separate the inside from the outside.	Separate one household from another.	Continuation of outside into inside. Removable outer shells. Garden continues into house. River flows under floor. Floor extends to outdoors. Passive appreciation of nature and environment.	A base for activity and interaction with environment, such as Japanese farm house. Or can be a base for interaction with other households.

ROOM

Specialized rooms (bedroom, dining) occupied by specialized furniture (beds etc.)	Specialized to individual user's needs rather than to generally categorized functions such as dining room.	Convertible. Furniture removable. Walls and partitions removable.	Convertible. Furniture removable. Walls and partitions removable.

SOCIABILITY

Socialize within homogeneous group. Hierarchy of groups, subgroups and supergroups.	Self-containment. Freedom from social obligations and freedom for individual caprice.	Mutual dependency. Concern over not disturbing equilibrium. Perpetuation of familiar relations.	Make new contacts, new networks, change patterns of interaction. Go beyond own group.

PRIVACY

Own group's privacy against other groups. Group solidarity. Concern with patent, copyright and other legal rights.	Individual insulation.	Maximum sharing of intimate concerns.	Less concern with privacy or property right, because interaction is seen as positive sum.

ACTIVITY

Hierarchically and homogenistically organized.	Up to the individual.	Nonhierarchical mutualistic activities to *maintain* harmony.	Generate new activities and new purposes through new contacts and new networks. Seek new symbiotic combinations and dissolve no-longer-symbiotic combinations.

Table 2 (*continued*)

Homogenistic	Heterogenistic		
Nonreciprocal	Isolationistic	Reciprocally causal	
Hierarchical	Independent-event	Homeostatic	Morphogenetic

CLARITY

Neat categories, clear without context.	Individual meaning is what counts.	Contextually interpreted, interdependent meaning.	Ambiguity is basic to further development and change.

DESIGN CHOICE

There is "the best design" for all persons.	Individualized design.	Traditional designs are considered to be results of most satisfactory equilibrium.	Generate new designs by interaction in new contexts.

PLANNING

By "experts."	Everybody makes own plan.	Plans are generated by members of the community and pooled together.	

DECISION PROCESS

Majority rule, consensus or "informing" the public in such a way that they will understand the "best" design.	Do your own thing. Let others alone.	Elimination of hardship on any single individual regardless of which way the decision is taken.	

the Chinese religion. The Hindu philosophy is also homogenistic and hierarchical. On the other hand the Mandenka (people of Manden) who live on and near the border between Senegal and Guinea in West Africa are morphogenetic (Camara 1975).

It is interesting to note that the Japanese philosophy has at least three underlying currents: The Jomon current which originated more than 9,000 years ago is morphogenetic; the Yayoi current which began about 300 B.C. is homeostatic; and the Yamato current which later came via Korea is hierarchical. The Jomon current accounts for the Japanese's view that nothing remains the same; hence their readiness to change. This contrasts with the traditional Chinese philosophy of oscillation in which the process returns to the same states. On the other hand, the Yayoi current is responsible for the Japanese's apparent rigidity, formality, and perfectionism, and the Yamato current is seen in the hierarchy consciousness of the Japanese. To add to the heterogeneity within the Japanese culture, the three currents have been distributed differently in different social classes. Until and including the feudal period the ruling class, which was small, was hierarchical and homeostatic, while the grass-roots culture of the farmers was equalitarian and reciprocally interactive. After the Meiji reform, the Yayoi and Yamato epistemologies have spread into the growing middle class, even though the Jomon current is still very basic in all social classes. Each person in the Japanese culture incorporates all three currents. The interaction between the Jomon and the Yayoi currents are also expressed in various forms of traditional and modern Japanese architecture (Tange and Kawazoe 1965; Tange 1972).

Furthermore, Japanese and the Mandenka philosophies are heterogenistic, while the Chinese philosophy is dualistic. Therefore the Chinese philosophy resembles the Greek logic on the surface, and it is this superficial resemblance which made the Europeans interpret the Chinese philosophy as having a "logical" structure, even though this interpretation contains some distortions. Similarly, Europeans recognized the Islamic and Hindu philosophies as "great philosophical systems" because these are hierarchical and homogenistic. One difference between the Christian philosophy and the Islamic philosophy is that the former has the dualistic structure of good and evil, while the latter is more unitary. In summary, the Islamic, the Hindu, and the Chinese philosophies, which the Westerners consider as "typically Eastern," have affinities to the Greek philosophy. On the other hand, the Jomon philosophy, the Mandenka philosophy, and to some extent the Navajo and the Eskimo philosophies constitute a different cluster, and have not yet been recognized as "philosophical systems" by Western philosophers. But by using the framework of the morphogenetic epistemology, this cluster can be formulated as philosophical systems (Maruyama 1977a).

Returning to Table 2, most of these concepts are self-explanatory. However, the concepts of space and objects in the Jomon culture require some explanation. In the primeval times in Japan, both space (locality) and matter were considered together under the concept of "mono," which also meant phenomena or vicissitude. Mono was permeated by "mononoke," similar to what anthropologists call "mana." There is no equivalent concept in the Western epistemologies. It is something like "forces," but *without* the Anaxagorean concept of "power substance." Eventually rocks came to be regarded as coalescence of mononoke. Much later the concept of personalized deities was born, and gradually rocks became abodes of the deities. Therefore initially the rocks represented space and a sort of "spiritual" quality rather than "matter," and only later turned into material objects (abodes). Even in this latter phase, the rocks were respected for their quality rather than for their size. Many ancient "shrines" in the form of rocks still remain, and the size of the rocks is rather small. Therefore in the Japanese epistemology and aesthetics, a rock is not a mass nor a material object, but represents space, spiritual quality, and process. Traditionally, rocks were considered to grow.

Similarly, the concept of space as something between masses did not occur. It was more like a locality permeated by mononoke. When the Japanese people became agricultural, the concept of land as property arose. About this time the concept of "shiki," a place reserved for a deity and his interaction with people, was developed. Again, a shiki was *not* defined as a space between masses, but was often marked by ropes spanned around it, or simply by laying white pebbles like a carpet. Thus "shiki" was not at all enclosed, but quite open and continuous to the areas around it.

In the Euro-American aesthetics, particularly in architecture, the mass opposes the space. The mass often symbolizes humans while the space is the nature to which they oppose. Forms are delineated by the physical contour of the mass, and the shape of the mass generates imaginary or real, straight shafts of space. The corners of the masses definite points, between which there is tension to be resolved.

The Yayoi principle, on the other hand, is characterized by the inter-penetration between the outdoor and the indoor, in which the concept of mass is meaningless. In the morphogenetic principle, a *flow* of imaginary curves is suggested by the *relative position* of objects, i.e., by the spatial relations rather than by mass. The rectilinear tension is an alien concept. Furthermore, the morphogenetic aesthetics is designed for multiple interpretations, while the homogenistic aesthetics aim at unambiguous and unalterable meaning.

But whatever the aim, an aesthetic object serves as a Rorschach test. The viewers or the critics see the principles they want to see. What they see is a reflection of their own epistemology rather than the epistemology of the creator of the object. For example, Edmund Bacon sees in a concave Chinese roof an expression of humble acceptance of heaven by man, basing this interpretation on his epistemology of mass opposing space (Bacon 1974). Or a French artist sees in a Japanese painting repetitions of certain curve forms. These interpretations usually involve dimension reduction (Maruyama 1969).

SYMBIOTIC. It is fallacious to believe that in order to get along people have to be of the same kind. Biology abounds in examples of organisms which get along together because they are different or even opposite. Take, for example, the relationship between plants and animals. The animals convert oxygen into carbon dioxide in their metabolic process. The plants convert carbon dioxide into oxygen in their photosynthesis. In this respect plants and animals do exactly the opposite, yet, they not only get along together, but they also need each other.

Some of the arguments which people in the homogenistic epistemology use against heterogeneity are: (a) differences would necessarily cause conflicts; (b) it would be impossible for several groups to gain at the same time (what someone gains must be someone else's loss). Both are fallacious. The first is fallacious because, in symbiosis, differences fulfill another's needs, which cannot be fulfilled by individuals of the same type. The second is fallacious because it is based on the assumption that everything is a zero-sum game. A zero-sum game is an interaction situation in which someone's gain is another's loss. In biology, only parasitism corresponds to the zero-sum game situation. Other types of interaction, such as symbiosis, antibiosis, and mutual antibiosis are not zero-sum games. In symbiosis, all parties involved can gain. In antibiosis, one party causes a loss to another party without gaining anything for itself. In mutual antibiosis, all parties cause a loss to one another.

We have seen that the random process tends to decrease structure and heterogeneity, while the reciprocal causal process can maintain and increase structuredness and heterogeneity by interaction. In our present society, however, there is another tendency which is a distorted mixture of random process and reciprocal causal process. It can be called separatism. It is a mixture of localization and the "do our own thing" philosophy: after localization has been achieved in a heterogenizing process, it turns into the isolationistic thinking discussed under the random process epistemology.

Separation has been advocated in some segments of ethnic and women's liberation movements as necessary for the "search for identity." It has also been advocated in many segments of youth movements which arose from the need to "drop out and turn inward." Separatism, though it might be necessary as a transitional step, has harmful effects, as in the case of the director of an encounter group institute who hates black people.

As noted earlier, the third phase of the development of the reciprocal causal models in science, which is to be characterized by the study of the processes of symbiotization of heterogeneity, is yet to come. Perhaps the remainder of the 1970s and the early part of the 1980s will witness an increase in our knowledge on the process of symbiotization of heterogeneity, both in science and in social implementation.

HARMONISTIC. The following incident illustrates the difference between harmonistic and hierarchical thinking. There was a culture in Africa which was based on a harmonistic philosophy. Its some 350 gods constituted the harmony of the universe. The purpose of the religion was participation in this harmony. One day a Christian missionary arrived and told the tribe members that he had brought them a god. The tribe welcomed the new god, expecting that it would become a part of the harmony. However, the missionary began advocating that there can be only one god and said that all other gods must be discarded. Had there been psychiatrists among the tribesmen, the missionary would have been diagnosed a genuine psychotic.

Those who advocate that behind different gods there is one true god do not understand the epistemological difference between non-hierarchical heterogenistic harmony and hierarchical homogenistic order. They are missing the basic point of harmonistic religions. It is not a matter of different names of the same god. The difference lies in the structure of the universe.

CONTEXTUAL. It is a frequent practice among Americans to ask abstract questions without context: "which color do you like best?" "Is murder good or bad?" Mead (1946) reports that the first question cannot be asked in England without specifying whether you are talking about the color of hats, shoes, cars, and so on. If you do not specify, people look at you as if you were an idiot. Ladd (1957) found that the second question could not be asked in the Navajo culture without specifying who killed whom and under what circumstances. I have found (1961b) also that the second question is impossible in Scandinavia for the same reason.

Many Americans who were stationed in Japan after World War II were puzzled by the fact that their Japanese friends' opinions seemed to change all the time. They concluded that either the Japanese were too polite to express their real opinions or they had no real opinions. The Americans did not realize that the Japanese people had contextual opinions rather than abstract opinions, and in addition that the manner of expression depended on the social context of communication. The ways the Japanese express themselves are highly contextually structured, predictable, and nonrandom. But the Americans, who were unable to see the context, interpreted them as random.

Similar errors are made by many social scientists, who proceed as if a response were independent of context. In the collection of social data, several types of transformation take place.

First, the distortion can be due to lack of *relevance resonance* (Maruyama 1961a, 1969) between the community people and the researcher. This occurs particularly in communities that are not middle class. In the middle class environment, data collection is generally accepted as a tool for direct or indirect improvement of the life of people from whom the data are collected. The purpose of data collection, as perceived by the community people coincides with their own purposes. The convergence of the researcher's and the community's purposes is called *relevance resonance*.

In middle class environments, relevance resonance, usually exists, not so in some other communities, such as ghettos, prisons, and ethnic minorities. The purpose of too many sociologists and anthropologists is either: (a) to provide material for academic theories, for which the community people become a utility item; to satisfy the researchers' curiosity or vocational ambition; to contribute to the researcher's reputation and promotion; or simply to produce salaries from the research; or (b) to promote whatever the researcher assumes to be relevant for the community people but may not be.

In simpler words, too often the researcher is an exploiter who is a part of the exploitative system and has dangerous power. Since he has more power than the community people, he cannot be gotten rid of easily. The only way to deal with him is either to keep him at a safe distance or to counterexploit him. The people in an oppressed environment live in a constant danger from the "system," and their survival depends on working out sophisticated methods to deal with exploiters. Prison inmates, for example, have several sets of well-worked-out phony information: one set to be given to sociologists, another to psychologists, etc. They have psyched out the researchers of different types, and are skilled at fostering the *delusion* of relevance in the researcher, as well as at playing stupid, in order not to arouse anxiety in the researcher. They can even fool prison psychiatrists. For example, they can play out a symptom of severe mental illness in front of a psychiatrist, and reduce the symptom from time to time in order to get a report of improvement.

The second type of transformation occurs because of lack of *criticality resonance* (Maruyama 1969). Some environments are full of dangers unknown to outsiders. The researcher may be unaware of these dangers and unwittingly pass the data to the wrong persons. When the community people are aware of the researcher's lack of awareness regarding these dangers, they must feed phony information to the researcher in order to protect themselves. The community people may perform an "isotope test" by giving some information to the researcher and tracing where it leaks out. Let me illustrate some of the dangers, taking prisons as examples. Primary danger sources are: guards, thieves, collectors of debts, murderers, homosexuals. Secondary danger sources are: informers who give real or purposefully fictitious information to primary danger sources to have them strike someone they don't like or to receive a reward from them. Tertiary danger sources: counterspies, killers of informers, false-jacketers (those who label an innocent man as an informer in order to have him killed by killers of informers). Fourth level danger sources: the false-jacketed (who must retaliate and kill the man whom he believes to be his false-jacketer), detectors of false-jacketers, and so on.

Even many of the professional social researchers are unaware of these contextual transformations. Less sophisticated data collectors, such as census takers, are subject to more elementary errors. For example, in the 1970 census many questions were asked about plumbing, apparently in order to discover what percentage of housing was substandard. But tenants of substandard housing are reluctant to disclose the plumbing conditions for fear of being evicted and being unable to afford any other place. They would, of course, like to have the plumbing improved. This fear is based on their repeated experience with urban renewal, which, according to the theory of middle class planners, is supposed to provide inexpensive housing and is therefore relevant to ghetto residents. But in reality, its effect is the opposite because it *deprives* ghetto residents of the only kind of housing they can afford, i.e., substandard housing. Consequently, by its design, the census, in all likelihood, collected phony data on plumbing in the substandard housing area where its questions about plumbing were aimed. The data collection defeated its own purpose because it lacked contextual thinking.

Many planners commit similar errors when they fail to use contextual thinking in arranging for community input, public participation, etc., and in interpreting the "data."

RELATIONAL. I have mentioned earlier the failure in communication I had with a physicist when he and I were discussing steady state and the differences between a waterfall and a lake. I did not know his criterion at that time. But, as it turns out, his perception was less relational than mine.

The perceptual difference in this example may seem merely academic, without practical relevance, but in many ways it does have important practical consequences. An obvious example is the ecological crisis brought about by the lack of relational perception. Another example is the psychological dilemma, if not crisis, encountered in the so-called self-actualization process in Western cultures. The very popular Maslowian "hierarchy of values," which is used by practically everybody in the field of social futuristics and planning, is very culture-bound. It is meaningless and irrelevant in many other cultures. It is regrettable that Maslow died in 1970 just when he began to be actively interested in other cultures, such as the Navajos. One more year of his life could have meant an important change in his conceptual formulation. The concept of "self-actualization" derives from atomistic thinking, in which the individual is perceived to be isolated and empty unless somehow fulfilled and actualized. In fact, this thinking presents great problems for Western cultures, in which the individual is cut off not only from nature but also from other individuals.

As a Japanese I can appreciate this problem. In the traditional Japanese culture, humans are a part of nature, inseparable from it. The scenery, the change of seasons, the rain, moon, and storms, all were part of the human experience. Traditional Japanese architecture is designed that human beings can be a part of the outdoors while sitting in the house. There are practically no walls. The inside of the house can immediately be transformed into the outdoors by removing the sliding walls and the partitions between the rooms. The gardens are designed to be nature in miniature. The unpainted wooden floor, wooden posts, and grass mats on the floor provide direct tactile contact with the bare foot and hand, visual stimulation, olfactory contact with the smell of wood and periodically renewable grass mats. While in the house, the Japanese sits and lays on grass mats, not on chairs or beds.

The Japanese live within nature in house or in garden. Traditionally the Japanese begin all letters to friends with a sentence or two describing the beautiful change of season, color of leaves, insect songs, snow, buds, etc. The individual is a part of ever-changing nature. One may feel fulfilled by walking in a forest, sitting in a mountain (not *on* the mountain as Westerners may prefer), caring for the trees in the garden, watching the moon from the living room with all the walls removed, listening to insects or the snow falling from tree branches. In such a setting, self-actualization is a very irrelevant, unnecessary, and artificial concept. Another fallacy is found in those "avant-garde" Americans who advocate what they call the "inner frontier" (mental) as opposed to the "outer" (physical) frontier.

POLYOCULAR. People in the nonreciprocal causal epistemology believe that there is *one* god, *one* truth, *one* logic, etc. Their universe consists of materials and substances, and they believe that there is an objective knowledge and that people should look for it. This point of view is very culture-bound. Objectification distorts, not necessarily because of what it measures, but because of what it does not measure, and because those things which can be measured must be interpreted in the context of those which cannot.

Though people who believe in objective knowledge do talk about different perspectives, their notion of perspectives is quantitative, as I discussed earlier. People in many other cultures are less concerned with material objects as such, less quantitative in perception, less obsessed with objectivity, and less preoccupied with deciding who is more objective and who is less objective. They take for granted that different individuals see the same situation differently.

Homogenistic thinking attributes the differences in interpretation or opinion to errors or lack of information. Hierarchical and competitive thinking see differences as conflicts. On the other hand, polyocular thinking regards differences as useful.

Vision with one eye has no depth perception. Vision with two eyes has depth perception, not because one of the eyes can see the back side of the object, but because the differences between the two images enable the brain to compute the dimension which cannot be directly perceived. This is precisely the reason why "objective" agreement to one view impoverishes our understanding. In the binocular vision, if you eliminate all parts in which the two images differ, what is left is *less than* a monocular vision.

For planners, engineers, and social scientists who believe there is only one truth, it would make them aware that there are many logics, contexts, and points of view from which the same thing can be interpreted. They should thus direct their efforts toward obtaining input from different parts of the community. They should consider different opinions as desirable sources of enriched vision, instead of avoiding, circumventing, or deflecting disagreements as unnecessary and undesirable interference.

Furthermore, polyocular thinking revolutionalizes the rationale and methods of social science. Until now most social scientists were bound by research methods borrowed from the physics of two or three centuries ago (Filstead 1972), believing that these were part of *the* scientific method. These methods required a lengthy training at the adequate level. Social scientists believed and deluded themselves into believing that the only persons qualified to do social research were those who had gone through the training, i.e., themselves.

If we take the polyocular point of view, these methods are no longer the only methods. In fact, it has been shown in many instances (Filstead 1972) that these methods are not only ethnocentric but also inadequate for use even in our own society. New conceptualizations, new research methods, and new theories must be developed by members of different cultures. There must be several types of research: (a) endogenous research done by insiders of a culture with their own conceptualization, foci of relevance, epistemological framework, methodology, research design, and data interpretation; (b) exogenous research; (c) endogenous polyocular research, team research with members from different subcultures within the culture; (d) exogenous polyocular research, team research with members from different outside cultures; (e) amphigenous polyocular research, a combination of endogenous and exogenous polyocular research.

Many people in the communities are experts on their own culture: the medicine men among the native Americans or the pimps and hustlers in the ghetto, etc. They are highly intelligent, articulate, and capable of developing their own types of research. The time of outsiders with doctorates parading as experts has passed.

PROCESS-ORIENTED. Let me begin this topic with an example. "Uncertainty" and "future shock" have become popular American terms. Why so much fuss? I think it is because American philosophy, based on the concept of substance, assumes certainty as the basis of life. Japan has undergone periods of rapid social transformation and social change without appreciable "future shock." This is partly because uncertainty and change are considered to be the basis of human life in Japan. Another example is the fallacy of static harmonism among many environmental-

ists. The natural systems are ever changing and evolving, and morphogenetic. Static systems do not exist in real nature.

TRANS-EPISTEMOLOGICAL PROCESS. This process is very difficult for persons
who are monopolarized. Monopolarization is the tendency in persons
brought up in the American-European nuclear family system (system of
family consisting of one father, one mother and their children), to
develop psychological dependency on *one* authority, *one* right theory,
one truth, and *one* god (Maruyama 1966).

For persons who are strongly monopolarized, it is a traumatic experience to be confronted with other ways of thinking. If these persons realize
that there are other ways of thinking, they feel as if the whole universe is
collapsing. Many people counteract this traumatic realization by reinforcing their belief in their truth and defending it as fiercely as they can. The
extremely patriotic conservatism with which some people oppose
counter-culture movements can be understood in this light. The
psychological defense mechanism against the *trauma of demonopolarization* is often disguised in the form of an intellectual argument. The
tendency to use this defense mechanism must be overcome. Painful as it
may be to some persons, the process of demonopolarization is the first
step in the trans-epistemological process.

The second step consists of *trans-spection*, the process of getting into
the *head* of another person. One erases as much of one's own epistemology as possible from one's head, and thinks in the epistemology of
another person. Instead of disagreeing, one tries to think exactly like the
other person. This process takes a long time for those who have never
gone through it before, but becomes easier as one acquires experience
and ability.

The third step is to let the other person trans-spect into one's own
epistemology. This is not as easy as it sounds. If you have never trans-
spected into other epistemologies, you would not even know how your
epistemology is different from others. You are not aware of something
which is very natural to you. For this reason, the third step should not
begin until the second is reasonably completed.

To illustrate why the third step should not be undertaken until the
second step has been reasonably completed, let me describe my own
experience. I was born and grew up in prewar Japan. I grew up thinking
with a reciprocal causal epistemology. In my grammar school years I was
much interested in science and mathematics. Science and mathematics
per se are not incompatible with the reciprocal causal epistemology. In
fact, as I realized much later, they are both useful tools for it.

In my senior high school years, which coincided with the fall of the
Japanese Empire, I became interested in philosophy, and eagerly read
Kant, Descartes, and other European philosophers. Kant was of particu-

lar interest to me because, like many other young people, I admired difficult theories. Finally, I got to the point of being "brainwashed" by European philosophies. I did not realize it at that time, but this was the beginning of my trans-spection into the nonreciprocal causal epistemology. I wanted to go to Europe but had no money. Finally I was able to borrow money from an American source and came to the United States, but regarded American philosophers as inferior to Europeans. I served two years in the United States Marine Corps as a private and a corporal during the Korean War, in order to become eligible for the G.I. Bill to go to Europe. (There were not many opportunities in the United States for a Japanese who graduated in mathematics from the University of California.)

After my military service, I went to Europe and my brainwashing, or more euphemistically my trans-spection, continued. I almost completely became an advocate of the nonreciprocal causal epistemology. Then two seminal works began to influence me. One was cybernetics (von Foerster 1949–1953) based on the deviation-counteracting equilibrating reciprocal causal models. The other was Gunnar Myrdal's theory of underdeveloped regions (Myrdal 1957) based on the differentiation-amplifying reciprocal causal models. I understood them quite naturally and became their advocate. To my surprise I found that it was very difficult for Europeans to conceptualize reciprocal causality. Those who knew mathematics had no difficulty. But those who did not know much mathematics had to break down the reciprocal causal relations into a succession of nonreciprocal causal relations in order to conceptualize them. Of course, such breakdowns were mathematically incorrect and ended in incorrect results. But that was the only way they could approximate the concept of reciprocal causal relations.

It was time for me to do the third step in the trans-epistemological process, i.e., to try to help Europeans and Americans trans-spect into the reciprocal causal thinking. I published my article "The Second Cybernetics: deviation-amplifying mutual causal processes," in 1963 in *American Scientist*, and I think I succeeded in getting the basic idea across to Westerners. Though the ideas contained in that article were quite natural to me, I don't think I could have expressed them in a way communicable to Westerners if I had not gone through the second step of the trans-epistemological process. If I had never come into contact with Westerners, I would not have felt the need to explain the reciprocal causality the way I did. And if I had not understood why it was difficult for Westerners to understand it, my article would not have been communicative.

There are many more epistemologies than the four I discussed in this paper, and there will be many more in the future. We need to develop methods of trans-epistemological communication for all these different epistemologies.

CONCLUSION

In this paper I have proposed the exploration of psychotopology and its applications to cross-disciplinary, cross-professional, and cross-cultural communication, particularly with regard to urban planning, environmental design, and other types of public works. I have discussed four epistemologies as examples. Many more exist, and they can be studied as psychotopology develops.

REFERENCES

BACON, E.
    1974   *Design of cities.* New York: Viking.
BALGOOYEN, T.
    1962   A study of conflicting values: American Plains Indian orators vs. the U.S. commissioners of Indian Affairs. *Western Speech* 26:76–83.
BATESON, G., *et al.*
    1956   Toward a theory of schizophrenia. *Behavioral Science* 1:25.
    1971   The cybernetics of "self": a theory of alcoholism. *Psychiatry* 34:1–18.
BINGSWANGER, L.
    1944–1945   Der Fall Ellen West. *Schweizer Archiv für Neurologie und Psychiatrie* 53:255–277; 54:69–117; 55:16–40.
BOLTZMANN, L.
    1898   *Vorlesungen über Gastheorie.* Barth.
BUCKLEY, W.
    1968   *Modern systems research for the behavioral scientist.* Chicago: Aldine.
BURK, R. A., J. M. ADAMS
    1970   Establishing rapport with deviant groups. *Social Problems* 18:102–117.
CAMARA, S.
    1975   Concept of heterogeneity and change among the Mandenka. *Technological Forecasting and Social Change* 7:273–284.
ELLENBERGER, H. F.
    1958   "A clinical introduction to psychiatric phenomenology and existential analysis," in *Existence.* Edited by R. May. New York: Basic Books.
FEUER, L. S.
    1959   Bearing of psychoanalysis upon philosophy. *Philosophy and Phenomenological Research* 19:323–340.
FILSTEAD, W.
    1972   The sociology of methodology. Mimeographed manuscript.
HOLLING, C. H.
    1976   "Resilience and stability of ecosystems," in *Evolution and consciousness.* Edited by E. Jantsch and C. H. Waddington Reading: Addison-Wesley.
JASPERS, K.
    1919   *Psychologie der Weltanschauungen.* Berlin: Springer.
KLUCKHOHN, C.
    1949   "The philosophy of Navaho Indians," in *Ideological differences and world order.* Edited by F. S. C. Northrop. New Haven: Yale University Press.

KUBIE, L. S.
1956   Some unsolved problems of the scientific career. *American Scientist* 41:3–32.
KUHN, T.
1962   *The structure of scientific revolutions*. Chicago: University of Chicago Press.
LADD, J.
1957   *The structure of a moral code*. Cambridge: Harvard University Press.
MANNHEIM, K.
1929   *Ideologie und Utopie* [Ideology and Utopia]. Frankfurt am Main: Schulte-Bulmke.
MARUYAMA, M.
1959   Communicable and incommunicable realities. *British Journal for the Philosophy of Science* 10:50–54.
1960   Relational algebra of intercultural understanding. *Methodos* 11:269–277.
1961a   Communicational epistemology. *British Journal for the Philosophy of Science* 11:319–327; 12:52–62; 12:117–131.
1961b   The multilateral mutual causal relationships among the modes of communication, sociometric pattern and intellectual orientation in the Danish culture. *Phylon* 22:41–58.
1962a   Awareness and unawareness of misunderstandings. *Methodos* 13:255–275.
1962b   Algebra of interpersonal interaction. *Methodos* 13:25–36.
1963a   The second cybernetics: deviation-amplifying mutual causal processes. *American Scientist* 51:164–179, 250–256.
1963b   Basic elements in misunderstandings. *Dialectica* 17:78–92, 99–110.
1963c   Generating complex patterns by means of simple rules of interaction. *Methodos* 14:17–26.
1965   Metaorganization of information: information in classificational universe, relational universe and relevantial universe. *Cybernetica* 8:224–236.
1966   Monopolarization, family and individuality. *Psychiatric Quarterly* 40:133–149.
1968   Trans-social rapport through prison inmates. *Annales Internationales de Criminologie* 7:19–46.
1969a   Epistemology of social science research: explorations in inculture researchers. *Dialectica* 23:229–280.
1970   Toward human futuristics. Paper presented at the American Anthropological Association annual meeting, San Diego, Ca.
1972a   Non-classificational information and non-informational communication. *Dialectica* 26:51–59.
1972b   "Symbiotization of cultural heterogeneity: scientific, epistemological and esthetic bases." Paper presented at the American Anthropological Association annual meeting, Toronto.
1975   *Endogenous research of prison culture by prison inmates*. University Microfilm Monograph N. LD0043.
1977a   Heterogenistics. *Cybernetica* 20:69–86.
1977b   New movements in old traps. *Futurics* 2:59–62.
1978   Ilya Prigogine and the epistemology of social science. *Current Anthropology*.

MEAD, M.
1946 An application of anthropological techniques to crossnational communication. *Transactions of New York Academy of Science* 2(9): 133–152.
1950 Experience in learning primitive languages through the use of learning high level linguistic abstractions. *Transactions of the seventh conference on cybernetics*. Edited by H. von Foerster. New York: Josiah Macy Jr. Foundation.
1964 *Continuities in cultural evolution*. New Haven: Yale University Press.
MILSUM, J.
1968 *Positive feedback*. New York: Pergamon.
MINKOWSKI, E.
1923 Étude psychologique et analyse phénoménologique d'un cas de mélancolie schizophrénique. *Journal de Psychologie Normale et Pathologique* 20:543–558.
MYRDAL, G.
1944 *American dilemma*. New York: Harper and Row.
1957 *Economic theory and underdeveloped regions*. London: Duckworth.
PRIBRAM, K.
1949 *Conflicting patterns of thought*. Washington, D.C.: Public Affairs Press.
REICHENBACH, H.
1956 *Direction of time*. Los Angeles: University of California Press.
RIEDL, R.
1976 *Strategie der Genesis*. Munich: Piper.
RUESCH, J.
1957 *Disturbed communications*. New York: Norton.
SHANNON, C., W. WEAVER
1949 *Mathematical theory of communication*. Urbana: University of Illinois.
SPEMANN, H.
1938 *Embryonic development and induction*. New York: Hafner.
TANGE, K.
1972 *Katsura*. New Haven: Yale University Press.
TANGE, K., N. KAWAZOE
1965 *Ise*. Cambridge: MIT Press.
ULAM, S.
1960 On some mathematical problems connected with patterns of growth figures. Lecture given at Stanford University.
VON FOERSTER, H., *editor*
1949–1953 *Transactions of Josiah Macy Jr. Foundation Conferences on Cybernetics*. New York: Josiah Macy Jr. Foundation.
WADDINGTON, C. H., *editor*
1969–1971 *Towards a theoretical biology*. Chicago: Aldine.
WAX, R. H.
1971 *Doing fieldwork*. Chicago: University of Chicago Press.
WIENER, N.
1948 *Cybernetics*. Paris: Herman et Cie.
1949 *Extrapolation, interpolation and smoothing of stationary time series with engineering applications*. Cambridge: MIT Press.
WRIGHT, S.
1931 Evolution in Mendelian population. *Genetics* 16:97–159.

Ethnicity as Identity: Individuals, Families, and Isolated Groups

Endogenous Research and Polyocular Anthropology

MAGOROH MARUYAMA

INTRODUCTION

One of the developments which will characterize the coming phase of anthropology undoubtedly will be the emergence of a large number of non-white anthropologists with non-Western perspectives, logics and methodology, who will enrich the field of anthropology.

Indications are already numerous. In 1969 the Native Americans, the Asian Americans, the Chicanos, and the black Americans have challenged the theories and the assumptions of white anthropologists at various national and regional anthropological conferences in the USA. In April 1970, at the annual conference of Society for Applied Anthropology, there was a proposal for Third World anthropology. In November of the same year at the annual meeting of the American Anthropological Association, the issues expanded beyond the question of ethnocentricism in anthropological research and touched upon sociocultural *logical pluralism* (assertion of the existence of many logics).

The indications are not limited to those manifested at formal meetings. On the community level, members of various ethnic minority groups are becoming increasingly expressive of their hitherto silent, but highly articulate awareness regarding the discrepancies between their own structure of relevance and what the researchers from outside perceive as relevance for the insiders.

Thus, the epistemological basis of anthropology as well as the ethnic composition of the anthropologistical community will soon undergo a radical change. This will have several profound consequences.

One of the consequences will be the *demonopolarization* of anthropology. Monopolarization (Maruyama 1966, 1969, 1972) is a tendency in persons who are brought up in a nuclear family system *or* in the

Western hierarchical, unidirectional, and homogenistic logic to develop strong psychological dependency upon *one* authority, and tend to believe in and seek *one* truth, *one* logic, *one* right theory, *one* answer, *one* god, etc., which they consider to be *universally* valid. Anthropology itself, which is supposed to be the least culture-bound of the disciplines, has nevertheless been afflicted with some degree of epistemological and methodological monopolarization. The main reason for this is not so much the fact that most of the anthropologists originate in one cultural grouping (European and white American cultures) but the fact that they have come from those cultures in which the tendency toward monopolarization was strong. Even if all anthropologists had come from a single culture, monopolarization would not have occurred as long as that culture was not predominantly monopolarizing (Iwata 1969).

The epistemological and methodological ethnocentrism in anthropology can be seen, for example, in the use of rank-order analysis in cultures whose basic epistemology may be a nonrankable universe. It can be seen also in the use of categorization techniques, especially in psycholinguistics, in cultures whose epistemology is basically relational, not classificational.

But a more pervasive influence of epistemological and methodological monopolarization can be seen in many anthropologists' inclination toward "objective" methods. This may occur at the metalevel even among those who recognize subjective realities. For example, those who study belief systems may recognize that belief systems are subjective realities. Nevertheless they may assume that if they can find ways to measure these subjective realities accurately, all anthropologists should be able to come to some agreement on the nature of any given subjective belief system. They may assume that there should be an objective understanding (by anthropologists) of subjective realities, i.e., they may believe that anthropologists can attain "*the* objective truth" about subjective realities.

Those who reason this way do not seem to realize that this assumption of the existence of "correct objective understanding" at the metalevel is itself culture-bound. They also do not see that what they attain by reducing the events to measurable shadows is *not the truth but only the communicability to their colleagues* who share the same belief system, i.e., who also insist on objectivity. Often communicability and subsequent agreement are mistaken for a discovery of "the truth."

Objectivization distorts, not necessarily in terms of what it measures, but more importantly in terms of what it does *not* measure as well as in terms of the absence of the contextual analysis in which the unmeasurables serve as the context for the measurables. Our education system, and more broadly our whole culture, brainwashes the social scientists into believing that the full objectivization is distortion-free and not culture-bound. Without appreciation of this distortion, many anthropologists have insisted that they, as outsiders and with "training," are more "objective" and more "qualified" than the insiders in obtaining the "correct truth."

The ideology of objectivization is as culture-bound, and therefore as subjective, as the perceptions of the insiders who have not been brainwashed by this ideology and training. On the metalevel the comparison of two perspectives — one by insiders and one by outsiders regardless of whether they are called objective or subjective — produces more insights into both cultures than the insistence on agreement on *one* so-called "objective" perspective, or the insistence on deciding which is right and which is wrong.

When anthropology was at the stage in which various cultures were studied by researchers from mainly one culture or from a small number of similar cultures, the emphasis on "objectivity" was necessary in order to counteract the ethnocentricism in the researchers. But at the next stage of anthropology in which anthropologists from many cultures become available, the emphasis can be shifted to *cross-subjective analysis* and to *polyocular anthropology*, even though the usefulness of the so-called "objective" anthropology will undoubtedly remain.

EPISTEMOLOGIES

Traditionally the term epistemology was used to designate philosophical discourses on the process of our cognition and cogitation as in, for example, Plato's *Theaitetos* or Kant's *Kritik der reinen Vernunft*. In these classic works, it was assumed that all humans had the same pattern of thinking. Therefore *one* epistemology was considered to be applicable to all human beings. Controversies over epistemology were fought in terms of the questions regarding the validity or invalidity of competing theories. It was assumed that a valid theory must be universally valid, and an invalid theory must be universally invalid.

Awareness of the culture-boundedness of epistemological theories arose only recently and was pioneered by Karl Mannheim (1928[1952]), T. S. Chang (1938), Karl Pribram (1949), Clyde Kluckhohn (1949), Gregory Bateson (1964), Maruyama (1961a) and others. However, the consideration of the individual variability of epistemological structures has a somewhat longer history (Kierkegaard 1884; Bergson 1889; Husserl 1913; Heidegger 1927; Jaspers 1919; Sartre 1943; Kubie 1956; Feuer 1959, Harvey 1966).

In this article the term epistemology is used in the sense of the underlying structure of reasoning of an individual or of members of a culture, which may not necessarily be made explicit or verbalized, but which manifests itself in various aspects of the life of the individual or the member of the culture. Since the structure of reasoning may vary from individual to individual, or from culture to culture, we speak of epistemologies for the purpose of this article.

Some of the aspects of life in which the epistemologies are manifest are:

1. Logical structure of verbal discourse
    Examples: Aristotelian deductive logic;
    Chinese logic of complementarity (Chang 1938);
    Nominalism vs. universalism;
    Mandenka logic of heterogeneity (Camara 1975).
2. Concept of time
    Examples: Balinese time as cyclic;
    Western time as unidirectional flow;
    Japanese time as ephemerality.
3. Structure of universe
    Examples: Hierarchical universe of Aristotle;
    Categorizational universe of Linné
    Competitive universe of Darwin;
    Navajo's mutualism between man, nature, spirits, animals, and ghosts;
    Symbiotic universe.
4. Religion
    Examples: Christian and Mohammedan monotheism with one god as creator, prime mover, omniscient, omnipotent, and "perfect";
    Early Greek anthropomorphic polytheism;
    Chinese religion as events and processes without god figure;
    Navajo religion as technical, aesthetic, and pragmatic practice to maintain harmony with nature, spirits, animals, and ghosts.
5. Social organization
    Examples: American "democracy" by assimilation and by majority rule over minorities (domination by quantity);
    Nonhierarchical societies of Navajos and Eskimos;
    Vertical mutualism of Japan (Maruyama 1972).
6. Scientific paradigms
    Examples: Unidirection cause-effect models;
    Mutual causal models (von Foerster 1949–1953; Wiener 1948; Milsum 1968; Buckley 1968; Maruyama 1963; Waddington 1968–1971; Riedl 1976);
    Random models and homogenization (Shannon 1949);
    Differentiation-amplification models and heterogenization (Maruyama 1978).

SEVERAL WAYS TO CONCEPTUALIZE POLYOCULARITY

Since there are many epistemologies as defined above, future anthropology must restructure itself with the recognition that not only the objects of research but also the researchers themselves may come from many epistemologies. This creates polyocular anthropology which incorporates different perspectives obtained with the use of different epistemologies. But the concept of polyocularity again varies from epistemology to epistemology.

Persons with a quantative epistemology may see polyocularity as additive combinations of segmentary perspectives, such as the construction of a map from successive aerial photos. Some persons with still another version of quantitative epistemology may see polyocularity as successive enveloping of high magnification pictures (microscopic pictures) by high condensation pictures (telescopic pictures). In fact, persons with natural science background tend to use this scale concept of perspective.

On the other hand, persons with a nonquantitative epistemology may see polyocularity as synthesis of several overlays on the same map or as synthesis of different photos of the same object taken with different color filters.

Furthermore, persons with a competitive epistemology may regard differences in pespectives as a conflict which must be resolved with a compromise, while persons with a complementary epistemology may view the differences in perspectives as noncontradictory and enriching useful information.

There are not only differences but also metadifferences between epistemologies. For example, a heterogeneistic epistemology can accommodate other epistemologies, while a homogeneistic epistemology must reject others. This is a metadifference. A heterogeneistic epistemology can become a meta-epistemology which includes other epistemologies as well as itself. But a homogeneistic epistemology cannot.

STEPS TOWARD POLYOCULAR ANTHROPOLOGY

There are several steps to be taken to attain polyocular anthropology:

1. *Endogenous research*: Each culture is studied by its insiders using endogenous epistemology, methodology, research design, and with endogenously relevant focus.

2. *Binocular vision*: Research by insiders and by outsiders can be juxtaposed to produce binocular vision, just as left and right eye vision combined produce three-dimensional perception not because the two eyes see different sides, but because the differences between the two images enable the brain to compute the invisible dimension.

3. *Polyocular anthropology*: A culture can be studied by research teams from several outside cultures. The results can be compared in order to produce an exogenous polyocular vision. If the culture is heterogeneous, it can also be studied by research teams from several inside subcultures. This will produce an endogenous polyocular vision. The subcultures may not be separate and self-contained entities, but may be interpenetrating, for example, the female and male subcultures. In most cultures females and males are not entirely separated. In fact, the pattern of the interaction between females and males characterizes these subcultures. Much of what the females do or think is a result of their interaction with the males and vice versa. In this sense, the female and male visions are like the overlays discussed above, not segmentary fields of vision. Likewise, endogenous polyocular vision should be understood in the sense of overlays, *not* in the sense of a collection of mutually exclusive segmentary fields of vision. When an endogenous and an exogenous polyocular vision are combined as in the *binocular vision*, we attain a polyocular anthropology.

ENDOGENOUS RESEARCH

The purpose of this paper is to discuss endogenous research which is the first step toward polyocular anthropology.

As defined above, endogenous research is conceptualized, designed, and conducted by researchers who are insiders of the culture, using their own epistemology and their own structure of relevance.

Though endogenous persons have been often used as data collectors or information sources by outside researchers, the work of endogenous persons as conceptualizers, selectors of the focus of relevance, theory makers, methodology makers, hypothesis makers, research designers, and data analysts is relatively new in white anthropologists' literature. This is largely due to the fact that only the works done in the academic format were recognized as acceptable research.

Only in a small number of cases efforts were made to conduct research in the endogenous format. For example, Worth (1967) and Worth and Adair (1972) had Navajos take films of their own life and edit them themselves in order to study whether there were structural differences between the films the Navajos made and a film a white anthropologist would make. Robert McKnight is currently conducting a literature survey of endogenous research recorded in the past. In this paper I will discuss three endogenous research projects which I have arranged or have been involved in: one in prisons (Maruyama 1968, 1969, 1975); one in black ghettos, and one on a Navajo reservation.

Both Adair and I found that the *less* educated or trained the endogenous researchers were by academic standards, the more insightful and interesting their products turned out to be. This, together with other criteria for endogenous researchers, will be discussed at the end of this paper.

The endogenous researchers in the three projects turned out to be superior to the academic researchers in three other aspects in addition to the epistemological considerations: (1) philosophy regarding communication; (2) relevance dissonance; (3) criticality dissonance. I will first discuss these, and then go into some of the products of the endogenous research projects, and conclude this article with a discussion of the successes and failures in the operation of the endogenous research teams.

PHILOSOPHY REGARDING COMMUNICATION

In addition to the epistemological differences between cultures, there are other considerations which, if not taken into account, distort research. One of them is the cultural differences in the philosophy regarding communication. I first became aware of this consideration while I was studying interpersonal communication behavior in Scandinavia (Maruyama 1961b; 1963). In Sweden, the main purpose of usual interpersonal communication is transmission of facts. In Denmark, on the other hand, the main purpose of usual interpersonal communication is perpetuation of a familiar atmosphere and a comfortable equilibrium of affect. The Swedes strive for factual interest and objective accuracy, while the Danes cultivate the art of not hurting one's own and others feelings. In Denmark, questioning and expression of knowledge or feelings are considered aggressive or inconsiderate and are avoided as much as possible except for specific professional purposes. Factual questions, even on impersonal matters, are impolite because they may reveal someone's ignorance. Explanations are also impolite because they assume that someone is ignorant enough to need an explanation. Factual discussions are avoided because a disagreement implies that someone is wrong. Intellectual conversations usually evolve around arts, literature, music, and other subjective topics on which disagreements cause no embarrassment. There are small circles of persons who engage in objective discussions. But they are a minority. Because the direct expressions of strong feelings are avoided, the Danes cultivate psychological projection, introspection, subjective interpretation, and the art of guessing one another's feelings. "Why should I try to understand anybody or anything when I don't even understand myself?" is a philosophy of communication common in Denmark.

There, the most enjoyable type of communication takes place when a small number of persons gather frequently at the same place, eating the same pastry, sharing the same gossip. Repetition of the familiar is the key to the Danish "Coziness" (*hygge*). Such communication is not focused on transmission of facts. It is oriented toward perpetuation of comfortable equilibrium.

A foreigner often makes the inevitable mistake in Denmark. With all good intentions he tries to win Danes' friendship by showing factual interests in Denmark, being inquisitive about Danish culture, and eager to explain his own culture and his point of view. An ordinary Dane may tolerate him for a while, but eventually will withdraw.

There are many other cultural differences in philosophy regarding communication. A research method imported from outside into a culture may encounter resistance to communication or produce purposefully phony responses.

RELEVANCE DISSONANCE

In the white middle class environment, data collection is generally accepted as a tool for direct or indirect improvement of the life of people from whom the data are collected. The purpose of data collection as perceived by the people coincides with the researcher's purpose. The convergence of purposes between the community members and the researcher as perceived by the community people is called *relevance resonance*. In the white middle class environment, there usually is relevance resonance because the researcher usually is from the white middle class and shares the goals and the purposes with the community people, and the community people perceive him to be so.

This is not the case in some other cultures. For example, in most of the Native Americans' (American Indians') perception, the purpose of too many anthropological researches is to benefit the academic community or the museum, to satisfy the researcher's curiosity or vocational ambition, to contribute to the researcher's reputation and promotion, or simply to produce salaries for the researchers. In fact, some anthropologists regard Native Americans mainly from the point of view of these people's utility for academic theories. Some other anthropologists satisfy their drive for territoriality and possessiveness by selecting a tribe and calling it "my tribe." Still others become self-appointed spokesmen "for" tribe members while not allowing them to speak for themselves. Such persons erroneously assume that tribe members are not intelligent enough to do so. There are also less pretentious do-gooders who satisfy their own psychological needs with a delusion that they are doing some good for the tribe. In any case, Native Americans see researchers as leading an extravagent life (by Native standards), made possible by a research salary. In this sense the researchers are exploiters and parasites unless they prove otherwise by producing practical results congruent with the endogenous goals of the tribe.

The discrepancy of goals between the community people and the researcher as perceived by the community is called *relevance dissonance*. When relevance dissonance exists, the research project is useful to the community people only as a means for hustle. The community people may counter-exploit the project, or may simply give phony information to keep the researcher happy and busy with himself. Oppressed people are very skilled and sophisticated in the art of survival. Often the researcher is convinced that his research is useful for the community people, who actually can contrive ways to make him believe so.

The phenomena of relevance resonance and dissonance were revealed more clearly in the prison project than in any other. Let me discuss this briefly.

Prison inmates often perceive the purposes of the academic researcher as: testing an academic hypothesis; proving and perpetuating a theory; producing publications as a tool for recognition, reputation, and promotion; gaining prestige of having worked with "criminals"; or simply earning a living from a research salary.

On the other hand, most of the inmates feel that research should be undertaken for the following purposes:

1. To make the public aware of the living and working conditions, physical, and mental treatment, and some inadequate or arbitrary procedures in the prison which often fall far below what the public is led to believe.

2. To make the society see, from an inside perspective, the environmental conditions that produce crimes and from which most of the inmates came.

3. If the inmate is suffering under specific injustice or abusive practice, to open a channel for rectifying the injustice.

4. To improve through public pressure the often substandard vocational and education programs in prison.

5. To express their feelings and opinions which they think are entitled to be heard by the public.

6. To have an opportunity to be considered as human being, to be listened to and respected by the interviewer, and to talk on a person-to-person basis with the interviewer.

7. To solve the inmate's psychological problems if the interviewer is a professional.

8. Through the interviewer, to obtain contacts for or means for self-improvement, such as books, legal service, counseling, discussion groups, etc. (The means available within the prison are often very limited. Some prisons even discourage or deny such means.)

9. To prevent young people in the society from becoming criminals.

Lack of relevance resonance produce phony information from the interviewee. The inmate detects the lack of relevance resonance in several ways: (1) noticing an instrumentalizing attitude in the interviewer; (2) giving reaction tests to the interviewer; and (3) observing the interviewer's action before and after the interview.

1. *Instrumentalizing attitude* of the interviewer manifests itself in one or several of the following ways:

a. Using pre-set tests or pre-set questions which do not accommodate what the inmate really wants to communicate;

b. Considering the inmate as a response machine without allowing interchange or independent contribution;

c. Considering the inmate as a statistical or clinical object;

d. Relying heavily on "official records" of the inmate, attributing more validity to official records than to the inmate himself;

e. Building his knowledge on books and theories, even though he is unacquainted with real situations;

f. Posing himself as an "expert" while discrediting the inmate's experience and insight as "unscientific";

g. Being distrustful of the inmate;

h. Being insensitive to, unresponsive to, or unaware of the inmate's feelings;

i. Lacking interest in or desire to know the inmate's point of view and concern;

j. Being evasive in expressing his own points of view, attitudes, feelings, and goals;

k. Being aloof;

l. Having a patronizing or condescending attitude;

m. Being naive regarding the way the prison operates;

n. Being apathetic or lacking a cause, involvement, and commitment.

2. The reaction test consists in (a) *value test* and (b) *click-in* test. In the value test, the inmate drops hints and observes the reaction of the interviewer in order to detect the interviewer's value orientation. In the click-in test, the inmate mentions some topic casually to see whether the interviewer catches its relevance and picks up the topic or remains unaffected by the topic. Examples of such topics are: police harassment, court appointed attorneys, school teachers, store owners, genocide.

3. The *action observation* method consists in seeing whether the interviewer puts in action what he promises or advocates; how promptly and energetically he does so; and how skillful he is in maneuvering through the obstacles.

When members of a culture perceive relevance dissonance with a researcher, they may feel exploited and may attempt counter-exploitation without letting him realize it. They can even nourish a delusion of his "relevance" to them in order to exploit him, to keep him happy at a safe distance, or to enjoy making him look foolish in their eyes without permitting him to be aware of it.

Endogenous researchers can set up research with purposes that are relevant to the members of the culture, and therefore relevance resonance can easily be obtained.

It is not impossible for a researcher from outside to attain relevance resonance with the members of the culture *if* he makes his purposes converge with theirs. But even this process can be facilitated greatly with help from endogenous researchers.

CRITICALITY DISSONANCE

Life in some cultures involves several types of dangers, of which the researcher may be unaware. The community people, who are *aware* that the researcher is *unaware* of the dangers, fear that the researcher may unsuspectingly let the data leak out to what the researcher assumes to be a safe place. In such cases the community people give phony data to the researcher for the purpose of self-protection, not necessarily for the purpose of deception. Such distortion of data due to data giver's awareness of the data collector's unawareness of the dangers is called distortion due to *criticality dissonance*.

The dangers that community members fear may come either (1) from persons connected with the authority system imposed from outside; or (2) from members of the community.

In both cases, the existence of the primary danger sources can be used as a leverage by those who manipulate the fear of the primary danger sources. These manipulators are the secondary danger sources. The term secondary does *not* mean less dangerous. In fact, the secondary danger sources may be as deadly or deadlier than the primary danger sources. Then there are those who manipulate the fear of the secondary danger sources. These are tertiary danger sources. To be more specific:

Primary danger sources: Livestock reduction agents, money collectors, thieves, policemen, prison guards, etc.

Secondary danger sources: Snitches (finks, informers) who give real or purposefully fictitious information to the primary danger sources for the purpose of having the primary danger sources strike the informer's rivals or for the purpose of being rewarded by the primary danger sources.

Tertiary danger sources: Counterspies, snitch killers, false-jacketers (those who label an innocent man as a snitch in order to have him killed by snitch killers).

Fourth level danger sources: The false-jacketed (who must retaliate and kill the man whom he believes to be his false-jacketer), detectors of false-jacketers, etc.

As in the case of relevance dissonance, the phenomenon of criticality dissonance can be illustrated most vividly by using the prison project as an example. Let me first discuss criticality dissonance in the prisons, and then give a comparative example from the ghetto project.

Criticality Dissonance in Prison Culture

1. DANGER FROM OTHER INMATES. The prison life is characterized by extreme scarcity of things and occasions which fulfill basic human needs. These needs range from material ones, such as cigarettes and toothpaste, physical needs of sex, to emotional needs, such as expression of manhood, proof of one's own worth to himself, recognition by others, autonomy, and privacy. Therefore, a conflict over one pack of cigarettes, one small insult, or inadvertent physical contact may lead to physical fights and murder, as we will see in the list of "Interpersonal and Individual Factors."

2. DANGER FROM PRISON GUARDS. There are two forms of danger from prison guards: harassment and abuse. Harassment is hostile behavior within legal limits or with a legal pretext on the part of the guards. Abuse is illegal hostile behavior on the part of the guards, such as physical assault or denial of medical care.

Let us emphasize that there are individual differences among prison guards. Some are calm. Others have tempers. Some are fair. Others are sadistic. Some are respected by inmates. Others are despised. Not all guards practice harassment or abuse. But what is relevant in the inmate life is that there are harassments and abuses which become the source of a realistic fear.

Harassment and abuse have three functions: message, harm, and provocation. The message is: "I hate you. I am doing this to you because I hate you. You hate me but you cannot do anything to me." The harm may be physical or otherwise: beating, shooting, suspension of a privilege, denial of a legal right, destruction of personal belongings, inconveniences, etc. Provocation has the purpose of inciting a hostile attitude in inmates to rationalize the guard's abuse which follows the provocation.

The direct harm may be negligible as compared to the message it intends to communicate and to the provocation it intends to create. The message and the provocation, much more than harm, create resentment and tension. Outsiders tend to see only the direct harm without realizing the message, the provocation and the resulting tension. This is why the outsiders are unaware of or unappreciative of the fear and the indignation in the prison inmates.

Common harassments. Guards are known to harass inmates in the following ways:

Shaking down: The guard stops the inmate and searches his pockets, etc. Probable message: "You are on the black list. Better be careful, or you will get busted."

Strip down: The guard orders the inmate to get completely undressed. This is usually done in full view of the prison population. Then the guard orders: "Pull up your balls (testicles)," "Spread your ass (rectum)," etc., pretending to search hidden objects under the testicles or in the rectum. The guard as well as the inmate and the onlookers know that there is nothing hidden under the testicles or in the rectum. Message: "I hate you especially. This is why I am humiliating you in front of everybody."

Cell search: The cell of an inmate may be searched for legitimate reasons, such as a check on narcotics or knives. But a cell search may be done for harassment. The search "squad" may cut up the mattress, tear the seams of clothes, slit the toothpaste tube, and scatter the family photos and religious symbols on the floor. The family photos or the religious symbols are often the inmate's only means of maintaining his tie with his family or of reminding him that he is an individual, not a number. If the squad drops these objects on the floor, the inmate feels as if his whole family or his whole individuality is slaughtered.

Cigarettes and toothpastes are purchased by the inmate at the canteen. If they are destroyed, it becomes a net loss. The inmate may owe some cigarettes to another inmate. If he is unable to repay, he may get stabbed. Clothes are "issue items," but the inmate is made responsible for their maintenance. The trousers and the jackets are stamped with the inmate's ID number. Though the uniform is the same, many inmates express their individuality by having their shoes shined and the trousers pressed and creased by inmates who work in the laundry, etc., paying them in cigarettes. If these clothes are destroyed, the inmate loses his pride in individuality as well as cigarettes which function as money.

A vicious variation of cell search is a "planted" violation. While the inmate is away from his cell, a guard places some illegal item in the inmate's cell. The guard then calls the squad to raid the cell. This is one of the ways the guard can get a clean inmate busted.

Delayed or denied pass: The guard may delay or withhold the delivery of a clinic pass or a visiting room pass. As a result, the inmate may miss his wife's visit or may not see her until near the end of the visiting hour. The wife may have traveled over a long distance and may have to wait hours in vain.

Unfair job assignments: Inmates' jobs range from manual labor to automechanic or file clerk. Some jobs serve as a vocational training. There are official criteria of eligibility for each assignment. For example, narcotic offenders may not be assigned to hospital duty. But unofficial discriminations may be practiced in spite of the official eligibility. Some jobs, for example cell assignment clerk, give the inmate a leverage over other inmates. Inmates, especially homosexuals, may bribe the cell assignment clerk to obtain a desired cell or cell partner. Such jobs are lucrative. These jobs may be obtained by bribing a guard or by doing him a personal favor. Inmates holding these jobs may also become a tool of guards to exercise favoritism on inmates.

Picking on trifles, called chickenshit beef: There are small violations which are usually tolerated, for example, taking a slice of bread from the mess hall left over on the tray, or possessing one extra pair of socks. A guard may single out an inmate and write him up for these usually tolerated violations. The inmates' phraseology for being given a chickenshit beef is "to be violated" by the guard. These beefs may cause the inmate to be transferred to a cell block with less privileges or delay his release.

Abuses: The usual form of abuses are physical attacks and refusal to issue a hospital pass, or intentional neglect to take a very ill or seriously injured inmate to the hospital. These are self-explanatory.

Tension: The tension created by harassment and abuse is underestimated by outsiders. Contrary to the general belief, when the prison authority tightens its control over inmates, there tends to be an increase of fighting and killing among inmates. When the guards begin stopping inmates to search for concealed knives or when the number of guards in the "yard" increases suddenly, tension strikes the prison yard like lightning. Inmates anticipate and prepare for an outbreak of violence. The percentage of inmates carrying a knife increases. Inmates, fearful and suspicious, are ready to attack anyone with the slightest real or imaginary sign of hostility. Under such conditions some guards tend to become trigger-happy. There was another consideration in the prison system where our project was conducted: Inmates are punished more severely for a possession of a hidden knife than for stabbing an inmate. When guards start shaking down inmates, some inmates stab anybody who happens to be nearby in order to get a lighter punishment. Completely innocent inmates may be stabbed under such circumstances. This adds to the fear and the tension.

Increase of harassment also contributes to an increase in resentment and frustration which, in displacement, finds an outlet in increased fights among inmates.

The prison staff may create tension among prison inmates for political purposes. For example, the prison administration may instigate one racial group against another in order to weaken the solidarity among the inmates. Or the prison guards may stage a riot among inmates in order to prove the need for increased budget or personnel.

3.   INFORMATION TO BE HIDDEN FROM OTHER INMATES.

a. *Number of cigarettes one possesses*: Cigarettes function as money in the prisons. If it is known that an inmate has many of them, he may be pressured to repay his debts, to make loans to someone, or to engage in wheeling and dealing as a partner. Or if it becomes known that his supply is depleted, his bluffing and bargaining power decreases.

b. *Amount of other items in possession*: To prevent theft, this information should be kept secret.

c. *Amount of debts*: If this is known, one may become the victim of loan sharks, or someone may offer financial help or physical protection from debt collectors in exchange for homosexual act.

d. *Amount of gambling gain*: If this becomes known, one may be pressured into repaying debts.

e. *Payment to protector*: If it is known that an inmate is paying someone for physical protection from an enemy, others may challenge the protector to take his business away.

f. *Plot against other inmates*: Plots for physical attack or for financial or sexual exploitation.

4.   SPIES FOR OTHER INMATES. A spy for other inmates, when discovered, is likely to be challenged to a physical fight.

5.   INFORMATION TO BE HIDDEN FROM THE GUARDS. There are reasonable as well as unreasonable regulations. The inmate may violate regulations for good or bad purposes. Inmates protect one another from punishment, harassment, and abuse. Inmate ethics require that an inmate would rather suffer a false accusation by guards than to disclose another's hidden facts.

6.   SNITCHES. Spies for the prison authority are called snitches. Snitching is the most despised and resented act among inmates. If a snitch is discovered, he may be killed or pressured into paying a large portion of his monthly allowance for several years to the person on whom he snitched. Sometimes a guard may spread a false rumor than an inmate is a snitch in order to get the inmate attacked by other inmates. Or the guards may set several inmates against one another by telling each of them that the others have snitched on him.

7.   INFORMERS AGAINST GUARDS AND PRISON AUTHORITY. Inmates who expose to outsiders the harassment, abuses, and other irregularities practiced in the prison are retaliated against by the guards and the prison authority. They may be punished or subjected to greater harassments and abuses. Their release may be postponed for several years. The prison authority tightly controls the information channels to the outside. Letters from inmates are censored. Visitors as well as the inmates who talk with

the visitors are registered. Thus the prison authority has several means to identify the inmates who have informed against prison authority. There-fore visitors who receive information from the inmates cannot publicly use it against prison authority for fear of retaliation. This renders the use of such information ineffective.

8.   RESEARCH PARTICIPANTS SUSPECTED AS SNITCHES. Inmates have good reasons to suspect that research findings can fall into the wrong hands. The researchers and the organizers or sponsors of research may make their best efforts to keep the data confidential. But they may be unaware of all the dangers of information-giving and all the complex channels of information leakage and may unwittingly pass information to someone who may snitch or slip. An inmate has no reason to give any information to anyone unless there is a very worthwhile cause for which he is willing to risk the danger which may result from the information-giving, and unless there is evidence (promise is not enough) of absolute confidentiality. At the beginning of our project the inmate researchers had to test me, and the inmate interviewees had to test the inmate researchers. "Isotope test" is a technique frequently used by inmates. First the inmate gives a person a piece of very safe or fictitious information, and observes where it will leak, just as an isotope is used to trace the path of materials in the body of an organism. If no leakage is found after several days, the inmate will give the person an additional dose of slightly more dangerous information and observe the results. The process is repeated. If at any stage there is an indication that the information has leaked to the guards or to the prison administration, the inmate will from then on give phony information. If information leakage is found at any stage during the research project, the inmate researchers as well as the inmate interviewees are suspected as snitches by the inmate population. If this happens, further interviews will produce phony information, and the inmate researchers and the earlier interviewees will risk physical danger, even death.

9.   ADMINISTRATIVE HARASSMENT. If the prison authority suspects that research is producing information that the prison authority wants to hide, the project may be administratively harassed or terminated, and the inmate researchers and the interviewees may be transferred to units or jobs which make them incapable of participation in further research activities. If individual guards fear the research project, they may harass and abuse the inmate researchers and the interviewees.

Aside from the leakage of hidden facts, there are some other considera-tions that cause the prison staff to resist research. A prison, like many other institutions, has a well-established tradition and a subtly main-tained equilibrium among its mutually opposing components. For example, the prison school teacher may disagree with the guards on the treatment of inmates, but both sides sustain a workable relationship buffered by elaborate routines. A new project of any type may upset the tradition and the equilibrium. Especially a research project using inmates as researchers may cause anxiety among the prison staff for the following reasons:

a. Research activities may upset daily routines. For example, (1) permitting inmates to go to a privilege area where the interview is held creates unwanted traffic; (2) taking them away from their daily assignments creates a shortage of manpower; (3) issuing passes to interviewees creates extra paperwork.

b. The administrative policy to permit the presence of a new type of project may alter the balance of power between conflicting factions within the prison.

c. Use of inmates as researchers may upset the traditional "place" (status) of inmates.

d. Those who regard certain parts of the prison as their personal territory may feel their psychological security threatened by the trespassing research project.

e. Those staff members whose self-image is built on "knowing the inmates" better than anybody else may feel their self-image challenged by the research project.

f. Those who are supposed to know the inmates but do not may fear that their ignorance or incompetence may be revealed by the project.

If the anxiety level becomes sufficienty high, the prison staff can harass the project or create inconvenience and difficulties to disable the project. If the anxiety level is kept to the minimum, the project may obtain a full cooperation of the prison staff. Our teams decided that the less conspicuous the project, the less anxiety it would create among the staff. We behaved as if ours was not a new type of project; we also took special care not to violate any rules or offend the prison staff. In the dining room I avoided sitting with white collar staff members who tended to ask me questions about the project.

Criticality Dissonance in the Ghettos

Similar dangers exist in the ghetto. For the sake of comparison let us list some of them here. Just as in the prisons, there are two sources of danger in the ghetto: other ghetto residents and legal authorities, such as policemen, probation and parole officers, social workers and shopkeepers.

1. DANGER FROM OTHER RESIDENTS. First, knife or gun fights may result from unpaid debts, insult, challenge to manhood, gambling, theft, or simply from accumulated frustrations. A materially insignificant matter

may have serious implications. For example, if someone owes you one dollar and refuses to repay, he may be testing you to see how far he can take advantage of you or can ignore your existence. If he gets away with $1 this time, he will try you for $10 next time. You must get the $1 back, even with a gun. The ghetto residents do not get much protective service from the police. A crime committed by one person against another in the ghetto is usually settled by a direct retaliation.

2.   DANGER FROM LEGAL AUTHORITIES. As in prisons, the ghetto residents experience much harassment and abuse from certain policemen, probation and parole officers. Furthermore, some policemen may receive bribes from gambling places, narcotic dealers, and pimps. They may "confiscate" into their own pockets, on the ground of suspicion, possessions or cash which ghetto residents have earned legally.

As in the prison, these harassments and abuses contain a message and provocation that create resentment and tension in the ghetto. There is an additional consideration in the ghetto which does not exist in the prison. It is loss of present and future employment due to arrests or confiscation without proof of guilt. Ghetto residents can seldom afford bail. Detention on grounds of suspicion or impounding of a car causes loss of job. Moreover, an arrest record will handicap a person in obtaining future employment even if he has been proved not guilty.

There is also what corresponds to "chickenshit beef" in the prison. For some arbitrary reason a parole officer may send a parolee back to the prison for a very minor violation or far-fetched violation. Certain types of violations are impossible to avoid because of some unrealistic regulations. For example, regulations may require that a parolee cannot associate with another parolee, a prostitute, or a member of "radical" organizations. A parolee, who has no choice but to live in a ghetto, cannot avoid running into such people. Usually violations of these regulations are tolerated. But they can be used for a "chickenshit beef."

Social workers and shopkeepers can obtain information on a ghetto person which he may want to hide from other ghetto residents or from the legal authorities.

3.   INFORMATION TO BE HIDDEN FROM NEIGHBORS
Money on hand, wins and losses in gambling: This information may be used to pressure repayment of debts, making new loans, refusing new loans, etc.
Working hours, hours of absence from home: This information may be used by thieves. The ghetto resident often leaves the radio or a lamp on while absent, in order to give the impression that someone is home.
Place of work: An example would best illustrate. A woman worked as a clerk at the City Hall and supplemented her income as a prostitute.

A neighbor told the City Hall that the woman was a prostitute. The woman lost the job, and the neighbor got the job. In this case it was dangerous to let City Hall know of her evening work; it was also dangerous to let her neighbors know of her daytime work.

Possession of small, handy appliances, such as a toaster, coffee maker, iron, or a small stereo set: these items attract thieves. The ghetto resident prefers to have a bulky stereo set which can be nailed to the wall in order to avoid theft.

4. INFORMATION TO BE HIDDEN FROM THE POLICE

Selling of narcotics, gambling: These may be necessary for income but are punishable.

Possession of guns: These are necessary for self-defense but possession is punishable.

Location of employment: The police often come to arrest a person at the place of his work. The employer, seeing the visible arrest, may fire him, or a few days of detention may cause another to take his job and leave him jobless even if he is later found not guilty.

Home address, names of friends and relatives, and location of hang-out places: Used by the police for arrest.

5. INFORMATION TO BE HIDDEN FROM THE SOCIAL WORKER

Employment: Until the 1969 revision of the welfare system, unemployment was usually a requirement for welfare eligibility. Underemployed persons needed welfare, yet had to keep the employment secret to the social worker.

Presence of husband or boyfriend: Often absence of husband was a requirement for welfare eligibility. Presence of a male visitor may be misinterpreted by the social worker and make the recipient ineligible.

Personal possessions of some monetary value: Items such as a stereo set, a television or a car often are counted against eligibility.

PROCEDURAL AND OPERATIONAL PROBLEMS, SUCCESSES, AND FAILURES

In the endogenous research, *how* the team is formed as well as *how* the team members related to one another and to other members of the community is extremely crucial. We have learned a great deal from our experiences in three projects, and experiences from earlier projects were fed to later ones. The prison project was the earliest, followed by the ghetto project. The Navajo project was the latest of the three. Let me discuss them in chronological order.

THE PRISON PROJECT[1]

At its formation in November 1965, the team was not a cohesive unit. The members were not well acquainted and distrusted one another. They had divergent goals, mostly self-centered. They did not know me, and they had to test me out. During the initial month the meetings looked like an encounter group or a group therapy session. Then gradually the team members started realizing that it was their own project, to be run in their way with freedoms they had been unable to exercise in the prison. They decided that if they did anything at all, it had to be meaningful to society and, especially, meaningful to themselves. Because they had been accustomed to prison life which was for most part meaningless, the participants found that the project created a new challenge and inspiration for them. By the second month a feeling of dedication, commitment, and group solidarity had grown. One member dropped out.

The first crisis came when a psychologist visited the team. He belonged to the prison project in a nominal capacity, though he was active on another project outside the prison. His name had been put on the project proposal mainly to facilitate its acceptance by the funding agency because of his reputation in his field. He lived 3,000 miles away from where the project was conducted and was mainly an absentee member of the project. He visited the prison teams occasionally during vacations — Christmas, Easter, and summer. His first visit was during Christmas vacation, when the team had just established group solidarity. He lectured down to the team members as to what they should do and how they should do it. When the team members politely and indirectly tried to suggest their ideas and their point of view, he rejected them as being unscientific. After his departure some team members said that they wanted to quit. But after some more encounter-group type meetings they decided to stick together and give it a try. The team decided not to follow closely the ideas dictated by the psychologist.

Next, one month was spent working out conceptualizations, focus of research, and a list of factors to be researched. As mentioned earlier, I needed only to function as a catalyst using the Socratic dialogue technique. At no point did I need to supply the team with sociological or psychological theories. The team produced highly sophisticated conceptualizations of their own.

After the completion of the factor list, the team devised an interview format, and conducted test interviews with other inmates to improve the format and their skills. The final format was in the form of discussion sessions rather than a question-and-answer interview, allowing as much

---

[1] There were several crises in the project from which we have learned a great deal, and which contributed to later sophistication of endogenous methodology. They are described in depth in Maruyama (1975).

time as the interviewee cared to spend. The interviewee was to be treated as the guest at the discussion sessions. When the data were tabulated at the end of the project, it turned out that the median length of the interviews was two days, the longest interview being seven full days.

In April the team started the interviews. First the team had to prove, by its performance, to the inmate population that it was not a snitch organization and that the interview was meaningful to the interviewees themselves. At the beginning, there was much suspicion and reluctance on the part of the interviewees. But as the interviewees went back to their friends and told them of their experiences with the team, word spread through the inmate population that the project was not only safe but was genuinely interesting and meaningful. Many inmates wanted to be interviewed. The team first completed the interviews of those who appeared on the official records of violence during the previous two years. Then the team interviewed those who were known in the inmate population for their violent tendencies, as well as those volunteers who met the criteria of violence. The waiting list of volunteers grew long. Eventually it became a prestige symbol for inmates in the yard to come up to the team members and talk on a buddy-buddy level as we crossed the yard. Some interviewees came with confidential notes they had especially prepared for the interview, and burned them up at the end of the interview session. In some instances the interviewees volunteered extremely dangerous information detrimental to themselves. The team thought it wise to erase such information from the tape after the interview, even though the interviewees had enough confidence in the team to let it be kept on tape. These indications, together with the quality and the quantity of the output of the team, were a proof of the success of the project.

There was another major crisis when a team member secretly false-jacketed another member as having been regarded as a snitch by some inmates in the past. This almost tore the team apart. But the members' dedication to the project was strong, and the painful wounds healed quickly. Then, during the peak of the team's production, some members became resentful of slow workers in the team. This was also resolved peacefully. Each of the occasional visits by the psychologist created some tension and resentment. But the team evolved a technique to deal with him, giving him what he wanted while carrying out their own project undisturbed. The team members took utmost care not to break any regulations and not to offend any guards. As a result, the guards were for the most part cooperative. Two team members' cells were shaken down by guards, but it became evident that it was not done to harass the project. The team completed its tasks at the end of August.

Successes of the prison project can be attributed to the following:
1. Allowing enough time (one month) for encounter-group type

meetings to develop group solidarity and sense of dedication at the beginning.

2. Permitting endogenous researchers' to design the project which was therefore meaningful to them.

3. Allowing enough time (three months) for conceptualization, selection of focus, research design, and test runs.

4. Allowing enough time (up to seven full days) for each interviewee to express freely his experiences and his point of view in a seminar atmosphere in which the interviewee was a guest, and studying the topic in depth.

5. Taking every precaution to prevent leakage of confidential information.

6. Allowing enough time (a few months) for the inmate population to gain confidence in the project.

THE GHETTO PROJECT

Even though the project produced 300 interviews, as a whole it can be regarded as a failure. It violated the first four of the six conditions of success just listed.

At the middle of June 1967, I was asked by an East Coast university whether I could organize a team of ghetto residents in the San Francisco area to conduct a pilot study for a nation-wide project it was contemplating. I discussed the matter further with the project director, and it turned out that the purpose of the project was to follow the fluctuations of tension in the ghetto to predict riots. The team had to be organized and put into operation quickly. It had to produce daily a large number of short interviews with people on the streets.

It struck me as a quick, shallow project. It also had a flavor of a snitch project. But the time was summer 1967. Riots had erupted in Tampa, Cincinnati, and Atlanta. Newark and Detroit were about to explode. There was some urgency. Therefore, I decided to accept the project and do the best I could.

I contacted two ghetto residents who had recently been released from prison, and asked them to organize a team of six ghetto residents quickly. One of the two was released just as the prison team was forming, and therefore knew very little about how the prison team operated. The other came out in August 1966, and had seen the prison team in operation for several months. In fact he wanted to join the team, but we could not add a new member at the midway point. In the summer of 1966, there was a hope for ghetto research patterned after the prison project. The then inmate was hoping to join that project after his release. Though there was no promise of funding, he took a chance and came to live in

Northern California, where the ghetto project had been proposed, instead of returning to his home town in Southern California. (A parolee, once having chosen a place of residence, must stay in the same locality.)

At the time that I asked the two to organize the ghetto team, there were some frictions between them unknown to me, and intrigues began immediately. Separately they began talking to me behind each other's backs. I could not spend much time figuring them out because of my busy schedule. Meanwhile the team was somehow put together, and after one week of confusion and orientation meetings, the members were on the streets interviewing. They had to produce a certain number of interviews daily; the quality was very poor.

As will be discussed under the criteria for the selection of endogenous researchers, the time restrictions at this stage of the project were quite detrimental.

At the end of July administrative procedures were finally settled, and funds began coming in at the beginning of August. Until then, the team members as well as myself contributed considerable sums of money out of our own pockets to supplement the small emergency "petty cash" advanced by the East Coast university. I was looking forward to spending more time with the team members after the financial procedures were settled. But at the beginning of August it was decided that our California project should seek separate funding from the federal government and that I should write the lengthy proposal. I spent three weeks of August working sixty hours a week writing the proposal and running the project. The East Coast university promised me that our project would get a three-year federal funding. Consequently I cancelled my teaching schedule for the fall semester. At the beginning of September, I was notified that funds were not forthcoming and that I should rewrite the proposal for a small operation. This meant that I had to go job hunting in the middle of September when most schools had already started, in addition to rewriting the proposal. My hope of working closely with the team members was gone again, and the team's performance deteriorated. The direct funding from the East Coast university depleted, and the team was kept going with a bare minimum budget. I ended up with two part-time jobs at two colleges, forty miles apart from one another and both thirty-five miles from home, teaching five days a week at one and two days a week at the other, totaling only 85 percent of full-time employment.

All I could tell about the ghetto team was that the members were competing at goofing off; only one of them remained conscientious. The operation of the team was finally closed in February 1968 for lack of funds. The team produced 300 interviews, each lasting from fifteen minutes to two hours. No new insights were gained except to confirm community tension and resentment. I suspect that most of the interviews were fictitiously made up by the team members. Almost everything about the project had gone wrong. (It must be added, however, that the East Coast university later provided me with funds to write up some parts of this project.)

THE NAVAJO PROJECT

Early in 1969, the Navajo Community College, the first Indian-controlled college, began its operation. In June 1969 its Navajo Culture Curriculum Development Project was organized. The purpose of the project was to collect teaching materials on the Navajo culture for Navajo students. The project consisted of a team of Navajo students and Navajo teachers, occasionally assisted by white students from other colleges. I was with the team for its first phase of operation, from June 8 to July 11, 1969.

During its first phase the team divided into four to six subgroups of two or three persons each. Each group was assigned a specific topic, such as historical places, medical and other plants, the effect of the Livestock Reduction Program, etc. (Mythology can be told only in winter by Navajo custom and thus was excluded during the summer phase.) Each team included one photographer and one who could operate a tape recorder. Each team went out into the field in a vehicle, usually a pick-up truck or a jeep, to seek out old men who were experts in history, medicine, etc. The interviews were taped in the Navajo language and later transcribed in written Navajo.

The most conspicious success of the project was the fact that the old experts, after being told of the purpose of the project, usually became quite cooperative. Indians are generally reluctant to give information to white researchers because they rarely feel relevance resonance. But when the Navajo researchers on the team explained to old interviewees that the information collected would be used to teach young Navajos and would not go to white man's museums or book shelves, the interviewees' usual response was: "It is nice[2] that young people want to learn about old tradition. We old people will die soon and there will be no one left to tell the old stories." Such was the relevance resonance that the project attained with old Navajos.

It must be mentioned that not all old men responded favorably. Some said that they were too busy to be interviewed. Some others, who were actually busy, set up an appointment for a later date and kept it.

Many Navajos attain a very old age. People over eighty are not uncommon. Consequently the generation gap is wide among Navajos. Some team members were over forty. Yet from the older people's point

[2]   In contrast to white Americans, Navajos seldom use the word good. Navajo epistemology has little or no good–bad polarization.

of view, their manner belonged to a younger generation. For example, "*yá 'át 'ééh*" — our equivalent of "how are you?" — widely used by the middle and young generations as a greeting, is strange to old people, and they may respond: "What do you mean? Do I look sick?"

In the eyes of the old people, the younger generation is lost from tradition. College students must look extremely young to men of eighty, and the idea that young Navajos want to learn about tradition seemed to strike the old men as a surprise. When telling an old story, the interviewees frequently added such comments as "Young people may not believe this and say that all this is nonsense. But this is the way I have heard it many years ago." On the other hand, such a comment may be also a part of the characteristic of the Navajo to allow for differences in individual opinions. Most of the interviewees ended each story by saying: "This is the way I tell it. Other people may tell it differently. But this is my version."

Another result of the project was that the endogenous researchers gained much new knowledge about old traditions. This contrasted with the prison project and the ghetto project, in which the researchers knew their culture thoroughly and interviews only added the details. In this sense the Navajo researchers, who were mostly under forty-five, were not strictly endogenous to the old tradition.

On the side of failures, there was the problem of hierarchical organizational structure which was alien to the Navajo culture. When an alien system is introduced, deviants tend to take advantage of it. Two students, who had been the heads of the student body, were appointed to run the project. It turned out that they were very authority hungry and dictatorial yet administratively incompetent. This may simply be due to their lack of experience. But judging from the way they interacted with other Navajos and from the opinion of other Navajos, I suspect that they were cultural deviants.

Another consideration is that precise planning is extremely difficult in a project in which the subgroups travel long distances (as far as 200 miles) into the field over rough terrain where people are seminomadic or frequently away for ceremonies at different places. Personally I enjoyed tracing medicinemen who were away at some remote patients' homes. In the process I learned much about the country and the people. Perhaps research in such a community should not be single-tracked. It can allow for unexpected byproducts and turn the seeming waste of time into productivity. For example, if a medicineman is not found at a distant hogan, his family may be interviewed instead on whatever topic they find relevant to them and are willing to discuss.

ABILITY OF ENDOGENOUS RESEARCHERS TO CONCEPTUALIZE

One of the resistances the endogenous research encounters is the professional researchers' scepticism regarding the untrained endogenous researchers' ability. Worth (1967) and Worth and Adair (1972) chose Navajos with a minimum degree of "Americanization" or formal education in their endogenous film project. In my prison and ghetto projects the average formal education level of the endogenous researchers was sixth grade, while the most of the Navajo researchers had high school education. Adair, Worth, and I found that the less contaminated the endogenous researchers by academic training, the more insightful their products are, and that the untrained researchers can be highly articulate and capable of research.

Of my three endogenous research projects, the prison project had participants with the lowest average of formal education. Therefore, let me use it to illustrate the ability of endogenous researchers with little formal education.

The prison project was conducted in two large state prisons. A team of endogenous researchers was formed in each of the two prisons. The overall objective of the project was to study interpersonal physical violence (fights) in the prison culture, with as little contamination as possible from academic theories and methodologies. The details of the research were left to be developed by the inmate researchers. Each team had the task of: (1) selecting the focus and conceptualizing the dimensions and the factors to be studied; (2) making a preliminary list of possible categories for each dimension or factor, and defining categories; (3) making preliminary data collection to see if these dimensions, factors, and categories were relevant and adequate, and adding new ones or eliminating unnecessary ones; (4) when dimensions, factors, and categories had been stabilized, designing an interview format, procedure, and interactional details to interview inmates known to be violent in order to analyze specific incidents; (5) developing a method to code the data; (6) trying out test interviews and modifying and improving interview format, procedure, and method; (7) conducting interviews; (8) coding the data; (9) analyzing the data.

Let me first reproduce here a part of the list of the factors and their categories formulated before the interview was designed. The two teams in the two prisons produced two different lists. All three members of the team in Prison A had only some grammar school education and very little reading in psychology or sociology, while two of the six members of the team in Prison B had some high school education, and another had had some exposure to lay psychology. Let us therefore take the list made by the team in Prison A. The list consists of the following eighteen dimen-

sions or factors to be looked into, each of which are further subdivided
into numerous categories:
1. interpersonal and individual factors leading to violence;
2. signals given prior to acts of violence;
3. how the signals were perceived;
4. reactions to such signals;
5. reasons for such reactions;
6. expected gains from the violent act;
7. degree to which the aggressor saw violence as the only alternative;
8. degree of communication skills;
9. involvement of others;
10. significance of spectators;
11. effectiveness of others in preventing violence;
12. extent of intended injury;
13. feelings before, at the moment, and after the violence, and present feelings about the incident;
14. how would you react to the same situation now;
15. subject's principles regarding violence;
16. sequential patterns leading to violence (use the diagrams provided);
17. fashions of violence in different prisons;
18. social climate which may vary between prisons as well as within a prison over time.

Due to the space limitations in this paper, we can reproduce here only the
categories for the first item: interpersonal and individual factors leading
to violence.

Coding Categories for Interpersonal and Individual Factors
(alphabetical)

Accumulated hostility from different sources
Definition: Several seemingly insignificant incidents occur with an
individual causing a build-up of anger or frustration.
Example: X didn't get that visit from his wife yesterday, his teeth have
been bothering him lately, a staff member searched him this morning, and
now Y bumps into him accidentally burning him on the hand with his
cigarette. This is too much for X so he attacks Y.
Boredom
Example: X gets tired of the same old routine and starts a fight with Y
to break monotony.
Bully
Definition: A person who pushes around people who appear to be
weaker.
Example: X cuts in front of Y everyday in the chow line because Y is

smaller. Y finally builds up the courage to tell X to quit; X, without further ado, beats the heck out of Y.

Challenge

Definition: One person invites another to fight for any reason.

Example: X is watching the television. Y walks up and changes the channel saying if X don't like it they can fight. X hits Y.

Cliques

Definition: A group of three or more individuals with the same principles who protect one another.

Example: Y slaps Z. Z tells his friends, and one of them, X, beats Y while Z and W stand around for support in case their friend X needs it.

Collector

Definition: One who collects debts for others on a percentage basis.

Example: Z loans Y one carton for two weeks at 100 percent interest rate (repay the double amount of loan). After two weeks Y is unable to repay. Z raises the interest rate to 200 percent and hires X to collect for 50 percent. Y is still unable to pay, or refuses to. X stabs Y.

Deliver message

Definition: One party relays a message for another party.

Example: X tells Y to tell Z to meet him behind the gym. Y tells Z. Z beats Y for not minding his own business.

Demonstrate not a fool

Definition: When a person indicates that others cannot run over him.

Example: Y makes fool of X by getting him to gamble on an event that has already happened and Y knows the result. X finds out and beats Y.

Disagreement

Definition: Persons cannot agree on issues and fight each other as a result.

Example: X stabs Y because Y did not agree with X that Mickey Mantle was the greatest baseball player in the world.

Displaced aggression

Definition: When it is dangerous or impossible to express aggression toward a person, the aggression may be expressed towards another person.

Example: X expects a visit from his wife and she doesn't show up. Y is unaware of this and bumps into X in the corridor. X stabs Y.

Dope

Definition: Narcotics, barbiturates, etc.

Example: Refusal to sell, acquisition by force, withdrawal frustrations, and debts.

Drinking

Definition: Under the influence of home brew (liquor made by inmates).

Example: X drinks home brew, becomes intoxicated, and stabs Y.

Explore reactions

Definition: One person agitates another just to see what he will do.

Example: X reads and tears up one of Y's letters for no apparent reason. Y asks X why. X beats Y.

Face saving

Definition: Avoidance of shame before other people.

Example: Y gets ahead of X in the chow line. Z tells X he wouldn't let Y do that to him. X smacks Y in the face.

False jacket

Definition: Untrue, derogatory labels.

Example: Y tells Z that X is a homosexual. When X finds out, he stabs Y.

Fear of being informed on

Definition: A person is seen by another doing an illegal act and is afraid he will tell authorities.

Example: Z sees X stab Y. X is afraid that Z will snitch on him, so X stabs Z.

Fear of being beat up

Definition: A person does something against his will for fear he will be harmed or killed.

Example: Y owes some cigarettes and can not repay. X tells Y to follow him to some obscure place. Y follows because he is afraid of X. X beats Y unnoticed. (Y wouldn't have been beaten if he had not followed X.)

Gambling

Definition: Wagering for cigarettes, money, or belongings.

Example: Cheating, betting more than a person has, refusal to pay losses.

Get down first

Definition: Getting in the first blow. Attacking because of fear of being attacked.

Example 1: Y tells X he is going to attack him on the following day at noon. X pipes (hits with a pipe) Y at 8 a.m.

Example 2: Y tells Z he is going to get him tomorrow at noon. Z tells his friend X: "I'm going to the board (parole board) and can't afford to get into any trouble." X jumps on Y the next day before noon.

Grudge

Definition: A fight that has been either postponed, or going on for a long time, and which finally comes to a serious violence incident.

Example: X and Y have been fighting each other since they were kids. They fought each other in another prison in another state. They fought each other on separate sides in a couple of gang fights outside. Yesterday Y hits X in the head with a sharp tin can. Five minutes later X sneaked up on Y while Y was busy eating chow and beat him severely about the head with a lead pipe.

Help friends

Definition: A person helps another in trouble because he is his friend.

Example: Y and Z become involved in a heated discussion. Y slaps Z. Later X holds Y while Z hits Y.

Homosexuals

Definition: This exists and is practiced (illegally) in institutions. There are female role player homosexuals. There are some who are considered married by the inmate population, and there are the free-lancers. This poses as many variations of problems as are actually happening outside among normal men and women: jealousies, triangles, irate husbands, fights for sexual rights, etc.

Example: H (female player) is approached by Y and asked for a date. H indignantly refuses stating he is married to X. At this moment X arrives on the scene, and when he finds out what is going on, he beats Y almost to death.

Hopeless outlook on life (Don't give a damn)

Definition: An inmate (possibly a lifer) decides there is nothing to care about since he already is in as deep as he can possibly get (life sentence).

Example: X, figuring he has nothing to lose anyway, beats the hell out of Y because Y seemed to be looking at him all the time.

Insult

Definition: One person degrades another justly or unjustly.

Example: Y tells X, "You are a bum, always were a bum, and you will always be a bum." X stabs Y.

Jealousy

Definition: Adverse feelings in a person who has not or does not get something another does.

Example: Y tells X he receives letters with money in them everyday. Further he says that he has not missed a draw (periodical cashing of personal funds) since he has been in prison. X calls Y a mama's boy and hits Y.

Loans

Definition: To lend something to someone expecting it back.

Example: X loans Y two packs of smokes for two weeks with no interest. At the end of two weeks Y refuses to pay. X stabs Y in the television room.

Mistaken identity

Definition: Picking the wrong party.

Example: X stabs Y in the movie room thinking it was W.

Misinterpretation

Definition: Taking an accidental act as intentional.

Example: Y is walking down the corridor thinking of his wife and bumps into X. X, thinking this was done on purpose, kicks Y in the testicles.

Misunderstanding

Definition: A person believes that another person has something against him when he really does not.

Example: X thinks Y is going to beat him up. Y has no intention of touching X. X sneaks up on Y and stabs him in the back.

No motive

Definition: A violent act is committed without apparent cause.

Example: When questioned by custody as to why he stabbed Y, X said he didn't have any reason.

No respect

Definition: Running over someone. (Acting as if the person's existence does not count.)

Example: Y steps on X's spit-shined shoes and fails to say "Excuse me." X stabs Y.

Opportune time

Definition: The best time to fight without being caught by custody.

Example: Y and X have been arguing for some time. Y wants to argue in the deserted television room. X, thinking this is a good time to straighten Y out, hits Y with a chair.

Outside influences

Definition: Events outside the prison contributes to violence in the prison.

Example: During Watts Riot, Y a Caucasian said to X a black: "We're on top now." X slaps Y and a riot starts.

Paid violence

Definition: Someone is paid to commit violence for another person.

Example: W gets into an argument with Z, but is afraid to fight him. So he pays X two cartons of cigarettes to fight Z.

Peace maker

Definition: Try to settle a dispute peacefully.

Example: W and Y are arguing. X asks them to break it up. W warns X to mind his own business. X stabs W.

Personality clash

Definition: When two or more persons are unable to get along because of similarity or dissimilarity in their personalities.

Example: X stabs Y because Y reminds X of himself.

Place saving

Definition: Two or more places are saved for a person in the canteen or movie lines or in the television room, etc.

Example: X goes into the TV room and asks Y for the chair next to him. Y informs X that the seat is saved for his buddy. X gets mad and slaps Y.

Political disagreement

Definition: Two parties disagreeing on political issues and policies.

Example: Y tells X that the governor is a bum. X disagrees and slaps Y.

Principles

Definition: Values that people have and are willing to fight for.

Example: Y calls X's mother "a dog" while they are standing in the chow line. X picks up a metal tray and hits Y. Y gets in the hospital.

Property destruction

Definition: Possessions of inmates are destroyed for various reasons by their enemies.

Example: To get even with X for slapping him, Y cuts up X's civilian shirt. Finding out who the cutter is, X pipes Y in the yard.

Protection

Definition: One pays someone to prevent being jumped on.

Example: W is paying Y four cartons a month for protection. X tells W, "I can protect you for two cartons a month." W stops paying Y and begins paying X. X and Y fight.

Protect friend

Definition: One person aids another because they are friends, and the latter is in trouble.

Example: Z tells Y that X is going to kill Z. Y offers to help Z. X hears of this and stabs Y and Z.

Prove self to others

Definition: A person feels as though he has to commit an act of aggression in order to prove to others his worth.

Example: X's friends tell him he is getting soft. X denies this, and to prove he is not getting soft, stabs Y in the chow hall.

Psycho

Definition: A person who is mentally ill and likes to commit acts of violence.

Example: Y owes Z three cartons and refuses to pay. Z is in hot water with the custody and cannot afford to get in fights. Therefore Z gets X, the local "nut," to jump on Y.

Race

Definition: Racial prejudice.

Example: X, a Mexican, jumps on Y, a Jew, because X doesn't particularly like Jews.

Reputation

Definition: Acts of violence committed by individuals for the purpose of being known by others as tough, vicious, and mean.

Example: X, having just got to prison, attacks Y in the chow line knowing he will be seen and build his public image.

Request not fulfilled

Definition: A person asks another to do something and the other party refuses for various reasons.

Example: X goes to clothing issue and requests a new shirt. Y, who is in charge of clothing, tells X he can't give him one because of rules, or because there aren't any. Later X, thinking Y wrong for not giving him a shirt, attacks Y.

Resent being told by others

Definition: One inmate telling another inmate what to do.

Example: X is talking loud while Y is taking a test in school. Y tells X to shut up. X broods about it later and attacks Y.

Resent custodial staff

Definition: To blame custodial staff for keeping him in prison or to have an authority problem and feel challenged when a person in authority orders him to do or not to do something.

Example: O tells X to move along and quit loitering. X moves but tells O he is an asshole. O asks for X's ID card. X begins to fight O.

Resent informers

Definition: Can't stand people who snitch on other people.

Example: Y is a known informer for custody. Y is also suspected of having informed on his crime partners. X, knowing this, purposely bumps into Y and starts a fight.

Restore self-image

Definition: Some individuals have a fixed image of themselves and will go to great length to restore this image even at the risk of their lives.

Example: X and Y are playing chess. Z is going by them and accidentally knocks the chess board askew, and moves on without another word. X thinks about it for a while and then goes looking for Z to kill him because Z dared to do this to him and not apologize.

Retain self-image

Definition: When a person sees himself as something and a situation occurs that causes him to think others will see him differently, he may fight.

Example: X is punching speed bag in the gym. Y asks if he can use the bag for a few minutes. Y hits the bag much better than X and appears to be a better fighter. Later X stabs Y to show who is the best fighter.

Revenge

Definition: Getting even for some real or imagined wrong.

Example: X, who arrived six months ago from another prison, stabs Y. A subsequent investigation reveals that Y was in the other prison and stabbed X there. Y came to this prison a few days ago.

Rumors

Definition: Rumors among inmates which grow into a fact.

Example: Clique S hears that Clique T is arming itself to fight Clique S. Clique S arms itself. When both cliques meet next time, they are ready.

Seek to impress others

Definition: One becomes involved in others' troubles for the purpose of impressing them.

Example: X has been wanting H (a homosexual) for months. X sees Y hitting H. H asks X for help. X stabs Y and impresses H.

Seeking acceptance by others

Definition: Wanting to belong.

Example: X sees that Clique B is very violent. He knows Y is an enemy of Clique B. X attacks Y in order to make a good impression on Clique B.

Self-defense

Definition: Forced to fight in order to survive.

Example: Y has been telling X he is going to kill him soon. In the morning Y hit X in the mouth and told him that tomorrow he will kill X for sure. X puts some food trays around his belly and under his shirt for protection, and arms himself. Next day Y challenges X and the fight is on. X kills Y.

Show off

Definition: Likes to be noticed.

Example: Y is showing off by loudly belittling X in front of people. X shows his resentment by stabbing Y.

Signify

Definition: To ridicule someone's appearance, work, or behavior.

Example: Z tells X in the visiting room that X's mother looks like she has been on a drunk. X smacks Z in the mouth. X's mother does not drink.

Teach lesson

Definition: Harming someone to teach in no uncertain terms not to do an act again.

Example: X loans Y some shaving cream. The next morning Y takes some without asking X. X hits Y to teach him to always ask before he takes something belonging to X.

Television

Example: Y changes the TV channel. X immediately changes the channel back. Y changes the channel again. X hits Y with a chair.

Theft

Example: Z is observed by X coming out of X's cell with two cartons of X's cigarettes. X stabs Z.

Want to stay in prison

Definition: Infractions committed to avoid release.

Example: X is scheduled to be released in two weeks. X begins a fight with Y in order to get locked up in isolation and lose his date.

Wheeling and dealing

Definition: Selling, loaning, bartering, gambling.

Example: Y sells X a wristwatch. The watch doesn't work. When X discovers this he asks Y for his smokes back. Y refuses. X stabs Y with a screwdriver.

ABILITY OF ENDOGENOUS RESEARCHERS TO RECORD, CODE, AND ANALYZE THE DATA

The total output of the two prison teams exceeded 1,200 single-spaced typed pages.

In addition to recording the eighteen dimensions or factors for 241 incidents, the endogenous researchers also recorded the following five items for each of the forty-two interviewees.
1. interviewee's overall pattern of violence;
2. variations in certain incidents from his overall pattern;
3. interviewee's philosophy of life and outlook on society;
4. description of the interviewee during the interview;
5. appearances and personal impressions.

Here are some examples from the output:

Examples from Coded Diagrams

Subject 36, Incident 8 (See Figure 1.)

Background: Subject had acquired a sizable bank roll (cigarettes) and had gone into "two for three" business, i.e., loaning out two cartons for the repayment of three cartons at the end of a two-week period, in other words, 50 percent interest.

Z and W were both in similar but separate business as subject, and they worked along with subject in the gym department.

Examples from "Principles"

Subject 36

1. *What would I fight for?* "As long as I have to die someday I would much rather die for a reason other than simply old age. It seems like a stupid senseless waste, you know, to die of old age. Since I'm going to die anyway, I would much rather die for something I believe in. Whether it was for a pack of cigarettes, or Mom's apple pie, or God and country, you know, I don't think it would be so much patriotism, or so much the value of the cigarettes, or anything else . . . I would be giving myself a reason for dying. Otherwise, I'm just going to die of old age, of cancer or something. I would just hate to die for nothing, you know, growing old. I would much rather die defending my pack of cigarettes."

When asked what would motivate him into getting himself into a hassle, he answered: "I guess false pride, possession, and beliefs. I've spent so many of my years in institutions where you don't really have anything . . . Everything belongs to the State. Ah, what little things you

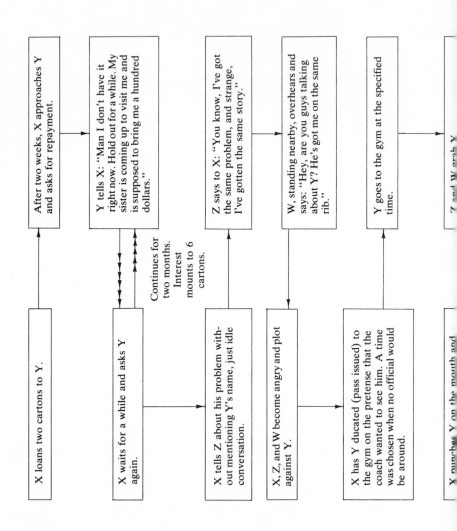

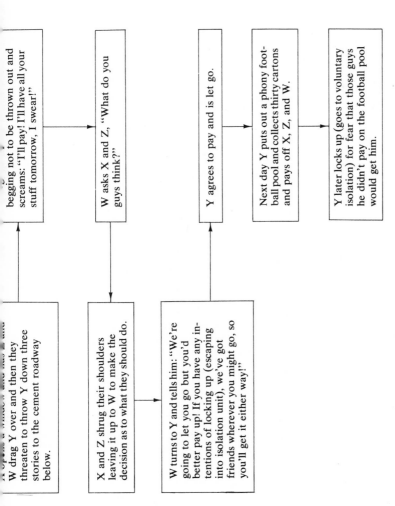

Figure 1.

have, such as cigarettes, or your canteen, or your word, ah, these are the things I would probably go down the river for," (i.e., to get killed).

2. *What would other people fight for?* "Basically the same things I would fight for . . . Pride, possession, and beliefs. If he believes something is right, he'll fight for it. In direct proportion to the degree in which he believes in it, will he respond to a threat to it. Naturally, if a guy don't think much of it, ah, he might just 'fat lip' a little. If he thinks a lot of it, he might fight you over it. But, if he's really hung up on it, he'll kill you for it." "You can bring any person, even an adult, into the penitentiary and here's a person that has led the good law-abiding life. You bring him in here to the big yard — this human zoo — and at first, what is repellent to him, over a period of time he will reach the point where he not only accepts it but, he can see why they're doing it . . . And then, he reaches the point where he condones it because he understands the need for doing it . . . And then, finally, he's doing it!"

Examples from "Patterns"

Subject 42

1. *Common patterns.* Subject states that his opponents in incidents 1, 2, 3 and 5 were bully-type persons who had agitated him by their ways. He claims that such people make him very angry. In every incident except 6, he says that the hostility built up before he decided to do something about it. He says further that in most encounters he can take a great deal of agitation until he feels that it must be stopped, then he becomes extremely angry and fights. In Incident 1 a homosexual was involved indirectly, and again in Incident 5 another homosexual was indirectly involved. The subject says that he does not like aggressive homosexuals, and their presence may have provoked him or made him angrier than he might otherwise have been. In almost every fight, there is an absence of any thought to use weapons (Incident 4 is an exception). He says that he was taught to fight fair, no weapons, no kicks, etc., and he follows this closely. The significance of these feelings come back strongly in Incidents 5 and 6, where he precipitates 6 as a result of the unfair fighting against him in 5.

2. *Variations.* In all incidents except 4 and 6, the subject's only intention was to get someone off his back. There was no intended damage. In 4, however, the intention was to kill. In 6 he seriously intended to hospitalize the victim if at all possible. In Incidents 1 and 2 it seems important to him that his opponents were bigger than he was. In Incident 3, the subject discloses that his opponent was very small, and that this is at least partially responsible for his not wanting to hurt the man. In other incidents there is no indication that size was important, but the subject

does state with some emphasis that there is no win in fighting a small man, and he also makes much of the fact that his opponents in 1 and 2 were bigger than he. (His own height is 6 feet 3 inches.)

Example from "Philosophy of Life and Outlook on Society"

Subject 41

1. *Has society been fair to you?* "No! Society is a bunch of shit. It isn't free." "I was brought up in an orphanage, an organization run by society." "They allowed my father to put me there." "The only thing I learned from the Catholic nuns was that 'might makes right.'" "They *force* you to do everything and physically punish you for all mistakes." "I stayed there nine years and learned to hate, become rebellious, and feel guilty for being so wrong all the time and for everything I did." "Society also owes me ten years, because they never looked at what led up to the killing (Incident 12)." "All the agitation that I had to take over the years." "The only thing society can do is to just leave me alone."

2. *What do you think people live for?* "People live for happiness, that is if they're honest about it." "Naturally it means different things to different people." "I guess it has to do with emotional contentment, and in being able to live half way decent, and having someone really care about you 100 percent."

3. *Is the world getting better or worse?* "Some aspects of the world are getting worse — like the civil rights movement. They're letting things get out of hand." "I hate them niggers." "If I had my way they would all be sent back to Africa and on the way thrown off the boat." "What's getting better? Well, the standard of living for one thing."

4. *What would you do when you get out?* "When I get out I'll try to make it, really try." (The subject was paroled the day after the interview was completed.) "My problem is to try to get along with people. In general they are phony." "I'll work, and I'd like to go into a business with my brother." "Piss on a marriage." "I'd like to help kids, train them in sports."

5. *What can society do to reduce violence?* "If society wants to reduce violence they should begin in the home." "Show kids affection." "Someone has to really like them for what they are."

6. *What would you teach your children about fighting?* "I'd teach my kids to never pick on someone weaker, or that couldn't defend himself."

DESCRIPTION OF THE INTERVIEWEE DURING THE INTERVIEW

The endogenous researchers in Prison B checked the following fifteen points on each interviewee.
1. Was S (interviewee) nervous or relaxed at the beginning of the interview.
2. Did he later become relaxed? How soon?
3. Did he speak spontaneously and continuously?
4. Were there moments when S was hesitant or evasive?
5. Did S try to impress the interviewers?
6. Was S repetitious or did he seem to dwell on a certain idea?
7. Was S interested in the interview? Did he seem to be preoccupied with something?
8. Did his narration seem to be prefabricated?
9. Did S tend to be abstract or did he relate concrete details? Did he illustrate his narration with hand movements, facial expressions, etc.? Was his narration vivid or dramatic?
10. Did he show much insight into himself?
11. Did he seem to gain insight during the interview?
12. Did he seem to have a pet theory about himself or to parrot his psychiatrist's theory on him? (If he has a psychiatrist in the prison.)
13. Did S's attitude change markedly during the interview?
14. Were there moments when S seemed to want to get out of the interview or take a break, possibly with the pretext of going to the rest room or to the water fountain?
15. Was there anything special about this S?

Example: Subject 42
1. Subject was a bit surly and obviously threatened when he first arrived. He was not nervous, but he was clearly not relaxed. Subject has a parole pending in the next few weeks, and he admitted that he was wary lest the interview have some effect upon the parole.
2. He did become more relaxed once the interview got under way. He remained slightly tense until after he had finished relating the first incident. His surly approach and mistrust was abandoned as soon as the purposes of the interview were thoroughly explained to him and before the interview was actually started.
3. At most times he talked spontaneously and continuously and with very little caution or suspicion. He did require a deal of coaxing or prompting before he would relate Incident 4. He claimed to be very ashamed of what happened here and did not like to talk about it. Having once related the incident, subject did inform the interviewers that he had intentionally left some embarrassing details out, but had revealed what he felt were the important points.

4. A time or two, he did pause before answering a question or continuing on the point he was on. This did not appear to be a result of any hesitancy to answer, however, but seemed to occur in order that he may organize his thoughts and present them in a manner that would be completely understood by the interviewers.

5. Subject did attempt to impress the interviewers during the early stages of the interview. The attempts were subtle however, and after one or two such attempts, he discontinued them. Also, he attempted to scare or bluff the interviewers shortly after his arrival for interview. It was at this time that he displayed his surly attitude and "tough-guy" role. He abandoned this approach completely and never returned to it.

6. He was not overly repetitious. On subjects or areas where there were repetitions, it was in order to clarify the matter and to attempt to be understood.

7. Nothing special seemed to preoccupy him. His attention was given to the task at hand, and to relate clearly and unambiguously.

8. His talk did not appear prefabricated. There were areas however, where he apparently "stretched" a point, and there were particular problems that he had given a great deal of attention to and discussed previously with other people.

9. Throughout the interview he related in concrete detail and was careful not to confuse the interviewers. He defined almost every statement that could have been misinterpreted or that may have projected a double standard.

10. He showed much insight into himself. Particularly so in Incident 4. While the subject himself offers these "deeper" reasons, it is significant that he has been reluctant to discuss them in the past. Also, on a couple of occasions the interviewers asked him whether or not there could have been some other reason for a particular aspect of his behavior, even offering what they thought about a certain point. Subject did acknowledge some of these, and let it be known that he had not seen it this way previously.

11. He did not appear to gain anything new from the interview. Previous to the interview, he had given a great deal of attention to his problems of the past, and had, by himself, gained a great deal of insight and knowledge of himself as to why he had acted in certain ways.

12. On several occasions he revealed that he had studied his problems from the psychological point of view. Moreover, he once worked for the psychiatric department here in the prison and for the chief psychiatrist. While he did not parrot a psychiatrist's analysis, portions of his statements did contain more than a sprinkling of psychiatric terminology and a definite awareness of how a psychiatrist might analyze him and his problems.

13.   Subject's attitude changed markedly during the interview. As pointed out before, he was surly at the beginning but became relaxed later. It should be pointed out however, that during the second day of interview the subject displayed a lack of interest that was a severe departure from his previous approach. Subject did not respond to questions readily, and while he did not convey the impression that he did not want to continue the interview, he did display a lack of enthusiasm that was marked in comparison to the previous sessions.

14.   Subject did not ask for a break or give any indication that he might like to leave or get out for a while.

15.   Subject acts as though he has made a sincere approach and attempt to evaluate himself and to correct his shortcomings that he once possessed. He is not a habitual criminal, having only the single arrest in his lifetime. In relating to the incidents, subject placed considerable emphasis on his dislike for aggressive and bullyish people. In more than one incident he fights because of this approach by others. It is also a fact, however, that the subject is himself aggressive and what might be termed bullyish. This may have been instrumental in bringing about some of the fights. Subject does not deny this, but it does not seem that he is fully aware of the impression he gives to others and how this may have been a strong factor in some of his fights. (6' 3", 235 pounds, Caucasian.) On this, he says, in part: "I may see the things I hate about myself in these bullies and aggressive people, and it may be that I attack the part of myself I dislike."

VALIDITY CHECK AND RELIABILITY

The inmate researchers devised several methods of validity check and reliability check and carried them out. These methods are discussed elsewhere (Maruyama 1969).

The numerous excerpts in the preceding pages indicate that persons without college or high school education can be very articulate and sophisticated in their ability to conceptualize and design a research and to record, code, and analyze the data.

The next question is whether the data obtained show any different insights as compared to the data obtained by social scientists from outside. The answer is affirmative. The insights gained are numerous. They are discussed in detail elsewhere (Maruyama 1968, 1969). The insights gained are on two levels: conceptual and factual. Examples are given below in a summary form.

Examples of Conceptual Insights

Some of the relations between categories made by inmate researchers make little sense as static classifications, but hold together if put into situational context of the prison culture. For example, "associations" is listed as a subcategory of "harm avoidance." Social scientists would rather put "associations" under acceptance. As has become clear in the data, the primary motivation in joining a group in the prison or in the ghetto is often to avoid being attacked by the same group. This is one of the significant epistemological differences between the middle class and the ghetto or the prison. "Harm avoidance," in turn, is listed as one of the major components of prestige. This is logical in a culture in which the ability to avoid physical attack is very important.

Another example is "defensive" which is listed as one of the subcategories of "anxiety." Other subcategories of "anxiety" are: "depression," "emotional instability," and "suicidal tendencies." "Defensive" seems to be out of place. But the data substantiate the connection: many individuals are unable to relate to others without defensiveness, and this inability frequently is a source of loneliness and its resulting anxiety.

Examples of Factual Insights

One of the findings is that there are many diverse types of philosophy of life and outlook on society among the violent individuals. I had expected that there would be some general philosophy of life and outlook on society with a smaller number of variations which would characterize violent individuals. But the number of diverse types found was much greater than anticipated. The diverse types found in the data are not amenable to neat categorization. But I have tentatively put them into the following groupings:
1. Subjects learned violence or exploitation in order to survive in their environment in childhood. Society is seen as individual against individual.
2. Conspiracy exists among individuals. One social group oppresses another.
3. Life centers around personal loyalty and individual efforts, buddy ties.
4. Traumatic experiences with or poor relations with parents are the most influential factor in the subject's worldview.
5. Life is dominated by a strong feeling of guilt.
6. No guilt is felt about violence. While some subjects enjoy violence others consider violence as the only ability they have without enjoying it.
7. Subjects fight for or in a clique or a group of individual friends.

8. Life goal is to get married and raise a family. No bitterness is felt toward society.
9. All of life is haphazard.
10. No incentive: the individual is happier in prison than outside.
11. The *main* factor in violence stems from homosexual relations.
12. Phony throughout the interview.
13. The *main* factor in violence is vocal hallucination (hearing voices).
    4, 15, 16. Three individuals with three unique types of philosophy of life and outlook on society.

Another example of the factual insights gained is that in most of the incidents the peer group acceptance model is inadequate. Two other models emerged as prevalent.

Dog-eat-dog model:
1. Each individual must defend himself *against* others in the "peer" group.
2. For each individual, other individuals are his enemies.
3. He would rather get away from other individuals, but there is no way out.
4. He fights for his defense, not for offense or for pleasure.
5. He tries to avoid the situations in which he has to fight.
6. He does not care whether he is liked by others. He would rather be feared.
7. The "group" is not formed by mutual attraction of its members. It is an aggregate *in spite of* its members.

In-or-be-killed model:
1. If the individual does not belong to the group, he is killed by the group.
2. The members do not have to like one another.
3. The members cooperate nevertheless, in order to produce collective power to fight individuals outside the group.

Another example of new insight is that the leader-follower model is inapplicable to most of the cases. In the incidents in which more than one individual cooperated, nonhierarchical partner relationship (whichever person gets attacked is helped by the other) and division-of-labor relationship (mostly in planned offense or defense) were prevalent.

Another insight gained is that in most of the fights (174 out of the total 241) the subjects fought alone without involving their friends.

CRITERIA FOR THE SELECTION OF ENDOGENOUS RESEARCHERS

Now that we have discussed the operational successes and failures of our past projects and pointed out for future projects several conditions for success, let me end this article with a list of criteria for the selection of future endogenous researchers.

1. Formal education is not required.

2. Because relevance resonance between the members of the culture and the project is most crucial, the most important criterion for the selection of endogenous researchers is the sameness of his own goals with those of the people in the culture. He must have a strong identification with the people, especially the grass-roots. Preferably he himself is a grass-roots member. He must not be an armchair philosopher or a hermit. He must not be an Uncle Tom. He must not be a do-gooder. He must not be one of those who alienate themselves from their own culture and identify themselves with an outside culture. But he may be bicultural, provided his identification is with his own culture. Monocultural, less "contaminated" persons, are preferable if available. Relevance resonance also requires some degree of experiential, existential, and commitment resonance. The endogenous researcher therefore must have lived in the grass roots, and must have shared experiences, feelings, interests, goals, and purposes with the grass-roots people, and must prove in action his commitment toward the goals of his people.

3. He must be industrious and must have the ability for dedication to what he undertakes.

4. He must be perceptive and must have the ability to relate to persons of all categories in his culture.

5. Certain skills, such as typing and driving, increase the efficiency of the work, and the team should include some persons who can type, drive, operate tape recorders, etc.

I must make here a special mention of the danger in delegating to someone the task of selecting and supervising the team members. I think anyone contemplating to start an endogenous research team should: (a) initially familiarize himself directly with different segments of the very bottom without going through intermediaries, get to know several individuals of each segment personally, and select team members from various segments. This will take several weeks. (b) Build the team from the bottom up, not from the top down; i.e., there should first be members who then elect the coordinator if needed, *not* first the coordinator who then selects the members.

Both (a) and (b) are important in: (1) reducing the unfair factional representation and favoritism in the selection of team members; (2) insuring equality, democracy, and mutuality among the team members; and (3) reducing the manipulation and the leverage the intermediary may exercise against the team members or against you, or both.

These considerations apply to both hierarchical and nonhierarchical cultures. In the ghetto culture, in which exploitation is a part of the epistemology, the manipulative tendency on the part of the intermediaries is expected to arise. On the other hand in nonhierarchical cultures such as Navajo or Eskimo, the whole concept of "coordinator" or "organizer" is foreign. In such cultures those who aspire to be or appear to act as coordinators or organizers tend to be deviants in terms of their own culture or at least nonrepresentative and tend to become disruptive sooner or later. Even if a nondeviant is given the role of organizer, he may malfunction due to his unfamiliarity with hierarchical roles. In all cases, direct selection of the team members without inter-mediaries is desirable.

In our ghetto project, however, the selection of team members was done by two intermediaries due to time limitation imposed by the funding agency. Thereafter the two exercised much leverage between the team members and myself, and I was unable to eliminate the intermediaries' manipulation throughout the project. The details of other failures of this project are reported elsewhere (Maruyama 1969).

Another policy I developed in a later project is to encourage each team member to use his own method congruent with his personal style.

CONCLUSION

I hope that this paper has sufficiently pointed out the rationale for endogenous research as the first step toward polyocular anthropology, and illustrated the capacity and contribution of endogenous researchers in my past projects. I hope it also has demonstrated the procedural and operational problems, successes, and failures we experienced, in such a way as to be useful to those who plan further explorations in endogenous research.

REFERENCES

BATESON, GREGORY
    1964   The logical categories of learning and communication. Unpublished paper. NIMH Grant K3-NH21-931.
BERGSON, HENRI
    1889   *Essai sur les données immédiates de la conscience.* Paris: Presses Univer-sitaires de France.
BUCKLEY, WALTER
    1968   *Modern systems research for the behavioral scientist.* Chicago: Aldine.
CAMARA, SORY
    1975   The concept of heterogeneity and change among the Mandenka. *Technological forecasting and social change* 7:273–284
CHANG, T. S.
    1938   A Chinese philosopher's theory of knowledge. *Yenching Journal of Social Studies* 1.

FEUER, LEWIS S.
1959 Bearing of psychoanalysis upon philosophy. *Philosophy and Phenomenological Research* 19:323–340.
HARVEY, O. J.
1966 *Experience, structure and adaptability.* New York: Springer.
HEIDEGGER, MARTIN
1927 *Sein und Zeit.* Tübingen: Niemeyer.
HUSSERL, EDMUND
1913 *Ideen zu einer reinen Phänomenologie und phänomenologischen Philosophie.* The Hague: Nijhoff.
IWATA, KEIJI
1969 *Toonan Ajia no Kokoro* [The Spirit of Southeast Asia]. Tokyo: Asia Economics Publishing Co.
JASPERS, KARL
1919 *Psychologie der Weltanschauung.* Berlin: Springer.
KIERKEGAARD, SØREN
1884 *Begrebet angest* [Concept of dread]. Copenhagen.
KLUCKHOHN, CLYDE
1949 "The philosophy of the Navaho Indians," in *Ideological differences and world order.* Edited by F. S. C. Northrop. New Haven: Yale.
KUBIE, LAWRENCE S.
1956 Some unsolved problems of scientific career. *American Scientist* 41:3–32.
MANNHEIM, KARL
1928 [1952] *Ideologie und Utopie* [Ideology and Utopia]. Frankfurt: Schulte-Bulmke.
MARUYAMA, MAGOROH
1961a Communicational epistemology. *British Journal for the Philosophy of Science* 11:319–327; 12:52–62; 12:117–131.
1961b The multilateral mutual simultaneous causal relationships among the modes of communication, sociometric pattern and intellectual orientation in the Danish culture. *Phylon* 22:41–58.
1963 Basic elements in misunderstandings. *Dialectica* 17:78–92, 99–110.
1966 Monopolarization, family and individuality. *Psychiatric Quarterly* 40:133–149.
1968 Trans-social rapport through prison inmates. *Annales Internationales de Criminologie* 7:19–46.
1969 Epistemology of social science research: exploration in inculture researchers. *Dialectica* 23:229–280.
1972 Symbiotization of cultural heterogeneity: scientific, epistemological and esthetic bases. *Third Symposium on Cultural Futuristics.* Washington: American Anthropological Association.
1975 *Endogenous research of prison culture by prison inmates.* University Microfilms Monograph N. LD0043.
1978 Heterogenistics and morphogenetics: toward a new concept of the scientific. *Theory and Society* 5:75–96.
MILSUM, JOHN H.
1968 *Positive feedback.* Oxford: Pergamon.
PRIBRAM, KARL
1949 *Conflicting patterns of thought.* Washington: Public Affairs Press.
RIEDL, RUPERT
1976 *Die Strategie der Genesis.* München: Piper.

SARTRE, JEAN-PAUL
 1943   *L'Être et le néant*. Paris: Gallimard.
SHANNON, C., W. WEAVER
 1949   *Mathematical theory of communication*. Urbana: University of Illinois.
VON FOERSTER, HEINZ
 1949–1953   *Transactions of Josiah Macy Jr. Foundation Conferences on Cybernetics*. New York: Josiah Macy Jr. Foundation.
WADDINGTON, C. H., *editor*
 1968–1971   *Towards a theoretical biology*, (four volumes). Chicago: Aldine.
WIENER, NORBERT
 1948   *Cybernetics*. Paris: Herman et Cie.
WORTH, SOL
 1967   The Navajo as filmmaker: a brief report on some recent research in the cross-cultural aspects of film communication. *American Anthropologist* 69:76–78.
WORTH, SOL, JOHN ADAIR
 1972   *Through Navajo eyes: an exploration in film communication and anthropology*. Bloomington: Indiana University Press.

Jívaro Headhunters in a Headless Time

HENNING SIVERTS

The Jívaro Indians of the Ecuadorian and Peruvian Montaña have for
a long time attracted the attention of anthropologists and laymen alike
due to their warlike practices and their habit of shrinking enemy heads
into miniature trophies.

This paper is an attempt at viewing Jívaro warfare and headhunting
as the core of "jívaroness" and source of ethnic maintenance. More
precisely, one could argue that the ideology underlying headhunting
represents the basic value orientation of the Jívaro and that the headhunting itself is one of the diacritical features exhibiting the Jívaro life style.

Together, the ideological underpinning and the headhunting-war complex constitute the cultural content that the Jívaro as an ethnic group
encloses (cf. Barth 1969: 14). The important point, however, is not so
much what is enclosed as the process of enclosing, i.e., how ceremonial
headhunting becomes the "source of ethnic maintenance." Thus, intertribal warfare, including resistance against the white intruders, was and is
considered a totally different undertaking from intratribal headhunting
raids.

Probably more than 40,000 Jívaro inhabit an area comprising some
60,000 square kilometers.[1] The region has difficult access, characterized
by rugged mountains and steep hills covered by dense tropical forest and
crisscrossed by swift-flowing rivers and brooks in an intricate fluvial net.
Some of the rivers and tributaries are navigable by canoes and balsa rafts
but, as Harner (1968) points out, travel by means other than foot is

---

[1] These figures are estimates based on various sources (Guallart 1964: 1970; Uriarte
1971, 1972; Varese 1970). It is further assumed that the Ecuadorian Jívaro groups occupy a
territory about the same size as the Alto Marañon region, i.e. some 30,000 square kilometers (Uriarte 1971).

difficult in large portions of the territory, where barely visible trails and paths tie settlements together.

Subsistence activities involve shifting horticulture, combined with hunting, fishing, and collecting of wild fruits and plants. The chief garden crops are yucca or sweet manioc (*Manihot esculenta*) and various species of plantains and bananas.

Although they form a linguistic and cultural entity — an ethnic group — they do not constitute a tribe if we take it to mean a permanent political group or corporation. The Jívaro are rather an aggregate of neighborhoods, called *jivarías* in Ecuador and *caseríos* in Peru, whose members consider each other as ceremonial foes or temporary allies within an all-embracing kin and affinal network. As headhunters, they recognize only Jívaro heads as worth taking and shrinking into /¢án¢a/ to be displayed and celebrated at the great victory feast following a successful headhunting expedition. In other words, a Jívaro is a potential /¢án¢a/ while all others, including the white people are just foreigners.[2]

At present when headhunting is no longer feasible and the victory feast cannot be performed, many Jívaro, reared as warriors, feel that their identity is being threatened, that their hallmark as a people is being lost. In spite of the fact that war parties are no longer organized and the concomitant ceremonial reassurance of commonness is a thing of the past, the fundamental values on which these activities were based are still shared by the majority of the Jívaro whether they live in Ecuador or Peru.

The implication of this observation seems to be that the Jívaro are aware of some "ethos," or, rather, a style of life, which they consider exclusively Jívaro. During my fieldwork among the Aguaruna Jívaros on the Peruvian side of the border, the subject of Jívaro unity and diversity was brought up repeatedly, even by the informants themselves.[3] For obvious reasons they showed concern for the future and wondered what would become of them all now that the military had got a foothold in their territory. They had no organizational means by which to mobilize all Aguaruna, not to mention other Jívaro groups, in order to resist the invaders and the colonists pouring into the area.

It is common knowledge that the Jívaro, until the recent past, have been able to unite in large and effective military operations, repelling attempts at conquest both on the part of the Incas, the Spaniards, and later the Peruvians and the Ecuadorians. The Jívaro themselves know this for a fact. That is why they are concerned; and that is furthermore why it seems pertinent to speak about the Jívaro as an ethnic group which is

[2]   Transcription of Aguaruna Jívaro words corresponds to phonemization proposals suggested by Pike and Larson (Pike and Larson 1964; Larson 1963).
[3]   Fieldwork was conducted in the Alto Marañon area between August 1970 and April 1971 and was supported by the Norwegian Research Council and Smithsonian Institution (Urgent Anthropology Program).

biologically self-perpetuating, shares fundamental cultural values, makes up a field of communication and interaction, and, finally, has a membership which identifies itself, and is identified by others as constituting a category distinguishable from other categories of the same order (cf. Naroll 1964).

The Jívaro do recognize the overt cultural forms signifying unity such as language, dress, house types, and technology. But, what is more significant, they assume existence of a set of common value orientations: "the standards of morality and excellence by which performance is judged" (cf. Barth 1969: 14).

The concept of /kakáham/ is a case in point. A /kakáham/ is a man who has killed several times, a *valiente*, and the Aguaruna still distinguish between the /kakáham/ and other persons. The former is likely to be an influential local leader. According to Harner, "the personal security which the Jívaro believe comes from the killing has some social reality. A man who has killed repeatedly, called the *kakaram* [i.e., /kakáham/ in Aguaruna] or 'powerful one,' is rarely attacked because his enemies feel that the protection provided him by his constantly replaced souls would make any assassination attempt against him fruitless" (1962). According to Aguaruna informants the /cimpuí/ or special chair is reserved for the /kakáham/ and the /nágki/ (the war lance) should be touched only by a person belonging to this category.

In other words, /kakáham/ provides us with a focal concept by which the Jívaro classify human beings and their actions. As an achieved status, /kakáham/ represents a valued end and a measure of success. Not all Jívaro became /kakáham/ but they certainly aspired to become one, and indeed a young man was marriageable only after he had proved his ability as hunter and warrior (cf. Stirling 1938: 110). Thus a Jívaro man is by definition a warrior, and the ideal career involves the recognition as /kakáham/ and later /wáhiu/, leader of men and organizer of war parties. The designation /kúhak/, derived from the Quechua–Spanish *curaca*, was probably reserved for those influential men who could muster a following among several local groups.

Thus the typical social categories refer to excellence of performance within a pattern of behavior focused on warfare and trophy making. These activities are still emphasized and until recently were made organizationally relevant. But the warrior ideal cannot be maintained much longer as the primary concern of men. The presence of troops, white settlers, merchants, and missionaries prevents the Jívaro from realizing in actual life the most important aspect of the Jívaro male role: being a warrior. Consequently individual men may consider themselves as only "part-time Jívaros," implying a gradual blurring of the image of virility and manliness assumed to underlie Jívaro behavior. "Since belonging to an ethnic category implies being a certain kind of person, having that identity, it also implies a claim to be judged, and to judge oneself, by those standards that are relevant to that identity" (Barth 1969: 14). According to the Jívaro way of arguing, social order is based on moral order, and the latter is composed of a series of demands and obligations derived from a set of beliefs about souls and esoteric power and the way to obtain it. Only Jívaro own the souls and control the power, and killing another Jívaro is a means by which power is attained; hence a claim to be judged as Jívaro is to kill another Jívaro, or in Karsten's words:

It is characteristic of the Jivaros that they especially wage war against tribes belonging to their own race and speaking the same language. To such an extent has this been the rule for centuries that the word, *shuara*, "Jivaro Indian," has become synonymous with the word 'enemy.' 'My enemy' in Jivaros language is *winya shuara* (1935: 276).

Vengeance and blood feuding, then, is the logical outcome, war parties are a natural tactical device, head trophies the overt and highly dramatic symbol of performance according to standards of morality, and military alliances are the long-term strategic solutions by which one may hope to maintain a reasonable balance between peace and war.

It is not clear whether the Kandoshi were included among Jívaro foes. They waged war on each other, but there is no evidence of head taking. Nevertheless, the Kandoshi are reported as fierce warriors and apparently showed great similarity in their war pattern and beliefs (Wallis 1965). In case Jívaro heads were severed and displayed among the Kandoshi and vice versa, we may assume, according to the argument pursued, that the Záparo-speaking Kandoshi and the Jívaro considered each other as participants in the same raiding game, sharing fundamental values about souls and power, i.e., "the assumptions about reality upon which they [the Jívaro] predicate" their warlike practices (Harner 1962). The implication of such a reciprocity would be the inclusion of the Kandoshi in a Jívaro–Kandoshi ethnic group.

One of my young Aguaruna informants offered a simplified "history" of the area to the effect that in the beginning all Jívaro were united against different foreign tribes, including eventually the white people. Then the Huambisa and Aguaruna started warring against each other and ultimately the Aguaruna split up into feuding units. Speculating over this version for a while, without grasping its meaning, it suddenly occurred to me that my friend was actually conveying a message, the interpretation of which might be the following: Formerly all Jívaro were potentially united, but, as we can all see, now they are separated in smaller groups. In other words, he tried to reconcile the facts relating to the present situation and the oral tradition referring to the great alliances of the past. A further indication of relative distance in time and space corresponding to some real or fictive alliance is found in the "tribal" designations handed down from an earlier period. All the people beyond Río Santiago were called /patúk/, comprising both the Huambisa and the Ecuadorian Untsuri Shuara. However, the Huambisa reserve the term /wampís/ for themselves and apply /patúk/ to describe the Ecuadorian Jívaro. The Achual are named /acuág/ by the Aguaruna.

Clearly this selection of "names" for peoples may reflect a particular alliance constellation or some vague notion about territorial groups. Dialect differences may also be involved. Indeed, we can expect a proliferation of names as long as every little *quebrada* [river valley] has its name by which also the group of people living there is known.

A temporary grouping of allies was given the name of the war leader or of the river on which he was residing. Thus, the Antipa may well have been an Aguaruna group distinguished from other Jívaro on account of a powerful leader by the name of Antipa. Today, nobody seems to remember the Antipa, but in 1899, when Up de Graff braved the Pongo de Manseriche, the Antipa were a powerful group which had joined forces with another Aguaruna group in order to attack the Huambisa further up on the Santiago River (Up de Graff 1923: 241ff.).

According to Up de Graff, fifty-five canoes containing some two hundred men were heading up-river "bent on a common mission (which needs no explanation)" (1923: 242). Not all raids counted such formidable forces, but apparently the Jívaro of those days were politically rather active, forming alliances and organizing war parties of considerable size. From Stirling's description we get the impression that the extension of influence assigned to any one *curaka*, or war leader, varied from time to time, implying the waxing and waning of alliances between smaller units.

The number of households under the influence of a given curaka is subject to a great deal of fluctuation. It frequently happens that a strong curaka will build up a fairly powerful group of warriors about him. A weak curaka or capito may have a blood-revenge killing to attend to but will find himself outnumbered by the enemy to such an extent that he is afraid to attempt a killing with his own group. In this event he is likely to call upon the strong curaka to arrange the killing for him with a gun or a woman. Often, too, a weak curaka, fearing that his group would not be able successfully to defend themselves against an attack from enemies, will voluntarily place himself and his group under the influence of the strong curaka in a loose sort of alliance. In this way the strong group tends to grow and to become even stronger until one curaka may have 8 or 10 lesser curakas more or less under his control. This state of affairs is usually not very permanent. Owing to the loose organization and lack of any real power on the part of the head curaka, the large group becomes unwieldy or develops diverse interests and it tends to split up again into independent units. Consequently, in as little as 2 or 3 years' time, the original head curaka may find that one or more of his former lieutenants are now stronger than he (Stirling 1938: 39).

Neither Up de Graff nor Karsten are specific in their treatment of alliance-forming and social organization generally. We have to rely on the work of Stirling from the 1930s and Harner's from a more recent period. Fortunately Stirling does go into some details on this point, documenting his generalized description of the political process by citing two cases of regional fusion and fission which he personally had encountered during field work in 1930–1931. The first example illustrates how military strength is related to personal power and, by implication, the physical and mental fitness of the leader or strongman.

Four or five years ago there was a strong chief on the Upano River named Tuki, known to the Ecuadoreans as José Grande. In the manner previously described, all of the curakas from Macas on the Upano River to Mendez on the Paute River became subchiefs under him until he was generally recognized as the strongest of all of the Jívaro curakas. However, he was beginning to grow old by this time and some of his subcurakas were strong men in their own right. About 2 years ago, Ambusha, who had been gradually gaining in power and becoming famous for his headhunting activities, split off with his own group, taking several curakas and their men with him. A little later Utita did the same thing. At the time of the writer's visit (1931), although Tuki was recognized by the Government of Ecuador as being head chief of the Macas-Mendez region, actually he had lost all power excepting that over his own family group and was in reality no more than a capito. These divisions of the organization, if it may be termed such, took place apparently without any ill feeling or formal announcements (Stirling 1938: 40).

The second case illuminates the demographical question in a strife filled society, by simply showing the repercussion of success.

In 1925 the Canga River and the upper Yaupe was very populous and prosperous. The Indians were a warlike group confident of their own strength and much feared by all of the Indians in the neighboring regions. The curaka of the Canga Jívaros was a well known warrior called Cucusha. Anguasha . . . another warlike leader, was head of the Yaupe group. The two had always been close friends and companions. During a period of 10 or 15 years they compiled a notable war record, each being credited individually with more than 50 heads during this time. Their raids extended to all of the tribes in the district and some quite distant, until they became the terror of the region. However, these constant raids under two such aggressive leaders began to take their toll of men. Although many victories were registered, they were constantly losing warriors, until eventually their numbers were appreciably reduced (Stirling 1938: 40).

The flexibility of organization which these excerpts suggest, is amply demonstrated in my own material on Aguaruna local groups and the process by which they are established and maintained. Just as the military alliances were subject to a developmental cycle, the house clusters (*caseríos*) and larger neighborhoods change through time in composition and numbers, corresponding to or reflecting ecological and demographical circumstances, individual mobility and independence being concomitant features. Genealogical data reveal that single persons and families have changed house sites several times not only within a settlement, but have also moved from one *caserío* to another far part. In so doing they have attached themselves to relatives and avoided traditional "enemies."

As I have argued elsewhere (Siverts 1971, 1972) the habitat requires mobility, and this moving about in search of suitable house sites, yucca gardens, hunting grounds and hunting partners is made possible by the linking of houses and settlements through genealogies. This linking of genealogies or rather fragments of genealogies constitutes an underlying framework of organization which, by extension, embraces all Jívaro in a kin and affinal network. Apparently the Aguaruna consider all other Jívaro, whether foe or friend, as somehow related. Personal experiences, implicitly shown in a statement such as, "my mother was a Huambisa," corroborates this notion.

The alliances of *caseríos* (or *jivarías*) were expedient activations of more or less extensive portions of the genealogical network, a measure which, by implication, established relative peace within an area. The lack of persistence of any particular alliance provided for constancy of the genealogical network itself which thereby was left unbroken as an organizational potential: new constellations of *caseríos* could always be established.

In view of the flexibility of organization, permitting the establishment of impermanent corporations, Jívaro invincibility in the past makes sense. The question has been asked how the Jívaro, preoccupied with the taking of each other's heads, could possible muster an effective resistance against intruders. And the answer must be one that takes account of the strategic advantage offered by the habitat itself as well as the military strength presented by the Jívaro as an ethnic group.[4]

It is this latter theme that is intimately related to the main problem of this essay, viz., the process by which "jívaroness" is maintained and the cultural boundary defended. From the Jívaro point of view this boundary is essentially one which separates /ćánća/s from non-/ćánća/s, and its territorial counterpart is recognized only insofar as the headhunting pattern or the conditions for pursuing this activity is threatened. Thus, the Jívaro make no territorial claim and they did let foreigners visit them and establish contact without showing hostility.

It was when they first felt that Spanish settlement and Spanish rule interfered with their own way of life and its esoteric basis that they acted; and they were able to act in concert since the underlying framework was all-encompassing, and potentially permitted the emergency mobilization

---

[4] How strong the striking power was is illustrated by the famous Jívaro revolt of 1559 when perhaps as many as 20,000 warriors under the leadership of Quiruba annihilated the town of Logroño, terminating Spanish rule in the Jívaro territory. Not even the Peruvians or Ecuadorians succeeded in making headway in this area some fifty years ago. At least they never won a decisive victory.

of all able-bodied men in a grand alliance transforming the Jívaro ethnic group into a corporation.

Such a complete fusion of antagonistic, feuding units may be seen as the automatic result as long as blood revenge and war were parts of daily life, the shifts in power continuous, and the alliance forming an ongoing, cyclical process.

Even as late as the 1930s, when Stirling visited the area, the following statement was probably appropriate:

The alliance between nature and the Jívaros has enabled these Indians successfully to repulse for 400 years the most determined efforts of the white man to establish himself in their territory. The many-faceted account of this prolonged struggle against military, theological, commercial, and territorial aggression constitutes one of the most colorful chapters in aboriginal American history (1938: 28).

The bulldozer and the machine gun have changed the situation. It is no longer possible for the Jívaro to control the area by watching the mountain passes or attacking isolated and vulnerable outposts.[5] The highway and the garrisons have put an end to the endless feuds, and prevented the most dramatic expression of "jívaroness." A further consequence of this state of affairs, is the retention of old grievances between former opponents without the natural outlet, leaving the underlying framework obsolete for corporation-forming purposes and hence leading to a situation of political inactivity and indecision.

And this indecision, combined with the distrust of fellowmen, has made it easier for the respective governments to launch their colonization projects, forcing the Jívaro, one by one, from their *chacras* [yucca gardens] and hunting grounds. It is symptomatic that the Aguaruna of Alto Marañon are so paralyzed that they have permitted the Peruvian authorities to back up a figurehead, hated by everybody.

There is only one case on record showing signs of political activity and a will to act *in corpore:* a group of armed men gathered in the Cenepa district in order to resist another round of DDT fumigation. For the first time, the "DDT gang"[6] met resolute and concerted action. They fled, and news about the success spread all over the region. Today, the "malaria-agency" people find it difficult to continue working in the area, which means one nuisance less to cope with.

However interesting this instance appears under the circumstances, it may not necessarily herald a new drive or revival of political activity on a

[5]   In 1951 a Peruvian garrison on the upper Morona was routed and practically everybody killed; and in 1925 the village and mission of Cahuapenas on the Apaga river were wiped out (cf. Stirling 1938: 28).
[6]   The "DDT gang" is short for the employees of the *Servicio Nacional de Eradicactón de Malaria* (SNEM) (see Siverts 1972).

large scale. It takes more to unite headhunters when there are no heads around to be taken; and in addition the prospects offered for Jívaro survival as an ethnic group are rather gloomy under the auspices of a "headless" minority policy.

REFERENCES

BARTH, FREDRIK, *editor*
  1969   *Ethnic groups and boundaries: the social organization of culture differ-
         ences.* Boston: Little, Brown.
GUALLART, JOSÉ MARÍA
  1964   *America Indígena* 24:315–331.
  1970   "Magia y poesía aguaruna: poesía magica y poesía lírica entre los
         aguarunas." Unpublished manuscript.
HARNER, MICHAEL J.
  1962   Jívaro souls. *American Anthropologist* 64:258–272.
  1968   Technological and social change among the eastern Jívaro. *Proceedings
         of the Thirty-seventh International Congress of Americanists*, 363–388.
         Buenos Aires.
KARSTEN, RAFAEL
  1935   *The head-hunters of western Amazonas: The life and culture of the Jívaro
         Indians of Eastern Ecuador and Peru.* Helsinki: Societas Scientarum
         Fennica, Comentationes Humanarum Litterarum.
LARSON, MILDRED L.
  1963   *Emic classes which manifest the obligatory tagmemes in major indepen-
         dent clause types of Arguaruna [Jívaro].* University of Oklahoma Sum-
         mer Institute of Linguistics, Norman, Oklahoma.
NAROLL, RAOUL
  1964   On ethnic unit classification. *Current Anthropology* 5:283–312.
PIKE, KENNETH L., M. L. LARSON
  1964   "Hyperphonemes and non-systemic features of Aguaruna phonemes,"
         in *Studies in languages and linguistics.* Edited by A. H. Marckwardt,
         55–67. Ann Arbor: University of Michigan.
SIVERTS, HENNING
  1971   "The Aguaruna Jívaros of Peru: a preliminary report." Mimeographed
         manuscript, University of Bergen.
  1972   *Tribal survival in the Alto Marañon: the Aguaruna case.* IWGIA-
         Document 10. Copenhagen.
STIRLING, M. W.
  1938   *Historical and ethnographical material on the Jívaro Indians.* Smith-
         sonian Institute of Washington, D.C., Bureau of American Ethnology,
         Bulletin 117.
UP DE GRAFF, FRITZ W.
  1923   *Head-hunters of the Amazon: seven years of exploration and adventure.*
         London: Herbert Jenkins.
URIARTE, LUIS M.
  1971   *Situación de genocidio, etnodicio e injusticia entre las tribus aguaruna u
         huambisa del Alto Marañon.* Comisión Episcopal de Acción Social,
         Cuadernos de Documentación 2. Lima.
  1972   "Algunos datos preliminares del censo aguarunahuambisa." Unpub-
         lished manuscript, Chiriaco.

VARESE, STEFANO, *editor*
  1970 *Estudio sondeo de seis communidades aguarunas del Alto Marañon*.
        Division de Communidades Natives de la Selva, Dirección de Com-
        munidades Campesinas. Series de Estudos e Informes 1. Lima Minis-
        terio de Agriculture.
WALLIS, ETHEL
  1965 *Tariri, my story*. Translated from Kandoshi by Lorrie Anderson. New
        York: Harper and Row.

COMMENT by *H. Siverts*

"Jívaro headhunters in a headless time": A short summary of points relevant for the discussion of warfare and warlike activities.

The present paper was not originally written as a contribution to a conference on warfare, but intended as a descriptive analysis of certain mechanisms generating ethnic consciousness as well as political awareness of boundaries. As stated in the abstract: "The paper focuses on headhunting as the dramatic expression of ethnicity among the Jívaro Indians of the Ecuadorian and Peruvian Montaña."

Although the paper is not specifically "on war" as a theme, the mere fact that the Jívaro used to indulge in warfare with great enthusiasm, make them as a group an ethnographic case highly relevant to a general treatment of hostility, conflict, and warlike military operations. What the Jívaro headhunting raids bring to the fore is the historical (ethnographical) importance of fighting as a way of life, so to speak.

Explicitly, I try to relate intratribal raids to intertribal warfare. Implicitly, I make use of a conceptual framework which is based on certain notions about the nature of social processes; the dynamics of maintenance. These underlying concepts include the key words of *choice* and *constraint in choice*, leading to a discussion of the relative merits of various sets of restrictions on individual choices. In my paper ecological restrictions constitute one such set while ideology represents another.

So much for the kind of anthropology I seem to be pursuing. Let me now turn to the crucial points in Jívaro warfare:
1. Ceremonial headhunting was an endemic phenomenon in the area in question: a recurrent and expected event.
2. Trophy hunting was considered highly rewarding in the Jívaro social ranking, indeed the very essence of being a Jívaro male.
3. Intertribal warfare was a distinct undertaking from trophy hunting, the primary purpose of the former being the protection of the latter. The extension of territory as such was no goal in itself.

Before summing up the line of argument suffice it to add a few notes on the area and its inhabitants.

Probably more than 40,000 Jívaro reside in an area comprising some 60,000 square kilometers. The region has difficult access. Travelling is done by canoes, balsa raft, and by foot. Subsistence activities involve shifting of horticulture, combined with hunting, fishing, and collecting of wild fruits and plants. The chief garden crops are *yucca* or sweet manioc and various species of plantains and bananas.

Although they form a linguistic and cultural entity, they do not constitute a tribe if we take tribe to mean a political group. The Jívaro are rather an aggregate of neighborhoods whose members consider each other as ceremonial foes or temporary allies within an all-embracing kin and affinal network. As headhunters they recognized only Jívaro heads as worth taking and shrinking into a trophy — to be displayed and celebrated at the great victory feast following a successful headhunting expedition. In other words: a Jívaro is a potential head while all others, including the white people are just foreigners.

At present when headhunting is no longer feasible and victory feasts cannot be performed, many Jívaro feel that their identity is being threatened.

In my argumentation I try to relate this apparent uneasiness shown by the present Jívaro to the infrastructure and the significance of raiding as a cementing force, politically speaking, as well as an expression of ethnicity. It is suggested that the headhunting ideology and the kin and affinal network tie all Jívaro in an ethnic group. This network provided the underlying framework for the establishment of temporary corporations or alliances, an expediency measure to cope with the problem of defense under conditions of dispersed living. Since alliance forming was dependent upon the emergence of great war leaders with limited life spans, the corporations were necessarily short-lived, permitting as it were, the constant activating of the underlying framework to form new alliances. By implication the limit set for fusion of traditionally hostile units is the totality of warriors recognizing each other's heads as trophies, i.e., the mobilization of the members of the ethnic group to form a corporation (a Jívaro nation).

Thus feuding and raiding is seen as the institution which generated the perpetuation of corporate units, their establishment and reforming, and the overall defense of Jívaro identity *vis-à-vis* the world.

It is symptomatic that the present state of affairs, characterized by the absence of headhunting, seems to be an era of political inactivity and indecision resulting in a fundamental weakness as far as political activity is concerned, constraining the opportunity to form alliances of sufficient strength to prevent an ever more massive intrusion of troops and settlers from other impoverished areas of Peru.

Opposition as a Component of Ethnic Self-Consciousness

B. F. PORSHNEV

In linguistics and ethnology attention is increasingly drawn towards the phenomenon of opposition. It is dealt with predominantly on the plane of logic or, speaking more broadly, of the theory of thinking; sometimes it is considered on a biological level. The theory of opposition tends to become increasingly formalized as a universal theory of symbols or a general theory of structures. The concrete facts which it draws upon, however, are found mostly in the field of ethnopsychology. The purpose here is to descend, to a certain extent, from the sphere of abstractions to earth, i.e., to show the phenomenon of opposition as one of the major problems (possibly even *the* major problem) of ethnopsychology.

In other words, I wish to contrapose this aspect of ethnopsychology against its more widespread interpretation.

From early times the minds of ethnologists were possessed by a myth, by the idea that ethnic groups, peoples, and nations are distinguished by innate and unvarying mental and cultural characteristics, by permanent specific traits. The ways of determining these mental characteristics have always remained unknown. Psychology could do nothing in the way of analysis or explanation with the conception of ethnopsychology which was reduced to a simple description of this or that set of allegedly perfectly static mental traits of people. Such descriptions were given at very different levels — from immature and superficial ethnic portraits to more or less scrupulously summarized field observations. But there always has existed and still exists the tendency to attach to a nation or an ethnos a psychological passport or identity card treated as something absolute. The historical changeability of the character and traits of an ethnos appeared here merely as a vexatious hindrance to ethnopsychology and was, as far as possible, kept out of sight.

In recent decades some ethnopsychologists have successfully marketed such "passports" to trusting military departments, on the basis that it is necessary to know the psyche of potential enemies and allies. In fact, this commodity had no scientific value and virtually no serious practical importance. Practically speaking, ethnopsychology, in the sense alluded to, turned out to be merely an enormous legend oriented toward nationalistic prejudices.

To counter this conception of ethnopsychology, which stands apart from modern psychological science and is at present dying out, another conception is being brought forward. This has at its core not the mental traits of each individual ethnos, each nation, but interethnic, international psychological relations. It is common knowledge that the psychological passports fashioned by the earlier ethnopsychologists were chiefly composed of appraising (i.e., positive and negative) characteristics, sometimes overtly, and sometimes under some kind of mask of objectivity. True science has absolutely nothing to do with the sort of approach that praises or blames individual peoples for certain qualities. This whole system of coordinates lies outside science. At the same time, such evaluations may themselves serve as objects of scientific study. It is possible to investigate the image a particular people forms of its own merits and demerits; its own evaluation of its qualities as well as that held by adjacent and other peoples; the stability or historical variability of these interethnic evaluations. The underlying reality which determines these evaluations is undoubtedly constituted of actual, objectively existing factors, those of mutual rapprochement, on the one hand, estrangement or contradictions between peoples, on the other.

Interethnic relations cannot, however, be reduced to mutually held images and evaluations. These relations largely permeate the inner cultural-psychological life of any community, its whole material and cultural everyday existence. A broad perspective of ethnopsychological and ethnocultural studies appears to open up in this direction.

Ethnographers and archeologists have already established by a number of examples the important fact that many phenomena of primitive culture carry, as it were, two simultaneous functions — that of separation and that of unification, i.e., they separate a particular group from any other group or groups, and unite the group's members with each other. This contraposition on the plane of social psychology I designate as the "we and they" principle, meaning that each "we" can only be built up through a comparison (contraposition) with a certain "they."

See, for example, how the French archeologist and ethnologist Leroy-Gourhan treats the problem of the history of dress. Two mutually contradictory processes are taking place here: that of ethnic disintegration, which has become especially intensive in recent times, and that of ethnic integration. The first consists in ousting local and regional stereotypes and the unification of forms of dress. Social differences are reflected in dress only through the price tags. On the contrary, the integrative function of dress consisted, and to a certain extent still consists, in linking an individual exclusively to his particular group, thus opposing him to members of other groups. According to Leroy-Gourhan, "To live in the dress customary in one's locality, as well as in one's social estate, means at once to feel oneself an element of the group, and to feel opposition against other groups. To live in a standard human uniform means a wide interchangeability of individuals as pieces in a universal 'macro-organism' " (Leroy-Gourhan 1965: 191). Leroy-Gourhan (1965) applies a similar principle to the treatment of certain other elements of material culture. However, we do not find in his works any attempt to expand this principle into a whole "philosophy of opposition."

The extremely interesting article by the Soviet ethnographer Tokarev (1970) represents, in my view, a step in this direction. Tokarev puts forward an identical principle for studying three basic elements of material culture: food, clothing, and housing. The author's interest lies not in the relation between man and material objects but in relations between men in connection with the material object. Meals taken jointly and consisting of strictly specified dishes and the consumption or rejection of particular kinds of food amalgamates people into a community to the degree that it separates them from other people.

Together with its function in social intercourse, food fulfills the function of social separation. For example, all peoples have been known to have customs forbidding or restricting meals between certain groups of people, e.g., men and women, members of different castes, social classes, religions. All kinds of prohibitions and prescriptions in matters of food and drink are considered from the same angle. A vestige of these food oppositions in our world is the preference for one's national or local dishes. Further, Tokarev demonstrates the application of this principle to the study of clothing: on the one hand, the differentiation and segregation of the sexes, of ethnoses, social strata, professions; on the other, the attachment of a person to his own community, to his "we." Dress, says Tokarev, plays the role of a social mark, stamping a person as belonging to a certain corporate body and contraposing him to those who do not belong to it. Thus, the function of dress as a socially and ethnically amalgamating factor is absolutely inseparable from its function of ethnic and social segregation.

Lastly, Tokarev turns to the role of housing. Here also, the author elucidates the social-ethnic aspect: the type of housing contraposes "we" against certain "they," furthering, at the same time, a distribution of relationships and functions within the "we" group. Similar to food and clothing, housing fulfills this double function: it unites people and separates them from others. The opposition "home-not home" is underlined among different peoples by different aesthetic and ritual methods. These may, in their turn, contrapose not merely a particular home against strangers, but all the homes in a particular community against different types of buildings, ornamentation patterns and symbols or, within any given ethnic group or settlement, men's houses against women's, dwellings of the nobility against those of common people, etc.

Thus, Tokarev isolates in his analysis of food, clothing, and housing the aspect of social opposition (separation-unification) from the aspect of their material functions (gratification of physical needs, etc.) and from the aspect of the levelling of all these social-ethnic features of material culture (Tokarev 1970).

Examples from different spheres of ethnic culturology and ethnic psychology are so varied and plentiful that the question is bound to arise as to whether a more universal generalization may be made. Can the opposition "ours-stranger's," "we-they" be a principle applicable in ethnology to any phenomenon of ethnic peculiarity, even though it belonged to the sphere of material culture, of rituals and collective concepts, and finally of language and gesticulation.

I have been unable to find any instance in which this aspect was not present. A local technological feature, though it is in many cases evidently determined by local environmental peculiarites, still reveals, as a rule, in its very traditionalism and in certain components lacking direct utilitarian value, the property of isolating "ours" from "not ours," from "strangers" who use somewhat different tools and methods of work. These "strangers" or "outsiders" are invisibly but psychologically present in all the practices of the ethnos.

Peculiarities of dialect and phraseology also serve to unify and to separate neighboring groups. Among theories on the earliest stages of human speech the hypothesis advanced by the Soviet linguist Abayev is deserving of attention. It suggests that the earliest words were designations given to themselves by primary human communities. These designations linked their members closer together and sharply contraposed them outwards, against non-members of the community. According to this hypothesis, these terms serve as the base for other denominational words. These terms act as a form of "appropriation" by the community of various elements of environment, again in contraposition to "not ours."

Imagine a line, or let us say a circle. The essence of opposition is the line itself and that which borders upon it on either side. In other words, the essence of opposition lies not in the interrelation of two elements but in one element which is itself a polar ambivalence. The point is not that a certain people possess a certain stable cultural element while its neighbor or neighbors do not have it or have it in a modified degree. No, it is the difference itself that constitutes the fact of culture.

Can it be that the totality of these differences, accumulated in the course of centuries, is identical with the specific culture of a given ethnos?

Here I allow myself only to suggest the possibility and the prospective value of such an extrapolation and of such generalization of inferences drawn by others from various elements or aspects of culture (mainly material culture). If such a generalization should, in the final analysis, turn out to be possible, it would tell us a great deal about the inner psychological mechanism of any and every national-ethnic self-consciousness.

Not that we would in any case reduce ethnic self-consciousness to this component. The contrary component must also be taken into account as no less important for concrete ethnocultural and ethnopsychological research. I mean the ever-present factor counteracting opposition, constituting an "opposition against opposition" — the factor of cultural borrowing, levelling of differences, the unification of various elements of culture. Such diffusion may act locally, or within vast regions, or, finally, on a global scale. Consideration of this side of the matter lies outside the scope of this article. But it must always be kept in mind in order to avoid any universalization of the principle of opposition even in the case of its widest possible extension, without exception, to elements of material, intellectual, and social culture of the ethnos.

In a general theory of social psychology I proposed (Porshnev 1970) a classification of all "we and they" situations into two forms. In one case, it is the side designated by the term "they" that is explicitly and specifically defined, while "we" merely means those who do not belong to this "they" community or category. In other words, in this case "we" has no positive definition of its own and is built up in the mind only through contraposition to the "they" category. It thus embraces all those who are not "they" (e.g., "not cannibals"). In the second case, it is only the community designated as "we" that has an explicit positive definition, while all the rest constitute an indefinite negative category constructed by means of the expressions "not we," "not ours." Of course, since both these extreme forms are possible and are observed daily in all spheres of life, an intermediate form is bound to exist where both extremes, i.e., both "we" and "they," have a precise definition. As an example of this, we may adduce the bilateral preciseness of such oppositions as "men–women" or "children–adults." The numerous cases of dual structure in archaic societies also belong here (Zolotarev 1964).

There exists, however, a widespread idea that it was the second form of opposition that was primary and original in the life of human communities. Thus, it appears natural to think that people begin by recognizing certain internal links between members of their group (community). In such a case, the idea of other human beings as different or contrasting could only arise as something secondary and derivative. In my opinion, this view is illusory. In the sphere of ethnic relationships it corresponds to a comparatively late condition, when some ethnic communities had undergone such numerical increase and territorial expansion that only a minute section of the population bordered upon other communities. Under such conditions, most people realize the culture, everyday life, mores, language, customs, aesthetic values of their own ethnic environment either in an ethnocentric manner, i.e., as inherently characterizing "people" in contrast to all others who are not quite "people," or as their traditional cultural heritage, distinguishing them from other people. Hence, the concepts which used to arise among ethnographers of the "soul of a people" inherent in a particular ethnos, independent of its actual relations with other ethnoses.

However, macro-ethnoses are a late phenomenon. If we look at the most distant past, there are sufficient grounds for picturing the population forming each ethnos as being so small and so nomadic that each individual member had contact of one kind or another with neighbors. For such an individual, linguistic and cultural differences were reproduced daily, precisely as differences. For instance, among certain Siberian peoples in the past a huntsman when leaving for the forest had the distinctive tattoo of his clan on his face and corresponding ornamentation on his weapons. He was also well acquainted with the tattoos and ornaments of members of other clans, recognized them immediately, and acted accordingly. In the same way, each member of an ethnos knew not only his own dialect but that of neighboring groups, even if he did not make use of the latter.

The hypothesis set forth here somewhat resembles, by the way, the hypothesis of "primitive linguistic continuity" advanced at one time by Tolstov (1950). But unlike Tolstov, I accentuate not the resemblance between any two adjacent primitive ethnic groups but the mutual oppositions, sometimes almost imperceptible, sometimes fairly important, which prevented these groups from merging into one another and confirmed their separateness. At the same time, I wish to stress, together with Tolstov, that such a model demands the concept of further migrational movements of tribes and peoples, i.e., the appearance at the borders of an alien ethnos, differing from those with whom the ethnic-cultural peculiarities originated.

This leads to the further inference that the essence of ethnic oppositions (whether ethnopsychological, ethnocultural, or ethnolinguistic) is the border itself. Ethnic self-consciousness of a community and the image it holds of another community will derive from this initial fact, from the very presence of the border between them. The characteristic of a border is that it belongs to both phenomena which it separates. And if these phenomena are not merely distinct from one another but mutually contradictory, then the border unites that which cannot be united. And beyond the border, the contrasting phenomena enter upon their own proper existence.

For the ethnopsychologist the ethnic border with its inherent paradox is evidently primary. This proposition is not a completely new one. Early in the present century Van Gennep (1909) made the following important generalization. The crossing of any border separating human beings — whether the threshold of a dwelling, an age limit, the line between the sexes, between night and day, winter and summer, the boundary between two mutually exclusive conditions — is regarded as a sacred act, while all that lies on either side of any such crossing belongs to the real, everyday world.

If we elaborate Van Gennep's ideas, in accordance with the present-day level of knowledge, we will perhaps come to the conclusion that the psyche and culture of an ethnos constitute an exceedingly complex totality of accumulated interethnic borders or lines of contact, partly internalized, half-obliterated, and devoid of the specific features of the crossing and its consequent ambivalence.

A corresponding phenomenon in genetic psychology is at present being investigated under the name of diplasty. It was first discovered in child psychology by Henry Vallon and designated by him as binary structure (in contrast to binary opposition). Later it was perceived in the genesis of all and any intellectual activity. The logical nature of diplasty is in opposition to the psychological operation of dichotomy, i.e., to the division in two — into "yes-no," "either-or." Dichotomy constitutes the mechanism of the nervous system of animals, logic, and computers. The operation of diplasty is in direct contrast to this: it is based upon the principle "both and," "both yes and no," "both that and not that." Thus diplasty stands in opposition to logical laws. From an emotional standpoint, diplasty corresponds to ambivalence of the emotions.

Evidently, the above analysis of ethnic oppositions leads us, on a new plane, to the fundamental phenomenon of the early phases in human psychological evolution to the phenomenon of diplasty.

In conclusion, I should add that if we confine ourselves to the sphere of ethnology and ethnopsychology, we may distinguish various degrees of opposition: from irreconcilable antagonism to peaceable differences (lack of identity), i.e., not opposition but rather comparison. Of course, with the advance of civilization, purely ethnic oppositions gradually lose the hue of irreconcilable animosity. And insofar as this takes place, the consolidation, the unification of ethnoses loses in intensity. Other oppositions — religious, for instance — have taken their place. However, on the basis of ethnic self-consciousness, we establish the universal psychological principle: all oppositions unite; all unifications oppose; the measure of opposition is the measure of unification.

REFERENCES

LEROY-GOURHAN, A.
 1965 *Le geste et la parole*, volume two. Paris: Albin Michel.
PORSHNEV, B. F.
 1970 *Sotsial'naia psikhologiia i istoriia* [Social psychology and history]. Moscow.
TOKAREV, S. A.
 1970 K metodike etnografischeskogo izucheniia material'noi kul'tury [Toward a methodology of the ethnographic study of material culture]. *Sovetskaya ethnographia* 4.
TOLSTOV, S. P.
 1950 Znachenie trudov I. V. Stalina po voprosam yazykoznania dl'a razvitia soretskoi etnografii [The role of works of I. V. Stalin on the problems of linguistics for the development of Soviet ethnography]. *Sovetskaya ethnographia* 4.
VAN GENNEP, A.
 1909 *Les rites de passage*. Paris: Librairie Critique, Emil Mourry.
ZOLOTAREV, A. M.
 1964 *Rodovoi stroy i pervobytnaia mifologiia* [Tribal system and primitive mythology]. Moscow: Nauka.

Ethnicity and the Family in the Soviet Union

O. A. GANTSKAJA and L. N. TERENT'EVA

The modern family is a gradually developed phenomenon brought forth by the entire social and cultural development of mankind. As a bio-ethnosocial microstructure, the family is part of all the basic systems of relations and connections: socioeconomic, state, law, population, ethnic, etc. The intrafamily relations (husband-wife, father-children, mother-children, children-children, etc.) and the relations between the family and other social institutions are regulated by the laws of the dynamic nature of these systems. As a social institution of an individual ethnicity, the family plays an important role in the socialization of the youth and, in particular, in the shaping of the young people's national self-consciousness.

With endogamy prevailing in areas densely populated by some individual nationality or ethnic group, the family reproduces the population of that specific area (Bromley 1969).

Socioeconomic factors, ethnic contacts, and mutual cultural influences, direct and indirect, result in the consolidation of components of one nation or closely related nations, natural assimilation, the integration of the multinational population of some historico-cultural regions and in the general process of the integration of the Soviet people. While studying the impact of these processes upon family life, one has to remember that in the past, in each historico-cultural region, nations with the same socioeconomic structure and religion evolved common foundations of marriage and family relations. Moreover, the dependence of these relations upon socioeconomic conditions and religion was reflected in the same or similar forms of family and marriage in nations situated in different historico-cultural regions and having no direct contacts with one another. However, ethnographic similarity found in marriage and family relations does not preclude some ethnic features that are only typical of some individual nation or a group of related nations. The family remains to this day a bearer of specific ethnic determinants. These include, in particular, some peculiarities of family etiquette, customs, rituals, relations among members of the family, etc.

The socioeconomic transformations and the cultural revolution carried out in the Soviet Union have brought about a society in which young people are free to associate with their contemporaries and choose their would-be husbands or wives. That is one of the factors in the integration of the Soviet people which promotes the stabilization of the structure of today's family. The coercion of a person into marriage is punishable by law, which protects the rights of those who enter into married life. Within the family, these rights are based upon the actual (for those who work) or potential (for students, for instance) economic independence of the adult members of the family.

Pre-marital relations among the youth show some specific features in different historico-cultural regions. Thus, most nations of the European historico-cultural region show more open (as compared to other regions) outward manifestations of love, friendship, and attachment between young people. The courtship etiquette allows manifestations of tenderness in the presence of relatives, friends, and even total strangers. In other historico-cultural regions, it is more restrained. In the countryside of Daghestan, for instance, open courtship is regarded as an offense to a girl unless it is followed by marriage. In the rural areas of Central Asia, during festivals or while visiting a place of entertainment such as a movie house, club, etc., young men and girls seem to keep each other at a distance; a young man and a girl walking around arm-in-arm would be an uncommon sight. It is noteworthy that the spreading of education among the nations of Soviet Central Asia has brought forth an epistolary declaration of love.

According to ethnographic data, ethnoregional peculiarities of courtship etiquette and premarital behavior among the youth are more pronounced in the countryside and in small towns than in big cities. Thus, young countryfolk from the Caucasus, Central Asia, and Kazakhstan who normally display much restraint in showing their emotions or in courting in the presence of other people, usually drop that restraint after they come to work or study in such big cities as Moscow, Leningrad, Novosibirsk, Kiev, Minsk, and others. When they come back home, however, they feel they should continue to adhere, although only outwardly, to the local customs — an indication of the impact of the ethnic and social environment. Young men and girls who stay in big cities gradually adapt themselves to the new norms of behavior. Such an adaptation is a reflection of the integration of multinational youth in big cities.

The development of new marriage and family relations in the Soviet Union are manifest in the changed marriage age (the minimum, prevalent, and average) which in the past varied considerably not only in different historico-cultural regions, but also with different nations within one such region. The general tendency that has appeared in the course of the integration of the Soviet people is toward the leveling of the marriage age; in some areas it is gradually going up, as in the Volga region, Central Asia and Kazakhstan, the Caucasus, Siberia, while in others it is going down, for example, in the Baltics where it used to be particularly high.

Of great interest are the ethnopsychological aspects of the standards for a marriage partner. The problem has been scantily investigated so far, yet some ethnographic material available allows us to conclude that some nations or groups of nations have some criteria in this respect. Thus, the Caucasian nations regard as positive such traits in a girl as dignity, restraint, modesty, and a reverential attitude toward older people. A bridegroom is also supposed to possess these qualities, as well as being manly, courageous, and able to conceal his emotions before others.

Similar criteria for a bride and a bridegroom are typical of the nations of Central Asia and Kazakhstan. In a young man, the Russians, Ukrainians, Belorussians, and Moldavians highly value the art of courtship (especially in the presence of other people), determination, loyalty in friendship, and such typically male qualities as strength, agility, etc. In a girl, they particularly value buoyancy, gaiety, artlessness, camaraderie, and also stamina, thrift, etc. The Lithuanians, Letts, and Estonians have a great regard for restraint in temperament and behavior, a young couple's ability to take care of each other, to keep house, etc. The age-old concepts, in some nations or groups of nations, of an ideal bride and bridegroom are alive to this day and exert some influence upon the choice of a would-be spouse.

The socialist system of the national economy, the Soviet law, the social transformations, and the cultural revolution have provided all the Soviet nations with a single basis upon which each new Soviet family is born, formed, and stabilized. The essential intra-ethnic nature of the Soviet family is an indication of the integration of the multinational population of the Soviet Union. Most Soviet families are monogamous, include members of two or three generations, and maintain close ties with near relations. Few nuclear families do not maintain these ties. Some of the spreading of the surviving forms of the family and the separation of young couples from their parents are due to the fact that prior to the Socialist revolution, the family, as a social organism, was at different stages of development in different historico-cultural regions and in different nations.

The number of children is an important determinant of a family's structure. To a certain extent, it determines a woman's ability to take part in Socialist production and her social activities at different periods of her life. Families with many children show some differences from families with few in the upbringing of the children, in relations among their members, and in the manifestations of the ties of blood. Whether or not the number of children may be regarded as an ethnic feature still remains a subject of controversy. It has been observed, however, that families with many children are common in Central Asia, Kazakhstan, Siberia, and the Caucasus, whereas typical of the European part of the country, and of the cities in particular, are familes with few children. It is noteworthy that in the Volga region, Tatar families generally have more children than Russian ones (Vasil'eva 1968:20).

One of the problems of present day ethnic processes is that of the interrelation between elements of the social and ethnocultural integration and the old traditional elements in family rituals and festive occasions. Each nation has some specific features of its own in this connection; this applies to nations (both close and distant ethnically) inhabiting a certain historico-cultural region or area (the Baltic Coast, for instance) and to nations separated geographically, but related in their origin. In the first case, a specific element of a custom or a festive ritual pertains to ethnic determinants of the culture of one nation. In the second case, it characterizes the culture of the nations of a specific region or area and, with related nations, is an ethnic determinant in a broader sense. In the third case, a similarity of a custom or ritual may be a result of indirect mutual cultural influences, but is more often typical of the same stage of the socioeconomic development of different nations in the past. It must be said that ethnic determinants are at the same time gradually developed phenomena that are typical of specific socioeconomic formations without their initial functional load.

Ethnosocial and cultural integration in the Soviet Union has been leading to a certain leveling of family customs and rituals and to a gradual disappearance of a number of survival forms. Instead, new traditions of family festivities and ceremonies, common to the entire country, emerge and spread. These include, for instance, komsomol' "red" (in Central Asia) and collective farm wedding ceremonies. Many nations have come to observe some occasions they never observed in the past: "silver" and "gold" wedding anniversaries, birthdays, school graduation day, seeing off young men called up for service in the Soviet Army, etc. New family customs are often born in big cities and then spread to the countryside.

Family rituals in regions inhabited for the most part by one nationality or ethnic group and in those inhabited by several nationalities, to a certain extent reflect the natural assimilation (if it actually takes place) and cultural integration processes. However, it is difficult to follow these processes because of the leveling of old customs and the spreading of new ones. It is known that cultural borrowings do not necessarily and immediately result in changes in the national self-consciousness of ethnic groups that are in contact with one another; that only takes place under specific conditions. Thus, for instance, many Russian inhabitants of the

Ukraine and Moldavia have retained their national self-consciousness, although their culture and, in particular, the wedding ceremony have been imbued with a number of elements typical of the Ukrainians or Moldavians. It is curious that at present, some parts of the Russian population of the Ukraine are indifferent to whether they are identified with the Russians or Ukrainians (Chizhikova 1968). Another example is the adoption by the Ossetians in Georgia and in Ossetia's lowlands of some elements of the Georgian wedding ceremony which testifies to their growing assimilation with the Georgians.

Nationally mixed families in the countryside, as a rule, adhere to the family customs of the national majority in their area, if one of the spouses belongs to it. In the city, such families are subject to integration with the national family customs of each spouse, with a general trend toward the leveling of these customs.

Family customs and ceremonies are unified in the process of the consolidation of the nation, (the merging of ethnographic groups, the disappearance of survivals of tribal differences) or of the integration of the multinational population of each historico-cultural region. Thus, many nations of Soviet Central Asia have a widespread custom of inviting professional musicians and singers and arranging sports contests to entertain guests.

The general trend in the development of the family structure in all the Soviet republics is toward a decrease in the number of authoritarian families and an increase in the number of families with the recognized equality among the parents, adult children, and other members of the family. This trend has been more pronounced in the cities than in the countryside. Some ethnic and regional differences exist with respect to the role of the head of the family and the nature of intrafamily and blood relations. These are manifest in the family etiquette which, to a certain extent is an accurate reflection of these relations. The domination of the husband has "suffered" most in the European historico-cultural region where most women are engaged in social production; yet here, too, this phenomenon has spread unevenly. Thus, Tatar families are less frequently headed by a woman (widows and divorcees not considered) than those of the Russians, Ukrainians, Belorussians, and in the Baltic nations. Tatar family etiquette includes elements that are meant to enhance the prestige of the husband as the head of the family. In keeping with the tradition, the wife tries in every way to show her respect for her husband, especially in the presence of guests, the daughter-in-law does so with regard to the father- and mother-in-law, etc.

In most of the European nations of the Soviet Union relations between the spouses are not determined by any strict rules of family etiquette. In the cities, blood ties are confined to near relations; in the countryside, blood relationships are maintained on a wider basis.

With the aborigines of Siberia, the head of the family is almost invariably the eldest man. This place can only be taken by a woman if she is a widow and the mother of underage children. Family etiquette demands a reverential attitude toward older people and includes a number of rules based on old customs. The authority of old people is incontestable. Ties of blood are much respected, as are mutual aid among relatives and the traditions of hospitality. Guests staying with a Yakut family, for instance, virtually become members of the family.

The dominating role of the eldest man is also typical of most families in the Caucasus. Even in families headed by young people, elders exert a marked influence upon the management of family affairs. Marked reverence toward elders is prescribed by one of the chief rules of conduct. Family etiquette includes some survival forms of conduct: thus, a daughter-in-law must shun older relatives of her husband, while in some families, younger women are not supposed to sit at the table with male guests. Ties of blood are maintained both with close and distant relations, including mutual support and hospitality. Hospitality is also shown to friends and acquaintances, as well as to strangers.

There are many similar features in the family and marriage relations of the nations of Central Asia and Kazakhstan. In this historico-cultural zone, elements of the integration of the family structure are interwoven with the traditional rules of family etiquette and with some survival phenomena whose origin dates back to the period of the domination of the large patriarchal family and even of its earlier forms. A marked domination by men is typical of the family life in this region. Yet here, too, the economic independence of the working women and youth provides the basis for equality in the family and, what is most important, enables them to decide their own destinies. According to family etiquette, juniors must be respectful to seniors, while wives must show marked respect towards their husbands and the husbands' older relations. The traditions of shunning other people and all kinds of taboos have lost their former meaning and if these are observed occasionally, it is only to keep up the tradition.

Ties of blood are as strong and extensive in Central Asia and Kazakhstan as in the Caucasus and in Siberia. One can see even today that the Turkmenians, for instance, have a greater regard for paternal family members, while the Kazakhs consider maternal relations more important. Contacts between relations are chiefly expressed in frequent visits.

Ethnic processes covering the entire system of intrafamily relations, traditions, and customs of the multinational population of the Soviet Union are also underway in the narrow sphere of marriages between persons of different nationalities.

In zones of ethnic contacts with multinational populations (borderlines between different ethnic areas, big cities, areas interspersed with populations of different nationalities, etc.) mixed marriages produce families which prove to be microenvironments for the processes of integration and natural assimilation. Among the factors determining the ethnic development in such families are language and national self-consciousness. The first factor reveals itself at the moment of the formation of a mixed family; the second factor appears when the second generation of this family decides the problems of its ethnic identity (Gantskaja, Terent'eva 1965).

In some mixed families, the language of one of the spouses falls out of use; in others, the two languages are spoken equally or almost so; in still others, the spouses speak some third language they both know. Language processes are accompanied in such families by the integration of elements of culture, everyday life, and traditions typical of the spouses' ethnicity. As a rule, such a family gradually evolves some specific features that distinguish it from the single nationality families the spouses come from. Children born in mixed families in most cases adopt one of the parents' languages, which is not necessarily the language in which the parents communicate, nor the mother's language. There are also bilingual children. For a number of reasons (the impact of the prevailing ethnic environment, the teaching in the state language of a specific national republic at the institutions of higher learning of that republic, etc.), the linguistic status of the second generation of mixed families may change substantially. The ethnic situation in mixed families becomes clear when children become of age and decide the problem of their nationality (when they get their passports) (Terent'eva 1969). An answer to this question in most cases reflects young people's national self-consciousness. At the same time, they fully realize that they are citizens of the Soviet Union (a manifestation of double self-consciousness: national and civic).

In different regions of the country, the process of the development of ethnic self-consciousness in young people has both common and specific features. Thus, in the major cities of the three Soviet Baltic republics, in families with one spouse of the local nationality and the other Russian (Group I), the proportions of children identifying themselves with the local and Russian nationalities are almost equal. In some places, however, especially in Tallinn, the former predominate.

This means that in Vilnius and Riga, the mixed families do not bring about any substantial changes in the second generation with respect to the ratio between the two interacting ethnic communities. This is more pronounced in Tallinn. In all other combinations of mixed marriages involving persons of the local nationalities (Group II), most young people identify themselves with the local nationality.

In the group of Russian-Ukrainian families (Group III) and in that of Russians and persons of other nationalities (Group IV), the young in all these cities give preference to the Russian nationality.

Here we observe three directions of assimilation processes with a varying degree of intensity. The first, which is the least conspicious, is directed toward a certain assimilation of Russians by Lithuanians, Letts, and Estonians; the second reveals itself in a far more intensive assimilation by the nationalities of these three republics of other nationalities; the third points to similar interaction between the Russians and people of other nationalities.

In other regions of the country, the processes observed in Group I are somewhat different; in Groups II, III, and IV, they are almost analogous to those in the cities of the Baltic republics. Thus, in Kiev, more than 60 percent of the children in Russian-Ukrainian families identify themselves with the Ukrainian nationality; in Minsk, the number of children in Russian-Belorussian families identifying themselves with the Belorussian nationality amounts to 40 percent. In Ashkhabad, on the contrary, almost 90 percent of the youth from Turkmenian-Russian families regard themselves as Turkmenians, while in Dushanbe, some 80 percent of the youth from the families of Group I identify themselves with the Tajiks.

The differences between those indices are still more striking in the autonomous republics of the Russian Federation. Thus, in Cheboksary (the Chuvash Autonomous Soviet Socialist Republic) only 2.2 percent of the youth born in Chuvash-Russian families identify themselves with the Chuvash nationality; 97.8 percent consider themselves Russians. The situation is very similar in Mordovian-Russian families; but the youth from Russian-Tatar and Tatar-Bashkir families generally identify themselves with the Tatars.

While studying the problem of national identification of young people from mixed families, we have taken into consideration the role played by some traditions, for instance, the tradition in some nations of identifying a child with the nationality of the father. An analysis of these data has shown that of all the nations under review, only the Turkmenians firmly adhere to that tradition, while it is not important among other nations. The solution by young people of the problem of their national identification is influenced by other factors. Thus, a direct relation has been observed between the direction of the process of assimilation and the extent to which the nationality of youth coincides with that of their fathers.

Hence, the national identification of youth from mixed families exerts a marked influence upon ethnic process. Under conditions of great mobility of the population and increased urbanization, the general increase in mixed marriages enhances their significance in the ethnic development of the Soviet population.

The family relations of the multinational population of all the historico-cultural regions of the Soviet Union show common features that have emerged and are still emerging in the process of the integration of the Soviet people, such as the equality of all the members of a family based on their juridical and economic equality in society, the emancipation of women, etc. These common features constitute the basis of the structure of the present-day Soviet family. The peculiarities of this structure in different historico-cultural zones and with different nations represent a complex combination of ethnic features, traditions, and survival forms typical of earlier stages of the socioeconomic development of populations.

REFERENCES

BROMLEY, YU. V.
  1969 Etnos i endogamija [Ethnicity and endogamy]. *Sovetskaya ethnographia* 6.
CHIZHIKOVA, L. N.
  1968 Ob etnicheskikh protsessakh v vostochnykh rajonakh Ukrainy [On ethnic process in the eastern regions of the Ukraine]. *Sovetskaya ethnographia* 1.
GANTSKAJA, O. A., L. N. TERENT'EVA
  1965 Etnograficheskoe issledovanie natsional'nykh protsessov v Pribaltike [Ethnographic research of national processes in the Baltic area]. *Sovetskaya ethnographia* 5.
TERENT'EVA, L. N.
  1969 Opredelenie svoej natsional'noj prinadlezhnosti podrostkami v natsional'no-smeshannykh sem'jakh [Determination of their national affiliation in nationality mixed families]. *Sovetskaya ethnographia* 3.
VASIL'EVA, E. K.
  1968 Etnodemograficheskaja kharakteristika' Semejnoj struktury naselenija Kazani v 1967 godu [The ethnodemographic characterization of the family, structure of the population of Kazan' in 1967]. *Sovetskaya ethnographia* 5.

New Developments in Family Life in the Countryside in Belorussia

V. K. BONDARCHIK and E. R. SOBOLENKO

The history of the family is inseparably linked with that of society. The family is a product of a certain social and economic system. The mode of production, being the determining factor of social development, influences the organization of the family indirectly, through relationships between production, economy, ideology, culture, and morality.

Assume particular degrees of development of production, commerce and consumption and you will have a corresponding form of social constitution, a corresponding organization of the family, of orders or of classes, in a word, corresponding civil society (Marx and Engels 1958:442).

The Great October Socialist Revolution which abolished the old social relations and replaced them by new socialist ones, also brought into being a new type of family which is characterized by full economic, legal, and social equality of all its members and democratic relations within the family. This was made possible, first of all, by the abolition of private property and social inequality in society and the establishment of new economic, sociodomestic, and legal conditions for the existence of the family.

The formation of a new type of family can be best illustrated by the example of the development of the rural family which prior to the revolution retained many patriarchal features and a conservative way of life. The factors which laid the basis for the reformation of the rural family along socialist lines were the abolition of private ownership of land, collectivization of agriculture, mechanization of farm jobs, emancipation of women, and the attraction of them into social production.

New features in the everyday life of the rural family are particularly manifest in the development of intrafamily relations. The economic independence of wife from husband and of adult children from father determined a new democratic character of relations within the family. These features in the development of the present-day family are common to all the peoples of the Soviet Union, specifically the rural family in Belorussia.

In this paper, based on concrete ethnographic investigations carried out in Belorussia, we shall analyze changes that have taken place in the form, size, and structure of the rural family and intrafamily relations.

Social and economic reforms in agriculture after the October Revolution and the first successes of the collective farm system tended to speed up the process of replacement of the traditional large family by a small one — the process which was started under capitalism — and to create all the conditions for the completion of this process. Collective farming made social production the main source of income of the peasant family. The fact that men and women, parents and their adult children are engaged in social production on an equal footing and get equal pay has given every married couple a chance to establish an independent household. The one-couple pattern of family, which has become widespread, has been influenced by a number of factors. The latter include the solution of the housing problem, pensions for the aged, the opening of public service establishments, kindergartens, crèches, and many other measures taken in the countryside to improve the welfare of the rural population. The typical rural family in Belorussia today is the small family consisting of two generations.

We have carried out a survey involving two farms, average in every respect and typical of Belorussia. One was the collective farm, Rassvet, in the Vileisky district, Minsk region, and the other the state farm, Novoselki, in the Petrikov district, Gomel region. In all, 1,397 families were polled. We found out that on the collective farm, two-generation families accounted for 64 percent and on the state farm, 76 percent. The rural family is increasingly becoming a nuclear family consisting only of parents and children. There are 53 percent of such families on the collective farm, Rassvet, and 57 percent on the state farm, Novoselki. A rather high percentage (about 12 percent) of two-generation families are incomplete families consisting of only one parent (usually mother) and children. Judging by the mother's age, most of these families were set up before the Great Patriotic War and are a result of family disorganization caused by war. Naturally, the percentage of such families keeps declining.

The number of three-generation families has decreased considerably compared with the prerevolutionary period. On the collective farm, such families account for 17 percent, and on the state farm, for 12.5 percent. But these families cannot be classed with large unseparated families since such a family usually consists of one marriage pair, their children, and one of the husband's or wife's parents. The young couple constitutes the economic and moral nucleus of such a family. Families that include two married couples living together are extremely rare now. Of the 1,397 families we polled only two had a two-marriage-pair pattern. At present the family includes, as a rule, only directly related persons. Families with collateral kin (sisters, brothers, husband's or wife's nephews or nieces) account for only 1 percent on the collective farm and for 0.5 percent on the state farm.

Speaking of the structure of the present-day rural family, it is also necessary to consider such an important characteristic of the family as its size. The typical family today is smaller than that of the prerevolutionary period. According to the 1897 census, the average rural family in Belorussia consisted of 6.8 members. The largest group in all Belorussian provinces was that of families of six to ten members. (*Pervaia vseob-shchaia perepis'*... 1897, 1899:4–5, 1904:15, 1903:15). This downward trend in the size of family in the countryside has grown markedly stronger since the first years of Soviet government.

According to the census of 1926, the average rural family in Belorussia consisted of 5.7 members (*Vseobshchaia perepis'*... 1929:72–73). The Civil War certainly contributed to the progressive reduction of family size, but fragmentation of the family was the main factor. This process in the countryside was particularly intensive in the post-war period, which is due largely to the urbanization of the Republic and the increased mobility of the rural population. According to the census of 1959, the average rural family in Belorussia was 3.8 members. (*Itogi vsesoiuznoi perepisi*... 1963:142–143). Our investigation showed that the average size of family both on the collective farm and on the state farm is 3.6 members. On the collective farm, first come families of four (28 percent); second, families of three (24.5 percent); third, families of two (23.5 percent); fourth, families of five (14 percent); and fifth, families of six and more members (10 percent). There is a somewhat different picture on the state farm where first place is shared by families of two, and six and more members (22.5 percent each), second place is held by families of four and five (20 percent each), and third by families of three (15 percent).

Thus, the state farm has more families consisting of five to six and more members (42.5 percent), and there are even families of eleven and twelve. The reason is the stronger large-family tradition which has always been characteristic of Polesye villages. At present, families of six and more members, although placing first on the state farm account for 22.5 percent of all families, whereas according to the 1897 census for Minsk province, such families accounted for 57 percent, and a still higher figure might be expected for Polesye. The number of small families has increased considerably there. At present families of two to three account for 37.5 percent, while toward the end of the nineteenth century there were only 14.4 percent of them in the province. So, the trends of development of the rural family do not vary much in Belorussia, local specifics being insignificant and due largely to the greater or lesser preservation of the old family life tradition.

As we see it, the reformation of Belorussian villages along socialist lines has speeded up the process of development of the rural family into a nuclear one. This process is characteristic of all industrially developed societies. In Belorussia, it started with the penetration of capitalism into agriculture, but the most favorable conditions were created for its development by the collectivization of agriculture which brought with it mechanization and industrialization of agricultural work.

The changes that have taken place in the form, structure, and size of the rural family are interconnected in many respects with changes in intrafamily relations. New developments in rural family life are particularly manifest here. This is evidenced by the social characteristics of the present-day family. Indeed, the social composition of the rural family mirrors the vast changes that have taken place in the social composition of the rural population during the years of Soviet government. The rural family today is not necessarily a peasant family. The percentage of employees, intellectuals, agriculturalists, and, accordingly, their families keeps growing in the countryside. On the collective farm families including employees or intellectuals account for 22.8 percent and on the state farm for 25 percent. To characterize a rural family one must know the social station of all its members. A family including peasants, employees, and intellectuals is a common thing now in the villages. Similarly, a purely peasant family includes members belonging to different social groups of the peasantry engaged in farm work of different types and at different skill levels. Of the families we polled on the collective farm, 30 percent are heterogeneous in social composition, while on the state farm such families account for 40 percent. As a rule, the younger generation is more socially advanced in such families, which is an indication of increased vertical mobility of the rural population, particularly from one generation to the next.

The family mirrors the great changes that are taking place in society. The high percentage of socially heterogeneous families testifies to a growing rapprochement between different social groups, the gradual narrowing of margins of difference in their ways of life, and the widening of vertical mobility channels.

The changed status of women is exerting a tremendous influence on the formation of new relations in the family. The new role played by the woman in society and family is determined by her economic and social position. Prior to the Revolution, the peasant woman was engaged in productive labor much less than the man, her work consisting mainly of servicing the family. The man was the producer of the good things of life and the bread-winner for the family. While earning her own upkeep and working for the family day and night, the peasant woman was still economically dependent on her husband, who was the sole owner of land and farm implements and was engaged in productive labor. The man represented his family before society and was responsible for it. It was only the man, as representative of the family, who attended rural meetings and took part in the election of local elders, i.e., it was through the man that the family kept in touch with society. Family law, general and codified, which was then in operation in Russia, legalized the woman's subordinate position in the family. The demand that the wife should "be in total obedience to the husband and gratify him in every way," taken almost word for word from the Rules of Propriety of the time of Catherine the Second, remained in force up to the October Revolution.

Man's authority over wife and children rested not only on the economic and legal basis. Morally, too, he had greater rights to this authority. Because almost all peasant women were illiterate in prerevolutionary Russia, the husband usually had a relatively better education than the wife. A father's education was, as a rule, on the same level as that of his adult sons. Greater social experience, practical know-how, and economic rights made the father the head of the family unit. Although the prerevolutionary peasant family in Belorussia was undoubtedly an authoritarian one, the man's authority in the family was liberal rather than despotic in character. All adult members of the family, women included, had a say in economic and family matters, although the last word was always that of the head of the family.

With the establishment of new socioeconomic relations, the social status of the peasant woman changed radically, affecting her position in the family and, hence, all intrafamily relations. Being engaged in social production on a par with the man and getting equal pay, the wife now shares with her husband the function of the family's breadwinner. In many rural families, a husband has the same social status as his wife. Forty-five percent of the families we polled are of this type. Not infrequently, the status of the wife is higher than that of the husband in rural families; that is, the wife has a higher level of education and is doing a more skilled job than her husband. There are 8 percent of such families on the collective farm and 12 percent on the state farm.

The rise in the educational standards of women tends to strengthen their position in society and consequently in the family. According to the 1897 census, 39.7 percent of men and only 17.1 percent of women were literate in the rural Belorussia.

The census figures for 1926 were 75.9 and 33.3 percent; for 1939 they were 88.9 and 65.8 percent; and for 1959, 99.4 and 98.6 percent. By 1970, illiteracy had been eliminated almost completely among people aged nine to forty-nine in the rural Belorussia. At present, the literacy figures for Belorussian villages stand at 99.7 percent for men and 99.6 percent for women.

Our findings also provide a good illustration of the improved educational standards in the countryside, particularly those of women. A majority of people in rural areas now have an elementary or seven-year education (72 percent). These are chiefly people above forty years of age who account for 68 percent of the adult population on the collective farm and for about 50 percent on the state farm. These groups, classified by educational level, include approximately equal numbers of men and women. Fifteen percent of the people on the collective farm and 22 percent of those on the state farm have a secondary, specialized secondary, incomplete higher, or complete higher education. Women predominate in this population group aged chiefly under forty. On the collective farm they account for 54 percent and on the state farm for 61 percent.

The woman's higher educational level has effectively increased her role in family affairs. It may be interesting in this connection to compare the level of education of husband and wife in the present-day rural family. In 70 percent of the families man and wife have the same level of education; in 17.5 percent of the families, the husband is better educated than the wife, and in 12.5 percent of the families, the opposite is true. To make clear the trend of change in this respect, we must consider the age of spouses. In families with couples above forty years of age, the husband has a better education than his wife, whereas in younger families (under forty) both partners have approximately the same level of education. All this has a considerable effect on the woman's standing in the family and gives her the right to share with her husband the role of breadwinner as well as that of moral leader of the family unit.

The status of adult children has also changed in the family. Now they are economically independent of their parents, even if they live with them. Very often children contribute more to the family budget than their parents because their education is, as a rule, higher than that of the parents, and they can handle more skilled and better paid jobs. We found in our survey that in almost one-quarter of the families, the social status of children is higher than that of parents, while families in which parents have a higher social status than children account for only 1 percent.

The changed status of the woman and adult children has transformed an institution such as that of the head of family. It was the man who was the head of the family in prerevolutionary villages. His economic, legal, and social functions were mentioned above. With the establishment of socialist socioeconomic relations in the villages, Soviet family law, and equal social rights for men and women, the functions of the head of family are shared by all adult members of the family. Being engaged in socially productive labor, all of them provide for the family. The family is linked with society not only through its head but, as a rule, through all its members. Soviet legislation has given the woman the right to decide, on a par with her husband, vital family matters and share responsibility for the family with him. Nevertheless, the institution of the head of the family continues in present-day villages, invested with new meaning. The main function of the head of the present-day rural family is that of organizing family life. It should be noted that this function, too, is often shared by husband and wife. Usually, both of them take part in family budget planning, deciding major family matters, rearing children, and distributing domestic chores.

The choice of the head of the family in the villages is usually a matter of tradition. In a majority of rural families, including those in which the wife holds a higher social status, the head of the household is the man.

The poll shows that on the collective farm 66 percent of those polled named the man as the head of the family and on the state farm 65 percent named the man as head. The percentages of families headed by a woman are 13 and 21.7 percent, respectively. A woman, as a rule, is the head of an incomplete family, even when she lives together with her adult children who hold a higher social status. That the institution of the head of family has merely retained the old form while acquiring a new meaning is evidenced by the role the head of the family plays in such family matters as budget planning and decision making on major family problems. The investigation shows that such matters in the rural family are now decided, as a rule, by both spouses. Thus, in 69 percent of the families headed by men, both man and wife are in charge of the family's money and in 78 percent of cases they make decisions together. Despite the viability of such an institution as the head of family, there is no ground for authoritarianism in the present-day rural family in Belorussia, and it is characterized by democratic relations between its members.

Our ethnographic survey of the collective farm in Northwestern Belorussia and the state farm in Southeastern Belorussia indicates that the development of new forms of family life in rural districts follows the same lines throughout the Republic with certain local variations. We found such local variations only in the size of family and the number of children.

As a result of social and economic reforms enacted during the years of Soviet power, a new family, basically different from the traditional peasant family of prerevolutionary Russia, has come into being. The present-day rural family in Belorussia is characterized by full economic and moral equality of all its members, democractic relations, and considerable authority for the woman. Significant changes have taken place in the form, size, and structure of the rural family. The prevalence of nuclear families among the rural population is also an indication of the democratization of intrafamily relations. The social composition of the rural family has changed, and it often comprises both manual and intellectual workers. The family's social connections have broadened and changed in character and its cultural and educational standards have risen.

The process of development of agriculture at this stage and the steady growth of mechanization and industrialization of farm labor make progressive developments the dominant feature of everyday life, family life included.

REFERENCES

Itogi vsesoiuznoi perepisi . . .
  1963   *Itogi vsesoiuznoi perepisi naseleniia 1959 Belorusskaia SSR* [Results of the all-union census of 1959, Belorussian SSR]. Moscow.
MARX, K., F. ENGELS
  1958   *Selected works,* volume two. Moscow.
Pervaia vseobshchia perepis' . . .
  1897   *Pervaia vseobshchaia perepis' naseleniia Rossiiskoi imperii* [First general population census of the Russian Empire]; 1899, volume five; 1903, volume twenty-two; 1904, volume twenty-three.
Vseobshchaia perepis' naseleniia
  1929   *Vseobshchaia perepis' naseleniia 1926* [General population census 1926], volume forty-four. *Belorusskaia sovetskaya sotsialisticheskaia republicka* [Belorussian Soviet Socialist Republic] Moscow.

Interethnic Families in the National Republics in the Middle Reaches of the Volga

E. P. BUSYGIN and N. V. ZORIN

Studies in the relations between different nationalities and their mutual influences are a major task of Soviet ethnography. These studies enable us to follow the development of socialist nations and nationalities, their integration, and the formation of a new historical community — the Soviet people.

Interethnic marriages resulting in a great number of interethnic families are an important factor in bringing people of different nationalities closer together.

This report contains an analysis of rural interethnic families in the Tatar and Chuvash Autonomous Republics. The report is based on material collected by ethnographic expeditions in 1965–1971 and on data obtained from village councils and registry offices. Interethnic families were surveyed in one hundred towns and villages; all were requested to fill in questionnaires. The data included the nationality of the husband and wife, their ages and occupations, the structure of the family, and the nationality of the children. Other questions touched upon the spouses' command of each other's languages, ties of blood, and ethnic peculiarities of their family life.

The middle reaches of the Volga are one of the multinational regions of the Soviet Union. The languages spoken there belong to three major groups: Slavonic (the Russians, Ukrainians, and Belorussians), Turkic (the Tatars, Chuvashes, and Bashkirs) and Ugro-Finnish (the Mari, Udmurts, and Mordvinians). In some areas and even in individual settlements, the population is made up of three or four nationalities. This is a result of a complicated historical process.

The Russians came to the Volga region *en masse* during the last half of the sixteenth century when the territory was annexed by the Russian state. Their advent had a tremendous impact upon the local life and culture and promoted the development of the productive forces in the region. Despite all kinds of barriers enforced by the ruling classes regarding the relations among different nationalities, the peoples of the Volga region established close economic and cultural links among themselves in all spheres of the material culture and everyday life (Busygin, Zorin 1960; Busygin 1966).

Marriages between different nationalities have been common in the Volga region beginning with the sixteenth century. G. I. Peretjatkovich, a well known specialist in the history of the Volga region, cites a letter by Metropolitan Germogene dating back to the late sixteenth century which says: "Many Russian prisoners and free men live amidst the Tatars, Cheremisses and Chuvashes, drink and eat with them and marry their women . . ." (Peretjatkovich 1877:266–267). Interethnic marriages in the eighteenth and nineteenth centuries were observed by the prominent linguist Shestakov who wrote that ". . . the peoples of the Volga region not only came closer together, but at times merged with the Russians and became Russian largely through marriages" (Shestakov 1884:1–2).

A substantial spreading of interethnic marriages over that period was observed in registers of the seventeenth century and in numerous local studies.

At the late nineteenth century, interethnic marriage became less common as a result of the development of capitalism in Russia, the appearance of the national bourgeoisie, and the growing national and regional isolation. According to the material collected by ethnographic expeditions, interethnic marriages at that time were an exception and, as a rule, due to specific circumstances. Such marriages were for the most part between persons of the same denomination and primarily between non-Russian men and Russian widows.

The Socialist Revolution of 1917 did away with all national, religious, and class privileges and restrictions. Autonomous national republics emerged in the Volga region. Large-scale economic development of the region resulted in the construction of a great number of industrial enterprises in the countryside, amalgamations of collective farms, transformations in agriculture, and the raising of the material and cultural standards of the rural population, all of which in turn changed its professional and social structure. At present, the rural population of this region includes a great number of specialists in different fields: teachers, doctors, agronomists, engineers, machine operators, etc. Today, there are twenty-two doctors and seventy-four middle-level medical workers per 10,000 of the population in the Kazan region; the respective figures for the former Kazan province were 1.6 and 1.4 (*50 let Tatarskoj ASSR* 1970).

During the Soviet period there have been changes in the national composition of the rural population in this region and an increase in the number of towns and villages with nationally mixed populations. Today, people of different nationalities reside in villages that formerly were entirely Russian, Tatar, Mordvinian, Mari, or Chuvash. Thus, in the village of Ronga which was Mari before the Revolution, today Mari account for 49 percent of the population, while the rest includes Russians, Tatars, Chuvashes, and Ukrainians; Tatars account for 30 percent of the population of the village of Tiulyachi which used to be all Russian. Also residing in this village are Chuvashes, Mordvinians, and Ukrainians. Today's collective and state farms often incorporate a number of villages with mixed populations. Many collective farms include men and women of three and even four nationalities: Russians, Tatars, Chuvashes, Mordvinians, and others. All these factors promote marriages among persons of different nationalities and the formation of interethnic families.

An analysis of the material available to us indicates that the number of interethnic marriages is steadily growing. According to local registry offices, in 1926–1927 mixed marriages accounted for 1.2 percent of all marriages in the Sura and Volga valleys (within the borders of the Tatar and Chuvash Autonomous Republics); the figure for 1949 was 6 percent and for 1967, 13.2 percent. Interethnic marriages have been observed among all the nationalities of the Volga region. Before the Revolution, marriages between persons of the orthodox religion and Tatar Muslims were prohibited by law (*Svod zakonov rossijskoj imperii* 1857:17); today, such marriages are quite common. Thus, in Tataria, on the right bank of the Volga, marriages between Tatars and persons of other nationalities amount to 21 percent of the entire number of interethnic marriages. In cities the figure is much higher. For instance, in Kazan, Russian-Tatar marriages account for 60 percent of all marriages between Russians and persons of other nationalities (Shkaratan 1970:13).

In the first years of Soviet power, interethnic marriages were observed largely among intellectuals (teachers, doctors, etc.). Today, these are typical of all the social groups of the rural population. This is shown in Table 1 which uses data from the western bank of the Kama in Tataria and for the Chuvash Autonomous Republic.

Despite widespread interethnic marriages, rural areas retain national preferences. This is shown by a comparison of the number of different types of marriage with their theoretical probability which depends on the number of brides and bridegrooms of different nationalities. Thus the number of actual marriages between Russian bridegrooms and Mordvinian brides is 23.8 percent of their theoretical number, while the figure for marriages between Russian bridegrooms and Tatar brides is 4.7 percent (Kucherjavenko 1969:139–144).[1]

In the villages surveyed, mixed families constitute 2 to 15 percent of the

---

[1]   The calculation is done by the method suggested by Gantskaja, Debets, and Pershits *Sovetskaja etnografija* 1966(3), 1967(4).

Table 1.   Occupations in interethnic marriages

Occupations	Percent of marriages
Both spouses are office workers	39.0
Both spouses are industrial workers	15.8
Both spouses are agricultural workers or collective farmers	18.1
One spouse is an industrial worker, the other an office worker	21.8
One spouse is an agricultural worker or collective farmer, the other an office worker	7.3
One spouse is an agricultural worker or collective farmer, the other is an industrial worker	6.3

total number of families. The structure of binational families with reference to the nationality of the spouses in the Chuvash Republic and on the western bank of the Kama in Tataria is characterized by the data in Table 2.[2]

As is seen from Table 2, in 35.3 percent of the binational families the husbands are Russians; in 33.2 percent, Chuvash; in 13 percent, Mordvinian; in 9.3 percent, Tatar; and in 9.2 percent, men of other nationalities.

Table 2.   Nationality of spouses in interethnic marriages

Nationality of wife	Nationality of husband								
	Russian	Tatar	Chuvash	Mari	Mordvinian	Ukrainian	Belorussian	Others	
Russian		7.0	28.6	0.6	11.4	4.4	0.5	1.7	54.2
Tatar	3.5		0.9		0.1	0.5		0.3	5.3
Chuvash	18.0	1.1			1.3	0.3	0.4	0.3	21.4
Mari	0.1		0.1						0.2
Mordvinian	7.5	0.5	1.5			0.1		0.1	9.7
Ukrainian	4.0	0.3	0.9		0.1				5.3
Belorussian	1.1		0.3		0.1				1.5
Others	1.1	0.4	0.9						2.4
Total	35.3	9.3	33.2	0.6	13.0	5.3	0.9	2.4	100%

Interethnic families with Russian wives account for 54.2 percent; Chuvash, 21.4 percent; Mordvinian, 9.7 percent; Tatar, 5.3 percent; etc.

As we can see from Table 2, Russian women marry men of other nationalities more often than Russian men marry women of other nationalities. The Chuvashes, Tatars, and other nationalities show an opposite tendency. The latter has also been observed by Vasil'eva in the city of Kazan (Vasil'eva 1968).

[2]   The table is based on a survey of 786 families.

Other areas of the middle reaches of the Volga show different figures from these because of the predominance of other nationalities. Thus, in the Tatar Autonomous Republic, the number of couples in which one spouse is a Tatar is four times as high as that in the Chuvash Republic. On the other hand, there are twice as many couples in which one spouse is Chuvash in the Chuvash Republic as compared to the eastern bank of the Kama in the Tatar Republic. The same reasons account for the low percentage of families with a Mari spouse.

Most married couples in interethnic families are in the middle and junior age brackets. They account for some 80 percent of all the interethnic families. With reference to the age of the husband, the interethnic families are differentiated as shown in Table 3.

Table 3. Interethnic families and age of husband

Age of husband	Percent of families
70 years and older	2.0
60–69 years	7.2
50–59 years	13.4
40–49 years	23.0
30–39 years	35.9
20–29 years	18.2
younger than 20 years of age	0.3

In the vast majority of interethnic families, the age of the wife is equal, or almost equal, to that of the husband. The families where the difference in the age of the spouses is from one to five years account for 70 percent of all the interethnic families in the given region. In the Russian-Russian families, they constitute 80 percent. An analysis of questionnaire material indicates that this difference is largely accounted for by the families within the middle and senior age brackets.

An analysis of the professional composition of the interethnic families shows that, as a rule, the occupations of the husband and wife are closely related. In a great number of families, both husband and wife are teachers, doctors, industrial workers, or collective farmers. However, there is a substantial number of families in which spouses have different professions and different qualification levels. In most cases, the qualification level of the wife is higher than that of the husband (he being a driver, while she is a teacher, etc.). This is also typical of the surveyed Russian families (Busygin, Zorin, and Zorina 1969).

The structure of the interethnic families in the territory under review is marked by certain peculiarities. Most of these families are simple. Complex families which include relatives of the husband or wife, constitute 24.8 percent. The same ratio between simple and complex families has been observed in the case of single-nationality families (Busygin, Zorin, and Zorina 1971). Most of the Russian complex families include the husband's relatives; this is less evident in the interethnic families, apparently, due to the weakening of patriarchal family traditions.

A student of interethnic families is, doubtless, interested in the way parents decide the problem of their children's nationality. That decision is not final, however, because when the children come of age they determine their nationality for themselves, yet it is indicative of the parents' national psychology. An analysis of registry materials and special questionnaires has shown that in the families with one Russian parent, the children, as a rule, are considered Russian (see Table 4). There are cases in which the homestead registers, one of the chief registration documents in the countryside, do not mention children's nationality. Sometimes within the same family the children are identified with different nationalities: the father's and the mother's.

Table 4.   Nationality of children in interethnic families

Types of family	Percent of children
Families in which the husband is Russian	
Children identified with father's nationality	88.2
Children identified with mother's nationality	9.4
Children's nationality undetermined	1.0
Children's nationality different	1.4
Families in which the wife is Russian	
Children identified with father's nationality	13.1
Children identified with mother's nationality	85.6
Children's nationality undetermined	1.3
Children's nationality different	0.0
Families in which both parents are non-Russian	
Children identified with father's nationality	29.0
Children identified with mother's nationality	24.6
Children's nationality undetermined	10.0
Children registered Russian	36.4

When neither of the parents is Russian, the children's nationality is often determined by the national republic in which the family resides. We have noted a number of cases in which non-Russian parents register their children as Russian. It also has been observed that a family's structure does not influence the national identification of the children.

As a rule, interethnic families maintain close ties both with paternal and maternal relations. These ties are expressed in reciprocal visits, especially on holidays or at family parties, in young couples doing all kinds of housework in their parents' homes, in helping each other out in buying things, in building a house, etc. Grandparents residing in the same town or village as their children usually help in raising the grandchildren.

Russian is the basic language in interethnic families. This is the case with 85 percent of all the surveyed interethnic families. The remaining 15 percent use both the Russian language and national languages either of both spouses or of one of them.

All the foregoing data corroborate the general laws typical of this country as a whole. The Russian language is actually becoming a common language of interethnic cooperation of all the nations of the Soviet Union (*Programma KPSS* 1962:314).

REFERENCES

BUSYGIN, E. P.
  1966 *Russkoe naselenie Srednego Povolzh'ja* [Russian population of the middle reaches of the Volga]. Kazan.
BUSYGIN, E. P., N. V. ZORIN
  1960 *Russkoe naselenie Chuvashskoj ASSR* [Russian population of the Chuvash ASSR]. Cheboksary.
BUSYGIN, E. P., N. V. ZORIN AND L. I. ZORINA
  1969 Struktura russkoj sel'skoj sem'i na territorii Marijskoj ASSR [Structure of the Russian rural family in the Mari ASSR]. *Geograficheskij sbornik* 4. Kazan.
  1971 Struktura russkoj sel'skoj sem'i v Tatarskoj, Chuvashskoj i Marijskoj ASSR [Structure of the Russian rural family in the Tatar, Chuvash, and Mari ASSR], *Struktura naselenija i gorodov Tatarii*. Kazan.
50 let Tatarskoj ASSR
  1970 *50 let Tatarskoj ASSR, Statisticheskij sbornik* [50 years of the Tatar ASSR, statistical collection]. Kazan.
KUCHERJAVENKO, N. N.
  1969 K voprosu izuchenija mezhnatsional'nykh brakov v Pravoberezhnykh rajonakh Tatarskoj ASSR [On the question of the study of interethnic marriages in the right-bank regions of the Tatar ASSR]. *Geograficheskij sbornik*. Kazan.
PERETJATKOVICH, G.
  1877 *Povolzh'e v XV–XVI vv.* [The Volga region in the fifteenth and sixteenth centuries] 1. Moscow.
Programma KPSS
  1962 Programma KPSS (*Stenograficheskij otchët XXII s'ezda KPSS*) [Program of the CPSU (Stenographic account of the 22nd session of the CPSU)]. Moscow.
SHESTAKOV, P.
  1884 Zametka o vlijanii russkogo jazyka na jazyki inorodcheskie [Note on the influence of Russian on languages of other families]. *Trudy IV Arkheologicheskogo s'ezda*. Kazan.
SHKARATAN, O. I.
  1970 Etno-sotsial'naja struktura gorodskogo naselenija Tatarskoj ASSR [Ethno-social structure of the urban population of the Tatar ASSR]. *Sovetskaya ethnographia* 3.

Svod zakonov rossijskoj imperii
  1857   *Svod Zakonov Rossijskoy Imperii* [Codex of laws of the Russian
         Empire] 10(1). St. Petersburg.
Sovetskaya ethnographia
  1966   *Sovetskaya ethnographia* [Soviet ethnography] 3.
  1967   *Sovetskaya ethnographia* [Soviet ethnography] 4.
VASIL'EVA, E. K.
  1968   Kharakteristika semejnoj struktury naseleniia Kazani v 1967 g.
         [Characteristics of family structure of the population of Kazan in 1967].
         Sovetskaya ethnographia 5.

Trends in Marriages Between Negroes and Whites in Chicago

ROBERT E. T. ROBERTS

RACIAL DEFINITIONS AND BOUNDARIES IN THE UNITED STATES

During nearly five centuries, millions of men and women have left the Old World, some as free immigrants and others as indentured servants or slaves, to settle permanently in the New World. New societies of varied racial and ethnic composition have emerged, exhibiting a degree of racial and cultural blending exceeding that of most of the older nations of Europe and Asia.

In the West Indies and most of the lands bordering the Caribbean, including the United States of America, the aboriginal population was eliminated or reduced to a small and powerless remnant and persons of European and African descent, including many of mixed ancestry of varying proportions, have long comprised almost the entire population of the area. Throughout most of the region, with the exception of Haiti, Negro slavery persisted well into the nineteenth century, and after emancipation the status of blacks and mulattoes remained inferior to that of whites.

In the United States a rigid system of status identification along with inherited and permanent inequality between Europeans and Africans and their descendants took form during the colonial era. The distinction between Caucasians, whether free or in bondage, and those of visible Negro descent, whether black or mulatto, slave or free, became a caste-like division between dominant whites and subordinate Negroes. Although the product of genetic mixture between Caucasian and Negro was commonly designated in legislation and in legal documents as mulatto, there was no recognized social division separating black from mulatto (Jordan 1969:167–178).

In most of the world, racial intermixture results in the formation of an intermediate group. Frequently the mixed group becomes a named, socially and often culturally separate and recognized division of the society, with consciousness of kind, group identification, and an intermediate position in the ethnic or racial hierarchy. In Asia and South Africa such groups have a long history and recognized place. Typical intermediate hybrid groups are the Anglo-Indians of India, Eurasians of Malaysia and Indonesia, and Cape Coloreds of South Africa (Stonequist 1937:10–53; Dover 1937; Gist, Dworkin 1972:25–102).

In Latin America and the West Indies there has been widespread race mixture, both in and out of marriage, and class and cultural factors override or mitigate the significance of color as a determinant of social status. Race, or color, along with other social attributes determines one's position in a class rather than a caste structure. Education, a professional or other high-status occupation, and wealth tend to offset the low status evaluation of dark complexion and Negroid physical characteristics. Light mulattoes have little feeling of identification with blacks. In Brazil and much of Spanish America one finds a color continuum rather than a sharp division of color categories such as white, mixed and black, and factors other than skin color and biological traits enter into racial designations. Known Negro ancestry does not preclude identification as white, and on the basis of color and appearance one brother may be classed as white while another is classed as colored (Pierson 1972:237–263; Degler 1971; Hoetink 1967).

Of the societies in the New World that have large populations of African descent, the United States alone adopted a rigid two-category system with no recognized intermediate color group. Here the rejection by whites of persons of known African descent, even if they are of predominantly European ancestry, is so complete that no distinction is made between colored and black. Apart from American Indians, Asians, and some Latin Americans, one is either white or black and no intermediate status is recognized. The United States Bureau of the Census, however, did enumerate Negroes under two subdivisions, black and mulatto, through 1920. Since then it has counted persons of any degree of Negro ancestry as Negro, although light colored Latin Americans and others of mixed ancestry who refuse to accept the designation of Negro are often enumerated as white. Afro-American, black, Negro, and colored have become designations for Americans of any degree of admitted Negro ancestry, and choice of term is determined by the preference of the speaker rather than by the complexion of the person described.

When a person's skin color, hair texture, or features call into question his racial identity, national origin and supposed absence or presence of African ancestry become supplementary clues. If the individual is of Asian origin, it is assumed that he is free of Negro ancestry and is either

Caucasian, Mongolian, or of "other race" such as East Indian. When legally-enforced racial segregation prevailed in the South, Asians, Latin Americans, and others of dark complexion were usually afforded accommodations with whites and even dark Negroes were known to gain service in hotels and restaurants when wearing a turban and affecting a foreign accent.

If rigid boundaries make American whites an exclusive group, American Negroes incorporate into their group persons of all degrees of mixture. The Afro-American ethnic group has no impermeable boundary line; rather, like a sieve of wide mesh, it permits easy entry and has absorbed and would accept as black anyone with any acknowledged or presumed Negro ancestry. Africans, West Indians, Latin Americans, and persons of predominantly European ancestry are freely accepted as members. There is a common understanding in the United States that "one drop of Negro blood makes a person a Negro" and the black community accepts as Afro-American persons of all shades of color and combinations of hair type and facial features, ranging from those indistinguishable from Europeans to those of unmixed Negro appearance.

The most conspicuous exception to this rule which defines the status of anyone in the United States of known or supposed black African ancestry, no matter how diluted, as Negro is in the case of Latin Americans who lack the two-category racial distinction and accept as white persons whose skin color, hair texture, or facial features depart from the somatic norm image of white in Anglo America.[1] The United States Census classifies Puerto Ricans and most Latin Americans as white unless the individual designates his race as Negro, Indian, or another non-white category. Most North Americans, and official records in cities such as New York and Chicago, classify Puerto Ricans of varying shades of color as a separate racial category, variously designated as Spanish-speaking, Latin American, or Puerto Rican.

In addition to persons of Latin American and other non-continental United States origin, some groups and individuals of known or suspected part-African ancestry resist classification as or association with blacks and seek recognition as white, American Indian, or another non-Negro identity. It has been estimated that approximately 70 to 80 percent of Negro Americans have some Caucasian ancestry, often mixed with American Indian genes as well (Herskovits 1930:177; Wirth, Goldhamer 1944:268–275; Reed 1969:762). Tens of thousands of Afro-Americans have the appearance of unmixed Caucasians and could by severing their ties to family, relatives, and friends cross the racial boundary and "pass for white." Crossing over, or "passing," normally requires concealment

---

[1] Hoetink (1967) examines and contrasts somatic norm image, somatic distance, and the differing boundaries which separate white from colored and colored from black in the Northwest European and South European or Latin variants of Caribbean societies.

of past identity and associations, discovery of which might result in rejection by whites and reverse boundary crossing with forced return to Negro status. Many or most fair Negroes of completely Caucasoid appearance are married to recognizable Negroes, have numerous close relatives and friends of darker complexion and Negroid appearance, and make no effort to be accepted as white. On the other hand, during the past three centuries unknown numbers of similarly Caucasian-appearing persons have concealed the African portion of their ancestry and crossed the boundary into the white group. As the result of this passing for white of one or more ancestors, hundreds of thousands of Americans who are recognized as white, and usually have no intimate social relationships with non-whites, have some Negro ancestry which is concealed from public knowledge and is often unknown to these individuals or their spouses and relatives. Such persons are, of course, everywhere identified as white and their marriages to white persons are not classed as interracial marriages (Wirth, Goldhamer 1944:301–319).

Finally, members of more than 200 variously mixed hybrid communities or groups, originating mainly in obscure seventeenth and eighteenth century blending of European adventurers and settlers with remnants of Eastern American Indian tribes and often with Negroes, located mainly in relatively isolated rural areas of the Southeast, though suspected of having some black ancestry, have persistently rejected Negro identity, refused to attend colored schools or churches, and sought and often secured recognition either as American Indian or white. For such groups to succeed in gaining acceptance as white or American Indian, it is necessary to deny having any African ancestry and to explain dark complexion and other questionable physical attributes as resulting from mixture of European ancestors with American Indians, Turks, Portuguese, or other swarthy forebears (Berry 1963; Berry 1972:191–212).

Described by some social scientists as "mestizos," mixed racial isolates or tri-racial isolates and known locally by dozens of usually unflattering appellations such as Red Bones, Brass Ankles, Jackson Whites, Issues, Cajuns, Croatans, Moors, Guineas, Yellowhammers, Wesorts, and Melungeons, these groups range in size from a few families to the more than 30,000 Lumbee Indians of Robeson County, North Carolina (Berry 1963; Frazier 1951:164–189; Griessman 1972). Separated from one another, usually refusing to marry or associate on intimate terms with blacks and being refused such association by neighboring whites, these communities constitute isolated endogamous pockets. Each such group can be viewed as a tiny subcaste intermediate in status between whites and blacks in the local social structure. Their persistent efforts to escape identification as Negro and to achieve recognition as white or American Indian may be seen as attempted boundary crossing by groups rather than by individuals. They may be viewed as similar in some respects to attempts, often successful after several decades or generations, of sub-caste units in India to avoid association and identification with other sections of a depressed caste with which they were formerly identified and to achieve upward mobility in the Hindu caste hierarchy.[2]

Ethnic, racial, religious, and class divisions are commonly found in modern societies and group boundaries are maintained by means of geographic separation, social distance, and rules of endogamy. In the United States racial identity is defined as permanent while religious and class status may be modified in a lifetime. There is considerable retention of ethnic identity and cohesion after several generations in the United States, despite loss of language and traditional culture, but many individuals of various European ethnic origins have severed ethnic ties and become part of the predominantly British dominant group. The once popular view that the United States was a "melting pot" in which diverse European immigrant groups would blend implied intermarriage and amalgamation of the white population at some time in the future, with a much longer time required for the assimilation and amalgamation of Southern and Eastern European Jews, Orthodox Christians and Roman Catholics than of Northwest European Protestants (Glazer, Moynihan 1970; M. M. Gordon 1964; Handlin 1951:286–300; Warner, Srole 1945).

Persons of American Indian, Asian, African, and other non-European ancestry were not considered to be eligible for absorption into the dominant white group and were disregarded by proponents of the melting pot theory. The white population was viewed as a superior race whose boundaries were to be protected from any intrusion of supposedly lesser breeds. Of all non-European racial types, Negroes were viewed as most inferior and undesirable and any mixture with them was seen as defilement of a superior stock. Blacks were wanted as slaves and, later, as servants and field hands, but law and custom defended the social and biological boundaries of the white group. There was considerable sexual contact between white men and black and mulatto women during the long period of slavery, but offspring of such unions were categorically defined as Negro and excluded from white society.

A boundary-maintaining system of racial caste replaced slavery in the South and legally-enforced segregation of schools, institutions, and places of public accommodation reinforced customary social distance and a system of so-called "racial etiquette" by which blacks were required to show deference to whites (Warner, Davis 1939:232–245; Davis, Gardner, Gardner 1941). Elsewhere in the United States residential segregation of Negroes has resulted in *de facto* segregation of schools, play-

---

[2] There is a striking parallel in the vigorous and persistent efforts of groups of marginal racial identity in the United States and sections of castes in India to use census classification to validate their claims to higher rank (Beale 1958:537–540; Srinivas 1966:89–117).

grounds, and neighborhood institutions, often reinforced by voluntary separation and discriminatory practices in hotels, restaurants, and other places of public accommodation (Drake 1965).

During the past two decades legislation has removed legal support for racial segregation throughout the United States and has strengthened the political and legal rights and occupational opportunities of racial minorities without effectively reducing the exclusiveness of the white majority in intimate social life and group membership. Blacks are entering occupations from which they were formerly barred and have made considerable headway in attaining political offices in the South as well as in the North. Restaurants, hotels and transportation facilities have been desegregated in most sections of the United States, and such segregation as remains in places of public accommodation is in defiance of, rather than with the support of, the law.

Most resistant to change throughout the United States have been attitudes which vigorously oppose intimate social relationships and marriage across the color line (Myrdal 1944:53–62). Most white Americans continue to exclude Negroes from their friendship circles and continue to support racial endogamy and to oppose, although often with less conviction or sense of shock than a generation ago, intimate social contact with blacks of a type which might give the appearance of condoning or encouraging intermarriage. In recent years, however, there has been some weakening of these attitudes and a considerable increase has occurred in Negro participation in previously almost exclusively white churches, colleges, and public accommodations and in more intimate social relationships including marriage.

At various times at least forty of the fifty states have had legislation prohibiting marriages between whites and Negroes (and frequently also between whites and various other "races"), and between 1910 and 1948 from twenty-six to thirty states, including all of the southern and border states and most of the western states, had such statutes. Between 1948 and 1967 fourteen states repealed their laws against intermarriage and the prohibitions of the remaining sixteen southern and border states were eliminated by the United States Supreme Court decision of June 12, 1967, in the case of *Loving v. Virginia* which held that the anti-intermarriage law of the state of Virginia was unconstitutional (Weinberger 1965, 1966; Sickels 1972).

NEGRO–WHITE INTERMARRIAGE DATA FOR THE UNITED STATES

Until recently there was very little published information, other than occasional newspaper and magazine accounts, often of a sensational nature, concerning the incidence of Negro–white intermarriage in the United States or the social characteristics of participants in such marriages.[3] Very few states or cities publish information on interracial marriages in their annual reports and in most states race or color of bride and groom is not entered on marriage application forms or is not compiled.

The most complete recording and compilation of marriage and divorce data by race in the United States has been for Hawaii, but a majority of this island state's inhabitants are Asians and Polynesians, and Negroes constitute less than 1 percent of the population and include a large number of military personnel and their families. The longest and most nearly continuous series of years for which interracial marriage data have been published for the continental United States is for Boston, Massachusetts, for the years 1855–1859, 1862–1871, 1873–1887, 1890, 1900–1907, and 1914–1938, and New York State, exclusive of New York City, for 1916–1964 (Wirth, Goldhamer 1944; Monahan 1971b, summarized in Tables 1 and 2).[4]

During recent years marriage record data on Negro–white marriages have been published for a number of widely separated cities, counties and states for varying periods during the past three decades. Table 3, below, gives the number of such marriages by year for Los Angeles County, California, for a period of approximately eleven years, beginning with

[3] For a description of hundreds of cases of sexual union and intermarriage of whites and Negroes in Europe, Asia, Africa, Latin America, and the West Indies from antiquity to modern times, as well as in the United States, see Rogers 1940, 1942, 1944, 1952.
[4] Other early tabulations of Negro–white intermarriages were published by Frederick L. Hoffman (1896) for Michigan for the years 1874–1893, Connecticut for 1883–1893, Providence for 1881–1893, and Rhode Island for 1883–1893; for Philadelphia for 1900–1904 (Wright 1912:174); and for the New York City boroughs of Manhattan and Bronx for the years 1908–1912 (Drachsler 1921). In addition to the Boston and New York State series, marriage record data on Negro–white intermarriages have been published for the years since 1912 as follows: California and Los Angeles County, 1948–1959 (Risdon 1954; Burma 1952, 1963; Barnett 1963; Heer 1966); Indiana, 1958–1959 (Pavela 1964); Iowa, 1940–1967 (Monahan 1970a); Kansas, 1947–1969 (Monahan 1971b); Michigan, 1953–1963 (Heer 1966); Nebraska, 1961–1964 (Heer 1966); Philadelphia, 1922, 1927 1932, 1937, 1942, 1947, 1950, 1960–1962, 1965, 1966 (Golden 1953, 1954, 1958; Monahan 1970b); Washington, D.C., 1931–1965 (Lynn 1953, 1956, 1967); and Hawaii, 1956–1964 (Heer 1966).
Major studies based on marriage records and intensive interviews with participants in Negro–white marriages have been published for Los Angeles County, California, (Risdon 1952, 1954); Philadelphia, Pennsylvania (Golden 1953, 1954, 1958, 1959); and Washington, D.C. (Lynn 1953, 1956, 1967); while Wirth and Goldhamer (1944), Heer (1966, 1967), Bernard (1966), McDowell (1971), and Monahan (1970a, 1970b, 1971a, 1971b) have made excellent statistical and interpretative analyses of available marriage data. In addition to the above, Cash (1956), Das (1971), Drake and Cayton (1945), Porterfield (1973), Roberts (1940, 1956), Smith (1960, 1966), and others have presented findings based primarily on research for dissertations. C. B. Day (1932), B. Day (1972), Gordon (1964), Halsell (1972), Hernton (1965, 1971), Larsson (1965), and Washington (1970) have written books on Negro–white sex relations and marriage in which case studies and interpretation are presented.

Table 1.   Negro–white intermarriages, Boston, Mass., 1855–1938

Years of marriage	Number of intermarriages				Percentage intermarried of all grooms and brides and by race			
	Groom Negro, bride white	Groom white, bride Negro	Total	Average per annum	Negro grooms	Negro brides	White grooms	White brides
1855–59			50	10				
1862–66			45	9				
1867–71			88	17.6				
1873–77			172	34.4				
1878–82			121	24.2				
1883–87			124	24.8				
1890			24	24				
1900–04	133	10	143	28.6	12.8	1.1		
1900–07	203	19	222	27.7				
1914–18	68	21	89	17.8	4	1.2	0.04	0.13
1919–23	42	5	47	9.4	2.7	0.3	0.01	0.08
1924–28	41	12	53	10.6	2.8	0.8	0.03	0.09
1929–33	36	4	40	8.0	3.2	0.4	0.01	0.09
1934–38	40	7	47	9.4	3.1	0.6	0.02	0.10
1914–38	227	49	276	11.0	3.2	0.7	0.02	0.10

Source: Hoffman 1896: 200; Stephenson 1910: 98; Stone 1908: 62; and Wirth, Goldhamer 1944: 277.

Table 2. Negro–white intermarriage, New York State, exclusive of New York City, 1916–1947

Years of marriage	Number of intermarriages				Percentage intermarried of all grooms and brides, by race				
	Groom Negro, bride white	Groom white, bride Negro	Total	Average per annum	Negro grooms plus brides	Negro grooms	Negro brides	White grooms	White brides
1916–18			25	8.3	2.0				
1919–21			55	18.3	3.6				
1922–24	88	32	120	40	4.8	3.5	1.3		
1925–27			96	32	3.3				
1928–30			105	35	3.4				
1931–33			74	24.7	2.5				
1934–36			63	21	1.7				
Totals:									
1916–37	424	145	569	25.9	2.9	2.4	0.7	0.01	0.05
1925–32	195	53	248	31	3.1				
1938–47	157	46	203	20.3	1.8	1.4	0.4	0.01	0.03

Source: Wirth, Goldhamer 1944: 278.

November, 1948, when the California Supreme Court found the state anti-intermarriage law to be unconstitutional.

Table 3.   Negro–white intermarriages, Los Angeles County, Calif., 1948–1959

Year	Groom Negro, bride white	Groom white, bride Negro	Total
1948 (Nov., Dec.)	6	0	6
1949	43	10	53
1950	30	16	46
1951	50	12	62
1952	45	13	58
1953	53	25	78
1954	61	30	91
1955	84	23	107
1956	77	27	104
1957	95	34	129
1958	111	35	146
1959	145	42	187
Totals, 1948–1959	800	267	1067

Source: Burma 1963: 163.

Marriage data for the state of California for the years 1955 and 1957–1959 indicate that 3.56 percent of Negro grooms and 1 percent of Negro brides married whites while 0.07 percent of white grooms and 0.27 percent of white brides married Negroes (Heer 1966:264, 265).

Monahan and Heer have been able to secure and have published data showing the percentages of Negro grooms and brides who have married whites and, for some states, of white brides and grooms who have married Negroes for selected years for several widely scattered states, as indicated in Table 4, below.

Monahan also presents data on interracial marriages in Iowa for the years 1940 to 1967 and states that from 1944 to 1967 there were 567,719 recorded marriages of which 7,988 included at least one Negro partner. Table 5, below, which groups the Iowa data into five consecutive time periods, is based on marriages of black men and women to non-Negroes, a predominantly but not exclusively white category.

The available interracial marriage data from city, county, and state records have come from a few cities and states and in sequences of relatively few years for most localities. Although there are gaps in the record and some inconsistency between reporting areas, it is possible to discern some uniformities and trends.

All of the available marriage record data for cities and states indicate that from 50 to more than 90 percent of Negro–white marriages have been of Negro men and white women. Prior to 1914 the proportions ranged from 78.8 percent in New York City from 1908 to 1912 to 91.4

Table 4. Negro–white intermarriages as percentages of marriages of grooms and brides, by race, selected states, 1947–1967

Year	Kansas Negro spouses	New York (excluding New York City) Negro grooms	New York Negro brides	Michigan Negro grooms	Michigan Negro brides	Michigan White grooms	Michigan White brides	Hawaii Negro grooms	Hawaii Negro brides	Hawaii White grooms	Hawaii White brides
1947	1.2	1.5	0.4								
1948	1.0	1.5	0.6								
1949	1.0	1.4	0.5								
1950	0.6	1.1	0.3								
1951	0.5	1.6	0.5								
1952	1.5	1.7	0.8								
1953	1.0	1.5	0.9	1.09	0.40	0.04	0.10				
1954	0.9	2.2	1.2	1.10	0.46	0.04	0.09				
1955	2.7	1.4	0.9	1.12	0.48	0.05	0.11				
1956	1.6	1.6	1.2	1.32	0.46	0.04	0.13	9.09	0	0	0.31
1957	1.7	1.2	1.1	1.37	0.14	0.01	0.14	13.33	0	0	0.47
1958	2.4	1.4	0.7	1.37	0.50	0.05	0.13	4.08	5.00	0.06	0.16
1959	2.6	1.8	0.7	1.62	0.40	0.04	0.16	9.80	8.33	0.11	0.36
1960	2.5	2.3	1.3	1.39	0.63	0.06	0.14	14.71	12.50	0.16	0.34
1961	3.7	2.8	0.7	1.76	0.48	0.05	0.18	16.00	8.00	0.11	0.52
1962	3.3	2.8	1.3	1.90	0.49	0.05	0.19	17.78	4.17	0.05	0.19
1963	4.0	3.3	1.2	2.34	0.77	0.07	0.23	14.81	9.38	0.14	0.43
1964	8.6	3.9	1.8					20.31	8.57	0.13	0.68
1965	6.0										
1966	6.7										
1967	5.8										
Totals:											
1953–63				1.53	0.48	0.05	0.15				
1956–64								13.53	6.82	0.09	0.43

Sources: Monahan 1971a: 110; Monahan 1971b: 98; Heer 1966: 264–265.

184   ROBERT E. T. ROBERTS

Table 5.   Percent of Negro marriages in Iowa which are mixed, 1940–1967

Years	Male	Female	Total
1940–42	3.08	0.81	3.84
1944–49	5.37	2.76	7.84
1950–55	6.14	1.75	7.69
1956–61	9.69	2.00	11.32
1962–67	13.88	3.73	16.67

Source: Monahan 1970a: 468.

percent in Boston from 1900 to 1907. Since 1914 a slightly larger proportion of interracial marriages have been of white men and Negro women. Proportions of Negro–white marriages in which black males married white females in recent years have ranged from approximately 51 percent (61 percent if Latin Americans are excluded) in Philadelphia from 1960–1962 and 1965–1966 to about 85 percent in Kansas during the years 1947–1967. Most of the available marriage record data showing sex and race of grooms and brides in Negro–white marriages in the United States are presented in Table 6, below.

The published marriage record data for cities and states in the Northeastern section of the United States, although scanty for the years before 1914, tend to indicate that the number and rate of Negro–white marriages, particularly of Negro men and white women, declined from a peak between the 1870s and World War I to a low point during the 1930s and 1940s. Data for the years since 1940 from several states in the Midwest and West as well as the Northeast and the District of Columbia indicate that the rate and number of interracial marriages between Negroes and Caucasians began to increase during the 1950s and was in a strong uptrend during the 1960s.

Before 1910 the vast majority of blacks in the United States lived in the South where, except for a few years following the Civil War of 1861–1865 (and somewhat later in Louisiana and Oklahoma), marriages of whites to Negroes were legally prohibited except in the District of Columbia. In 1910 Negroes constituted from 0.1 to 3.5 percent of the population of the northern and western states, and less than 1 percent in eighteen states. Less than 10 percent resided in states that permitted their marriage to Caucasians. As late as 1940 only 20 percent of the black population lived in states which permitted interracial marriage. Until the 1960s the law in most states and custom supported by strong social sanctions elsewhere prevented more than a tiny fraction of whites and blacks from transgressing the rule of racial endogamy.

The data presented in Tables 1 through 4 indicate that with few exceptions Negro–white intermarriages constitute less than 1 percent of total marriages in the cities and states for which information has been

Table 6. Negro-white marriages by sex and race of grooms and brides

Years	Area	Number of Negro-white marriages	Marriages of Negro males-white females		Marriages of white males-Negro females	
			Number	Percent of all Negro-white marriages	Number	Percent of all Negro-white marriages
1874–1893	Michigan	111	93	83.8	18	16.2
1883–1893	Rhode Island	58	51	87.9	7	12.1
1908–1912	New York City (Manhattan and Bronx)	52	41	78.8	11	21.2
1900–1907	Boston	222	203	91.4	19	8.6
1914–1938	Boston	276	227	82.3	49	17.7
1916–1937	New York State (excluding New York City)	569	424	74.5	145	25.5
1922–1947	Philadelphia*	41	24	58.5	17	41.5
1948–1959	Los Angeles	1,067	800	75	267	25
1955–1959	California	1,173	921	78.5	252	21.5
1931–1965	Washington, D.C.	818	523	64	295	36
1947–1969	Kansas			85		15
1953–1963	Michigan	1,132	864	76.3	268	23.7
1956–1964	Hawaii	74	59	79.7	15	20.3
1962–1967	Iowa**			79		21
1960–1962, 1965–1966	Philadelphia	245	124	50.6	121	49.4
1960–1962, 1965–1966	Philadelphia***	197	120	60.9	77	39.1

Sources: Wirth, Goldhamer 1944: 282; Monahan 1970a, 1970b, 1971b; Lynn 1967: 429; Golden 1953; Heer 1966: 264–265.

Key: * 5 year intervals, including 1922, 1927, 1932, 1937, 1942, and 1947.
    ** All non-Negro included with white.
    *** Excluding Puerto Ricans and Mexicans.

published. Fewer than 1 percent of white grooms or brides marry blacks or other non-whites. The highest rates of intermarriage of Negroes have been at times and places where they constituted a small fraction of the population, thus requiring proportionately few white marriage partners. Thus, in 1900–1904 when 12.8 percent of Negro grooms married white women and 1.1 percent of Negro brides married white men in Boston, the population of the city was but 2.1 percent black and relatively few whites violated the rule of racial endogamy. The highest recorded percentage of Negro outmarriages has been in Hawaii where from 1956 to 1964, 13.53 percent of Negro grooms married Caucasian women and 6.82 percent of Negro brides married Caucasian men, but only 0.09 percent of white grooms and 0.43 percent of white brides married Negroes.

As the black population of the larger cities of the United States increases while the white population remains stable or declines, the proportion of white men and women who intermarry is likely to increase even if there is no increase in the percentage of Negroes who marry whites. The most spectacular increase in numbers and proportion of whites to intermarry in a large city has probably been in Washington, D.C. where Negro–white marriages increased from fifteen during the five year period from 1931–1935 and eight during 1936–1940 to 177 from 1956 to 1960 and 493 from 1961–1966, representing an increase of from one in 10,000 marriages in 1935 to 150 in 10,000 marriages in 1965. This increase was concurrent with a transition from a white to a black majority in total population (Lynn 1967:430–431).

It is probable that variations and changes in rates of interracial marriage are the result of a number of factors, including: sex ratios; relative size of the racial groups; degree of residential, institutional, and occupational segregation; similarity or difference in culture, education, occupation, and income; and changes in attitudes toward out-groups and degree of opposition to intermarriage. Few people would be expected to entertain the idea of interracial courtship or marriage in a state or community in which such action might be penalized by imprisonment and strong social sanctions, such as ostracism, loss of opportunity for employment, or physical danger. The high rate of Negro–white intermarriage in Hawaii may be attributed in part to the racial harmony which characterizes that state as well as to the high Negro sex ratio occasioned by the presence of men in military service.

Wirth and Goldhamer (1944:279) attribute the very high rate of Negro–white intermarriage in Boston at the turn of the century to the role of that city as a center of abolitionist activity during the anti-slavery movement, and the subsequent marked decline in intermarriage to the weakening of such traditions and sentiments in the present century. It is not unlikely that the extremely great increase in Negro–white marriages in Washington, D.C., during the past two decades is related to the elimination of racial segregation in hotels, restaurants, theaters, and other places of public entertainment and accommodation and increased contact at places of employment as previous job restrictions were removed.

The decline in rates of marriages of blacks to whites in the North during most of the first half of the present century would appear to be related to the large influx of rural southern Negroes from about 1915 to midcentury and their concentration in almost solidly black urban areas with accompanying segregation of schools, institutions, and recreational facilities. Anti-Negro sentiment and stereotypes were strong during this period. The increase in marriages of blacks to whites during the past two decades coincides with a weakening of racist attitudes and with the civil rights movement which, supported by legislation and court decisions, has eliminated much of the former segregation and discrimination against blacks. There has been increased interracial contact in recent years in colleges and universities and in a wide range of work settings from which Negroes were almost entirely excluded a generation ago. On the other hand, there has been a counter trend toward voluntary separation on the part of many blacks.

The variations in intermarriage rates and in the proportion of white men as compared to white women who marry blacks from one city or state to another are not easily explained. The available marriage data do not indicate why the intermarriage rate is higher in Boston than in Philadelphia or in Iowa than in neighboring Nebraska or Kansas, or why in Philadelphia white men marry Negro women almost as frequently as black men marry white women while in most other cities and states for which marriage statistics have been published many more white women than men contract such marriages.

In contrast to whites and Negroes, American Indians, Japanese, Chinese, Filipinos, and "other races" have high outmarriage rates and it is not uncommon to find such rates to equal inmarriage rates in some localities. The 1970 United States Census of Population gives the following percentages for existing marriages of endogamous and interracial pattern for the various "races" in the nation, based on a 5 percent sample (see Table 7).

It can be seen that American Indians, Japanese, Chinese, Filipinos, and other Asians and Polynesians (the census category, other race, includes Koreans, East Indians, Hawaiians, and most other Asians and other non-whites, while Mexicans, Puerto Ricans, and other Latin Americans are usually classified as white) intermarry proportionately from ten to thirty times as frequently as do Negroes and that when they intermarry they usually select white marriage partners and rarely Negroes.

The only interracial marriage data for the entire United States was published in the census of population for 1960 and 1970 (United States

Table 7.   Racially endogamous and interracial marriages, United States, 1970*

	Percent of total	Spouse of same race	Race of spouse (percentages)						
			White	Negro	American Indian	Japanese	Chinese	Filipino	Other race
Race of husband									
White (40,740,647)	91.4	99.6	99.6	0.1	0.1	0.1	—	—	0.1
Negro (3,393,555)	7.6	98.5	1.2	98.5	0.1	—	—	—	0.1
American Indian (119,783)	0.3	64.2	33.4	1.3	64.2	0.2	0.1	0.2	0.7
Japanese (119,069)	0.3	88.6	8.3	0.1	0.1	88.6	1.1	0.5	1.3
Chinese (86,581)	0.2	86.5	8.3	0.4	0.1	2.8	86.5	0.6	1.4
Filipino (64,233)	0.1	66.5	24.4	1.1	0.7	3.1	0.8	66.5	7.4
Other race (73,706)	0.2	62.7	29.4	1.2	1.0	2.4	1.6	1.6	62.7
Race of wife									
White (40,714,129)	91.3	99.7	99.7	0.1	0.1	—	—	—	0.1
Negro (3,371,464)	7.6	99.2	0.7	99.2	—	—	—	—	—
American Indian (125,980)	0.3	61.0	35.6	2.3	61.0	0.1	—	0.4	0.6
Japanese (157,851)	0.4	66.8	28.0	1.1	0.1	66.8	1.5	1.3	1.1
Chinese (85,239)	0.2	87.8	8.1	0.4	0.1	1.5	87.8	0.6	1.4
Filipino (58,691)	0.1	72.8	20.9	2.0	0.4	1.0	0.9	72.8	2.0
Other race (84,220)	0.2	54.9	36.1	2.3	0.9	1.8	1.4	2.6	54.9

Source: U.S. Bureau of the Census, *Census of Population 1970:* PC (2)-4C: 262.
* Total of 44,597,574 married couples.

Bureau of the Census 1966, 1972). Despite the fact that all of the seventeen southern and border states made marriages between whites and Negroes (usually classified as anyone having one-eighth or more, but in some states any amount, of Negro or African ancestry) a criminal offense until 1967, the Census reports show that 39.7 percent of such existing marriages were found in the South in 1960 and 20.6 percent in 1970. There is considerable doubt as to the accuracy of these figures, particularly those for 1960 which also show a total of 25,913 existing marriages of white husbands and Negro wives and only 25,496 of Negro husbands and white wives in the United States. The census data differ from the data derived from city and state marriage records in that they include all rural as well as urban areas and common law marriages (which constitute legal marriages in several states), consensual unions, and perhaps less formal relationships in effect at the time of census enumeration, as well as regularly licensed marriages. Marriages entered into in other sections of the country or abroad were counted in place of residence at the time of census enumeration.

The 1970 census, however, shows fewer Negro–white intermarriages in the South than in 1960, and a majority of such marriages in all regions of the United States except the South are of the Negro husband–white wife combination, distributed by region as shown in Table 8.

The 1970 census data on existing Negro–white intermarriages, excluding the South, appear to be reasonably close to the patterns indicated by marriage record data for the non-southern regions of the United States. In all major geographic regions fewer than one in 1,000 white men marry Negro women and fewer than one in 500 white women marry black men, and, except in the West where Negroes are a relatively small proportion of the population, fewer than 2 percent of black men or women are married to whites. The census count also indicated that whereas of intact marriages entered into during the preceding decade there were only 7,534 of Negro husbands with white wives and 6,082 of white husbands and Negro wives in 1960, the comparable figures a decade later for marriages contracted between 1960 and 1970 had risen to 16,419 and 7,352 (U.S. Bureau of the Census 1972:262).

NEGRO–WHITE MARRIAGES IN CHICAGO, 1882–1969

The United States census reports give limited information concerning existing Negro–white marriages while most other published data on interracial marriage reveal some social characteristics of brides and grooms at the time of marriage, omit later periods in the family cycle, and give no information concerning children of such marriages. Most of the field studies of interracial marriages made by graduate students and other

Table 8. Number and percent intermarried of Negro and white husbands and wives by geographic region, United States of America, 1970

Region of residence	All married couples	Number interracially married			Percent intermarried of all husbands and wives, by race			
		Husband Negro, wife white	Husband white, wife Negro	Total	Negro husbands	White wives	White husbands	Negro wives
Northeast	10,647,480	12,435	8,096	20,531	1.9	0.13	0.08	1.3
North Central	12,563,107	10,758	4,525	15,283	1.5	0.09	0.04	0.6
West	7,619,806	11,744	3,862	15,606	4.5	0.17	0.05	1.6
South	13,767,181	6,286	7,083	13,369	0.35	0.05	0.06	0.4
Total, United States	44,597,574	41,223	23,566	64,789	1.2	0.10	0.06	0.7
United States, excluding South	30,830,393	34,937	16,483	51,420	2.2	0.12	0.06	1.0

Source: U.S. Bureau of the Census 1972, 262–267.

scholars have been based on interviews with fewer than fifty couples during a single time period.

In the following pages the writer will present findings based on a longitudinal study of 530 interracial marriages in Chicago and nearby suburbs, including 173 of white men and Negro women and 357 of Negro men and white women and the children of these unions. Intensive field-work was conducted during three extended periods, 1937–1939, 1951–1955, and 1964–1969,[5] and the marriages studied were entered into over a period of 88 years, from 1882 to 1969.

Table 9.   Chicago Negro–white marriages by period of study

Period of research	Number of families in sample		
	White husbands and Negro wives	Negro husbands and white wives	Total
Phase 1: 1937–1939	35	121	156
Phase 2: 1951–1955	24	33	57
Phase 3: 1964–1969	114	203	317
Total	173	357	530

Marriages of white persons to Negroes have never been separately recorded in Chicago and interracial couples and families do not constitute an organized group. As their numbers and location are not known and they are dispersed in varying proportions in many of the city's neighbor-hoods and suburbs, it was not possible to secure a random sample of such families. The 530 families included in the present study were located by the writer and his students through the assistance of many individuals but mainly through referral by interracial couples whom we interviewed. The tables presented below are based on information given by members of families discovered in this way who were willing to be interviewed and complete a questionnaire. Approximately 75 percent of the couples who were contacted cooperated in the research. Although it was not possible to secure a random sample, the 530 families may be regarded

[5] The research was supported in part by a Social Science Research Council Faculty Research Grant and a Roosevelt University research leave during February to September, 1966, and a faculty award and use of the facilities of the Social Research Center of the American University in Cairo in 1970–1971. Questionnaires were completed by members of 530 interracial families in Chicago and suburbs and approximately 400 husbands, 500 wives, and 120 children were interviewed, mainly in their homes, nearly half by the writer and others by approximately 100 of his students. Special mention is deserved by the writer's wife, Iris R. Roberts, and by Claudia Evanchuk Kafer, Linda Curtis, and Elworth Taylor, all of whom conducted numerous interviews and helped in other ways, and by Eleanor Glowe who programmed and secured computer printouts of most of the data from the 530 sets of questionnaires. Regina Holloman and St. Clair Drake read the manuscript and made helpful suggestions.

as a reasonably representative sample of Negro–white families in Chicago.[6]

On the basis of information given by persons who were interviewed since 1937, it would appear that in proportion to the number of marriages in which there were Negro partners the intermarriage rate was highest between about 1880 and 1920, declined markedly during the next three decades, and increased during the 1950s and 1960s. There appears to be a definite trend in the sex and race combination of marriage partners in Chicago, with the proportion of interracial marriages in which the husband is white and the wife is Negro increasing from approximately one in six in the late nineteenth century to more than one in three during the past two decades, as indicated in Table 10, below.

Table 10.   Chicago Negro–white marriages by period of marriage

| | Marriages in Chicago sample | | | | |
| | White husband, Negro wife | | Negro husband, white wife | | |
Period of marriage	Number	Percent of intermarriages	Number	Percent of intermarriages	Total
1882–1899	4	16.7	20	83.3	24
1900–1919	14	25.0	42	75.0	56
1920–1939	28	25.7	81	74.3	109
1940–1949	12	21.1	45	78.9	57
1950–1959	48	35.0	89	65.0	137
1960–1969	67	45.6	80	54.4	147
Total 1882–1969	173	32.6	357	67.4	530

The social structure of Chicago and its suburbs is not unlike that of other urban areas of the United States, with a primary division into two endogamous racial groups. Blacks and whites share the definitions of whites as a closed group with numerous ethnic subdivisions and of Negroes as including persons of all shades of color and degrees of racial mixture as long as some African ancestry is admitted. Whites possess greater prestige, power, and privileges than blacks and the two groups are

[6]   In the present study the writer attempted to locate families of intermarried whites and blacks of all socio-economic, occupational, and educational backgrounds and to exclude doubtful cases in which the fact of marriage or the racial identity of either spouse was uncertain. Transient non-marital unions, dubious marginal cases of near-whites, Latin Americans, and others whose racial identity was ambiguous, and couples in which one partner was passing as white and the couple was not known to their associates as interracial were excluded. No Puerto Ricans and only two persons of Mexican ancestry are included. Seven of the 530 unions lacked legal marriage ceremonies but were of several years duration. All but four of the Negro wives and five of the Negro husbands were visibly Negroid.

separated by rather marked residential and institutional segregation and both regard intermarriage as a violation of group norms.

From Chicago's establishment in the 1830s until about 1915 Negroes comprised between approximately 1 and 2 percent of the city's population. Chicago was predominantly a city of European immigrants and their children, residing to a large extent in ethnic neighborhoods and participating in ethnic churches, lodges, athletic clubs, and other social organizations. Ethnic consciousness and institutions, language and cultural barriers, and the early acceptance by immigrants of prevalent American racial attitudes served to separate whites and blacks and to reduce intimate social contacts, courtship, and marriage across racial boundaries.[7]

Before 1910 the "Black Belt" and other areas of Negro residence were interracial in character and blacks were found scattered in many predominantly white neighborhoods. Chicago's black population doubled during the great migration from the rural South during World War I, and thereafter residential segregation of Negroes became the rule. By 1940 the great majority of the city's blacks were concentrated in six or seven almost solidly Negro neighborhoods in which contacts with whites in other than economic and administrative relationships were minimal. The proportion of the city's population that was Negro doubled between 1910 and 1920 and between 1920 and 1940, and quadrupled between 1940 and 1970 when it reached 32.7 percent of the total, as indicated in Table 11, below.

Table 11.   Total and Negro population of Chicago,1837–1970

Year	Total population	Negro population	Percent of population Negro
1837	4,180	77	1.8
1840	4,470	53	1.2
1845	12,088	140	1.2
1850	29,963	323	1.1
1860	109,260	958	0.9
1870	298,977	3,696	1.2
1880	503,185	6,480	1.3
1890	1,099,850	14,271	1.3
1900	1,698,575	30,150	1.9
1910	2,185,283	44,103	2.0
1920	2,701,705	109,594	4.1
1930	3,376,438	233,903	6.9
1940	3,396,808	277,731	8.2
1950	3,620,962	492,265	13.6
1960	3,550,404	812,637	22.9
1970	3,366,957	1,102,620	32.7

[7]   For a history of Chicago's major ethnic groups and Negro community see Drake and Cayton (1945), Roberts (1965), and Spear (1967).

Despite a high degree of residential and institutional separation, social distance, and attitudes in support of racial endogamy, a fraction of 1 percent of Chicago's marriages involve crossing of the boundary between blacks and whites. Information provided by members of 530 interracial families makes possible an examination of trends and patterns in such marriages. This will be done through a series of tables in which the marriages will be grouped into two time periods and separated by sex and race: marriages entered into between 1882 and 1939 and those entered into between 1940 and 1969 for white husbands, Negro wives, Negro husbands and white wives, with the following totals which will be reduced in cases of no response to any of the questions.

Table 12.   Totals for tables based on two marriage periods and race and sex of spouses in Chicago sample

Period of marriage by year of marriage	Husband white, wife Negro	Husband Negro, wife white	Totals
Period 1: Marriages, 1882–1939	46	143	189
Period 2: Marriages, 1940–1969	127	214	341
Totals	173	357	530

Tables 13 to 22 will examine the ancestry and social background of the 530 husbands and 530 wives in the present study, excluding in each table

Table 13.   Racial ancestry of Negro spouses

Biological ancestry	Husbands			Wives		
	Married 1882–1939	Married 1940–1969	Total	Married 1882–1939	Married 1940–1969	Total
Not stated	56	60	116	11	25	36
Unmixed Negro	3	28	31	1	12	13
Negro + American Indian	20	30	50	2	12	14
More Negro than white	13	36	49	4	23	27
More Negro than white + American Indian	11	30	41	11	28	39
Approximately ½ Negro and ½ white	10	12	22	6	8	14
½ Negro, ½ white + American Indian	9	6	15	2	8	10
More white than Negro	10	4	14	5	6	11
More white than Negro + American Indian	11	8	19	4	5	9
Total, omitting not stated	87	154	241	35	102	137

those who failed to give a response to specific questions. We will first note that in physical appearance and ancestry the white husbands and wives are predominantly of Northern European type while the Negro husbands and wives range from almost Caucasian to unmixed black African phenotypes with a majority of those who responded possessing more Negroid than Caucasoid ancestry.

Table 14. Skin color of Negro spouses

Skin color	Husbands			Wives		
	Married 1882–1939	Married 1940–1969	Total	Married 1882–1939	Married 1940–1969	Total
Very dark	12	11	23	2	4	6
Dark brown	40	33	73	9	25	34
Medium brown	35	100	135	12	44	56
Light brown	29	31	60	11	29	40
Tan, light	15	31	46	7	20	27
Fair and can pass for white	1	3	4	2	3	5
Totals (excluding no response)*	132	209	341	43	125	168

* Tables which follow will omit "no response" category from totals.

Table 15. Ethnic or national origin of white spouses

Ethnic or national origin	Husbands			Wives		
	Married 1882–1939	Married 1940–1969	Total	Married 1882–1939	Married 1940–1969	Total
Old (predominantly British) American	12	23	35	32	49	81
British (recent)	6	18	24	11	19	30
Irish	6	9	15	14	13	27
German	4	16	20	34	27	61
Scandinavian	3	6	9	10	10	20
French	1	3	4	5	5	10
Italian	4	7	11	4	17	21
Jewish	1	23	24	9	30	39
Polish	1	5	6	4	8	12
Other Slavic	0	4	4	8	2	10
Other	5	12	17	3	9	12
Totals	43	126	169	134	189	323

Table 16.   Generations resident in the United States, white spouses

Generations resident in United States	Husbands			Wives		
	Married 1882–1939	Married 1940–1969	Total	Married 1882–1939	Married 1940–1969	Total
0, came to U.S. age 18 or over	9	3	12	16	33	49
0, came to U.S. before age 18	6	2	8	22	6	28
1	6	28	34	33	27	60
1½ (1 parent foreign-born)	4	12	16	13	13	26
2	1	28	29	13	41	54
3 or more	13	52	65	33	86	119
Totals	39	125	164	130	206	336

Table 17.   Place of birth of husbands and wives, by race

Place of birth	White husbands	Negro wives	Negro husbands	White wives
Chicago and suburbs	65	59	74	100
Other North and West	55	28	59	155
South and border states	25	71	189	20
U.S.—no state indicated	2	5	20	3
Total, United States	147	163	342	278
Canada	0	1	1	8
Germany	2	0	0	27
Italy	4	0	0	10
Other Europe	14	0	0	31
West Indies, Latin America	0	8	9	0
Asia, Africa	3	1	4	0
Total, Foreign born	23	10	14	76
Totals	170	173	356	354

Table 18. Age at marriage by race of husbands and wives

Age at marriage	White husbands			Negro wives			Negro husbands			White wives		
	Married 1882–1939	1940–1969	Total	Married 1882–1939	1940–1969	Total	Married 1882–1939	1940–1969	Total	Married 1882–1939	1940–1969	Total
Under 19	1	1	2	6	12	18	2	2	4	29	10	39
19–21	0	13	13	3	29	32	7	19	26	32	55	87
22–24	3	28	31	3	34	37	26	37	63	18	61	79
25–27	6	26	32	7	14	21	13	38	51	14	36	50
28–30	7	15	22	5	9	14	19	32	49	15	18	33
31–35	3	23	26	2	20	22	17	46	63	14	17	31
36–40	6	10	16	8	7	15	14	22	36	3	14	17
41–45	2	2	4	1	1	2	8	9	17	2	2	4
46 and over	10	8	18	0	0	0	12	7	19	7	1	8
Totals	38	126	164	35	126	161	118	210	328	134	214	348

Table 19.   Difference in age of husband and wife, by race

Difference in age of husband and wife	White husbands, Negro wives			Negro husbands, white wives		
	1882–1939	Married 1940–1969	Total	1882–1939	Married 1940–1969	Total
Husband older by:						
15 or more years	6	8	14	11	11	22
10–14 years	8	10	18	18	30	48
6–9 years	5	21	26	16	41	57
4–5 years	4	15	19	18	16	34
2–3 years	1	22	23	21	35	56
½–1.9 years	3	21	24	12	33	45
Same age	2	12	14	4	16	20
Wife older by:						
½–1.9 years	0	7	7	5	7	12
2–4 years	4	6	10	2	12	14
5 or more years	1	4	5	8	8	16
Totals	34	126	160	115	209	324

Table 20.   Years of schooling completed by husbands and wives, by race

Years of schooling completed	White husbands			Negro wives			Negro husbands			White wives		
	1882–1939	Married 1940–1969	Total	1882–1939	Married 1940–1969	Total	1882–1939	Married 1940–1969	Total	1882–1939	Married 1940–1969	Total
0–8	19	4	23	18	4	22	60	13	73	65	10	75
9–12	6	24	31	9	28	37	28	48	76	38	64	102
13–15	2	20	22	7	57	64	13	66	79	7	70	77
16	4	28	31	1	19	20	6	27	33	4	34	38
17 or more	2	50	52	1	18	19	7	55	62	2	35	37
Totals	33	126	159	36	126	162	114	209	323	116	213	329

Class of occupation	White husbands			Negro wives			Negro husbands			White wives		
	1882–1939	Married 1940–1969	Total	1822–1939	Married 1940–1969	Total	1882–1939	Married 1940–1969	Total	1882–1939	Married 1940–1969	Total
Unemployed, housewife	15	4	19	36	51	87	28	9	37	107	84	191
Professional, manager, proprietor, official	13	63	76	2	31	33	24	95	119	7	58	65
Clerical, sales	5	19	24	2	22	24	10	21	31	8	43	51
Skilled, semi-skilled	5	17	22	1	1	2	20	43	63	3	6	9
Service and unskilled	4	3	7	2	7	9	35	25	60	8	5	13
Student	0	17	17	0	15	15	0	16	16	0	16	16
Totals	42	123	165	43	127	170	117	209	326	133	212	345

Table 22. Previous marital status, by race.

Previous marital status	White husbands			Negro wives			Negro husbands			White wives		
	1882–1939	Married 1940–1969	Total	1882–1939	Married 1940–1969	Total	1882–1939	Married 1940–1969	Total	1882–1939	Married 1940–1969	Total
Single	20	94	114	16	87	103	56	120	176	79	153	232
Divorced	7	29	36	15	36	51	30	75	105	28	52	80
Widowed	12	3	15	6	2	8	11	7	18	18	6	24
Total	39	126	165	37	125	162	97	202	299	125	211	336

The preceding tables fail to support several of the assumptions which have been made concerning participants in interracial marriages. It has been suggested that the foreign born would be heavily represented among white marriage partners in Negro-white marriages because they lacked racial prejudice, did not share the usual concern of white Americans with maintaining endogamy and guarding group boundaries, or were unaware of the social stigma and penalties such a marriage might entail (Cavan 1969:206–207; Golden 1953:179). Yet our data indicate that in Chicago a majority of the intermarried white husbands and wives were second and third generation Americans and more often of older than of more recent immigrant groups. There is an overrepresentation of men and women of British and German background and underrepresentation of those of Polish and other Slavic origins. More than 95 percent of the Negro husbands and wives were born in the United States and black husbands were disproportionately of southern birth. A large percentage of the foreign-born white wives who married after 1940 and who came to the United States as adults, particularly those born in Germany and Italy, met their husbands while the latter were in military service in Europe. More of the white husbands were born in the South of the United States than in foreign countries and could hardly have been unaware of American racial attitudes. Several of the white husbands who married before 1940 came to Chicago to marry Negro women whom they had met in the South.

Table 18 indicates that there are relatively few teenage marriages among the 530 couples studied and that the age at marriage is higher than for in-group marriages of whites or blacks. An increase in the proportion of youthful marriages between white men and Negro women can be noted for the period after 1939, however. Table 19 indicates that a large proportion of the couples vary considerably in age. This may be related to the high proportion of husbands who had been previously married and might be expected to marry younger women. The white spouses were more often previously single than the Negro spouses.

Merton (1941), Van den Berghe (1960:62), and other scholars have theorized that intermarriages would be mainly of low status whites who would exchange high caste position for the gains of marriage to economically, professionally, and educationally superior Negroes. Pavela (1964:211), however, found that in Indiana in 1958 and 1959 Negro and white spouses in interracial marriages were roughly equal in educational and economic status. Bernard (1966) also concluded that in 1960 educational homogeneity was typical of Negro–white marriages. The 1970 United States Census also indicates that Negro men and women who marry whites are of higher average educational attainment than those who marry blacks, but are of roughly equivalent schooling to that of their spouses (U.S. Bureau of the Census 1972:283–288).

Tables 20 and 21 show far more contrast between the educational and occupational attainment of the couples who married after 1939 and those who married before that year than between Negro and white spouses. Most of the couples who married before 1939 were interviewed in the late 1930s while those who married after 1939 were interviewed in the 1950s and 1960s when educational and economic opportunities were much improved. Many of the husbands and most of the wives were not employed during the Depression years while in the later periods there were few unemployed husbands and most of the wives were employed outside the home. The contrast is most marked in years of schooling completed. Very few of the husbands or wives who married before 1940 had attended college and a majority had not completed elementary school. A majority of the husbands and wives who married after 1939 had attended college and a larger number than in the general population had seventeen or more years of schooling. There were very few college graduates in the earlier group, but of those who married after 1939, thirty white husbands, six Negro wives, thirty-four black husbands, and eighteen white wives had master's or higher degrees.

A comparison of years of schooling completed by the husbands and wives studied who were married before 1940 with census data for the Chicago metropolitan area for 1940 indicates that the interracially married white and Negro men and women exceeded their counterparts in the general population in educational attainment, and those who married between 1940 and 1969 extended this trend (see Tables 23 and 24).

The number of children born to the 530 families at the time of study totalled 885, a rather low figure, but as many of the wives had had children by previous marriages and married late while others were recently married and could be expected to have children in the future, this cannot be interpreted as a measure of fertility. Tables 25 and 26 indicate marital status of the 530 intermarried couples and numbers of children born.

Very little has been published concerning the children of Negro–white

Table 23. Years of schooling completed by intermarried husbands and wives, married 1882–1939, by race, by percentages

Years of schooling completed	White husbands	Negro wives	Negro husbands	White wives
0–8	57.6	50.0	52.6	56.0
9–12	18.2	25.0	24.6	32.8
13–15	6.1	19.4	11.4	6.0
16	12.1	2.8	5.3	3.5
17 or more	6.1	2.8	6.1	1.7

Table 24.   Years of schooling completed by persons 25 years old and over, by race and sex for Chicago metropolitan district,1940, by percentages

Years of schooling completed	Foreign-born white		Native-born white		Negro	
	Male	Female	Male	Female	Male	Female
0–8	80.9	84.9	46.3	45.9	71.7	67.7
9–12	13.2	13.1	36.2	41.5	21.2	26.4
13–15	2.3	1.2	7.8	7.0	3.6	3.5
16 or more	3.0	1.0	9.4	5.2	2.5	1.8
not reported	0.6	0.7	0.4	0.3	0.9	0.6

Source: U.S. Bureau of the Census 1943, Vol. II, Part 2: 653.

marriages in the United States. The normal expectation is that they will identify as Negro and be accepted as such by Afro-Americans regardless of their color and other physical characteristics. Taylor (1969), in a study of 100 children of Negro–white marriages in the Chicago area concluded that the majority of these children preferred Negro identity and did not experience any serious problems in being accepted. However, nearly one-third of the children in his study as well as of the 885 children in the writer's study were sufficiently Caucasoid in appearance to be mistaken for white by persons unfamiliar with their parentage. In Tables 27 and 28 data are presented which indicate the extent to which group boundary crossing has been practiced by adult children of Negro–white marriages.

As children under 16 years of age may be considered to be too young to leave home and change their racial identity the examination of question-naire responses concerning passing for white was limited to older sons and daughters of the couples studied. It can be noted that only a few children of the marriages entered into after 1939 had entered white

Table 25.   Present marital status of intermarried couples

Marital status	White husbands and Negro wives			Negro husbands and white wives		
	Married 1882–1939	Married 1940–1969	Total	Married 1882–1939	Married 1940–1969	Total
Married and together	33	97	130	75	165	240
Separated	6	13	19	16	7	23
Divorced	1	14	15	11	34	45
Husband dead	3	1	4	22	7	29
Wife dead	2	2	4	6	0	6
Husband and wife dead	1	0	1	11	0	11
Totals	46	127	173	141	213	354

Table 26.   Numbers of children born to intermarried couples

Number of children	By white husbands and Negro wives			Negro husbands and white wives		
	Married 1882–1939	Married 1940–1969	Total	Married 1882–1939	Married 1940–1969	Total
0*	0	0	0	0	0	0
1	5	28	33	27	52	79
2	6	44	50	28	88	116
3	9	24	33	54	51	105
4	8	8	16	24	64	88
5	15	10	25	45	25	70
6	6	6	12	42	12	54
7	7	7	14	7	35	42
8	8	0	8	24	8	32
9	9	0	9	9	9	18
10	10	0	10	20	0	20
11	0	0	0	22	0	22
14	0	0	0	14	0	14
15	0	0	0	15	0	15
Total born	83	127	210	331	344	675

* Number of couples without children was 25 in column 2, 61 in col. 3, 86 in col. 4, 49 in col. 5, 70 in col. 6, and 119 in col. 7.

society, but this is partly because many were still living with their parents and were barely approaching adulthood. It would appear that as they grow older a considerable number of this group will elect to cross over into the white society.

In Table 28 we note that only four of the children of the second period in our study had married at the time the research was conducted. The marriages which did take place indicate that approximately twice as many sons as daughters of Negro–white marriages selected white partners. More than 10 percent of the children who married selected white wives or husbands, indicating that marriage to whites is more likely for children of interracial marriages than for children of two black parents.

SUMMARY AND CONCLUSIONS

This article is an attempt to define and indicate the boundaries of the groups described as white and Negro or black in the United States, to summarize the published data on marriages between whites and Negroes in the United States, and to present results of a study of 530 such marriages in the Chicago area.

Unlike the more typical color continuum or three-category (white, colored, and black) racial classification of Latin America and the West Indies, a rigid two-category racial system evolved in the United States, with no provision for an intermediate status for persons of mixed racial

Table 27. Racial identification of Caucasoid-appearing children of intermarriages

| | Children of white–Negro and Negro–white marriages | | | | | | | | |
| | Sons | | | Daughters | | | Sons and Daughters | | |
Racial identification	Of 1882–1939 marriages	Of 1940–1969 marriages	Total	1882–1939	1940–1969	Total	1882–1939	1940–1969	Totals
Lives as Negro	23	5	28	29	8	37	52	13	65
Passes for white at work only	2	1	3	6	0	6	8	1	9
Leads dual life	4	2	6	1	0	1	5	2	7
Lives as white	11	2	13	6	4	10	17	6	23
Total over 16 and could pass for white	40	10	50	42	12	54	82	22	104

Table 28. Race of spouse of children of Negro–white marriages

| | Children of marriages between whites and Negroes by time period of parents' marriage | | | | | | | | |
| | Sons | | | Daughters | | | Sons and Daughters | | |
Race of spouse	1882–1939	1940–1969	Total	1882–1939	1940–1969	Total	1882–1939	1940–1969	Totals
White	14	1	15	7	1	8	21	2	23
Passable Negro	1	0	1	2	0	2	3	0	3
Negro	81	1	82	107	1	108	188	2	190
1 white, 1 Negro	1	0	1	1	0	1	2	0	2
1 white, 1 Chinese	0	0	0	1	0	1	1	0	1
Total married	97	2	99	118	2	120	215	4	219
Never married	85	248	333	55	219	274	140	467	607
Totals	182	252	432	173	221	394	355	471	826

descent. Racial endogamy was supported by strong public opinion and social sanctions throughout the continental United States and was required by law in most states until the late 1950s. Although state legislation prohibiting interracial marriages was voided by a decision of the United States Supreme Court in 1967, more than 98 percent of Negro brides and grooms and 99.6 percent of white brides and grooms in the United States marry persons of their own race. American Indians, Filipinos, Japanese, and other Asians have outmarriage rates from 30 to 80 times greater than those of whites.

Examination of previous research and published records of Negro–white marriages reveals considerable variation in intermarriage rates from place to place and at different periods of time. During the late nineteenth and early twentieth century a high percentage of Negro grooms married white brides in Boston and other localities of the North where Negroes constituted but 1 or 2 percent of the population. Then as large numbers of predominantly rural poor blacks migrated to northern cities from the South between about 1915 and 1950, the Negro population of these cities became increasingly concentrated in inner city neighborhoods and had little social contact with whites. There was a decline in intermarriage rates during this period. During the 1950s and 1960s, racial segregation and discrimination came under strong attack from black and white civil rights advocates, court decisions, and legislation, and there was increased contact and social interaction between whites and Negroes in many localities. There has been a reversal of the decline in marriages between whites and Negroes and a considerable increase in such marriages since the mid-1950s in most of the cities and states for which intermarriage data are available. There has also been some increase in the proportion of such marriages in which the husband is white.

The writer's study of 530 Negro–white marriages in Chicago was conducted during three periods, 1937–1939, 1951–1955, and 1964–1969, by means of questionnaires and interviews with husbands, wives, and children of marriages entered into between 1882 and 1969. In 173 of these families the husband was white and in 357 he was black. The black husbands and wives were mainly of predominantly Negro genetic composition with some Caucasian and American Indian mixture and ranged in complexion from fair to very dark, with four of the wives and five of the husbands having the appearance of Caucasians. The white husbands and wives were of a wide variety of nationality origins, but mainly of British and North European background.

Comparisons of couples married between 1882 and 1939 and those married between 1940 and 1969 indicate a number of trends. There was a decline in foreign-born white husbands and wives although there was a considerable number of European war brides, a decline in husbands and wives of Irish ancestry, and of wives of German ancestry, and a marked increase in Jewish husbands and wives. A larger proportion of marriages entered into by white men and Negro women before 1940 were of persons over 35 years of age and there was a marked increase in marriages of white husbands and black wives under 25 years of age after 1939. There was a marked decrease in the number of husbands and wives of both races who were widowed at the time of their present marriage and a marked increase in the number of white husbands and black wives who were not previously married.

There was a considerable increase in the proportion of husbands and wives married after 1939 who were employed as clerks, professionals, managers, proprietors, and officials and a marked increase in working wives. The most marked change between the older and younger groups was in years of schooling completed. More than half of the black and white husbands and wives who married before 1940 had no more than eight years of schooling while of those who married between 1940 and 1969 only 3.2 percent of the white husbands, 4.7 percent of the white wives, 6.2 percent of the black husbands, and 3.2 percent of the black wives had completed eight or fewer years of schooling. Over 65 percent of the husbands and wives who married after 1939 had completed at least one year of college.

Nearly one-third of the 885 children of the families studied were completely Caucasian in appearance. Of 105 who appeared to be white and were over sixteen years of age, thirteen sons and ten daughters have completely identified or "passed" as white, three sons and six daughters pass for white at work but not otherwise, and six sons and one daughter lead a dual life, being known as white to some associates and as Negro to others.

Of 222 marriages of children in the families studied, sixteen sons and ten daughters married whites, while there were 84 marriages of sons and 111 of daughters to blacks and one to a Chinese man.

REFERENCES

BARNETT, LARRY D.
    1963   Interracial Marriage in California. *Marriage and Family Living* 25:424–427.
BEALE, CALVIN L.
    1958   "Census problems of racial enumeration," in *Race: individual and collective behavior*. Edited by Edgar T. Thompson and Everett C. Hughes, 537–540. Glencoe, Ill: The Free Press.
BERNARD, JESSIE
    1966   Note on educational homogamy in Negro–white and white–Negro marriages, 1960. *Journal of Marriage and the Family* 27:274–276.

BERRY, BREWTON
  1963   *Almost white*. New York: Macmillan.
  1972   "America's mestizos," in *The blending of races*. Edited by Noel P. Gist
         and Anthony Gary Dworkin, 191–212. New York: Wiley-Interscience.
BURMA, JOHN H.
  1952   Research note on the measurement of interracial marriage. *American
         Journal of Sociology* 57:587–589.
  1963   Interethnic marriage in Los Angeles, 1948–1959. *Social Forces*
         42:156–165.
CASH, EUGENE
  1956   *A study of Negro–white marriages in the Philadelphia area*. Unpublished
         Ph.D. dissertation, Temple University.
CAVAN, RUTH SHONLE
  1969   *The American family*, (fourth edition). New York: Crowell.
DAS, MAN SINGH
  1971   A cross-cultural study of intercaste marriage in India and the United
         States. *International Journal of Sociology of the Family* 1 (special issue):
         25–33.
DAVIS, ALLISON, BURLEIGH B. GARDNER, MARY R. GARDNER
  1941   *Deep south*. Chicago: University of Chicago.
DAY, BETH
  1972   *Sexual life between blacks and whites*. New York: World.
DAY, CAROLINE BOND
  1932   *A study of some Negro–white families in the United States*. Cambridge:
         Peabody Museum, Harvard University.
DEGLER, CARL N.
  1971   *Neither black nor white: slavery and race relations in Brazil and the
         United States*. New York: Macmillan.
DOVER, CEDRIC
  1937   *Half-caste*. London: Martin Secker and Warburg.
DRACHSLER, JULIUS
  1921   *Intermarriage in New York City*. Columbia University Studies in His-
         tory, Economics, and Public Law 94 no. 213. New York: Columbia
         University.
DRAKE, ST. CLAIR
  1965   The social and economic status of the Negro in the United States.
         Daedalus Fall issue: 771–814.
DRAKE, ST. CLAIR, HORACE R. CAYTON
  1945   *Black metropolis: a study of Negro life in a northern city*. New York:
         Harcourt Brace.
FRAZIER, E. FRANKLIN
  1951   *The Negro family in the United States*. New York: Dryden.
GIST, NOEL P., ANTHONY GARY DWORKIN
  1972   *The blending of races: marginality and identity in world perspective*. New
         York: Wiley-Interscience.
GLAZER, NATHAN, DANIEL P. MOYNIHAN
  1970   *Beyond the melting pot: the Negroes, Puerto Ricans, Jews, Italians, and
         Irish of New York City* (second edition). Cambridge, Mass.: MIT Press.
GOLDEN, JOSEPH
  1953   Characteristics of the Negro–white intermarried in Philadelphia.
         American Sociological Review 18:177–183.
  1954   Patterns of Negro–white intermarriage. *American Sociological Review*
         19:144–147.

1958   Social control of Negro–white intermarriage. *Social Forces* 36:267–269.
1959   Facilitating factors in Negro–white intermarriage. *Phylon* 20:273–284.
GORDON, ALBERT I.
1964   *Intermarriage: interfaith, interracial, interethnic*. Boston: Beacon.
GORDON, MILTON M.
1964   *Assimilation in American Life*. New York: Oxford.
GRIESSMAN, B. EUGENE, *editor*
1972   The American isolates. *American Anthropologist* 74:693–734.
HALSELL, GRACE
1972   *Black/white sex*. New York: William Morrow.
HANDLIN, OSCAR
1951   *The uprooted*. New York: Grosset and Dunlap.
HEER, DAVID M.
1966   Negro–white marriage in the United States. *Journal of Marriage and the Family* 28:262–273.
1967   Intermarriage and racial amalgamation in the United States. *Eugenics Quarterly* 14:112–120.
HERNTON, CALVIN C.
1965   *Sex and racism in America*. New York: Doubleday.
1971   *Coming together: black power, white hatred and sexual hang-ups*. New York: Random House.
HERSKOVITS, MELVILLE J.
1930   *The anthropometry of the American Negro*. New York: Columbia.
HOETINK, H.
1967   *The two variants in Caribbean race relations*. London: Oxford.
HOFFMAN, FREDERICK L.
1896   *Race traits and tendencies of the American Negro*. New York: Macmillan.
JORDAN, WINTHROP D.
1969   *White over black: American attitudes toward the Negro 1550–1812*. Baltimore: Penguin Books.
LARSSON, CLOTYE M., *editor*
1965   *Marriage across the color line*. Chicago: Johnson.
LYNN, SISTER ANNELLA
1953   *Interracial marriages in Washington, D.C., 1940–1947*. Washington, D.C.: Catholic University of America.
1956   Some aspects of interracial marriage in Washington, D.C. *Journal of Negro Education* 25:380–391.
1967   Interracial marriages in Washington, D.C. *Journal of Negro Education* 36:428–433.
McDOWELL, SOPHIA F.
1971   Black–white intermarriage in the United States. *International Journal of Sociology of the Family* 1 (special issue): 49–58.
MERTON, ROBERT K.
1941   Intermarriage and the social structure: fact and theory. *Psychiatry* 4:361–374.
MONAHAN, THOMAS P.
1970a Are interracial marriages really less stable? *Social Forces* 48:461–473.
1970b Interracial marriage: data for Philadelphia and Pennsylvania. *Demography* 7:287–299.

1971a Interracial marriage in the United States: some data on upstate New York. *International Journal of Sociology of the Family* 1:94–105.

1971b Interracial marriage and divorce in Kansas and the question of instability in mixed marriages. *Journal of Comparative Family Studies* 2:107–120.

MYRDAL, GUNNAR
1944 *An American dilemma: the Negro problem and American democracy*. New York: Harper.

PAVELA, TODD H.
1964 An exploratory study of Negro–white intermarriage in Indiana. *Journal of Marriage and the Family* 26:209–211.

PIERSON, DONALD
1972 "Brazilians of mixed racial descent," in *The blending of races*. Edited by Noel P. Gist and Anthony Gary Dworkin, 237–263.

PORTERFIELD, ERNEST
1973 Mixed marriage. *Psychology Today* 6(8):71–78.

REED, T. EDWARD
1969 Caucasian genes in American Negroes. *Science* 165:762–768.

RISDON, RANDALL
1952 *Selected problems arising from interracial marriages in the metropolitan zone of Los Angeles City*. Unpublished M.A. thesis, University of Southern California.

1954 A study of interracial marriages based on data for Los Angeles County. *Sociology and Social Research* 39:92–95.

ROBERTS, ROBERT E. T.
1940 *Negro–White intermarriage: a study of social control*. Unpublished M.A. thesis, University of Chicago.

1956 *A comparative study of social stratification and intermarriage in multiracial societies*. Unpublished Ph.D. dissertation, University of Chicago.

1965 "Chicago's ethnic groups," and "The Negro community," in *Chicago Lutheran planning study*, volume 1. Edited by Walter Kloetzli. Chicago: National Lutheran Council.

ROGERS, J. A.
1940, 1942, 1944 *Sex and race*, three volumes. New York: J. A. Rogers.

1952 *Nature knows no color line: research into the Negro ancestry in the white race*. New York: J. A. Rogers.

SICKELS, ROBERT J.
1972 *Race, marriage, and the law*. Albuquerque: University of New Mexico.

SMITH, CHARLES E.
1960 *Negro–white intermarriage in metropolitan New York*. Unpublished Ph.D. dissertation. New York: Columbia University.

1966 Negro–white intermarriage — forbidden sexual union. *Journal of Sex Research* 2:169–178.

SPEAR, ALLAN H.
1967 *Black Chicago: the making of a Negro ghetto 1890–1920*. Chicago: University of Chicago.

SRINIVAS, M. N.
1966 *Social change in modern India*. Berkeley: University of California.

STEPHENSON, GILBERT THOMAS
1910 *Race distinctions in American law*. New York: D. Appleton.

STONE, A. H.
1908 *Studies in the American race problem*. New York: Doubleday Page.

STONEQUIST, EVERETT V.
1937   *The marginal man*. New York: Charles Scribner's Sons.
TAYLOR, ELWORTH
1969   *Children of Negro–white marriage: a study of social identification and acceptance*. Unpublished M.A. thesis. Chicago: Roosevelt University.
UNITED STATES BUREAU OF THE CENSUS
1943   *Sixteenth Census of the United States: 1940*. Population, volume II, part 2. Washington, D.C.: U.S. Government Printing Office.
1966   *Census of population: 1960, marital status*. Washington, D.C.: U.S. Government Printing Office.
1972   *Census of population: 1970, marital status*. Washington, D.C.: U.S. Government Printing Office.
VAN DEN BERGHE, PIERRE L.
1960   Hypergamy, hypergenation, and miscegenation. *Human Relations* 13:83–90.
WARNER, W. LLOYD, W. ALLISON DAVIS
1939   "A comparative study of American caste," in *Race relations and the race problem*. Edited by Edgar T. Thompson, 219–245. Durham, North Carolina: Duke University.
WARNER, W. LLOYD, LEO SROLE
1945   *The social systems of American ethnic groups*. New Haven: Yale.
WASHINGTON, JOSEPH R., JR.
1970   *Marriage in black and white*. Boston: Beacon.
WEINBERGER, ANDREW D.
1965   "A reappraisal of the constitutionality of miscegenation statutes," in *Man's most dangerous myth* by Ashley Montagu, 402–426. New York: World.
1966   Interracial marriage—its statutory prohibitions, genetic import, and incidence. *Journal of Sex Research* 2:157–168.
WIRTH, LOUIS, HERBERT GOLDHAMER
1944   "The hybrid and the problem of miscegenation," in *Characteristics of the American Negro*. Edited by Otto Klineberg, 249–369. New York: Harper.
WRIGHT, RICHARD R.
1912   *The Negro in Pennsylvania: a study in economic history*. Philadelphia: A.M.E. Book Concern.

Changing Patterns of Ethnic Identity and Prestige in East Africa

W. ARENS

The typical sociocultural unit of investigation for anthropological studies of African populations has been the "tribe." If defined at all, it usually has been employed to refer to an aggregation inhabiting a specific territory and sharing a set of common cultural traits. For purposes of analysis, a tribe has been recognized as distinct in relation to other groups of the same type. For East Africa at least, other groups, such as the Arabs, Shirazi, Persians, and the Waswahili (plural of Swahili people) which do not conveniently fit the characteristics of a tribe, have received much less attention by anthropologists. Even studies of cities in Africa have focused on the maintenance of tribal identity as an adaptive mechanism to the urban milieu (cf. Cohen 1969).

Although the concept of tribe is a mainstay, its theoretical value has recently come under severe criticism because of its vagueness, imprecision, and oversimplicity (Fried 1967). Even a cursory review of the monographs devoted to the social or cultural study of a tribe leads to the conclusion that such charges are more than warranted. Fried has further suggested that what others have accepted as tribes in Africa and other parts of the Third World were actually of recent origin. They emerged in reaction to contact with colonial powers, which intentionally or unintentionally adopted a policy of divide and rule in dealing with their subject populations (Fried 1967:15–17). Gulliver, in discussing the relationship between British rule in East Africa and tribalism, has echoed this sentiment, writing that ". . . the net effect of the colonial era was a marked heightening of tribal consciousness and a deepening of tribal differences" (1969:16).

The purpose of this essay is not to raise anew the issue of the true meaning or the overall value of the concept of tribe. Rather, this discussion accepts the proposition that, at least during the period of colonial rule, the European administration regarded groups of people as belonging to tribes. As a direct consequence, the indigenous population came to accept this definition of the situation. Colonial officials, after all, did not have to grapple with the task of providing a meaningful definition of the term, but rather were faced with the practical problem of organizing people so that they fit into the vague European model of a tribe. Through the imposition of a system of indirect rule and by following the dictates of their folk model, the administration played its part in stimulating the emergence of tribes. The creation of Native Authorities, the appointment of chiefs and headmen, the establishment of reserves, the ban on national political organizations, and in some instances the imposition of pass laws that restricted movement were early manifestations of this policy. Argyle probably has provided the most concrete example of this phenomenon on the basis of his research among the Soli of Central Africa. He reports that "during my own fieldwork, I was told emphatically by one old chief that he and his people had not been Soli and had not thought of themselves as such, until the District Commissioner said they were in 1937" (1969:55).

Because the creation of tribes seems to have been one of the implicit interests of colonial rule, the European administrators also accorded a certain amount of grudging respect and prestige to those subjects who acted as if they were members of tribes. Those individuals who restricted their sense of identity and loyalty to a localized area and who maintained traditional attitudes and customs were "proper natives." Whole groups that exhibited these characteristics were considered to be less troublesome in many ways than those that attempted to "westernize." As indicated, during this period the ideology of tribal identity was also influencing the native inhabitants when, in some instances, culturally related but politically disparate groups joined together and sought common symbols of their new identity (cf. Stahl 1969).

Although administrative and political needs were efficiently fulfilled by encouraging tribalism, the economic demands of colonialism required a quite different response. European investments in land, industry, and commerce required a work force to be drawn from the African population; such a process stimulated the emergence of multitribal urban centers. The European presence also allowed for a greater degree of internal rural migration on an individual basis as some Africans sought to take advantage of virgin agricultural land in other parts of the colony. The emergence of these migrant, polyethnic communities, although a direct by-product of the colonial system, was treated with some suspicion, and they were considered to be a disorganized mass of "detribalized" Africans.

Fieldwork carried out in Mto wa Mbu, a polyethnic rural community in Masai District of northern Tanzania, during 1968–1969, provided the opportunity to contrast official attitudes and policies toward the tribal and nontribal population during the colonial and independence periods. The community was first settled by a handful of migrants in the early 1920s in an unoccupied, but potentially fertile, agricultural area on the western boundary of Masailand. Over the years other migrants arrived from less favorable parts of the country in a steady stream until the population had reached 3,500 by 1969. The inhabitants represented approximately seventy different tribal backgrounds but used the term Waswahili to define the ethnic composition of the community. The Masai on the plains just outside of the settlement also referred to the villagers of Mto wa Mbu as Waswahili. The term Waswahili has been defined in various ways in the anthropological literature (Eastman 1971). Most persons who identify themselves or are identified by others as Waswahili speak Kiswahili as a first or second language. However, adherence to Islam, also commonly associated with the Waswahili, is not universal. Waswahili is best thought of as representing a group of people exhibiting a certain cosmopolitan lifestyle and having cultural traits unrelated to a specific locality within East Africa (Arens 1975). As we can see the group does not even meet the minimal definition of a tribe because today locality is not involved, although it seems to have been in the past (Prins 1967).

Although the colonial system may have been largely responsible for creating conditions favorable to the founding of Mto wa Mbu, the official attitude toward the village could best be described as disinterested. For example, the total amount of information available on Mto wa Mbu during the era of British rule consists of two brief mentions in the District Book and a small file largely concerned with matters pertaining to the years just prior to independence. During this period the administrative projects and services were directed primarily toward the Masai. This focus was quite natural because the overwhelming majority of the residents of the district were Masai and their problems should have assumed paramount importance. This concern reflected not only a practical approach to government but also a philosophical orientation which stressed the value of the continuity of indigenous societies. In addition, many European officials had a positive attitude to the Masai, whom they considered to be a proud, independent people unwilling to change their traditional ways. Paradoxically, other groups more responsive to changes and showing an inclination toward "westernization" were less admired and also presented greater administrative problems. It was not that the colonial government was unconcerned with improvements in the territory but rather that its policies were aimed at producing gradual changes without radically upsetting the mode of life of the peoples involved or affecting traditional relationships between various groups (Bates 1965).

Mto wa Mbu provides a striking contrast to this situation because it was established during the colonial era and had a polyethnic population which de-emphasized tribal identity. As an anomalous agricultural community within an immense area populated by cattle-keeping people, it was all but overlooked during the British administration of the district. Also, because it was populated by migrants from other areas and therefore lacked a traditional political structure, it had to be dealt with differently from other parts of the district. Along with the lack of a traditional system of authority, the mixture of residents meant that a single body of customary law could not be applied in the community. This problem further compounded the confusion and aura of untidiness which surrounded the settlement. The response of district officials was to appoint one of the local residents *jumbe* (an office which entailed the responsibility of maintaining law and order, hearing cases, mediating disputes, and collecting local taxes). During the entire period, no development projects were initiated, few services were provided to the residents, and official visits by administrators were infrequent. The same conditions prevailed for all other such "alien" agricultural settlements in Masailand.

With the coming of Independence in 1961, the situation altered radically. The departure of the British and the installation of an African administration was accompanied by a discernible shift in attention by the new regime away from the scattered homesteads and hamlets of the countryside towards more densely populated rural settlements like Mto wa Mbu. For the Masai District, this meant that the numerous pastoralists dispersed throughout the area were no longer of greater significance than the inhabitants of the agricultural settlements, which had emerged during the years of British rule.

This shift in orientation and values was due to a number of factors stemming generally from policy decisions formulated at the national level by the new government. First, the Tanzanian government decided to encourage rural rather than urban industrial development. Because the overwhelming majority of the rural residents are small-scale cultivators, an emphasis was placed on agricultural development. Second, this program of rural development involved an attempt to provide for the inhabitants of the countryside greater social services than they had previously received under the British. This meant encouraging more compact rural settlements and giving those already in existence more importance as centers for these services. It was decided that, for economic and administrative purposes, these central locations could more efficiently serve the needs of the inhabitants of the village and surrounding countryside (Nyerere 1967). Mto wa Mbu was a natural site in light of the policy because it already exhibited the necessary characteristics for the implementation of the new goals. Third, a reorganization of the governmental structure, involving the creation of smaller administrative units below the district level, resulted in the creation of the Mto wa Mbu Division, with the community serving as headquarters for a large area, including a portion of the outlying Masai plains. In effect, part of traditional Masai country fell under the jurisdiction of Mto wa Mbu; previously the opposite had been the case.

In addition to these explicit policy formulations, other factors underlie the increased importance of these communities. The replacement of British officials by Africans was also accompanied by a change in attitude toward the Masai. The typical African administrator does not see the Masai and other conservative groups as "noble savages" but rather as backward peoples lacking the proper consciousness necessary for contributing to the growth of a modern progressive nation. As an indication of this attitude, the new administration has subjected the Masai to programs that encourage them to wear trousers and shirts in place of their traditional cloaks and to stop piercing their ears and practicing other customs that are considered barbaric by many other citizens.

This attitude was vividly illustrated in 1968 on the occasion of the official opening of the new homes constructed in Mto wa Mbu by the government's National Housing Corporation, part of the rural development program. On the appointed day, a number of important regional party and government officials were on hand to participate in the ceremony. Hundreds of local residents had gathered at the site. A few dozen Masai, who had been coaxed into the village by the TANU party chairman for the occasion, also lingered on the fringes of the crowd in a group. During the ceremony, one of the government speakers took it upon himself to castigate the Masai for their relative backwardness. He compared them to the people of Mto wa Mbu, whom he described in positive terms because of their concern for change and improvement. The villagers listened with pride and glee, but the Masai were not amused by his references to them. The turnabout in official position on the Masai could not have been more clearly conveyed to all concerned.

Finally, the fact that these communities were important rural outposts during the independence movement and at present give firm support to the party has not been lost on the government. For example, the Masai and other such groups in the vicinity, such as the Iraqw and Wambugwe, took little interest in political matters during the colonial era. But the residents of Mto wa Mbu organized the first local branch of TANU in the district, from whence it spread to other small settlements. The response of the government has been to involve these centers of strength in the machinery of rural development and administration.

All these factors resulted in the establishment at Mto wa Mbu of a local court with two trained magistrates and a police post, the opening of a dispensary with a small hospital, and the expansion of the primary school. The increased importance of the community was also reflected by an influx of government employees and various other officials, such as two rural development officers, an agricultural and fishery officer, a health inspector, a village executive officer, and others whose primary duties were related to the developmental needs of Mto wa Mbu. The presence of these individuals in addition to the school staff, medical personnel, court officials, policemen, and nearby employees of a national park has also produced a group of residents who are dependent on the goods of the local economy. In the decade since Independence, the village has taken on a new vitality and is rapidly becoming an important center in northern Tanzania.

The present situation can be contrasted with the one during the colonial period when the inhabitants of Mto wa Mbu were left to their own devices. The community has always, even during the era of British rule, reflected what was new and changing in the country. However, under the European administration, it was ignored in favor of what was traditional and stable. After Independence this growing village has been recognized as representative not only of what was new, but also of what was desired, and has thus been given strong government support. Mto wa Mbu reflects the new Tanzania; the surrounding countryside represents the old. This reality is understood and appreciated by the residents of the community. They consider themselves to be forward-looking and in many ways citizens of a new country as compared with the neighboring Masai and Iraqw, whom they see as relics of the colonial past.

The changeover in administrative and developmental emphasis was accompanied by a discernible shift in attitude regarding ethnic identity in Tanzania, with specific reference to tribal and nontribal affiliation. As mentioned, the residents of Mto wa Mbu referred to themselves as Waswahili, a nontribal distinction. Other polyethnic rural villages in Tanzania use similar terms of ethnic identification. The prestige accorded these terms has undergone a reorientation over time and is of significant concern.

More important, all aliens, whether originally from the same areas or from a number of different ones, will generally form a loose community based on social interaction in opposition to the original inhabitants. As a result of this social circumscription, a different lifestyle develops. In Tanzania, because of historical circumstances, one of the inevitable results of occupying an alien status is by necessity the use of Kiswahili (the *lingua franca* of East Africa). In addition, in immigrant multitribal communities, beliefs often associated with a specific type of traditional social structure are abandoned while others are adopted. The acceptance of Islam is a case in point, but conversion to Christianity is a similar indication as well. As world religions, both provide a basis for interaction across ethnic boundaries. They result in a broadening of social horizons and an identification with larger social groupings bearing no relationship to a specific territory.

In Weber's terms (Gerth and Mills 1958), the "social estimation of honor" associated with the Waswahili has an interesting and changing history. In the past, particularly during the colonial period, the prestige accorded this status grouping was low. The failure to be identified closely with a particular locality and culture, a tribe in other words, carried with it a negative social value. It meant a lack of pedigree, a blank genealogy, and the absence of a legitimate rationale for living in a particular community. To the Africans it implied that the individual was possibly a descendant of a slave and, therefore, a social inferior. The colonial administration considered a Mswahili (singular form) as someone who was not living with his "own" people and, consequently, was a potential deviant or troublemaker of some sort. It is not surprising, therefore, that during the colonial era few were willing to identify with the status. Those few who did so were resigned to their inferior position in the community.

Today, in independent Tanzania the situation has been reversed dramatically. Many of the social characteristics of a Mswahili, which were devalued during the colonial era when "tribalism" as we know it was fostered, are today highly appreciated and encouraged. The failure to identify with a specific, local cultural group, the willingness to take up a new residence, the disregard of tribal differences, and the acceptance of one of the world religions are all in accord with the developmental policies of the state, which considers "tribalism" an anathema. Those individuals characterized by this lifestyle were incipient nationalists prior to the first stirrings for independence, and it is not surprising that polyethnic centers, both rural and urban, were the outposts of the independence movement. Today, it is these individuals who also identify most closely with the state. Consequently, the social esteem accorded the Swahili lifestyle has increased tremendously over the past decade and the communities associated with it have been rewarded by the national government. At the same time, the number of people claiming the status for themselves has multiplied since Independence.

In Mto wa Mbu, the residents often contrasted their Swahili culture and outlook on life with that of the surrounding Masai, Iraqw, and Wambugwe. These self-identified Waswahili of Mto wa Mbu consider their lifestyle far superior to that of those they refer to as "tribesmen." Their status is superior because to them it represents sophistication and modernity. They see themselves as the bearers of a new culture in Tanzania and as the wave of the future; the tribesmen represent to them an archaic lifestyle more befitting the colonial and precolonial periods.

Within the community itself, as one would assume, there is great cultural variation in many respects. Nevertheless, as opposed to the immediate outside world, they see themselves as a single people, and not just because of the few shared common cultural features, such as the Swahili language. More significant is their agreed-upon perception of their common nontribal status in a modern nation. It is this social fact that serves as a communal binding force.

CONCLUSION

This essay has attempted to illustrate the flexible character of ethnic identity in Tanzania by contrasting the situation during the colonial and independence periods. At the present time it is difficult to assess the significance of tribes as a principle of organization for the precolonial era. However, events which have taken place since independence just over a decade ago clearly underscore the notion that ethnic groups and identification are by no means permanent fixtures. In Tanzania this process has involved an ideological and organizational de-emphasis on tribal identity and a corresponding emergence of the Waswahili as a more positive ethnic category because it is more closely associated with the nation than with any particular locality within it. The processual character of ethnicity in recent years indicates that Fried's comment (1967) regarding tribes as a response to the era of European political dominance is by no means an idle suggestion.

The preceding discussion is not meant to imply that traditional tribal identity is completely insignificant in modern Tanzania. In some situations, such as at the level of interpersonal relations, shared ethnicity may be a relevant consideration for the actors. Even in Mto wa Mbu, where "tribalism" was actively discouraged, it was still possible to observe the manner in which a certain segment of the population emphasized their common tribal background in instances of economic competition. However, at the national level, Tanzania has been able to defuse the issue of tribalism, especially as compared to its neighbors in East Africa (Bennett 1969). For example, it seems that in Kenya today, to identify oneself as a Kikuyu or Luo is still a matter of some relevance, if not in fact of national ideology. However, it must be noted that this variety of "tribalism" is quite different from that of the colonial period. In independent Africa, common ethnicity and tribal solidarity is often employed as a conscious strategy by the participants in the struggle for scarce economic and political rewards (cf. Cohen 1969). To define this phenomenon as a form of "tribalism" directly resulting from a traditional precolonial state of affairs is simplistic and misleading. The tribal factor, which is so readily apparent, often serves to obfuscate a developing class struggle in which ethnic and economic positions may coincide.

Possibly the clearest example of the flexible character of ethnicity in East Africa as a response to external factors is provided by the example of the "Arab" community of the Kenyan coast. During the colonial period, this ethnic label conveyed far greater prestige than that of any African tribal identity. As could be expected, many claims to this distinction were often rather dubious. Individuals, whose families had lived on the coast for centuries, who spoke little if any Arabic, and who were physically indistinguishable from Africans, sought to include themselves in this category. Such attempts were not always accepted by others, especially those who considered themselves to be "pure Arabs" physically and culturally (Lienhardt 1968). With the advent of Independence, however, many of the same individuals who had previously claimed to be Arabs reverted to Africans, as the status of Arabs declined.

The examples discussed in this essay indicate that individuals or groups in many instances can choose identity from among a number of alternatives; ethnicity, therefore, is not necessarily a fixed form. The ethnic label selected and employed will depend upon situational factors involving a consideration of the expected relative gains to come from the choice. A comparison of the situation in colonial and postcolonial East Africa has shown that the relevant factors may change very rapidly. Thus, it is to be expected that ethnic groups may expand or contract in a short period of time.

REFERENCES

ARENS, W.
1975 The Waswahili: the social history of an ethnic group. *Africa* 45: 426–438.

ARGYLE, W. J.
1969 "European nationalism and African tribalism," in *Tradition and transition in East Africa*. Edited by P. H. Gulliver. London: Routledge and Kegan Paul.

BATES, MARGARET L.
1965 "Tanganyika: changes in African life," in *History of East Africa*, volume two. Edited by V. Harlow and E. M. Chilver. London: Oxford University Press.

BENNETT, GEORGE
1969 "Tribalism in politics," in *Tradition and transition in East Africa*. Edited by P. H. Gulliver. London: Routledge and Kegan Paul.

COHEN, ABNER
1969 *Custom and politics in urban Africa*. London: Routledge and Kegan Paul.

EASTMAN, CAROL
1971 Who are the Waswahili? *Africa* 41:228–236.

FRIED, MORTON H.
1967 "On the concepts of 'tribe' and tribal society," in *Essays on the problems of tribe*. Edited by June Helm. Proceedings of the American Ethnological Society.

GERTH, H. H., C. WRIGHT MILLS
1958 *From Max Weber: essays in sociology*. New York: Oxford University Press.

GULLIVER, P. H.
  1969   "Introduction," in *Tradition and transition in East Africa*. Edited by
          P. H. Gulliver. London: Routledge and Kegan Paul.
LIENHARDT, PETER
  1968   *The medicine man*. Oxford: Clarendon.
NYERERE, JULIUS
  1967   *Freedom and unity*. London: Oxford University Press.
PRINS, A. H. J.
  1967   *The Swahili-speaking peoples of Zanzibar and the East African coast*.
          London: International African Institute.
STAHL, KATHLEEN M.
  1969   "The Chagga," in *Tradition and transition in East Africa*. Edited by
          P. H. Gulliver. London: Routledge and Kegan Paul.

SECTION THREE

Contact, Acculturation, and Boundary Maintenance

Region, Religion, and Language: Parameters of Identity in the Process of Acculturation

MAHADEV L. APTE

INTRODUCTION

Anthropological studies of the phenomenon known as acculturation or culture contact generally entail many prerequisites and subsequent analyses of its several relevant features (Beals 1953; Herskovits 1938; Redfield et al. 1936). Among the prerequisites are the ethnographies of the two or more societies which come in contact and the duration and nature of such contact. For instance, is the contact between two societies of equal status or is one society dominant? Is the contact due to geographical contiguity or to migration, etc. Analyses may focus on such aspects as the following: (1) changes that may occur in the observable cultural traits of the populations in contact: for example, changes in clothing, diet, marriage patterns, agricultural and other occupational techniques, ceremonial behavior, family structure, child rearing, etc.; (2) attitudes of the members of each society toward such material changes: their acceptance of, or indifference or resistance to them; and (3) consistency or discrepancy between objective changes and subjective ethnic identity.

The aim of this paper is to describe briefly an extended culture contact situation resulting from the migration of one community to a different linguistic region and to analyze the ethnic identity problems faced by its members.

Although a single criterion for a distinct collective identity, such as language, may be available to the members of a minority community, other criteria may be equally influential. Often the choice of a particular

Fieldwork on which this paper is based was done in the state of Tamilnadu in South India from September 1971 to July 1972. I am grateful to the American Institute of Indian Studies for a Senior Research Fellowship which enabled me to undertake the research.

criterion or the different priorities given to various criteria is the result of socially relevant factors (Barth 1969:15) and motivations of the minority community members. In populations which are already stratified, culture contact over an extended period may develop into congruence of codes and values, if structural parallels exist in the ascribed social status of various groups within the two populations. In such cases, change in ethnic identity from one group to its structural counterpart is conceivable.

In the South Asian region there exists a caste and/or *varṇa* structure which can be considered a special case of a stratified polyethnic system. Migrants from one region to another may therefore find it convenient to acquire the sociocultural identity of structurally parallel caste or *varṇa* groups in the dominant population in the new region.

The main thesis of this paper is that, in the South Asian context, groups with high ascribed social status, namely Brahmans, easily adapt to the regional identity because they can readily associate themselves with the Sanskritic Great Tradition[1] shared by most regions in South Asia. Similar opportunities are available to groups with low ascribed social status only if comparable groups exist in the dominant population. If, however, the structural parallels do not exist, or if a group is desirous of upward social mobility and seeks the goal of higher social ranking, then the factors emphasized in ethnic identity may be an affiliation to a broader reference group outside the new region and a continuation of religious practices emanating from the original home region. Thus the available criterion of language for the retention of a distinct identity for a whole community may be superseded by other criteria such as religion, region, or *varṇa* status.

BACKGROUND

The community under discussion is that of the Marathi-speakers (also Mahrattas) in the state of Tamilnadu in South India, which consists of about 50,000 people. Marathi, an Indo-Aryan language, is spoken by approximately 41 million people in the state of Maharashtra on the west coast of India. Tamil, the official language of the state of Tamilnadu, belongs to the Dravidian language family and is spoken by approximately 37 million people.

The present-day Marathi-speakers in Tamilnadu are in most cases

---

[1]   Starting with Redfield (1955), anthropologists who have worked in South Asia have generally recognized two distinct traditions. These are known as Great Tradition and Little Tradition. The former generally refers to existing Sanskritic literature consisting of religious scriptures and other works on philosophy, law, polity, literary criticism, and epistemology in general; and to the pan-Indian religious ideology and practices emanating from this literature. The latter refers to localized innovations and interpretations of the great body of Sanskritic religious and secular literature.

descendants of Marathi-speakers who immigrated approximately 200 years ago. The initial migration into Tamilnadu was due to the establishment of a small Maharashtrian principality in Tanjore District toward the end of the seventeenth century. The Maratha kings ruled Tanjore District and some of the surrounding areas for about 150 years. There were later migrations of Marathi-speakers during the nineteenth century. Although Marathi-speakers are scattered all over Tamilnadu in small numbers, they are primarily concentrated in four districts, the largest group being in the city of Madras.

There are three major caste groups among the Marathi-speakers in Tamilnadu: Deshastha Brahmans, who were closely connected with the Tanjore kings as administrators and priests; tailors, who appear to be later migrants; and Marathas,[2] who are Kshatriyas [warriors] and were the ruling caste of the Tanjore kingdom. The Brahmans, although still living in large numbers in the city of Tanjore, are now concentrated in the city of Madras. Their migration from Tanjore District to the urban center of Madras began about seventy years ago. The tailors have spread all over Tamilnadu and have sizable groups in many major cities. A large number of them live in the city of Madras. Except for a few scattered families who are related to the former Tanjore kings and still live in Tanjore City and the surrounding areas, the Marathas are mostly concentrated in the northern part of Tamilnadu and are primarily agriculturists. They also have a sizable population in the city of Madras.

LINGUISTIC PROFILE OF THE COMMUNITY

Members of the Marathi-speaking community still use their native language, but it is generally restricted to the home and to interaction with the immediate and extended family. The preferred second language is Tamil, the state language of administration. Most members of the community speak Tamil with native fluency and seem quite at home conversing with Tamil-speakers in all types of social interaction. Thus the community is clearly bilingual, although the individual members are aware that they can be identified as a separate linguistic group. The objective criterion of separate language usage is sufficient to distinguish the Marathi-speakers as a separate community from the rest of the Tamil population (Vreeland 1958:86) and this seems reinforced by the subjective criterion, namely the awareness of their distinct linguistic identity on the part of the Marathi-speakers. This is also substantiated by the fact that since the

---

[2]   Everywhere in India except in the state of Maharashtra, all Marathi-speakers are known as *Marathas* or *Mahrattas*, irrespective of their sociocultural background, including caste. Within Maharashtra, however, the term is used only to refer to a caste group with Kshatriya status.

taking of censuses began in 1891, the number of Marathi-speakers has not altered in any substantial way.

SEPARATE GROUP IDENTITIES WITHIN THE COMMUNITY

Although the objective criterion of language exists to separate the Marathi-speakers as a community distinct from the dominant population, the separate group identities within the community seem much more influential and dominant than the common identity. These collective identities are based on caste status, socioeconomic conditions, distinct historical and sociocultural traditions, and religious ideologies. The three caste groups in the community appear isolated from each other; each has its own formal organizations, and there is very little contact and communication among them (Apte 1974). Each group seems motivated in a different direction and appears to respond differently to the existing sociocultural, political, and economic conditions. Marathas as a caste group are not relevant to this discussion. Judging by their sociocultural and historical background, however, they show characteristics similar to those of tailors rather than of Brahmans. Thus the major distinction appears to be between Brahmans and non-Brahmans. Each of these groups exhibits different trends of ethnic identity, as reflected in their attitudes and actions discussed below.

Brahmans

Brahmans as a group within the Marathi-speaking community in Tamilnadu are the most advanced in terms of education, prestige, jobs, and income. As late as the 1930s many of them owned land and had influential positions in the social structure of villages, primarily in Tanjore District. Even today many are absentee landlords and have ancestral houses and property there. Their efforts to organize themselves as a community and especially to help their group members get higher education go back to the beginning of this century. In 1912 an educational fund was established to give financial support to young Brahman boys and girls for higher education. The association has thrived through the years and now has substantial endowment funds. The majority of the Brahmans interviewed had finished school and many of them have college degrees. This educational level has been achieved not only by the younger generation but also by the previous two generations.

In terms of economic conditions, the Brahman group seems much better off than its non-Brahman counterpart. Brahmans hold the highest percentage of white collar and professional jobs and also have a higher average income than the tailors or the Marathas. Many of them hold high administrative positions in private firms and in state and central government offices. The number of Brahmans who are engineers, doctors, lawyers, and college or university professors is also quite high in comparison to the numbers of tailors or Marathas holding such jobs. Available sources indicate that the situation was the same in the 1930s.[3] Thus it is obvious that Brahmans as a group are socioeconomically more advanced than tailors.

Until recently, the Brahman group in the Tamil population enjoyed a long period as a political and cultural elite. This was due, to a considerable extent, to their religious domination of the rest of the population, to their superior position as the inheritors of the Great Tradition of Hinduism, and also to their favorable attitude toward Western education (Béteille 1969:66–67, 165; Hardgrave 1966:213). All the Marathi-speaking Brahmans shared in this elite status and the advantages which accrued from it.

The Marathi Brahman group has a great deal in common with its counterpart in the Tamil population, the Tamil Brahmans, with whom they share a number of rituals, religious rites, and extensive philosophical and classical literary knowledge, all part of the Great Tradition of Hinduism. They practice a number of religious restrictions similar to those followed by Tamil Brahmans, reflecting their common beliefs in pollution and purity. The divisions between Marathi Brahmans are closely linked to those between Tamil Brahmans, and are based primarily on religious and philosophical interpretations of Vedic texts. The two major religious sects among Tamil Brahmans are that of the Smarthas [worshipers of Shiva and believers in *advaita* philosophy] and that of the Shri Vaishnavas [worshipers of Vishnu] (Béteille 1969:71). The Marathi Brahmans follow the same two sects, although the majority of them appear to be Smarthas and the distinction does not exist to the same rigid degree. More Brahmans in the Marathi-speaking community in Tamilnadu know the Devanagari script than non-Brahmans, not because they read Marathi literature but because they read Sanskrit religious scriptures.[4]

In recent years the social, political, and economic domination by the Brahmans in Tamilnadu has suffered a considerable setback because of the development of non-Brahman political forces, especially those in the Dravida Munnetra Kazhagam Party which now controls the state legislature. As a result, the Brahman community generally feels discriminated against with regard to higher education and jobs in government services

[3] The economic inquiry undertaken by Rao and Rao (1937) included observation of family size, education, type of occupation, income, housing, and food consumption among Brahmans and non-Brahmans in the Marathi-speaking community in Madras. The conclusion of the inquiry was that Brahmans as a group were socioeconomically much better off than non-Brahmans.

[4] Both Marathi and Sanskrit are written in the Devanagari script.

(Béteille 1969:164–168). The Marathi Brahmans share this feeling with the Tamil Brahmans and complain about the deliberate discrimination against them and the lack of opportunities in various fields, even for qualified persons. Thus the Marathi Brahmans seem to identify themselves more with Brahmans in South India and to have little affinity with the Maharashtrians in Maharashtra.

Tailors

The tailors as a group appear to be more evenly distributed throughout Tamilnadu than the Brahmans, although they too are concentrated in large numbers in the four northern districts including Madras. They are more recent arrivals than the Brahmans. Most of them started their migration to the south with the British army camps approximately 150 years ago.

The majority of the tailors continue their traditional occupation, either in their own tailoring shops or working for others. Those who are not tailors are in related businesses, such as cloth selling or buying. The level of education among the tailors is low, and they fall into a much lower income group than the Brahmans. Very few of them hold white collar jobs and even fewer are in any high-status professions. No caste group comparable to the Marathi tailors exists in the dominant Tamil population. (Their only competitors are the Muslim tailors.)

The tailors are organized into formal associations in almost all towns in which they live in substantial numbers.[5] The goals of all tailor organizations appear primarily to be caste solidarity and high *varṇa* identity. The usual pattern of such organizations is to form a committee of active members of the community, to collect funds, and to help the community members in whatever way possible. Most of the tailors' associations in various towns own buildings specially constructed so that they can be rented out for marriages and other special ceremonies. These buildings are provided without charge to community members for religious or other functions but are rented to those outside the community. Often such buildings are the primary source of income for the associations.

The tailors seem to desire a high *varṇa* identity. Because of their traditional occupation they are included in the third category of *vaishya* of the classical fourfold *varṇa* division. They claim Kshatriya status, however, by calling themselves Bhavasara Kshatriyas. They have myths which suggest that originally the tailors were Kshatriyas [warriors]; but in order to survive during a mass destruction of the Kshatriyas by a Brah-

---

[5]   Tailors are concentrated in large numbers in the following cities and towns of Tamilnadu: Coimbatore, Kumbhakonam, Madurai, Salem, Tirapattur, Vellore, and Walajah Pet. There are voluntary associations of tailors in all of them.

man in ancient times, they concealed their Kshatriya identity and pre-
tended to be dyers and tailors, as advised by a goddess. They have
imitated many of the religious and cultural practices of the upper
*varna*s. Thus their efforts seem to be directed toward a broader and
higher *varna* identity and the status associated with it. All associations of
this kind in Tamilnadu are known as Bhavasara Kshatriya Associations.

The organizational pattern among the tailors in Tamilnadu is a microcosm of similar but larger-scale activities undertaken by the tailors and
dyers in all parts of south, west, and north India. These groups started
their organizational attempts at the national level as early as 1911, when
the first all-India Conference of the Bhavasara Kshatriyas was held in
Dharwar in Mysore State. Since then the tradition of holding such conferences has continued, the last one having been held in Poona, Maharashtra
in December 1972. The main office of the all-India organization known
as Akhil Bharatiya Bhavasara Kshatriya Mahasabha [All-India Bhavasara Kshatriya Association] is located in Bombay. Histories of the
Bhavasara Kshatriyas have been written in which elaborate origin myths
are told and their claims to Kshatriya status are justified. The primary
emphasis of the national organization is to encourage caste organization
in various parts of the country and to encourage self-help among caste
members toward better socioeconomic and educational status. The
prominent members of the communities in different parts of India have
built temples and hostels for students and have undertaken other similar
activities for the benefit of the tailor communities. A monthly caste
newsletter called *Bhavasar Jyoti* is published from Poona, Maharashtra.

The religious ideology and behavior of the tailors connect them closely
to their original home region of Maharashtra. Tailors are worshipers of
Panduranga or Vitthal, a deity associated with an old and popular religious sect in Maharashtra, the Vārkarī sect (Deleury 1960). This particular sect still survives and has a large following all over Maharashtra. One
of the important marks of affiliation with this sect is the semiannual
pilgrimage to Pandharpur, where the oldest temple to this deity is located.
From the thirteenth to the sixteenth century, a number of Marathi saints
composed devotional songs in praise of the deity, and these are still
popular among Marathi-speakers both within and outside Maharashtra.
One of these saints, Namdev, was a tailor. He is one of the most popular
saints and is said to have traveled as far north as Punjab to spread the
worship of Panduranga and the philosophy of his religious sect. The
tailors in Tamilnadu seem closely associated with this religious sect partly
because of Namdev. In many Tamil cities and towns with a large tailor
community, temples to Panduranga have been built and are usually under
the control of the local community associations.[6] In many others, there

[6] There are Panduranga temples in Coimbatore, Kumbhakonam, Madras, Vellore, and
other cities in Tamilnadu.

exist active *bhajan* [devotional song] groups which meet every week to sing the devotional songs in praise of Panduranga composed by Namdev and his contemporaries.

Thus the tailor community appears to retain its regional religious identity which has a reference point outside Tamilnadu. At the same time the tailors are interested in upward social mobility for their whole caste group and have attempted to achieve it by claiming a higher *varna* status, as described earlier.

CONCLUSIONS

These rather brief descriptions of the two groups within the Marathi-speaking community in Tamilnadu clearly suggest that language, although retained by the community members in the home environment even after an absence from the homeland of more than 100 years, does not play a significant role in creating a conscious ethnic identity for the entire community. Instead, each group appears to have a distinct focus of self-identity and emphasizes different criteria for it. The Brahmans lean toward their counterparts in the dominant population for ideological reasons and also because of common bonds at the economic, educational, and sociocultural levels. The tailors emphasize the *varna* identity within the framework of pan-Indian social structure, and their regional affiliation to their homeland in terms of their religious behavior. There is very little communication and interaction between Brahmans and tailors. Each group is thus self-perpetuating and uninterested in relating itself to any other status group within the minority community objectively identified as such. This conclusion is further supported by the existence of separate voluntary associations for each group, separate residential areas,[7] and separate modes of religious, occupational, and educational behavior.

The primary *raison d'être* for these different groups thus appears to be the socially ascribed status, which determines the nature of self-identity and motivation for either assimilation into or distinctness from the dominant population of Tamilnadu. The primary parameters of identity in this culture contact situation appear to be caste, religion, and region rather than language, although language is the main objective criterion distinguishing this community from the dominant population.

---

[7]   In the city of Madras, Brahmans are primarily concentrated in such areas as Mylapore and Triplicane. The tailors, however, are scattered through all parts including some suburban areas.

REFERENCES

APTE, MAHADEV L.
1974   Voluntary associations and problems of fusion and fission in a minority community in south India. *Journal of Voluntary Action Research* 3(1):43–48.

BARTH, F., *editor*
1969   *Ethnic groups and boundaries: the social organization of culture difference.* Boston: Little, Brown.

BEALS, RALPH
1953   "Acculturation," in *Anthropology today.* Edited by A. L. Kroeber, 621–641. Chicago: University of Chicago Press.

BÉTEILLE, A.
1969   *Castes: old and new.* Bombay: Asia Publishing House.

DELEURY, G. A.
1960   *The cult of Vithoba.* Poona, India: Deccan College.

HARDGRAVE, R. L.
1966   "Religion, politics, and the DMK," in *South Asian politics and religion.* Edited by Donald E. Smith, 213–234. Princeton, N. J.: Princeton University Press.

HERSKOVITS, M. J.
1938   *Acculturation: the study of culture contact.* New York: J. J. Augustin.

RAO, T. RAMCHANDRA, B. R. DHONDU RAO
1937   "South Indian Maharashtrians," in *Silver jubilee souvenir.* Edited by N. R. Kedari Rao. Madras: Mahratta Educational Fund.

REDFIELD, R., R. LINTON, M. J. HERSKOVITS
1936   Outline for the study of acculturation. *American Anthropologist,* (n.s.) 38:149–152.
1955   The social organization of tradition. *The Far Eastern Quarterly* 15(1):13–21.

VREELAND, H. H.
1958   "The concept of ethnic groups as related to whole societies," in *Report of the ninth annual round table meeting on linguistics and language study.* Edited by W. M. Austin, 81–88. Georgetown Monograph Series on Languages and Linguistics 11. Washington, D.C.: Georgetown University Press.

Contrasting Value Orientation of Peasant Communities and its Persistence into Modernization

BERTALAN ANDRÁSFALVY

The ethnological problems of Europe cannot be investigated without historical research. Likewise the economic and political problems of the historical change of populations cannot be investigated without using ethnographic materials.

The area of this investigation is the hilly region of the Meçsek in southern Transdanubia, Hungary (where the maximum elevation is 682 meters). It is a limestone area, covered in varying thicknesses by clay and yellow soil. In the valleys are meadows; on the hillsides and hilltops are vineyards and woods. The plowed fields are in sheltered spots and the steep slopes are covered with forests. It is called *Hegyhát* "Hill region" and *Volgység* "valley land" and consists of seventy-six villages, some large, some small.

A few Slavic place names lead to the supposition that some Slavic peoples still lived in the wooded parts of the hills in the ninth and tenth centuries when the Hungarians, coming from the east, settled there. In the Middle Ages, southern Hungary was a densely populated, productive land. In the *Hegyhát* and *Volgység* there was about the same number of villages as there is now, but their populations were smaller than in the fertile plains, and probably poorer. The expanding Osmali Turkish empire reached the territory of Hungary at the end of the fifteenth century. In 1526, at the defeat of Mohacs, the Hungarian king and the greater part of his army died on the battlefield. In 1534, the town of Pécs — the economic, religious, and administrative center of the region — was occupied by the Turks, and thus the *Hegyhát* and the *Volgység* fell completely under Turkish domination. For 150 years most of the country was a constant field of battle. During this time the more productive and abundant regions of the plains were destroyed. In 1686, when the Turks were driven out of Hungary, the most densely populated regions of the devastated country were those few areas where the inhabitants could find refuge in forests or marshlands. Meanwhile the abundant productive plains had become practically uninhabited.

In the territory of the *Hegyhát* and *Volgység*, forty-four villages were listed in a register dating from 1711. The least fertile hilly regions were the most densely populated. In 1714 new inhabitants came to the depopulated area: Southern Slavs, then large numbers of German settlers (coming from various regions between the Rhineland and Lower Austria). In the *Hegyhát* they first settled in the flatter and more fertile regions of the north. Later immigrations resulted in a few entirely German villages within the Hungarian territory.

The most conspicious trait is the growth of German-speaking groups within those villages which formerly were inhabited only by Hungarians. Old registers show how this happened. In the Hungarian village one or two German artisans appeared as well as small farmers and usually a miller. Within a few decades each bought a plot and his name appeared in the register as a serf paying tax on his land. Meanwhile, additional German artisan farmers appeared in the village and all endeavored to acquire land.

After a hundred years the German population had become more numerous than the Hungarian in several villages. By 1900 there were only ten villages left where hardly any Germans lived, and only thirty-one villages remained where the majority was Hungarian. Twenty villages may be regarded as German, and in fifteen villages the Germans were already in the majority. Of the thirty-one villages where the Hungarians were formerly in the majority, the Germans had gained a majority in seven by 1941. In 1900 the number of Hungarian and German inhabitants was equal. The Southern Slav population did not reach ten percent of the whole population even at the time of their settlement. Many a Southern Slav family moved on during the eighteenth century, and those remaining rapidly decreased in number and became assimilated, moving back to Yugoslavia during the period between the two wars. During World War II some of the Germans took a stand for Hitler and the ideas of his empire. In 1946–1947 half of the Germans were resettled in Germany and in their place refugees and displaced Hungarians coming from Rumania, Czechoslovakia, and Yugoslavia were settled and given land, along with landless folk coming from other parts of the country.

Doubtless the German settlers arriving in the eighteenth century received special privileges; the local estate owners, mostly of German origin, as well as the administration, directed by Austrians, granted them favors which were not granted to native Hungarians. Even so, the vital expansion and growth of population, which meant simultaneously the restriction and impoverishment of the Hungarians, cannot be explained by these factors alone. In addition to the demographic features and the historical economic statistics, the contrasting value orientation of the two cultures with their power to direct behavior must be considered. The value orientation of these two cultures will be contrasted, making use of various data: nineteenth century descriptions, recent investigations and observations, interviews, and recordings of personal memoirs.

The difference between the two cultures cannot be accounted for simply by the difference in the mode of life between settlers and native inhabitants although that is part of it. The settlers were not bound by inherited tradition, while the behavior of the natives was bound by often irrational conventions and values. The myth of "ancient land," which gives an illusion of security but really provides no defense against poverty if production cannot keep up with modern standards, altered to cope with increasing demands. (With some variations, the contrast between German settlers and Hungarian natives may be found everywhere within the Carpathian Basin and also everywhere within Eastern Europe.)

The purpose of the investigation was to establish what ideals, what conceptions of desirable behavior, stood behind the two differing patterns. Both ideals may be distinctly outlined. The ideal of the Hungarian peasants of the eighteenth and nineteenth centuries was the country nobleman, the rural estate owner, magnanimous and extravagant; keen on fine clothes and fine horses; fond of festive occasions, music, company, gay merrymaking, hospitable, spending freely, and extraordinarily proud of all these qualities. The Germans, as settlers, aimed wisely to collect capital and their ambition was expansion. Their ideal was a calculating, thrifty, diligent citizen, taking every advantage of the opportunities arising from the blunders of others, a clever entrepreneur, a capitalist.

Before contrasting the two value orientations according to their differing ideals, the questions arises: where do these ideals originate? It is difficult to formulate the answer in a satisfactory manner. The feudal hierarchy of Western Europe arrived in Hungary belatedly and never developed in such a stable manner as elsewhere in Europe. Hungarian serfs lived in a freer way than did their fellows in western parts of Europe. Only after the peasant revolution of the sixteenth century was an attempt made to abolish the right of migration and even then it did not completely succeed. Within certain restrictions the serfs had a right to fish and to hunt, and certain acts of personal subordination were no longer practiced, such as the *ius primae noctus*. Hungary lagged behind Western and Central Europe in industrial and urban development.

Further improvement in endeavors to catch up and to eliminate the drawbacks of late development, seen at the beginning of the rise of an urban bourgeois class, were made impossible, first by the peasant war of 1514 then, from 1526 on, by the country-wide war. The 150 years of war was a period in which it was impossible for a class of citizens who did not belong within the boundaries of feudal society to develop or for their ideals to be formed. In contrast, this period offered constant possibilities for achieving distinction through military deeds, for rising socially through courage. A simple peasant without rights could become a soldier and later a nobleman. It was evident that for the mass of peasants no alternative for rising socially (or the illusion of doing so) existed, so they could have no other social ideal. After the Turkish wars, the Wars of Liberty (first of Ferenc Rákóczi in the eighteenth century, then of Lajos Kossuth in the nineteenth century) again created the possibility of achieving military noble virtues — irrational, uneconomic virtues. A similar social development led to similar value orientation among Poles, also. The heroes of Hungarian fairy tales and the figures shown in folk art — highwaymen with courageous qualities befitting a knight — also reflect this conception.

Meanwhile, the representatives of rational and successful bourgeois-capitalist virtues befitting traders and artisans, were mostly foreigners, Germans or Jews, despised because of their behavior and because of their foreignness, envied for their wealth and their success. This conception reflects the opinion of the feudal gentlemen, too, not only the peasants. Even after the liberation from feudal ties, the peasants, the former serfs, admired only those who had more land; in the eyes of peasant youth the most respected man was one who excelled in desirable and extreme manifestations of the nobleman's way of life. Being thrifty was equated with being mean and selfish; diligence equated with greed. All these qualities were despised and considered ridiculous.

The German settlers brought no fortune with them and hardly any beasts or fowl, only the simplest of agricultural tools. Even if there were farmers among them who had had land of their own in Germany, in a foreign climate, on unknown soil, and among unknown conditions, their farming experience had little value. The majority of them were landless peasants, day-laborers, rural craftsmen, agrarian proletarians who had found it hard to make a living at home. For a century their farming was in no respect more advanced than that ⅽ the native Hungarian peasants, either in quantity or in quality. Yet they brought along a different attitude toward production. The aim of producing commodities, a more advanced purpose than the aim of being self-sufficient, of achieving economic independence, along with farming in a rational manner as well as the system of inheritance, insured spectacular advancement for the settlers within a few decades. It was spectacular advancement for this manner of farming, and the qualities and virtues that belonged to it were in the eyes of the ancient inhabitants not only foreign and unknown but truly despised. The system of inheritance by the eldest son insured that the whole of the farm, the peasant estate, would be under the ownership of only one son. To pay the brothers their share of money, it was necessary to collaborate in a regular and well-planned manner in order to save and collect capital until the time came to divide the inheritance. The younger brother, who had learned a trade and received his inheritance in money, had such a fortune on his hands that he was able to establish a livelihood of his own and could buy real estate, as no Hungarian peasant could ever do. The Hungarian peasant, eager to buy the expensive and glittering articles of luxury which were offered in a world turning modern, wanting to imitate the gentlemen also in this respect, was at the same time a largely self-sufficient farmer in an anachronistic way and could easily receive the necessary loan from a German to keep up his prestige. But he was not in the economic position to pay back the loan. (The situation is similar to the time of the discoveries, when the white man bought big plots of land from the natives for but a few handfuls of colored beads.)

It is probable that the diligent, ambitious type of German living in the *Hegyhát* region, eagerly reacting to the possibilities of the market and making utmost use of his time and energy, developed into such an extreme example of his type through the spectacular success of his endeavors. The result was that this territory, which was originally less fertile, by the end of the nineteenth century surpassed the neighboring regions, including those where Germans were farming on better soil.

In the eyes of the *Hegyhát* Germans, the behavior of the Hungarians — easy-going, full of pride, prodigal, loving pomp, pathos and prestige — seemed just as ridiculous as the German thrift seemed in the eyes of the Hungarians. During the two centuries they lived side by side, the contrasting value orientations did not approach each other; they were not on the same level. Even though they depended on each other, the two systems became a challenge to each other. In many instances the Germans were apt to induce certain behavior on the part of the Hungarians which they could then make use of for their own profit and advancement. At the same time the Hungarians also induced the Germans to behave in an extreme manner by assuring them ground to advance. It is not surprising that Hungarian peasants also tried to keep up their nobleman-gentleman status through birth control (this they could also learn from the impoverished gentlefolk).

Though the origin of the two contrasting value orientations may be argued, their existence is a fact. The two systems are contrasted below; the traits among the *Hegyhát* Hungarians are listed first, then those among the *Hegyhát* Germans. The lettered items are approximate pairs of values. The sequence of the items is of no importance.

The value orientation and behavior of the *Hegyhát* Hungarians may be characterized as follows:

a. Every son received an equal share of the inheritance; to grant one or the other of the descendants an unreasonable advantage was considered unjust and unfair. It was considered equally unfair to send a child off to become an apprentice to an artisan, especially to a foreigner, or to be a servant. That was considered to be excluding him from his legitimate rights, his ancient heritage.

b. The farm aimed to be self-sufficient, to produce everything necessary and not be obliged to purchase anything. This aim was out of date by the nineteenth century and though only partly accomplished could still be observed in the twentieth century. Furthermore, the farmer tried to produce his own implements partly because of a lack of money. Occasionally the farmer was ready to accept any sort of odd job — day labor, transport, etc.

c. Such a self-sufficient type of farming with many kinds of work was characterized by rigid division of labor between men and women within the Hungarian peasant family. The wives and the daughters were busy spinning and weaving, as mentioned in descriptions of the last century. Contemporary authors considered it really curious that even those Germans who lived among Hungarians did not imitate them in the craft of weaving. And the Germans who lived in their own villages did so to an even lesser extent. If the size of the farm was larger than the family was able to handle, the Hungarians preferred to rent their land, but they did not allow their womenfolk to work in the fields.

d. Being self-sufficient insured a certain constancy of production and was an obstacle to reacting quickly and efficiently to the demands of the market. Even at the time when wine was much sought after, the Hungarians did not enlarge their vineyards. And when wine could not be sold at a profit, they did not reduce the size of the vineyards.

e. The size and beauty of the crops and beasts was a question of prestige, not just of income, as they belonged to the everyday surroundings. Four oxen in the yoke, a team of fine horses, a beautiful crop of wheat were matters of pride.

f. A large portion of the family income went into non-profitable investments and dead stock. A great deal was spent on clothing, especially that of the women. The clothes of the Hungarians reflected the age and condition of their wearers (maiden, bride, young woman before her first child, a young mother, a mother-in-law, a woman in mourning); various seasons and holidays (Advent, Christmas, Lent, Easter, Whitsuntide, the first and the second day of a holiday, the first Sunday of the month); the costume even reflected the time of the day (the forenoon of a holiday, an afternoon dance). Until 1848, serfs went to perform labor for their feudal lord dressed in clean, semi-festive clothes. The garments of the Hungarians were made of valuable materials: expensive silk, velvet, often costing the price of a cow. The value of the wardrobe of a Hungarian peasant woman was several times more than the price of the clothes of a German woman richer than herself.

g. Not only did Hungarians buy finer and more expensive clothing than the Germans, but also costlier crockery. The German makers of faience (for instance in the village of Hetvehely) worked especially for Hungarian customers. The potter of Óbánya made fancy ware for the Hungarians and simple and cheaper pottery for the Germans. This was also true of such commodities as carriages and harnesses.

h. Among the Hungarians there were many occasions for celebrating, for making a holiday, beginning with the obligatory feasting after making a sale, including frequent visits to the local inn and playing cards. A Hungarian man went to have a drink in the inn even if he had sufficient wine at home, just for the sake of the company and for the sake of prestige. A religious holiday, the occasion of family festivity (weddings, christenings, funerals), those types of jobs where the work was done in company (bringing home the corn, the grape harvest, corn husking, spinning) were all celebrated expensively with merrymaking and drinking.

i. Variety of food, a better kitchen, but without economy, was typical of the Hungarians. The saying was "Cake at Christmas, bread at Easter, and what-to-eat at Whitsuntide?" There were certain prestige dishes which had to be served on certain occasions. Pure wine was served to guests and laborers, the farmer drank pure wine himself. Wine diluted with water was despised, and considered a German drink. Bread had to be white wheat bread.

j. Exogamy was typical of the Hungarians, which meant that, especially in the small village, the bride should be brought from another village. Choosing a mate, the meetings of the young people, the wedding, and then visiting all the relatives required a good deal of time and money.

k. Diligence was not the most appreciated quality. The most highly valued qualities were: physical beauty, the beauty and cleanliness of clothing, hospitality, generosity, making merry in an easygoing way, full of pathos and prodigality, controversy with authority, being in the opposition, courage and daring, pride and cleverness.

l. There was broad interest and mobility, readiness to travel, to go to a fair, a circus, a movie, an amateur theater, to make a pilgrimage. Noisy frankness, rivalry in making donations, splitting up in parties, feuds were other characteristics.

m. Making use of situations for prestige was another.

Following, are the corresponding items of behavior of the Germans:

a. Inheritance was by the eldest son, only one child inheriting the real estate. The other brothers received their share, the approximate value in money. This was closely connected with the fact that most sons learned some trade. Until the division of the estate took place, the whole family collaborated to enrich their wealth.

b. The German peasant farmer strove to produce for the market.

c. The division of labor according to sex was not as distinct as it was among the Hungarians. German women and girls did not spin or weave, though in the middle of the last century they were ready to mow and plow like men.

d. Production was always rapidly altered to suit the demands of the market, and the Germans always strove to produce those commodities which were most sought after and most profitable. Thus they also became tobacco growers in the middle of the eighteenth century, and when wine was much sought after, they enlarged their vineyards to ten or twenty times their former size. When wine became difficult to sell, they cut back their vines within a few years, leaving barely ten percent.

e. Prestige was less important than productivity. Germans were not ashamed of putting a cow under the yoke and were the first to make use of new kinds of animals, such as the heavy, draft horses, work animals with which one could not travel fast. (Driving at top speed was an important matter for Hungarians!)

f. The income of the family was spent on useful investments, on increasing the productivity of the farm, on modern improvements. Compared to this, clothing was of secondary importance. The clothing of the Germans was not as varied as that of the Hungarians and was made of cheaper material. In a few villages both girls and old women wore black for weekdays and for holidays.

g. The household utensils were simpler, more practical and, compared to those of the Hungarians, poorer.

h. There were fewer holidays, fewer celebrations at family festivities. The inn was visited less often, and at a ball they drank wine brought from home.

i. The Germans had duller food with cheap ingredients such as potatoes, porridge, dumplings. They used less spice. There was more economy and saving for the season of field labor, and there were no prestige dishes. Pure wine was rarely consumed. It was sometimes drunk at weddings, but usually it was diluted with water. Even the producers of wheat ate rye bread, for it was cheaper, and when it dried out less was consumed. In the second half of the last century, rye bread was considered a German food.

j. They were endogamous. Brides were rarely brought from another village. Thus it was cheaper to visit relations and took less time.

k. The almost inhuman cult of diligence meant that the productive energy of man became the most highly esteemed value. The most honorable description was "hungry to work," it was the subject of bragging and sentimental reminiscences of youth. Women knitted even when sitting on the cart going off to the fields. They got up earlier than the Hungarians which was noted as early as the last century. From early childhood their life was nothing but striving for a better living, coupled with harsh frugality — no poetry and no joy.

l. They had narrower interests, mostly in useful, practical things (technical books, for example) and less feeling for literature, theater, and movies. They were reserved in expressing opinions, did not disagree with authority, and were obedient loyal citizens. They had a feeling of solidarity with the causes of their own group. The latter traits might have developed out of their position as a minority.

On some occasions, the same situation was used by the Hungarian to establish his prestige and by the German for economic gain. The anecdotes presented here give a picture of Hungarian and German behavior together.

The following case happened at the end of the last century and has almost become a legend. A Hungarian farmer, although he was able to thresh his own corn, had a German do it instead. The German was glad to have the work. Asked why he hired the German, the Hungarian answered, "Don't you know that God created the German to serve the Hungarian?"

The German expressed his admiration for the fine clothing of the Hungarian, and for his festivities, and loaned him money to increase his pomp, at the same time taking a profit which made it easier for him to get established in the village.

The Hungarian despised the "hungry" German. The Hungarian judge of the village, Magyarszék, leaned out of his window and seeing a German in the street who had recently moved into the village, took out a banknote to light his pipe, saying, "Let that hungry German get yellow with envy." When this judge died a pauper, his house and estate were bought by the Germans who had settled in his village.

After World War II, the displacement of the Germans from the country and the socialist reorganization of agriculture created a new situation in the region of *Hegyhát*. However, the contrasting value orientation of the two groups of people, and their different historical experience have their effect to this day and may still be observed.

Nigeria's 250 Ethnic Groups: Realities and Assumptions

AJATO GANDONU*

The grouping of human beings into reference units is a most complicated exercise for which no satisfactory rule of thumb has been devised by anthropologists and others interested in the science of man. Nevertheless the need for some system of grouping members of the specie remains. It is on the basis of such divisions that generalizations become imposed on sections of the specie. At the national level a citizen's claim to his country may depend upon prior affiliation to such a group. At various times and in various contexts loaded terminologies — such as the family, clan, community or village, tribe, people, nation or race, in increasing order of complexity — have been featured as favored descriptive words. Some of these terms (e.g., tribe) have become so distorted in their usage that they have lost currency as objective terms for describing human groups. In its place the term "ethnic group" has become a favored alternative for analytic and descriptive purposes.

Trends observable in the anthropological literature during the last ten years indicate a positive effort in the social sciences to group people according to racial origin, cultural background, and kinship affiliations, playing down the prejudiced, subjective nature of earlier researchers. In this respect an ethnic group has become the favored grouping which identifies a number of related persons organized in social contexts. The confused terminologies with which earlier anthropologists had identified and described man, especially in underdeveloped countries, are responsible for the many misconceptions imposed upon indigenous peoples to the point of bringing disrepute to anthropology in the post-colonial era.

One fact remains valid about human groupings: there is always a need

* The author's family name changed from Amos to Gandonu officially on January 1, 1975. References in bibliography are under the name of Amos. The author's first name remains the same — *Editor*.

to refer to a group of people, at least for the purpose of generalizing about it. Since the validity of generalizations depends on the meaning one attaches to the group, it becomes of primary importance from the point of view of interdisciplinary communication to adopt as objective a criterion as possible for the groupings.[1] The present confusion arising from unstandardized use of terminologies among social scientists is not only unsatisfactory for academic purposes, it often leads to mistaken identities in the field.

What constitutes an ethnic group? In the answer to this question lies the crux of the confusion that has plagued anthropologists over the years. Ethnicity tends to describe human grouping on the basis of language, territorial identity, common ancestry (kinship ties), and a hazy concept of cultural affinity. From a combination of these variables, emerges a blurred image, shrouded in a multi-colored cloak of tribe, nation, ethnic group, clan, or community. In the place of such a hazy image, it is hereby proposed that anthropologists and others interested in the study of man in groups adopt a common terminology. One such terminology is the ethnic group. An ethnic group should comprise a people who can be identified as sharing a language, common ancestry (as variously preserved in oral tradition or history), and possibly, a territory to which they would lay claim of ownership.

While members of an ethnic group in most cases are known to identify with a language, it is noteworthy that field samples may deviate from this requirement. An ethnic group may have adopted the language of a neighboring ethnic group or conqueror to the extent that its own language becomes extinct or forgotten. Examples from Nigeria, however, indicate that it is a rare occurrence and may be found only in extreme cases where economic and political influence of the supplanting group operated long enough. Such is the acculturation one observes among the Efut who have adopted Efik in place of their own language during the past seventy years.

---

[1] A grouping based on birth or genealogical origin seems the most reasonable for our purpose. It is an objective criterion in so far as it relates to a social (mutually exclusive) unit, recruiting membership by a naturally determined channel (i.e., members belong on account of their being born into the group). The smallest of such natural social units is the family (ego, father and mother, and so on to include the extended family). Beyond this is the lineage, which in the case of Nigerians, has been shown to be patrilineal almost always. A number of related lineages constitute a village (a residential unit), assuming the absence of stranger elements. A number of settlements related by common ancestry or descent and often occupying a known territory, creating and using a means of verbal communication (language) and possessing a cultural identity (exclusive learned behavior) constitute the practically remotest possible social unit — an *ethnos* or "people." In this paper the term ethnic group refers to this ultimate group whose members acknowledge the same territorial, cultural, and historical identity, among other things. There is no restriction as to the size of population or territory as these merely reflect the fortune and historical circumstances of each ethnic group over time. It is not a simple alternative simile to "tribe" — a term that deserves to be dropped because of the confusion it has caused in earlier anthropological writings (see Amos 1968a).

Territorial identity is a normal requirement whose usefulness becomes obvious when it comes to "pinning" the ethnic groups to the ground or locating them in the field. However, ethnic groups that are nomadic in nature, e.g., some Fulani groups in Nigeria, are not necessarily tied to land areas. The group retains identity in other respects (language, religion, economic way of life, social organization, and history). The territorial identity is subject to principles such as survival of the fittest in land occupancy. The size of land occupied by ethnic groups varies according to the fortunes of that ethnic group in resisting eviction by more powerful ethnic groups. In Nigeria, for example, fights over ethnic territories have constituted major traditional interethnic conflicts which hamper the drive to multiethnic nationalism. Ethnic territories are jealously guarded. Their size and location reflect the strength or misfortune of the ethnic groups whose homelands have been lost or gained in conflicts with neighboring groups.

The sociocultural identity of all members of an ethnic group is of primary importance. For it is such intangible identity that binds seemingly unrelated groups together in the absence of territorial contiguity or linguistic affinity. It usually takes the form of an oral tradition that links the origin of one group to the other and may be further strengthened by ceremonies of social significance. The identity of all Yorubas as related brothers, in spite of territorial and dialectical differences, is an outstanding field example (Amos 1968a).

In each of these criteria — language, territorial, and cultural affinity — there is also the need for careful evaluation of the "truth" indicated by the various inputs. In the sifting and winnowing exercise involved, efforts are made to distinguish between true and falsified links.

Once the variables have been agreed upon, it is then possible to arrive at ethnic groupings that would genuinely represent some standard definition within which a generalization would be valid and field tests could be more uniformly applied. What emerges in the working definition would be a balancing of linguistic, territorial, and cultural identity, backed by an acknowledged linkage of historical or cultural affinities between subgroups. In other words, it is important that clear distinctions are made in the minds of fieldworkers as to the standard meanings of tribe, people, community, nation, or race in the context of the study. The result could be an agreement on ethnic group as the largest possible grouping of people sharing a common identity in ancestry, way of life, and territorial claims.

As far as possible, people of similar ancestry, cultural trait, and social structure are grouped together. Relationships and differences are identified and appreciated with a view to recognizing the sources of conflict and cooperation or affiliation between groups which must competitively share a given environment on accepted principles of rights in land and resources. All of these factors would be considered along with the need for balancing between "space surplus" and "space deficient" groups of an ex-colonial emergent nation.

The nature of ethnic groups derives from the basic requirements of their members to remain as a group in perpetuity. For this purpose all the institutions of the ethnic group are geared to ensuring three features:

1. Communication between members; this necessitates maintaining an exclusive language. All recruits to the group are taught this exclusive means of communication (the average Nigerian normally becomes bilingual by the age of five).

2. Interrelationship between group members — the social structure contains details of how people are recruited into the group. The recruitment procedure normally covers the "blood relationship" whose claim to membership of the group is established by common descent, and the affinal groups whose claim originates from relating by marriage or similar circumstances. The former is either patrilineally or matrilineally decided. In Nigeria patrilineal descent is the system common to most groups. Effective recruitment by marriage varies between groups. In most cases, the affines retain membership of their descent groups. It is therefore a common practice to restrict membership of an ethnic group to patrilineally descended individuals.

3. The territory occupied by an ethnic group is perhaps the strongest locational identity of the group. It is referred to as the land, country, or territory of the ethnic group. Since it sustains the group's livelihood and represents the arena in which the ethnic group's existence may be observed, a major collective function of the group involves maintaining the group's territorial integrity. The group becomes attached to its ethnic territory and defends it against intruders. Most of the wars in which an ethnic group becomes involved originate from the need to acquire better territory (if the group considers itself strong enough) or in defending what land area the group already holds. A study of the peopling of Nigeria prior to European partitioning of West Africa reveals a process of interethnic movements which jointly produced the present pattern of ethnic territories in Nigeria.[2] The stronger, better organized groups suc-

---

[2]   Prior to the partitioning of West Africa (pre-1880s) each ethnic group (which as a warring unit, secured or lost territories) moved freely into and within the well-watered and agriculturally favored lands of the Niger-Benue river systems. It was that process of inter ethnic movement or competition for land resources, and the subsequent intervention by European colonial powers, that by 1900 became set into the present pattern of ethnic homelands of Nigeria. With the advent of Pax Britanica, ethnic groups were no longer free to raid others for territorial expansion or displacement; everyone seems to have become forced to remain where they were at the time the new rulers arrived. However, by this time the "best lands" in terms appraised in those days as "good agricultural land and less difficult country" had already been occupied by the strongest or more successful ethnic groups (Fulani-Hausa, Yoruba, Igbo, Tiv, Kanuri and Nupe). The Jukun, for example, could no longer recover the vast territory they had lost to intruding ethnic groups in the old rule of the game of "might is right."

ceeded in occupying the more desired land areas, while the least attractive lands became the hideout and abode of the less powerful or less organized ethnic groups. Thus, the Fulani by raids and conquests have spread themselves into many parts of the former northern region, displacing such formerly powerful groups as the Jukun and the Mambilla. The Ijaw have had to restrict and adapt themselves to the Delta area, while the relatively inaccessible rock faces of Jos plateau and Kukuruku highlands have become sanctuaries for many small ethnic groups fleeing from the Fulani and other aggressors. Through the notorious slave trade, interethnic wars and epidemics, many ethnic groups have suffered irreversible decline and others have even become extinct.

During British colonial administration, ethnic territories in Nigeria became stabilized and remained relatively so in the period 1900 to 1966. In the past six years following the political restructuring of Nigeria,[3] ethnic boundaries are becoming better defined both in the interest of internal peace and for ease of political administration. Many ethnic groups who felt suppressed by larger groups have felt themselves resurrected by the new state structure of Nigeria. It is this new feeling that sparks off interest in the study of Nigerian ethnic groups, their territories, and membership identities. For each Nigerian ethnic group, apart from exercising influence over a given geographical area, constitutes a cultural unit which contributes in its own way to the rich mosaic of the Nigerian cultural fabric. One of the effects of the last civil conflict (June 1967 to January 1970) is that it identified ethnicity as a major element in Nigeria's political makeup. The importance of ethnic territories as the final unit of group identities also became apparent. The whole question of

[3] In May 1967, the military head of Nigeria, then Lt. Col. Gowon, at the verge of civil war, abolished the old universally condemned unproportionate but powerful regions. In their place he set up the twelve states. It had the far-reaching effect of splitting the giant "Hausa North" into six states, the Yoruba contiguous western region into two states, the "Igbo dominated Eastern region" into three states. The Midwestern state, with its many ethnic groups, was left intact. This action (creation of states) was received by most of the long neglected 247 ethnic groups as a blessing and a liberation from the alleged oppression they had suffered under supertribe politics which "had written them off as minority groups to be justifiably ignored."

As work on ethnic boundaries was largely non-existent or was previously hindered by the "supertribe" politics of pre-coup Nigeria, the internal boundaries resulting from the states' creation are not as accurate as they might have been; particularly at the ground-level delimitation of "divisional" boundaries.

Some confusion, arising mostly from the atmosphere (imminent civil war) in which it was created, the poor publicity and poor awareness of the realities by Nigerians and outsiders alike, was encountered by the sponsors of the states system, and many have questioned the basis of the exercise. However, there is no doubt today that the state boundaries are etching themselves deeper into the ground and, given careful management, may well form the internal administrative framework of a united Nigerian nation, where no ethnic group is oppressed by others. It is best seen as a political halfway house (particularly in the atmosphere of 1967) between straight forward unitary government rocked by internal dissension between three apparently selfish ethnic groups and a multitude of independent mini-nations breaking off from the Nigerian Federation.

grass roots loyalty and national consciousness stood revealed in the ethnic factor. Poor knowledge of the ethnic groups in the past had led to wrong political assumptions and frustrated developmental policies. The same lack of knowledge influenced the course of the last civil war and continues to affect natural development plans of the country.

THE NIGERIAN SCENE

Nigeria has been described as the "home of a hundred kings."[4] It is also an acknowledged micro-Africa where no less than 150 ethnic groups live together and exercise influence in various geographical units of the country. This diversity in the ethnic composition of Nigeria has the adverse effect of giving observers the impression that Nigeria cannot possibly be one nation. However, the ethnic groups by any standards do not constitute "nations" as such. Indeed the groups vary in population size and land resources. In many cases, evidence abounds to substantiate claims of inequality of initiative and drive between ethnic groups. Some ethnic groups for example are known to be more progressive than others, but it is dangerous to emphasize this seeming difference in character traits before thorough unprejudiced research has been carried out on each ethnic group.[5]

Up to the moment of presenting this paper, there is no agreement on how many ethnic groups really make up the Nigerian nation. Perhaps once we agree on a working definition, the air of confusion will clear sufficiently to identify the groups and locate them on a Nigerian map. One recurrent message researchers must face is that overloaded or derogatory terms, such as tribe, are inadequate to describe Nigerian human groups. Conscious effort has to be made to remove the confusion arising from inconsistent definitions and general ignorance.

[4] Nigeria has been described as the "Republic of a hundred kings" by Jane Watson (1967).
[5] Claims of inferiority traits in one ethnic group or the other appear to be deeply rooted in the minds of members of every ethnic group against their neighbors (sometimes even deliberately inculcated), possibly as a self protective device used for keeping the group united in the face of rivalry between groups. Calling a neighboring group by a derogatory name (Bariba for Borgu by the Yorubas, Unenge for Igbo by the Efiks, Kaferi or "pagan" for non-moslem northern ethnic groups by the Hausas) is the most common form of abuse. The Nigerian groups have been most successful in discouraging peaceful intermarriage and other forms of social contact or intermingling, other than in trade and purely economic exchanges. More unfortunately, earlier researchers, missionaries, and administrators in Nigeria did not sufficiently resist the temptation to take sides with "their people", e.g., Lord Lugard's attachment to the Hausa ethnic group blinded him considerably to the possibility of any virtues that might exist among southern peoples, particularly Yorubas and Igbos (Perham 1963).

The Biafran propaganda drew much inspiration and form during 1967 through 1970 from this sort of interethnic mutual animosity, by which its organizers could be accused of defrauding world sympathy against Federal Nigeria.

ABSENCE OF DETAILED FIELDWORK

The paucity of fieldwork on Nigerian ethnic groups is more apparent than real. For the wealth of material a researcher can assemble from several sources (colonial archives, missionary reports, travelers' diaries, military intelligence and, in recent years, commissioned feasibility reports of development agencies and census reports) is massive. However, these sources are rather scattered and uncoordinated. Even the Nigerian government has not made a conscious effort to assemble these sources for useful research purposes. The researcher must on his own account hunt out the sources and fill in missing links from his own field knowledge. In any case, there is hardly an adequate substitute for detailed fieldwork in Nigeria. The fieldworkers often encountered such practical problems as accessibility to some ethnic territories, paucity of funds for fieldwork, and political sensitivity which is touched off whenever a stranger undertakes investigation in ethnic territories other than his own. The recent political upheaval also added to the practical problems. The dust of the civil war had not quite settled in certain parts of the country at the time the author undertook some of the fieldwork for this paper. Consequently, it was essential to tread gently in the various ethnic territories and weigh one's field questions carefully to elicit maximum cooperation from informants and avoid any sensitive questions that would incite suspicion which can upset the whole exercise.[6]

REVIEW OF PREVIOUS WORK

Prior to the publication of Daryll Forde's ethnographic survey, efforts made in the study of Nigeria's ethnic groups were scanty and isolated. The monographs edited by Forde were systematic studies and covered many but not all ethnic groups. Even in that impressive work, problems of confused definitions were left unsolved and wrong identities were preserved in the groupings used. For example, Forde believed that Ibibios and Efiks were one and the same people — a belief which featured in the literature until recently. It is a typical example of how undue reliance upon the linguistic factor as evidence of ethnic identity led to the wrong categorization of human groups in Southeastern Nigeria (see Map 1).

Many anthropologists were employed by the colonial government for the purpose of documenting the native peoples. On the basis of such

[6] In this respect, the author gratefully acknowledges help received from foreign scholars, friends, relations, colleagues, and contacts in various Nigerian ethnic territories. In particular the help provided by the Nigerian Research Center in Lagos and the many undergraduates in Lagos University who responded to questionnaires used in sample derivation were crucial to the success of this survey of Nigeria's ethnic groups.

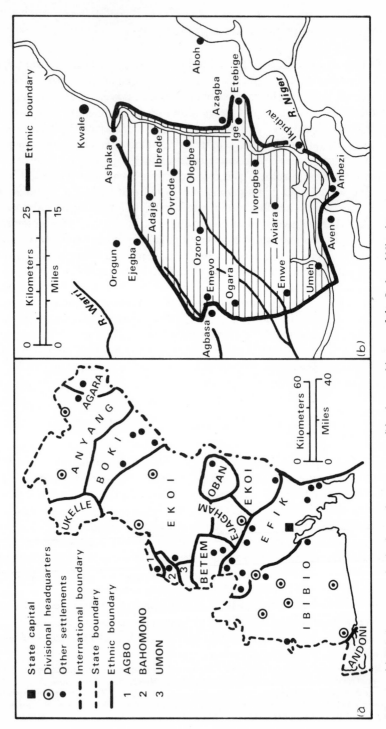

Map 1.   (a) Ethnic-group territories in southeastern state;   (b) ethnographic map of the Isoko of Nigeria

documentation, convenient administrative units were created, and from selected centers of such administrative units, government policy was implemented. This logical procedure of first dividing the people up into convenient groups and ruling them became the notorious divide-and-rule policy of the British Administration in Nigeria. Whatever misgivings Nigerians may now harbor against this policy, it remains a fascinating system (at least from the point of view of the colonialists) which served the needs of empire-builders such as Lord Lugard and his successors. Indirect rule in the Northern States involved the devolution of power within the native authority. Pax Britanica throughout the new territory (Nigeria) was effectively maintained after an inventory of the many diverse people caught within the framework of Nigeria had been taken.

It is doubtful however whether the complete range of Nigerian ethnic compositions has been fully explored, even today. The picture one has is more a sketchy appreciation of which group occupies what part of the country. It is therefore of current necessity to continue the effort of finding out more about the ethnic groups which have proved either inaccessible to previous workers, e.g., the Zumperi of the eastern borderlands, or were given mistaken identity on the basis of lack of knowledge by previous workers, e.g., the Isoko who were thought to be Urhobos or the Egun who were only recently recognized as a subgroup of the Yoruba.

Until now, most of the field knowledge we have about the majority of Nigeria's ethnic groups we owe to the army of anthropologists and related workers who worked in Nigeria during the colonial period. They appear to have done the best of a bad job, involving themselves directly in the affairs of the ethnic group to the point of identifying themselves completely with the groups they were studying. Forde (1964) among the Yako; Nadel (1942) among the Nupe; the Bohannans (1953) among the Tiv; Green (1947) among the Ibo; Meek (1925) among the Jukun; Bascom among the Yoruba; Talbot among the Ijaw; Bradbury (1957, 1959, 1964) among the Bini (Edo); Hill (1972) among the Hausa; Greenberg (1955, 1960) among the Kanuri; Lloyd (1954, 1963) among the Itshekiri; Boston (1963) among the Igala; Waddel among the Efik; Brice-Smith among the Mumuye; and Jones (1963a, b) among the Ibibio. These are just a few of the better known works, but an army of workers have in various capacities documented a large number of Nigerian ethnic groups. The information accumulated from such sources concern the ethnic groups' way of life, location, peculiarities, language, and history.

Earlier division of Nigeria's peoples on basis of race, language, and migration source was responsible for the misleading pattern which yielded such terms as Bantu, Semi-Bantu, Niger-Congo (Greenberg 1955); Kwa-Kru, Benue-Congo, Nilo-Saharan, and Western Atlantic groups. The dominant factor for these groupings was linguistic. A more consistent procedure is to group the peoples of Nigeria in ethnic territories that reflect the geographical distribution of the various human groups. Such a division would relate each Nigerian ethnic group with its natural habitat which can be placed in historical perspective from the period A.D. 1000 to 1885 when most of the territorial acquisitions appear to have taken place.[7]

Murdock's monumental work (1959) stands out as the most comprehensive attempt at mapping the ethnic groups in Africa as a whole. The Nigerian scene adapted from his Africa map is shown in Map 2 for comparative purposes in this paper. Murdock's impressive effort is limited and in parts actually ruined by the absence of field knowledge and

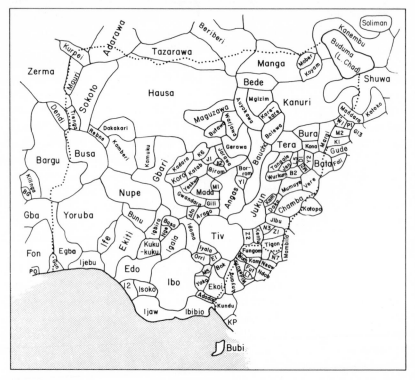

Map 2. Ethnic territories after Murdock (1959). An example of wrong assumptions and armchair exercise

[7] Since 1885 ethnic territories have tended to stabilize and mass movements outside recognized homelands since the time of British colonial intervention has not been known. However, minor boundary disputes of very local nature between neighboring ethnic groups, e.g., Igbo vs. Idoma, Yoruba vs. Borgu, Chamba vs. Jukun, Gwari vs. Hausa. Even a nomadic ethnic group like the Fulani has been less mobile (as a group) when it comes to moving permanently into recognized ethnic territories of other ethnic groups. In some cases, such as the Efik-Balundu, ethnic boundaries have coincided with international territorial boundary between, first British and German colonial powers and later the resulting newly independent nations of Nigeria and Cameroons.

confused terminologies. Murdock lists about 100 groups in uncertain ethnic territories. In Southwestern Nigeria for example, he split Yoruba-land into such inconsistent groupings as Ijebu, Egba, Ife, Ekiti, Gun (Egun) and Yoruba (presumably Oyo). Thus Murdock's map epitomizes the grand confusion that plagues anthropologists in their attempt to map ethnic groups before adopting standardized terminologies or assembling accurate field knowledge.

Two official ethnographic reports (Temple 1969; Talbot 1969) which appear jointly to cover the whole of Nigeria by 1926 deserve important mention in this paper. Each was commissioned by the colonial adminis-tration, was edited by a competent authority of the time, concentrated on one of the two parts (North or South) of Nigeria which became amalga-mated under Lord Lugard, and was considered important enough to be republished in 1969 by Frank Cass of London.

Although these documents tried to cover all known ethnic groups in their respective territories of reference, the reporters did not attempt a serious mapping exercise but were quite content with generalized descriptions of the countries or lands occupied by the groups they described. Temple's compilations appear to be more thorough, in that authorities (field personnel made up of missionaries, government an-thropologists, members of Lugard's army, and local personages) were quoted for as many of the ethnic groups described as available.

The Nigerian Federal Surveys (an agency of the Federal Government) has produced a number of maps under such titles as "Nigerian Tribes," "Nigerian Language Groups," "Languages and Dialects of Nigeria," and "Administration Map of Nigeria." Most of these maps appeared between 1967 and 1971. However, their inaccuracy is well known and in many cases errors which accumulated from previous works are faithfully re-peated, even perpetuated in these government maps. Despite the low degree of accuracy in these maps (viz., the erroneous location or misspel-ling of ethnic groups on the map) they serve the useful purpose of being base maps for more detailed fieldwork which one hopes will eventually lead to more accurate mapping of the ethnic groups. (The missing factor remains the absence of direct government support for such scholarly investigations.)

The impression a researcher gets after wading through these existing sources and appreciating their limitations is that once the initiative is taken to make a more accurate, fieldwork-validated map of the ethnic groups, the various government agencies would benefit from drastically revising their old maps.

THE ETHNIC GROUPS AND WHERE THEY ARE

Writing in *Focus* in 1964, Barry Floyd,[8] a geographer, made the following
introductory remarks about Nigerian peoples.

Nigeria has a heterogeneous and polyglot citizenry divided into many cultural and
linguistic groups which number millions e.g. the Hausa; others e.g. the Eggon
of Bauchi Province and the Kerekere of Western Bornu number only a few
thousand.... Between them at least 200 discrete languages are spoken within the
country. Counting dialects the total must reach several hundreds. These could
have caused serious communication problems but for English and Hausa.

Floyd's map was the earliest to show accurately the location of groups
such as Efik, Jibu, Chamba, Koyan, Maguza, Duky, Gwari, Lere,
Kalabari, and Yauri, although it used the wrong cognomen, such as
"Bariba" (a Yoruba derogatory name for their Borgu neighbors) without
proper checking.

As late as 1970, another *Focus* report on Nigeria was commissioned by
the Association of American Geographers, possibly to update the previous work by Floyd. The new authors, Professors John Willmer and
Charles Lyons made the points that the population of Nigeria is noteworthy because of its cultural diversity. They wrote that there are more
than twice as many "tribal nations" in Nigeria as there are member states
in the United Nations. They note that tribal affiliations are perpetuated
despite the urban environments because of the social clubs called tribal
unions. They estimated that there are about 400 linguistic groups in
Nigeria. The Willmer and Lyons report benefited a great deal from the
intense interest the world showed in Nigeria's three-year civil war which
ended just before the report was written. The authors had learned a great
deal more about the ethnic diversity of the Nigerian nation and its potent
effects on Nigeria's political and economic policies. Perhaps based on
those experiences the authors were more hesitant about presenting maps
that give the impression of accurate location of Nigerian groups. The civil
war and its consequences had proved to hitherto uninterested scholars
that knowledge of Nigeria's ethnic composition has been both inadequate
and mispresented even at official levels. It has become necessary to see
beyond the three super ethnic groups (Hausa, Yoruba, and Ibo) who for
twenty years had overshadowed more than 247 ethnic groups. The minority groups, so-called, now claim attention and a right to be mapped within
their ethnic territory.

[8]   Barry Floyd is currently of the Department of Geography, University of Durham,
England. His book on "Eastern Nigeria," published in 1969 during the Nigerian civil war,
qualifies as one of the richest sources for any researcher interested in the three eastern states
of Nigeria.

The author's survey was carried out in 1972 with two clear objectives: (1) to find out how many ethnic groups Nigeria actually contains; (2) to locate each ethnic group territorially on a map to reveal its exact extent. (A checklist of the ethnic groups in Nigeria is presented in Appendix 2.)

The task involved searching through all available records, colonial ethnographic reports, and maps. The merits and limitations of these sources have already been related in this paper.

Actual field investigations followed. The author seized every opportunity to travel widely in Nigeria and visit ethnic territories. In each case a number of the people and ordinary villagers were interviewed. A prior visit to each state capital was followed by series of tours into the interior armed with information received from the state governments and educational establishments. Sometimes proper escort was sought and obtained from friends in government agencies. In other cases, students on vacation were sponsored to visit their people in the more remote areas and bring back usable information for the survey. In every case the author made it a point to meet and interview at least one member of all the ethnic groups mapped for this paper. It was a most rewarding effort despite the expense, and provided the much cherished opportunity to collect one's information "straight from the horse's mouth."

The survey also involved a systematic examination of all settlements listed in Appendix 1 of this paper with a view to ascertaining ethnic claims for each. From that exercise, selected settlements were grouped under ethnic group (Appendix 3); the survey was subsequently used as ground control for demarcating the ethnic territories shown on the finished map. For simplicity the settlements are represented in dots (squares and abbreviated letters for state capitals). They are reference points on the ground and should serve as basis for any subsequent adjustment of ethnic boundaries as more knowledge becomes available.

A trial survey based on responses from 1,000 university students, drawn mostly from the first year group in Lagos University in March 1972, proved rather unrepresentative. Only eighteen ethnic groups were found in the sample. However, the exercise revealed the universal applicability of the ethnic concept to all Nigerians. Everybody belongs to one (often the father's) group even in the case of married women; there has been very little intermarriage; in some very large ethnic groups such as the Yoruba, Ibo and Ijaw interviewees felt affiliated to lower order (subethnic) groups, e.g., Ijebu, Egba, Ijesha for Yoruba; Ika, Ngwa, Awka for Ibo; Nembe, Okrika or Kalabari for Ijaw. The students' responses, despite their unrepresentativeness (see Appendix 4), are potentially useful for further investigation, especially if extended to cover students in all Nigerian universities or members of the Youth Corps. Respondents from the least known ethnic groups emerge from such surveys.

ETHNIC TERRITORIAL CLAIMS

Nigeria's lands may be divided into the following surfaces:

1. The Southwestern Niger-Atlantic block forming the largest single contiguous ethnic territory occupied by the Yoruba in the Western and Lagos States with considerable overspill into Kwara State. Within the same block but set deep into the rain forest and the remote rugged Afenmai highlands are the Edo, Itshekiri Urhobo, Isoko, Ika-Ibo, Igbirra, and Kukuruku cluster of ethnic groups which constitute the Midwest State with overlap into Kwara State.

2. The Southeastern Niger-Benue block which stretches from the eastern banks of the Niger to the frontier zones of Cameroon mountains. This block also contains the entire Cross River basin and the southern tributaries of the River Benue. The largest single ethnic group within this block is the Igbo group (in a densely populated contiguous land area), completely enclosed within the East Central State boundaries. The Ibibio group occupy the Atlantic foreland, their territory wedged like a southward based triangle between the southwestern banks of the Cross River and the Andoni River of the eastern delta system. The Tiv, Idoma, and Igala occupy the southern plains and slopes of the Benue River in what constituted the southern borderlands of the old Northern Region. The Cross River lands and western slopes of the Cameroon mountains contain the relatively complex cluster of ethnic groups. There the Efiks who once spread their commercial and political influence to all the lands of the Cross River basin and beyond, now occupy only the lower trough of that river, southeastwards to Nigeria's boundary with Cameroon Republic at Rio del Rey (a boundary which also coincides with the Balundu-Efik ethnic boundary). Between the Cross River estuary and the highland slopes of the Cameroon mountains the Ekoi and their related subgroups (e.g., Ejaghan, Mbembe, and Obanlike) claim uncontested ownership. But the upper basin of the Cross River is shared in strips and pockets of territory between the Agbo, Bahomono, Umon, Boki, Ukelle, Uyanga and Anyang, who together share the South Eastern State with Ibibio, Efiks, and Ekois up to Obudu highlands.

3. The Niger Delta complex constitutes another habitat which has almost become the exclusive territory of the Ijaw (Ijo); but within the Rivers State, one also finds the Andoni, Ndoki, Ikwere, and Igbo ethnic groups sharing the habitat. The Kalabari, Okrika and Nembe are, contrary to earlier belief, merely subgroups of the Ijo ethnic group and should be classified as such.

4. The southern Lake Chad Basin and Bornu high plains — the largest single contiguous ethnic territory here is the Kanuri ethnic group, but pockets of Fulani and Hausa strongholds are also large enough to be mapped clearly in the area. The Kerikeri, Yedina, Bole, Bedde, Manga,

Gamergu, Tera, Babur, and the ubiquitous Fulani also have ethnic territories in this region.

5. The Adamawa, Mambila, Shebsi, and northeastern (Sardauna Province) mountainous borderlands are some of the most inaccessible ethnic groups. The Mumuye, Mobber, Mambila, Higi, Zumperi, and Shuwa have their ethnic territories here. The easternmost spread of the Fulani is indicated in the section of Adamawa highlands occupied by them. This region is also among the least developed part of Northeastern State because of poor accessibility and inadequate knowledge of the region's economic resources. Population is generally low in the region and all the characteristics of a frontier zone can be observed among the ethnic groups found in the area — part transitory, part repellent.

6. The central highlands, culminating in the Jos plateau — here is the most complex cluster of ethnic groups. The nature of the rugged topography combines with the history of interethnic conflicts which deprived the groups of less difficult land areas earlier on, to produce the observed conglomerate of diverse ethnic groups in this region. The Jukun who were known to have colonized these areas extensively, now control only a modest size of territory under pressure from among others, the Fulani ethnic group. The Birom are the next largest group to the Jukun in this region. The other ethnic groups which make up the observed cluster each occupy very small land area ranging from 1,000 sq. km. among the Mada to less than 140 sq. km. for the Kuleri in relatively difficult country. A mere 40,000 sq. km. of Benue-Plateau State is divisible into ethnic territories between as many as forty ethnic groups (see ethnic territories from Bashar to Yeskwa and Birom to Migili or Arago at northern Tiv borderlands). They have all been brought under the administrative umbrella of Benue-Plateau State, along with the Tiv, Idoma, and others.

7. Hausaland; all the high plain stretching from the upper reaches of River Gongola in the east and the northern slopes of the Jos central high plateau, across Kano State to the banks of Sokoto River constitutes the ethnic territory of the Hausa; it is not at all as contiguous and exclusive as Yoruba, Ibo, or Nupe ethnic territories. However, it is within this block that Hausa and Fulani peoples have dominant territorial claims. Interspersed among these two are other ethnic groups such as the Ningi, Warja, lying between Bauchi and Kano; the Maguza whose territory appears to form a rimlike bracket opening towards Kano; the Zamfara and Darkarki who occupy northern Kontagora and Zamfara River basin; the Bugale (Buzu), Barebari and Asbini to the east and south of Katsina. Hausaland as mapped by Morgan and Pugh (Geography of West Africa) and reproduced by Hill (1972), claims much larger territory than is borne out in the present ethnic survey. However, until the question of whether Hausa is more a language than a people is resolved, maps of the Hausa ethnic territory will continue to vary according to the input used by each

researcher. What is less disputable is that the efforts of empire builders such as Lord Lugard over the sixty-year period in which Hausa reigned as the *lingua franca* of these parts of Nigeria had the added effect of obscuring the ethnic identities of the non-Hausa elements whose territories lie here. In addition, the contemptuous reference to indigenous non-Moslem groups in these parts as pagan further suppressed ethnic identities and make a researcher's work more difficult on this topic.

8. West of the central plateau from Nasarawa Division along the northern banks of the Niger to Sokoto River; this largely comes under Northwestern State and is dominated by Gwari and Nupe ethnic territories, with wedges and "inlier" stumps of such other ethnic territories as the Koro, Bassa, Kamuku, Ganagana, Duka, and Kamberi and clusters of Hausa elements.

9. The western frontier and Niger River lands constitute a final habitat identifiable in this survey. Shared administratively between Kwara and Northwestern States, this fringe zone contains ethnic territories of the Borgu (known to Yorubas as Bariba), Bussa, Kamberi, Kyenga, Yauri, and Adar.

MIGRATIONS, TERRITORIAL CLAIMS AND RESOURCE COMPETITION

There is overwhelming evidence in the field and in available literature to show that the ethnic groups have shifted territories a good deal in the past one thousand years.[9] When the various myths and legends fostered by Nigeria's political history are carefully examined and discounted, one cannot escape the conclusion that only very few of the many ethnic groups in Nigeria today are indigenous to the territory now known as Nigeria. Ethnic groups have lost or gained lands and have moved around within the country. However, even the Fulani appear to have "settled" in clearly

---

[9]   Few of the present ethnic groups were actually "indigenous" to Nigeria, if one mapped meticulously the position of each ethnic group 1,000 years ago. Evidence in the field and in literature in support of migration routes and interethnic territorial movements continue to accumulate as research progresses. Remnant villages, for example, may be identified from modern Cameroons, across mountain passes and the bend of the Cross River into present Igbo homelands. Efik migration, traced most rigorously by such native researchers as Efiong Ukpong Aye and others, helped sort out confused facts about Ibibio and Efik separate identities. Links between Idoma and Aragos, Jukun and Birom, Hausa and Fulani, and of course the various Yoruba subgroups have become apparent from field and research documents. Ethnic territories as mapped in this survey, represent the facts as one finds in the field today (ethnic territorial claims). They may be regarded as fairly stabilized land units. They await the welding force of a nationalist government able to render unnecessary the need for each ethnic group to cling to given ethnic territories or homelands. When that is achieved all Nigerians would feel free to regard anywhere else as "home" in the Nigerian nation.

identifiable parts of the country to which they lay claim, often according to their political strength.

It is significant that constant change in resource appraisal has tended to favor those groups who, until recently, only found safety in remote, less desirable parts of the country. Oil wealth, for example, has turned the remote delta region of Nigeria into areas of economic advantage. This contrasts with the earlier period when agricultural land was seen as more desirable and the larger ethnic groups established themselves in the then fertile plains and valleys of the country. Today, Iboland, Hausaland, and Yorubaland, for example, are at slight disadvantage in mineral resources which increasingly have boosted the Nigerian economy in recent years. Alas, a redistribution of ethnic territories, which might benefit the large or hitherto strong ethnic groups, cannot now be effected through the pre-colonial rules of "might is right." New rules of the game must now be sought within the framework of Nigeria's nationalist goals. Such a rule would necessarily operate on the basis of "unity through mutual respect."

The neglect suffered by many parts of the country, e.g., the so-called "minority areas" of the country (especially Gwariland, Ijawland, and the Cross River communities) during the last civilian regime, should not be repeated in a properly conceived development program based on locating the right activity in the right place irrespective of whose ethnic territory might benefit most.

Now that the ousting of weaker groups by stronger ones has virtually ceased, the need for a sharing of resources among all ethnic groups in the country is at a premium. Besides, it occasionally becomes necessary, as Nigeria develops economically, for a whole ethnic group to lose its territory for a national project, such as new dams (the Bussa ethnic group had to move) or for a federal capital (as the Gwari who were moved to make room for Kaduna earlier on may lose more of their territory if Abuja emirate becomes accepted as the site of the new federal capital).

The present distribution of ethnic groups bears evidence of the influence of Nigerian land forms on migration routes, diffusion of agricultural innovation, and pattern of interethnic conflict earlier in Nigeria's history. In the present survey also, time as a factor in the primogenetic occupation of ethnic territories was considered important enough to lead to the use of historical sources for deciding conflicting claims to territory. For example, it was not easy to decide on exact demarcation lines between Gwari and Hausa, Ibo and Ijaw, Jukun and Fulani, Kanuri and Hausa, or Ekoi and Efik, because length of occupation at the frontier zones posed serious field problems as to the validity of claim. This problem of earlier settlers versus late arrivals threatens the accuracy of the seemingly rigid boundaries between ethnic groups. It is a maxim that nature abhors lines or rigid boundaries but geographers adore them. With that firmly planted in the reader's mind, all seemingly rigid ethnic boundaries shown on the final map (of the survey) should be seen as transition zones and lines of interethnic contact rather than exclusive borders. However, the land tenure system in most of the ethnic groups is so significant that the elders or leaders of each ethnic group have fairly clear knowledge of where the group's territory ends and their neighbor's begins. Rivers, streams, ridges, and swamps tend to serve as boundaries. There are very few unoccupied lands throughout the country. Even forest reserves and similar parts are known to be in a people's ethnic territory. Land disputes and occasional wars arising from conflicting land claims further strengthen this attachment to ethnic homelands.

THE CASE OF FOUR SAMPLE ETHNIC GROUPS

The points discussed so far in this paper about the nature and location of Nigeria's ethnic groups are reflected variously on the following well-known ethnic groups, viz., Hausa, Igbo, Yoruba, and Efik. Each has a history of extra Nigerian origin. The first three constituted the "super-tribes" which nearly succeeded in imposing their supremacy through modern politics. The last one (Efik) was one of the so-called minority tribes and was for a long time misgrouped under the Ibibio because of mistaken identity and unscholarly oral tradition. The three larger groups each number over 10 million and have spilled over into more than two Nigerian states. The Efiks however are all contained within the Southeastern State. The three larger groups are also characterized by a multiplicity of dialectic groups but acknowledge (in each of the three) a standard central language identity. In all cases, each of the four ethnic groups consider themselves one-people, speaking a single language with recognizable mutually intelligible dialects, acknowledging a common oral tradition as to migration routes and source of origin or ancestry, and thinking of themselves as sharing a single basic culture. Each also regards certain parts of Nigeria as its homeland which does not necessarily correspond with political units. The problems and evolutionary changes each of these four groups experiences epitomizes the situation all Nigerian peoples have to grapple with as Nigeria moves towards nationhood and as development plans aim at opening up hitherto neglected areas of the country.

THE QUESTION OF NUMBER

This survey may not have succeeded in settling the question as to how many ethnic groups are in Nigeria, but it is certainly an improvement on previous knowledge and sets a standard for more accurate ethnographic mapping of Nigeria. So far contemporary Nigerian ethnic groups, mapped according to ethnographic principles, indicate that when factors of political expedience, prejudice, and uncontrolled guesswork are excluded, we do not really have 250 ethnic groups. Moreover, only very few real tribes in the anthropological sense actually exist in Nigeria today. As the researcher, the census man, the missionary, the development planner, the Nigerian Youth Corps, the taxman, and the oil explorer penetrate farther into remote ethnic territories of Nigeria, more details are likely to become available for improving the map presented here.

CONCLUSION

Socioeconomic research on Nigeria will for a long time rely upon a thorough understanding of Nigeria's ethnic problems. On the basis of such thorough knowledge, one may find valuable explanations, among other things, to the pattern of the nation's power politics; the unequal distribution of resources and amenities; the problems of internal administrative boundaries; and, the problems of developing a nationalist ideology amidst such diversity of cultures.

There is a problem of resolving the demographic manifestation of earlier assumptions and the need for halting unnecessary annihiliation of uninvestigated cultures in Nigeria. There is also the urgent need for a rapid documentation of all ethnic groups, and conscious efforts to abstract culturally valuable materials of all Nigeria's ethnic groups to build a richer cultural mosaic into Nigerian nationalism should be encouraged. Whatever success is achieved in such efforts would hold far-reaching implications for Nigeria's internal political units. The free circulation of peoples through temporary migration depends upon better interethnic understanding. On matters of national economic development, it is hoped that the ethnocentricity, which led to wrong decisions in the location of economic activity and provision of modern amenities where they were needed most, would be replaced by a conscious effort to plan for the national good. Such a feeling could be generated by replacing current mutual distrust among the ethnic groups with mutual respect for one another's contributions to the nation's strength.

The inputs for deciding on which people constituted an ethnic group relied upon evaluating similarities and relationships in language, settlement and land-use pattern, social structure, legal system, cultural peculiarities, and territorial claims among other factors. Raw materials for some necessary factors such as demographic details must await a properly conducted census (expected in November 1973). Because the present survey is not expected to be the last work on Nigerian ethnic groups, a

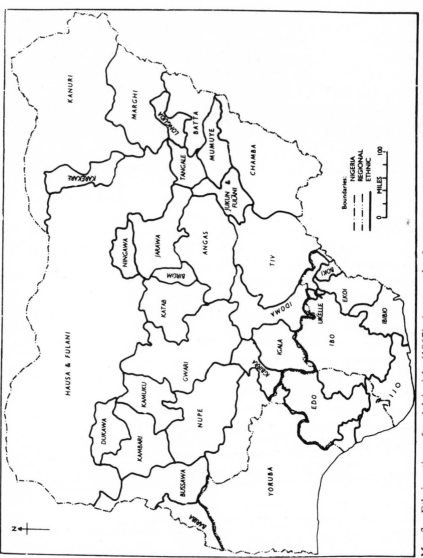

Map 3. Ethnic nations after Adejuyighe (1967). An example of wrong assumptions and perpetuated errors

continuous addition and improvement to the results achieved so far is contemplated.

The author hereby presents for adoption, a map of the ethnic groups as documented from the results of the 1972 survey. It is offered to fellow scholars and all interested Nigerians for further improvement and as a basis for future constructive academic debates. There are still many unknowns and the exact number or identity of Nigerian ethnic groups may elude us a little longer. Given adequate resources and with effective interdisciplinary coordination of efforts in this field, better results can still be achieved. Comments, corrections, and additional field information are always welcome by the author.[10]

Ethnicity, despite its sensitive character, remains a valuable source for understanding the science of man in Nigeria. What is presented, as the product of the present study, in a form open for constructive challenge and improvement, is a map representing what is known as against what is assumed about the ethnic composition of the Nigerian nation. It is the picture as perceived by one researcher (armed with a multidisciplinary approach) in the wake of Nigeria's hopeful evolution into one nation.

[10] Reports and inquiries from scholars should be addressed to the Nigerian Research Centre, P.O. Box 3148, Lagos, Nigeria.

APPENDIX 1: NIGERIAN ETHNIC GROUPS SURVEY 1972/73—GROUND CONTROL

List of Nigerian Settlements: 1. N.W. Sector

Araba	Maiyema	Kaoje
Binji	Kebbi	Raha
Argungu	Mahuta	Yelwa
Buri	Kende	Giro
Birnin Kebbi	Fanna	Bin Yauri
Gulma	Dakingari	Fogge Is.
Gwandu	Fokku	Sulka
Jega	Koko (N.W.S.)	Auna
Bunza	Duku	Bussa
Kamba	Shanga	Babana
		Kenugbe

Nigerian Settlements: 2. N.E. Sector

Matsena	Katagum	Potiskum	Duhu	Ako	Goniri
Meori	Gamawa	Zadawa	Nafada	Kafareti	Damaturu
Gumsi	Ijdubo	Sade	Bajoga	Gungura	Damhalwa
Kumaganum	Katama	Tikau	Doho	Zalanga	Biriri
Nguru	Gwio Kura	Daura	Hirina	Gwaram	Dampehi
Yusufari	Geidam	Fika	Wuyo	Shani	Bornu Yassu
Wadi	Madara	Caabarin	Deba Habe	Meringa	
Gashua	Azare	Darazo	Kumo	Biu	
Gorgoram	Yanda	Fagam	Garho	Yan	
Hadejia	Jajere	Jamari	Gombe	Gaanda	

Nigerian Settlements: 3. Eastern Sector

Pindiga	Numan	Jalingo	Gashasha
Kumo	Girei	Mutum Biyu	Mayo Daga
Yuli	Dong	Gandole	Lissam
Futuk	Yola	Gassol	Bissanla
Tula	Billa	Dampar	Nama
Kaltungo	Mayo-Faran	Bakundi	
Dadiya	Mayo-Lope	Kogin Baba	
Kirim	Lau	Toungo	
Zurak	Lankoviri	Gandole	
Kiri	Kona	Serti	

Nigerian Settlements: 4. Southernmost Sector (Delta and S.E.)

Yenagoe	Okrika
Otokpott	Bori
Buguma	Abak
Degema	Eket
Abonnema	Opobo Town
Brass	Oron
Kula	Calabar
Ifoko	Mkpanak
Bonny	Ikang
Port Harcourt	

Nigerian Settlements: 5. East of Niger River

Abocho	Tahum, Bele	Oturkpo	Nike	Ihiala	Ahoada	Obudu
Bopo	Ihugh	Nsukka	Enugu	Orlu	Elele	Iso Bendiga
Makurdi	Igbor	Okwoga	Amagunze	Okigwi	Ogwe	Obubra
Ibi	Boju Ega	Opi	Ahegbe	Mberubu	Aba	Ikom
Riti	Boju	Aku	Udi	Afikpo	Umuahia	Ugep
Wukari	Ezume	Ukehe	Anam	Oguta	Abakaliki	Oban
Kado	Otukpa (Al Owuno)	Oju	Awka	Orodo	Arochukwu	Itu
Yonov	Idah	Igumale	Onitsha	Owerri	Bende	Uyo
Gboko	Enugu Ezike	Effiuma	Nnewi	Ovoro	Afikpo	
Katsina Ala		Eha Amufu	Okija	Omoho	Ogoja	

Nigerian Settlements: 6. West of Lower Niger River

Lafiagi	Lokoja	Siluko	Obiaruku
Pategi	Okene	Uhi	Warri
Erufu	Ikole	Ubiaja	Usoro
Isanlu Makutu	Ado Ekiti	Auchi	Ughelli
Oro Agor	Ikerre	Ogwashi-Uku	Burutu
Osi	Ikare	Benin City	Forcados
Irele	Ishua	Asaba	Amassama
Kabba	Akure	Koho (M.W.S.)	
Agbaja	Idanre	Sapele	
Akutupa	Ifon		

Nigerian Settlements: 7. N.E. Nigeria

Bisangana	Ngala	Auno	Garkida	Mijilu
Arepe	Rann	Masba	Mubi	Michika
Baga	Kala	Yajua	Gombi	Gulak
Mongonu	Malum Maja	Damboa	Zummo	Madagali
Gashagar	Gulumba	Konduga	Song	Kumshe
Zari	Marte	Maiduguri	Malabu	} Border lands
Kukawa	Dikwa	Gwoza	Girin	
Ngetera	Titiwa	Kaburi	Ribadu	
Gubio	Yerwa	Askira	Gandira	
Gujiram	Chobol	Uba		

Nigerian Settlements: 8. S.W. Sector

Wama	Gwanara	Ago-Are	Fiditi	Ondo	Ado
Yashikera	Shaki	Otu	Iwo	Ijebu-Igbo	Badagry
Eban	Agboho	Ilero	Ede	Ijebu-Ode	Lagos
Kaiama	Ibgetti	Oke-Iho	Ogbomosho	Ishara	Okitipupa
Gwasero	Badesadu	Iseyin	Ikirun	Shagamu	Gbekebo
Jebba	Lanwa	Eruwa	Oshogbo	Epe	Mahin
Sadu	Paiye	Igbo-Ora	Ilesha	Abeokuta	
Kishi	Ilorin	Ibadan	(proper)	Ilaro	
Okuta	Offa	Ilora	Ikire	Agege	
Ilesha	Ila		Ife	Ikeja	
(Kwara State border)			Gbongan		

Nigerian Settlements: 9. Central Area (Niger—Benue Confluence)

Mashegu	Lapai	Gwi	Garahu	Jos	Kwolla
Zungeru	Gbangba	Kwali	Keffi	Wamba	Shendam
Wushishi	Minna	Buga	Karu	Lafia	Gerhawa
Bokani	Kafin	Toto	Kafanchan	Doma	Pankshin
Lemu	Kuta	Baro	Vom	Gidan Rai	Wase
Mokwa	Guni	Koton Karifi	Jemaa	Giza	Dengi
Enagi	Kachia	Umaisha	Bokhos	Awe	Amper
Bida	Kagarko	Loho	Sha	Azara	Dawahi
Badegi	Abuja	Rafin	Panyam	Obi	Boi
Agaie	Zuba	Nasarawa	Bukuru	Assaikio	Lere
		Gabas			Bogoro
					Bununu
					Mato
					Kwande

Nigerian Settlements: 10a. North Central Sector

Kahmao	Isa	Jangero	Katsina	Yashi	Anka
Guru	Sonobo	Faru	Jibiya	Jikamshi	Gummi
Gada	Gandi	Kaura Namoda	Dankama	Chafe	Zamfaru
Gilbedi	Dingyadi	Talata Mafara	Mashi	Dawaki	Dan Dume
Kaddi	Bodinga	Dosara	Bumbum	Kano	Dan Gulbi
Gigane	Denge	Maru	Dan Yashi	Malumfashi	Dan Sadau
Asara	Chadi	Gusau	Daura	Bakori	Bena
Gwadabawa	Maradun	Rawuya	Pimi	Funtua	Danja
Goronyo	Shikafe	Runka	Yamil	Dan Gulbi	Dabai
Rabah	Galadi	Ummadau	Wagini	Birnin Tudu	Zuru
					Rijau

10b. North Central Sector (continued)

Ghaba	Kajuru	Dutsan Wai	Gagarawa	Marahu
Kontonkoro	Kaduna	Anchau	Gumel	Zalau
Zaria	Rigachikun	Gajale	Kazura	Zungur
Birnin Gwari	Soba	Dan Gora	Maigatori	Zaranda
Ibeto	Ikara	Garko	Keffin Hausa	Bununu
Kusherike	Afago	Kano	Jamaar	Yamrat
Kontagora	Kauru	Kunya	Disina	Bauchi
Tegina	Lere	Baure	Birnin Kudu	K. Madaki
Alawa	Zalau	Babure	Ningi	Foggo
Kushaka	Marahu	Gwarzo	Burra	Ringim
				Gaya

APPENDIX 2: 1972 SURVEY—LIST OF NIGERIAN ETHNIC GROUPS

Adar
Afo
Agara
Agbo
Akoko
Ndoki (Akwete)
Angas
Ankwe
Anyang
Arago
Asbina
Aworo
Ayu
Babur
Baburawa
Bahomono
Balama
Bambara
Basa
Bashar
Batu
Bedde
Beriberi
Betem
Birom
Bole
Boki
Borgu
Bunu
Bugale
Burum
Bussa
Bura
Chamba
Chawai
Cheke
Dakarki
Dede
Dimmuk
Duka
Edo

Efik
Efut
Egedde
Ejaghan
Ekoi
Eggon
Ekuri–Unyanga
Fulani
Gaanda
Ganagana
Gamergu
Gobir
Gunga
Gwandara
Gwari
Gwoza
Hausa
Higi
Ibibio
Ibo
Idoma
Igala
Igarra
Igbirra
Igon–Igbe
Ijaw (Ijo)
Ikwere
Ikulu
Ishan
Isoko
Itshekiri
Jaba
Jara
Jukun
Kadara
Kagoma
Kagoro
Kaje
Kalabari (Ijo)
Kamakuru
Kamberi

Kanumbu
Kanuri
Katab
Kentu
Kutev
Kamaton
Kamuku
Karekare
Kilbi
Koro (Korot)
Kuleri
Kwoi
Kyato
Kyenga
Kukuruku
Laro
Lindiri
Linguda
Longude
Lungu
Mada
Maguza
Mama
Mambila
Mandara
Mango
Manchok
Margi
Mbembe
Miango
Migili
Mobber
Montol
Mumuye
Nasarawa
Ndiri
Ndoro
Nembe
Ngizim (Ngizem)
Ningi
Ninzam

Nupe
Obanlike
Ododor
  (Ododop)
Oron
Ora
Ososo
Panchama
Pankshin
Qua
Ribina
Ron Sura
Rukuba
Saya
Shokshok
Shuwa
Tangale
Tera
Tiv
Turi
Ukelle/Iyalla
Umon
Urhobo
Utum
Utuur
Verre
Waja
Warja
Wurkum
Yagba
Yako (Ekoi)
Yauri
Yedina
Yergam
Yerkwa
Yoruba
Yungur
Zamfara
Zumperi

APPENDIX 3: SETTLEMENTS (TOWNS AND VILLAGES) OF NIGERIAN ETHNIC GROUPS (as identified in the field within ethnic territories)

YORUBA
- Cotonu
- Porto-Novo
- Lagos
- Otta
- Ilaro
- Odofa
- Abeokuta
- Ijebu
- Ibadan
- Oyo
- Ilesha
- Ilorin
- Patako
- Ilesha (proper)
- Ondo
- Owo
- Okitipupa
- Mahin
- Omu–Aran
- Makutu–Isnalu
- Kabba
- Okeluse
- Igbaja
- Shonga
- Idoba

KAMBERI
- Konkwesso
- Raha
- Ukata

KYENGA
- Zagga ⎱ West of and within
- Kamba ⎰ Gwandu Division

YAURI
- Kaingiwa
- Lemu
- Bunza (on Sokoto River)

DAKARKI
- Makuta
- Duku
- Rijau
- Sakaba
- Kotonkoro
- Wasagu
- Danrenge

DUKA
- Kwimu
- Ibeto

EDO (BINI)
- Benin City
- Akotogbo
- Siluko
- Sapoba
- Auchi
- Sabongida–Ora
- Iki
- Irrua
- Ubiaja
- Igarra
- Oshin
- Agenebode
- Illushi

ITSEKIRI
- Inyangu
- Warri
- Koko

URHOBO
- Orerokpe
- Elume
- Sapele
- Ugheli
- Abraka

ISOKO
- Ozoro
- Ivrogbo

IGBIRA
- Okene
- Aja–Okuta
- Lokoja
- Gerinya
- Koton–Kerifi
- Umaisha

NUPE
- Egboro
- Ndeji
- Pategi
- Mokwa
- Bokani
- Enagi
- Dakomba
- Katcha
- Baro
- Kulfo
- Manegi
- Bida
- Agaie
- Kataregi
- Lafiagi
- Zungeru

KORO
- Kafin

KAMUKU
- Uregi
- Tegina
- Kagara
- Kurigi (at border with Gwari)

ADAR
- Kurdula
- Makwia
- Tangaza
- Kalmalo (at border with Hausas North of Sokoto Road)

ZAMFARA
- Kebbi
- Gummi
- Donho
- Ragam
- Dan Gulbi
- Anhar
- Mukuchi

IGALA
- Idah
- Itobe
- Adoru
- Ankpa
- Ayangba
- Abejukolo
- Oguma

BORGU
- Kaiama
- Okuta
- Gwanara
- Karunji
- Yashihere
- Nikki (in Dahomey)
- Samia ⎱ Northern
- Kaoje ⎰ Borgu

BUSSA
- Wawa
- New Bussa
- Babana
- Kubi

GUNGA
- Akwana

GOBIR
  Kurawa
  Isa
BUGAJE
  Kusada (Ungawa at border)
GWARI
  Abuja
  Minna
  Kaduna
  Orehi (last border village of south
    Gwariland)
  Badeggi (border)
  Karu (seat of Sudan Interior
    Mission)
  Kuje
  Gawo
  Zungeru
MAGUZA (open scissor-shaped)
    across N.W.S., K.S. and N.C.S.)
  Gusau
  Dutsi–Ma
  Mara
  Yashi
  Chafe
  Kankara (at border with Fulani)
ASBINA
  Land between Dutsi & Katsina
BAREBARI
  Enclave of Maguza—no settlement
    of importance marked
DAN–GUNU
  Gurmana
  Kusherik
  Kushaka
  Kwali
  Gani (border with Koro tribe)
  Zaria
  Gwagwada
  Antu
  Kagarko
  Kurugi
  Bilawari
  Kidandan
  Kwambana
  Dan–Sadan
  Daniya Bakwoi
  Riga Chikur
NINGI
  Burra
  Ningi (and possibly Tibchi at border
    with Warja)

MANGA
  Maigatari
  Gumel
WARJA
  Bunga
  Miya
  Lame
  Tibchi (on border with Ningi)
RIBINA
  Rahama
  Kakowa
BIROM
  Jos
  Bukuru
  Bachit
JARA
  Toro
  Bununu
  Tafawa Balewa?
RUKUBA
  No specific settlement shown on map.
    Neighbors of the Katab and Berorn
KATAB
  Z. Katab
  F. Chawai
JABA
  Kachia
KAJE
  No main settlement—occupy strip
    along the Kaduna–Kafanchan
    Road
KADARA
  Occupy lands between Gwani and
    Jaba—no main settlement but found
    east of Kachai
NINZAM
  Jemaa
  Nunku
YESKWA (along Nasarawa to
    Kaduna Road)
  Gitata
MADA
  Akwanga is main town
EGGON
  Kagbu
LINDIRI
  Wamba
MAMA
  Sha
AYU
  Sandwiched between Birom and
    Mama. No main town.

KULERI (Sandwiched between
   Mama and Angas)
   Monguna Ama
RON SURA
   Panyam
WAYA
   Boi
   Lere
BURUM
   Yuli
BASHAR
   Bashar
   Wase
   Zurak (on border with Wurkum
      tribe)
YERGAM
   Gerkawa (also possibly Pinau)
WURKUM (down to the Benue
      River. Forms border with Fulani
      and Jukun)
   Angule
   Muri
ANKWE (lies between Wase and
      Shemankar streams)
MONTOL (between Deg and
      Wase streams near tributaries of
      Benue)
   Shendam
   Yelwa
DIMMUK (between Angas and
      Montol)
   Kwabsak
   Mushere
JUKUN
   Pinau?
   Mato
   Ibi
   Wukari
   W. Bokk
   Kam
   Gassol
   Yakola
   Tunga (at border with Tiv on
      Benue)
MIGILI
   Lafia
   Obi
ARAGO
   No significant town; only village
AFO
   Indo
   Gofa

BASSA (between Igbiras and
      Gwaris)
   Ugia
   Abaji
KUTEV
   Takum
GWANDARA
   Keffi
   Rafin Gaba
   Assaikio (and possibly Doma)
TIV
   Gboko
   Makurdi
   Tunga
   Azara
   Udei
   Keana
   Arufu
   Kado
   Katsina Ala
   Kasinbila
   Shangeu
   Abinsi
   Shanger Tier
KENTU
   Fali
ZUMPERI
   Bissaula (also Badji in Cameroon)
   Nama
MAMBILA
   Gashaka
   Mayo Daga
NDORO (between Mambilas and
      Kentus)
   Baissa
CHAMBA
   Donga
   Suntai
   Kogin Baba
   Maio Butale
   Taraba
LARO
   Toungo
   Koncha (in Cameroon)
DAHAKARI
   R. Kordo
   Nyibango
VERRE
   Karaki
MUMUYE
   Jalingo
   Mankin
   Mayo Faran
   Gandole

CHEKE
  Malabu
  Belel
HIGI
  Holma; Womdiu?
TURI (between Holma and Mubi)
  Small enclave. No main town.
  Part in Cameroon.
MANDARA
  Madagali
  Michika
BACAMA (near the Benue.
    Opposite Ballas.)
  Lamido
TANGALE
  Biliri
  Tutuk
  Dadiya
WAJA
  Galengu
  T. Banle
TERA (middle Gongola basin)
  D. Kowa
  Kumo
BABUR
  Meringa
  Badir
GAMERGU
  Dumboa
  Buni
  Mulgwe
MARGI
  Ashira
  Bui
KANAKURU
  Shari
BURA
  Kwaya
GANDA
  Gombi
KILBA
  Garkida
YUNGUR (on the south bank of the
    Hawal stream, tributary of the
    Gongola)
  No established settlement.
GWOZA
  Madagali
KAREKARE
  Potiskum
  Jakusho
  Gorgoram

SHUWA
  Bama
  Gulumba
  Kumshe
  Dikwa
  Ngala
  Rann
  Jibe
BEDDE (across the Gana stream)
  Dapchi
BOLE
  Damagum
IDOMA
  Oturkpo
  Otukpa
  Iga Okpaya
  Ntonkan
  Loko (on the Benue)
EGGEDE
  Oju
ANYANG
  Ogoja
  Obubra
KANURI
  Maiduguri
  Bida
  Kukawa
  Arege
  Bosso (in Niger by the lake)
  Dagay (in Niger by the lake)
  Gashagar (on Yobe River)
  Geidem
  Gazabure
  Gashua
  Matsena
  Nguru
  Hadeja
  Kangama
  Mallammaduri
  Birniwa
  Fika
  D Kargum (Shuwa?)
UKELLE/IYALLA
  Enclaved between Egedde, Ibo,
  Anyang, Boki and Yako
BOKI (right into Cameroon)
  Onya
  Nsadip
  Bamba

EFIK
  Calabar
  Ikang
  Odukpani?
  Itu
  Asang
  Umon
  Efiat
IBIBIO
  Uyo
  Eket
  Opobo
  Abak
  Ikot Ekpene
  Ebughu?
  Part of Itu
IKWERE
  Bor
  Part of Port Harcourt
NEMBE
  Nembe
  Brass
KALABARI (are they Ijaws?)
  Egbema
  Degema
IJAW
  Bonny
  Opobo
  Yenagoa
  Otwan
  Akassa
  Ekenie
  Kulama
  Aggi
  Forcados
  Ekeremor
  Okrika
AKWETE
  Sandwiched between Ibo and Ijaw–
    Kalabari.
EKOI
  Ugep
UTUUR
  A small inlier at Tiv territory on
    west bank of River Katsina Ala close
    to town of Katsina Ala.
QUA
  Territory between Calabar and
  Ikang.
EFUT
  Within Efik territory, restricted to
  Calabar and mixed with the city.

IBO ⎫
  Asaba ⎪
  Ogwasiuku ⎬ Ika–Ibo
  Agbor ⎪
  Ossissa ⎪
  Kwale ⎭
  Aboh ⎫ Aboh?
  Ahoada ⎭
  Ubumimi (Akwete or Ngwa?)
  Onitsha
  Ogurugu
  Nsukka
  Enugu
  Eha Amufu
  Ete
  Obolo
  Awka
  Orlu
  Owerri
  Okigwi
  Awgu
  Afikpo
  Abakaliki
  Aboomege
  Ndibulofia
  Aba
  Umuahia
  Bende
  Arochuku
AKOKO ⎫ All said to be in Afenmai's
OSOSO ⎬ rugged country. Minute
ORA ⎭ villages in rock enclaves.
                          ⎫ The two
AWORO – near Lokoja ⎪ are con-
YAGBA – at Isanlu– ⎬ troversial
           Makutu ⎭ towns
NGIZEM ⎫
MANGA ⎪
MOBBER ⎪ located around
MARGI CHIBUK ⎬ Chad Basin.
MARGI KILBA ⎪
YEDINA ⎭
KANEMBU
EJAGHAM (in South Eastern
    State)
FULANI
  Katsina
  Nasarawa
  Kajuru (S.E. of Kaduna)
  Bital
  Yola
  Mutom Biya
  Fulore
  Gombi
  Numan

HAUSA
  Kano
  Daura
  Soloto (with Fulani)
  Kontagora
  Birnin–Kebbi
  Argungu
  Katsina (with Fulani)
  Fokku (Kyanga or Hausa or Fulani
    in N.W.S.)
  Zaria
  Azare
  Bauchi
  Gombe
  Naboro (Fulani?)
  Lanzai (Fulani)
  Nafada (Fulani)
YAKO
  Ugep ⎤
  Nko   ⎬ They are usually
  Nkani ⎟ regarded as Ekois
  Ekuru ⎦
BETEM
  Main town: Betem and Ehom.
  They share half of Akankpa Division
    with the Ejaghams.
UKWUANI
  They are Ibos in Midwestern State
ISHAN (they are a subgroup of the
    Bini)
  Main towns: Ubiaja and Irrua.
BAHOMONO (settlements on the
    Cross River south and east sides)
  Ediba
  Usumitong
  Anong
  Afafanyi
  Ebom

AGBO (neighbors of the
    Bahomono)
  Lekuleku
  Adadara
  Letatama
  Lebuma
  Itigidi
  Igbo–Ekureku
  Igbo–Imabana
  The Ntezi, isolated group 14 miles
    on Enugu–Abakaliki Road are
    also said to belong here.
ORON
  Squeezed by Efik and Ibibio
    influences to point of near
    absorption by both
IGARRA (in Midwestern State)
  (a) Scattered villages, many
      dialects; akin to the Igbiras;
      according to their oral tradi-
      tion, they originated from
      Kwara.
  (b) They assume Yoruba names,
      – e.g., Mr. Lawrence Osho at
      Unilag comes from a village 20
      miles near Northwest of Auchi
      on Ikare–Auchi Road.
EJAGHAM
  Under Ikom Division with sections
    spread into southern half of
    Akankpa.
MBEMBE (contains Obanlike too)
EKOI (accommodates)
  Ododops
  Ukelle
  Akaju
  Ekuri

APPENDIX 4: UNIVERSITY OF LAGOS STUDENTS, MARCH 1972, ANALYSIS OF ETHNIC GROUPS SURVEY QUESTIONNAIRE

1. Yoruba	131	10. Birom	1
Ilaje	1	11. Urhobo (Sobo)	11
Ilesha	3	12. Isoko	6
Egba	6	13. Fulani	1
Ijebu	14	14. Ibibio	6
2. Bini (Edo since 1440 A.D.)	17	15. Igbirra	4
Ishan	6	16. Gwari	1
3. Ibo	43	17. Ijumu	1
Ika	2	18. Igara	1
Ukwani	1		
4. Itshekiri (Jekri)	5		
5. Efik	2		
6. Ijaw	6		
Nembe (Brass)	1		
Kalabari	1		
7. Ora	2		
8. Tiv (Munchi)	1		
9. Nupe	1		

Note: Total response in subsample = 275
Total number of ethnic groups represented = 18
Number of students stating only subethnic groups = 42 out of 275

APPENDIX 5: SPECIMEN OF STUDENTS' QUESTIONNAIRE FOR SAMPLE SURVEY

Name: . . . . M/F* (cross one)
Course of Study: . . . .
Your Place of Birth: . . . .
Father's Ethnic Group: . . . .
  His village or town: . . . .
    State: . . . .
Mother's Ethnic Group: . . . .
  Her village or town: . . . .
    State: . . . .
Your Own Ethnic Group: . . . .
  Your village or town: . . . .
    State: . . . .
Your Spouse's Ethnic Group (married or engaged): . . . .
  His/Her village or town: . . . .
    State: . . . .

N.B. The information you supply on this form will be treated with the utmost confidence. You are supplying essential data for a proper study of Nigeria's ethnic groups (tribes). How many and where? Please do so sincerely.

REFERENCES

AMOS, A.
  1968a "Modern Yorubas in cultural transition," in *Proceedings of the VIII International Congress of Anthropological and Ethnological Sciences*, volume 3. Tokyo.
  1968b "Oral tradition in reconstructing the African past," in *Proceedings of the VIII International Congress of Anthropological and Ethnological Sciences*, volume 3. Tokyo.

ADEJUYIGHE, O.
  1967 "Aspects of the political geography of Nigeria with particular reference to the problem of unification." Unpublished Ph.D. dissertation, Durham University.

BOHANNAN, P., LAURA BOHANNAN
  1953 "The Tiv of Central Nigeria," in *Ethnological survey of Africa*. London.

BOSTON, J.
  1963 Notes on the origin of the Igala. *Journal of the Historical Society of Nigeria* 2(3).

BRADBURY, M. R.
  1957 *The Benin kingdom and the Edo-speaking peoples of S. W. Nigeria.* London: I.A.I.
  1964 "The historical use of comparative ethnology with specific reference to Benin and Yoruba," in *The historian in tropical Africa*. Edited by J. Vansina et. al. London.

BRADBURY, M. R., P. C. LLOYD
  1959 *The Benin kingdom and the Edo-speaking peoples, etc., plus the Itshekiri.* London: I.A.I.

FLOYD, B.
  1969 *Eastern Nigeria: a geographical view.* London: Macmillan.

FORDE, DARYLL
  1964 *Yakö studies.* London: I.A.I.

GREEN, M. M.
  1947 *Igbo village affairs.* London.

GREENBERG, JOSEPH H.
  1955 *Studies in African linguistic classification.*
  1960 Linguistic evidence for influence of Kanuri on Hausa. *Journal of African History* 1(2).

HILL, POLLY
  1972 *Village Hausas.* Cambridge: Cambridge University Press.

JONES, G. I.
  1963 European and African tradition on the Rio Real. *Journal of African History* 4(3).
  1963 *The trading state of the Oil Rivers.* London: Oxford University Press.

LLOYD, P. C.
  1963 The Itshekiri in the nineteenth century: an outline of social history. *Journal of African History* 4(2):207–231.

LLOYD, P. C., A. F. C. RYDER
  1954 "Don Domingos, Prince of Warri—Portuguese contact with the Itshekiri. *Odu*.

MEEK, C. K.
  1925 *Northern tribes of Nigeria.* 2 volumes. London: Frank Cass.

MURDOCK, G. P.
1959 *Africa: its people and their culture history.* New York: McGraw-Hill.
NADEL, S. F.
1942 *Black Byzantium: the kingdom of Nupe in Nigeria.* London: Oxford University Press.
PERHAM, M., *editor*
1963 *The Diaries of Lord Lugurd*, volume 4. Evanston: Northwestern University Press.
TALBOT, P. AMAURY
1969 *Southern Nigeria: an official report based on the 1921 census*, (four volumes). London: Frank Cass. (First published in 1926.)
TEMPLE, O.
1969 Notes on the tribes of Northern Nigeria. An official report compiled by O. Temple and edited by C. L. Temple. London: Frank Cass. (First published in 1921.)
WATSON, JANE
1967 *Nigeria: Republic of a hundred kings.* Living in Today's World. Champaign, Ill.: Garrard.

The Chinese Community in Canada before 1947 and Some Recent Developments

W. S. CHOW

The Chinese have been present in Canada for more than one hundred years. Before 1947 the population consisted mainly of immigrants from rural China, forming a closely knit and homogeneous community. The date 1947 is significant in that it marks the beginning of a new type of immigrant — from cosmopolitan Hong Kong. This article deals with the Chinese emigration from their homeland, their popular image, occupations, social organizations, a life history, and the social change in the community after 1947. The sources of data are library research, personal background, and informal conversation with the elders of the community.

EMIGRATIONS

Most of the Chinese in Canada came from the Pearl River delta in the Province of Kwantung. Their emigrations overseas were apparently an unplanned result of poverty and overpopulation in China and the opportunity for travel offered by proximity to the sea. Furthermore, knowledge of the countries abroad existed in Canton from a very early period. Already in the Tang Dynasty (A.D. 618–907) there were official superintendents of merchant shipping at Canton. According to the *Hsin Tang Shu* written by a Tang geographer, Chinese merchant ships sailed frequently between Canton and the Persian Gulf. Recent archeological excavations show in detail the living quarters of the Arab enclaves in Canton. European traders, when they went to China, usually went to Canton, and overseas opportunities naturally came in there. Contact with countries of the British Empire was secured through the Crown Colony of Hong Kong established one year after the end of the Opium War (1840–1842).

However, emigration was not easy and was regarded as a capital offense by the Chinese government before 1859. The traditional attitude of the government towards emigration might be seen in the words of Emperor Ch'ien Lung (1736–1796), when he was told of the Batavia Massacre on October 10, 1740, in which ten thousand Chinese were said to have been killed by the Dutch in Java. The Emperor said, "The court has nothing to do with the deserters of the Heavenly Dynasty, who would even leave the ancestral home and graveyards in order to seek for wealth abroad" (Chui 1965:141). The government was unable to enforce the emigration law however; those who ventured overseas did so at their own risk, and had to rely on themselves and their own power of organization to protect their interests.

By the second half of the nineteenth century, many had emigrated as indentured laborers. They were recruited by the agents of the coolie brokers of Hong Kong to work for a number of years overseas with the understanding that they could return to China at the end of their contract and that their ash residue would be sent home for burial if they should die in the foreign land.

The emigrants to the New World knew very little about the country beyond the fact that their destination was Gold Mountain, as San Francisco was called, where they were to work for twenty to twenty-five dollars per month for a number of years; for these benefits they returned a fee to the coolie broker, and, of course, they would have to pay for their passage home. Some people went to the New World as a result of their contact with the returning overseas Chinese who provided them with the means to go abroad. The ideal of an emigrant was to amass a fortune and to see himself back to his birthplace where he could bring glory to his relatives and ancestors. But such an ideal was seldom realized.

The earliest Chinese immigrants came to North America when gold was discovered in California in 1840. By about 1858 some of them had migrated north to the Fraser and Cariboo valleys, where gold was also discovered. The first considerable immigration to Canada was to British Columbia, in connection with the construction of the Canadian Pacific Railway project. The contractor, the Ondertonk Company, found difficulty in securing enough white labor for the construction in the mountainous section. Through the coolie brokers in San Francisco and Hong Kong, the contractor brought in ten shiploads of about six thousand laborers from Hong Kong in 1881 (Berton 1971:109). Between 1881 and 1884, during the construction, over 15,700 Chinese laborers arrived in the province (Royal Commission of Canada 1969:21).

Meanwhile anti-Chinese sentiments were spreading on the West Coast of the continent. It appeared to both the provincial and federal governments that the Chinese laborers contributed to the economic development of British Columbia insofar as there was a labor shortage; however, it was claimed by a large part of the public that white labor would be attracted if the Chinese were not present. Consequently, on the completion of the Canadian Pacific Railway, parliamentary actions culminated in the passage of legislation in 1885, stipulating that, as a condition of entering Canada, Chinese laborers would be required to pay a head tax of fifty dollars. In 1901 this head tax was increased to one hundred dollars, in 1904 to five hundred. This was paid by all Chinese immigrants "except consular officers, merchants and clergymen and their families, tourists, men of science, students and teachers" (*Canada year book* 1930:175).

At the turn of the century, countries with populations of European ancestry, including the United States, Canada, New Zealand, Australia and Mexico, began to restrict Chinese entry. In Canada, the Chinese Immigration Act of 1923 restricted the entry of persons of Chinese origin (see Table 1), irrespective of citizenship, "other than governmental representatives, Chinese children born in Canada, merchants and students" (*Canada year book* 1930:174ff).

In spite of the head tax, the Chinese population in Canada continued to rise until 1931. However, from then on the population began to decline. Between 1931 and 1951 there was a drop of 13,991 in population (see Table 2). Of these, many had returned to China and the rest had died in Canada. On the basis of the 1941 census, the sex ratio of the Chinese population was 7.8 males to one female; by 1951 this had changed to 3.7 males to one female, i.e. before 1947 the Chinese in Canada were mostly men who were either single or who had left their wives in China.

Table 1. Arrivals of immigrants of Chinese origin, 1901–1966

Year	Arrivals
1901	2,544
1910	2,302
1915	1,258
1920	544
1924	674
1925–1946	16
1947	21
1948	76
1950	1,476
1958	2,630
1959	2,586
1960	1,402
1961	894
1962	876
1963	1,571
1964	3,210
1966	5,178

Sources: Canada year book 1937: 205, 1942: 156, 1947: 133, 1950: 189, 1952–1953: 169, 1961: 188, 1965: 211, 1967: 221, 1968: 235.

Table 2.   Population in Canada of
Chinese origin, 1881–1951

Year	Population
1881	4,383
1901	17,312
1911	27,831
1921	39,587
1931	46,519
1941	34,627
1951	32,528

Sources: Canada year book 1947: 118,
1952–1953: 149; *1961 census of Canada*
1964: Bulletin 1, 3–9 and Table 114–2.

THE POPULAR IMAGE

In the early years, the popular image of the Chinese arrivals was generally harsh and unfavorable. In appearance all individuals looked alike: same faces, modes of dress, and pigtails. Irrespective of the context, the individuals were often seen to represent the totality. Thus the arrivals were characterized as a broad mass of "atheistic heathens," "opium smokers," "sodomists," and "gamblers." They were also accused of having no regard for the sanctity of oaths and of falsifying tax records to their own benefit. The following quotation from the *Report of the Royal Commission on Chinese immigration* (1885:13) is fairly representative of the various testimonies given to the Commission:

The Chinese know nothing of our institutions, except the prisons. They do not know or care about citizenship, only to evade the merest duties or burdens of it. . . . As a rule they are ignorant, slavish, submissive, and often brutish in their manners, living in hovels, poorly fed, worse clad, over-worked, profane and immoral in the extreme.

The negative stereotypes of the Chinese in the early twentieth century were epitomized in Doctor Fu Manchu, a character made popular by the fiction published in the 1930s by the Irish-American writer Sax Rohmer. This character was the embodiment of the crafty evil Chinese: revengeful, sinister, wicked, the commander of a host of thugs and slaves, and a master of oriental drugs.

However, there were the exceptional few whose opinions of the Chinese were sympathetic and favorable. Scores of missionaries, medical doctors, and governmental officials praised the Chinese as being honest and law-abiding. The Chief Justice of British Columbia, Sir Matthew Begbie, for example, testified to the Royal Commission on Chinese Immigration that they are "notoriously excellent tenants . . ." and that the "pilfering by Chinese manservants is really quite inconsiderable" (Royal Commission of Canada 1885:73).

In any case, the stereotypes of the Chinese began to change to one of general approval by the 1930s. It appeared to the public that the Chinese were hardworking, persevering, kind towards children, respectful towards elders, and law-abiding. The Chinese then became the people of curio shops, laundry shops, and exotic dishes. The goodness of the Chinese was well reflected in Pearl Buck's book, *The good earth*. In the 1940s, the war effort in China seemed to gain the admiration of the people in North America, and the Chinese immigrants became a part of the popular image of fighting China and the heroic allies in Asia.

OCCUPATIONS

During the construction of the western section of the Canadian Pacific Railway, thousands of Chinese workers were employed by the railway contractor. The reasons for their being employed were:

1. Due to the railway boom in the Far West of the continent, there was little white labor available, this having been drawn mainly from San Francisco.

2. The employment of the Chinese laborers saved the contractor millions of dollars. White laborers demanded a higher wage — one dollar fifty to one dollar seventy-five per day, in comparison to the one dollar per day wage of the Chinese. Besides, contracts made with the Chinese labor agents required the laborers to buy their provisions from the railway store where the prices were inflated; otherwise, the laborers would only be paid eighty cents per day (Berton 1971:197).

3. The laborers formed good working relationships with the foremen and other railway officials, and were regarded as reliable, cooperative, and efficient. Moreover, the Chinese laborers were directly under the control of a number of Chinese headmen. If a laborer was discharged because of misconduct, his headman was always in a position to find a substitute (Campbell 1923:45). Consequently, in spite of the protests from the press across Canada and the widespread anti-Chinese sentiments in the West, the employment of the Chinese appeared to the contractor as the best solution for his labor problems.

Work in the mountainous section was hazardous. Frequently, tunnels had to be dug in the old rocks; men had to be lowered hundreds of feet down the faces of the steep cliffs; the roadbed had to be hewn slowly and gradually. During the summer, the bush was infested with mosquitoes; still the laborers worked on with typical peasant industry. However, they could not withstand the severe Canadian winter. Many of them had to stop work by the end of November.

On top of the physical danger, scurvy and tuberculosis were rife. The death-rate among Chinese workers was high. As the Royal Commission on Bilingualism and Biculturalism (1969:21) notes: "It has been said that a Chinese is buried beneath every mile of track of the railway through the mountains of British Columbia."

Each time a section of the railway was completed a number of laborers were discharged, so that by the end of 1884, when the project was near completion, most of them were paid off and were no longer wanted as maintenance men. Many who came from San Francisco and Seattle returned to the United States. Many who wished to return to China did not have the means to do so and settled in Canada, at least temporarily.

The Manitoba Free Press on November 19, 1887 reported the arrival by stagecoach in Winnipeg of the first three Chinese to open a laundry business. They probably represented the exceptionally adventurous few who wandered away from the community in Vancouver. Migrations to the east did not start until 1890 and Montreal was the main focal point of settlement. By 1901 there was a Chinese population of just under a thousand in Montreal. Toronto, which became the main focus for migration in later years, had a Chinese population of about one-half that of Montreal. Migrations to the prairies did not start until 1901, when the wheat boom, which was characterized by rapid urbanization, favorable economic circumstances, and a huge inflow of European settlers was well under way. While the rapid phase of western settlement was over by 1913, Chinese migrations to the prairies continued into the late 1910s. If the dispersion period of the Chinese population in the United States occurred between 1880 and 1910 (Lee 1949:426), the dispersion period in Canada occurred between 1890 and 1920. The time lag of ten years apparently reflected the different timing of urbanization in the two countries. After 1920, the Chinese population in Vancouver was no longer attracted to the other Canadian cities (see Tables 3 and 4).

According to the 1931 census (see Table 5), the occupations of the Chinese ethnic group were predominantly in the category of personal service which included mainly cooks, domestic servants either in private households or hotels and restaurants, cafe and lunch-counter keepers. Next in importance was agriculture, which included many farm laborers and truck gardeners in British Columbia. Trade was third in importance, about one-half of the persons in this category were listed as owners and managers of wholesale and retail stores. Of minor importance was food manufacturing. This included the salmon canning industry in Vancouver and the making of Chinese food, catering mainly to the Chinese restaurants and consumers. It should be noted that by 1931 the laundry business (commonly a Chinese enterprise in Canadian cities early in the century[1] and often known as the "traditional occupation" of the Chinese

---

[1]   According to the figures given by the Chinese Consulate, Chinese persons engaged in the laundry business numbered 14,000, and those in the restaurant business 9,000 in 1924 (Cheng 1931:196).

Table 3. Distribution of Chinese population in Canadian provinces, 1901–1941

Provinces	1901	1911	1921	1941
British Columbia	14,885	19,568	23,533	18,619
Alberta	235	1,787	3,581	3,122
Saskatchewan	41	957	2,667	2,545
Manitoba	206	885	1,331	1,248
Ontario	732	2,766	5,625	6,143
Quebec	1,037	1,578	2,335	2,378

Sources: Canada year book 1912: 24, 25, 1922–1923: 160–161; Eighth (1941) census of Canada 1946: II, 283–317.

Table 4. Distribution of Chinese population in Canadian cities, 1921, 1941

Cities	1921	1941
Vancouver	6,484	7,880
Calgary	688	799
Edmonton	518	384
Winnipeg	814	762
Toronto	2,134	2,559
Montreal	1,735	1,865

Sources: Canada year book 1922–1923: 162; Eighth (1941) census of Canada 1946: II, 508–511.

Table 5. The important occupational groupings of gainfully occupied Chinese in Canada in 1931

Occupations	Number of persons	Percentage
Service	21,095	52.4
(personal service)	(14,564)	(36.2)
Manufacturing	1,054	2.6
(food products)	(744)	(1.8)
Trade	2,733	6.8
Lumbermen	649	1.6
Agriculture	4,718	11.7
Other	10,014	24.9
Total occupations	40,263	100.0

Sources: Seventh (1931) census of Canada 1936: VII, 430–443.

immigrants) was no longer important. Laundry machines had displaced the Chinese laundry business.

A number of factors severely limited the choice of occupations. The immigrants spoke very little English and lacked the proper background for many jobs in the urban settings. Furthermore, people tended to seek jobs from those who had kinship and territorial ties in China. However, having said this, one has to acknowledge that commercial firms and social institutions of the host society tended to exclude the Asians from participation. The Rev. S. S. Osterhout of the United Church, Superintendent of Oriental Missions West of the Great Lakes (1927:40–41) wrote:

The chief difficulties arise as the [Chinese] graduates from high school and universities emerge into commercial life. Here discrimination is marked. . . . There are few industries which are open to them except those carried on among themselves, such as the green grocer stores, Oriental shops, laundries and cafes. . . .
Not only are Orientals of Canadian birth denied full entrance into industrial life, but their access to clubs and even some churches is greatly restricted.

Under these conditions, the Chinese created occupations that supplemented those of the other ethnic groups, and that were clearly adapted to the urban settings. For example, the Chinese hand-laundry business catered to customers who liked their washing and ironing to be done meticulously, and became famous, as Wright (1955:158) wrote: "for removing grease and coal dust from a railman's overalls, starching a clerical collar, and expertly stiffening the front of a dress shirt." The Chinese restaurants catered to customers who would like their food prepared somewhat differently, if not in an exotic manner. Furthermore, their curio shops and restaurants were often tourist attraction centers. Even truck gardening was adapted to the metropolitan life. In short, the larger the metropolis, the larger was the clientele available for the Chinese enterprise. This perhaps explains the choice of Montreal as the first target of migration after Vancouver as well as the migration to the prairie cities while the wheat boom was well under way, and also explains the failure of the prairie cities to attract more Chinese from Vancouver after the rapid phase of development was over.

SOCIAL ORGANIZATIONS

The Six Companies of San Francisco

The Six Companies, transliterated as the Sam Yup, Yung Wo, Kong Chow, Wing Lung, Hop Wo, and Yan Wo, are relevant to this study, even though they were situated in San Francisco. Their functions were manifold. First, they were coolie brokers; through them, the Canadian Pacific Railway and the Central Pacific Railroad recruited a large body of laborers from China. Besides receiving payments from the railway contractors, the Companies, according to the testimony given by Colonel Bee, who proclaimed himself as the Consul of China in San Francisco, collected a fee of two dollars fifty cents to ten dollars from the individual workers. The actual amount one had to pay depended on how many of one's countrymen were represented in the company; the more countrymen one had in the company, the less one had to pay (Royal Commission of Canada 1885:19). That what one had paid would benefit one's countrymen certainly implied the *Landsmannschaft* nature of these Companies.

The indentured laborers were honor-bound to fulfill their quota of "work years" in North America. Absconding, which was very common among the indentured laborers from China working in Malaya, probably seldom occurred here. Besides being capable of using coercive force and violence, the Companies had close connections with the shipping companies on the West Coast. Any attempt by indentured laborers to get on board any ship without the approval of the Six Companies would certainly end in failure.

According to the testimony of one American person who had ten years residence in China and who was "active in the United States Consul" in Hong Kong, "All coolies returning to China complain of the extortions, deception, and arbitrary conduct of the Companies here" (Royal Commission of Canada 1885:189). If this had been the experience of the returning overseas Chinese, their counterparts in North America who could not speak English and who were totally uninformed about the host society would have to look towards the Six Companies for protection and perhaps as the focus of loyalty.

These Companies often acted as representatives for the whole Chinese community in the United States. In a letter to President Grant of the United States, the presidents of the Six Companies wrote, "In the absence of any consular representative, we the undersigned, in the name and on behalf of the Chinese people now in America, would most respectfully present for your consideration the following statements regarding the subject of Chinese immigration to this country"[2] (as quoted by Baldwin 1890:40).

Among the Chinese, the Companies were often responsible for the arbitration of disputes between segments of the community. The Companies maintained private hospitals, and if someone should fall sick at the job site, a team would be sent to look after him. However, in the case of the indentured laborers of the Canadian Pacific Railway, the Companies failed to provide adequate medical attention.

Lastly, these Companies were commercial firms which monopolized a good proportion of the trade between China and San Francisco. They also handled the remittances made by the Chinese sojourners to their kin at home. The Companies reached the height of their power during the 1870s and early 1880s. In British Columbia, their social control over the Chinese was diminished with the completion of the railway construction.

---

[2] Probably written in 1875, date not cited by Baldwin (1890:40). China did not accredit a diplomatic representative in the United States until 1878.

•

The Associations

Wherever there were Chinese living overseas, associations or guilds began to spread. These associations were not an overseas invention. In China fellow provincials, for example, living in a strange part of the country tended to group together and form associations. Travellers, merchants, and, in the case of the capital, examination-taking students, would on arrival call on these associations for guidance. Among the overseas Chinese in the various parts of the world, dialects, territorial origins, surnames, and clans were often the associational modes of recruiting memberships, whatever the professed aims of the associations might be: recreational clubs, reading rooms, provincial guilds, surname associations, professional societies, and so forth. The modes of membership recruiting were directly related to the detailed features of the local ethnic community and the lines of cleavage.

Linguistically the Chinese population in Canada was relatively homogeneous, as it was drawn mainly from the six counties at the Pearl River delta in Kwantung where the dialects were fairly similar. Therefore dialect was not an important basis for forming associations. However, people grouped themselves according to their territorial origins. A few associations were publicly known as *tung hsiang hui* [territorial associations]; the Chung Shan Lung Cheng Tung Hsiang Hui of Vancouver was one such example. Some associations, though known as dramatic societies, recreational clubs, and so forth, contained dominant county groups in their membership. Territorial origins seemed to be the membership recruiting factor in these associations.

In the traditional society all those who bore the same surname were regarded as being patrilineally related. This bond united all those using the same Chinese character for their surname, regardless of what part of China they came from. The surname was traditionally exogamous and remained so to a great extent. This surname group could be said to be the widest clan group and was based upon a largely fictitious common unilineal descent. The surname group was subject to segmentation into innumerable local groups. These local clans, often occupying a single village or groups of villages, had an organized structure under the leadership of a recognized head.

Among the overseas Chinese, including those in Canada, the surname group as a whole took the place of the local clan in traditional China. The immigrants came from the various local clans and they did not group themselves in such a way as to duplicate the kinship structure in the homeland on a miniature scale. They formed associations on the basis of surnames in the various Canadian cities in which they lived. Examples were: Lin Hsi-ho Tang for the Lin clan, Kuan Lung-hsi Tang for the Kaun clan, Huang Chiang-hsia Tang for the Huang clan, Li Shi Kung-suo for the Li clan, and so forth.

The general activities of the associations were not related to clan or territorial matters *per se*. A family life was mostly absent for the sojourners, and marriages did not occur very often. Performance of rituals and care of the ancestral temples and tombs were left to the kin in the native land. In general, the associations were looked upon as sources of financial and moral support, for example, in the event of death, or business, or legal difficulties. Mutual protection was particularly necessary at the turn of the century when anti-Chinese riots broke out sporadically in British Columbia.

The activities of the associations were often for purposes of recreation and entertainment. They might include music, dramas, boxing and swordplay, lion dance, mahjong, and so forth. Scores of these associations had libraries where Chinese publications could be read. A few associations sponsored afternoon or evening classes in which the Chinese language was taught to children and English to adults.

Generally speaking, these associations functioned less on the principle of clanship than on what Hammond (1972:5) termed "institutionalized friendship." In the homeland, kinship was the important governing principle that regulated with whom one should show respect, cooperate, exchange gifts, and so forth. However, emigration had disengaged a person from his social milieu as well as from the expectations and norms of his native society. In particular, he was relieved of the jurisdiction exercised by the elders of the local clans. Clan rules and traditional writings on moral principles frequently warned against prostitution and gambling as vices that would ruin one's family and make one a liability to the clan. The fact was that at the turn of the century, prostitution and gambling were much more widespread among the overseas Chinese, including those in Canada, than in southern China.

A number of associations in Canada were so preoccupied with mahjong, fantan, and other gambling activities that they had the appearance of professional gambling dens. For example, Palmer (1972:61) reported that in the late thirties there were fourteen gambling establishments in the small Chinese community in Lethbridge, and that the proceeds were said in court hearings to be used for welfare purposes among the elders. In the forties police action stopped the widespread gambling activities whether they occurred in the actual gambling dens or in the associations. Prostitution and gambling among the immigrants can be explained in terms of the predominantly male community and even more importantly, in terms of their disengagement from the traditional social network that helped the individuals in the selection of approved modes of behavior.

A prominent association with lodges across Canada was the Hung Men Hui, also known as the Chi-kung Tang and Chinese Freemasons. Its origin was traceable to the Triad Societies in China. These were secret and illegitimate organizations widespread in southern China during the nineteenth century. They existed not as groups of outlaws hidden in the hills, but as functional parts of the local communities. Their chief slogan was, "Overthrow the Ching and restore the Ming." These organizations were the direct result of hostility between the Han and Manchu ethnic groups in China.

The Hung Men Hui was also widely distributed among the overseas Chinese in Southeast Asia and Hawaii, and in Canada evidently many of the early immigrants were Hung Men members. They remained anti-Manchu and observed the rituals of the Hung Men, which consisted of series of solemn oaths aimed at creating a sworn brotherhood. However, the organization was no longer secret and the activities of the Hung Men were normally similar to the other associations in the community. Still, at the turn of the century, they carried out their anti-Manchu objective insofar as they gave financial and moral support to the Republican revolution. The founder of the Republic, Sun Yat-sen, was in Vancouver in 1897 and in San Francisco in 1904, and on both occasions he launched successful fund-raising campaigns with the members of the Hung Men. Today in Canton city, China, on the marble of a monument commemorating the 1911 Canton Uprising, are carved the names of the various lodges of Hung Men Hui in Canadian and American cities. The Hung Men maintains a daily newspaper in Vancouver, makes significant investments in real estate, and remains a well-financed and well-supported association in Canada.

In the 1910s an ancillary organization of the ruling political party of Republican China, known as the Chinese National League, was formed in various cities in Canada. One of the primary objectives of this organization was to keep the overseas Chinese in close touch with China. The activities included the initiation and organization of important national events such as observance of the National Day, the anniversaries of the Canton Uprising, and so forth. The organization also maintained three daily newspapers in Canada.

The ruling political party of Republican China, the Kuomintang, was deeply interested in the wealth of overseas Chinese. At the outbreak of the Sino-Japanese War, the Kuomintang launched a world-wide fund-raising campaign among overseas Chinese. In the United States, Lee (1960:150–155) reported that during the 1930s and 1940s the so-called "voluntary taxes" imposed by the nationalist organizations became so burdensome that many Chinese left the city in order to avoid excessive contributions. In Canada the Chinese National League established a front organization known as the Chinese Patriotic League to take charge of the "China Relief Fund." While contributions were made in part voluntarily, the fund-raising campaign also involved group pressure and probably imposition of fines. For example, during 1940 Chinese persons in Winnipeg who failed to make prompt contributions towards the fund might receive a notice that read, ". . . The deadline has now been extended for two weeks. If you fail to contribute by that date, you will be punished. . . ."[3] The Chinese Patriotic League was disbanded at the end of the war. Ordinarily, the activities of the National League were very similar to those of the other associations, which might involve an afternoon school for children, a movie show, and perhaps for some members a game of mahjong.

A LIFE HISTORY

Mr. Li, a resident of Winnipeg, was born in the county of Hsin Hui, Kwantung in 1882. He was a peasant until 1913 when a relative returned from Canada for a visit and told him of the opportunities there. The returnee also offered to lend him five hundred Canadian dollars which he could use to clear the head-taxation on entry into Canada. He decided to leave his wife, children, and kin and set sail for Canada, with the hope of returning in a few years' time. He followed his relative to Hong Kong where they took the British liner, the "Russian Queen," bound for Vancouver. In Vancouver, they went to a hostel housed above a grocery shop, where the agent for the Canadian Pacific Railway in the community was also located. After three days, they went to Moose Jaw, Saskatchewan. Together with one hundred Chinese workers, they were employed in an *abattoir*. In his later days, he still recalled the foreman as a kindly person, and that floor and carcass washings were done by the Chinese workers, while the Canadian workers did the skinning and butchering. He worked for ten hours per day at thirty cents per hour. In 1914, he was hired by the Canadian Pacific Railway for repairing the construction. He remembered that many of his Chinese friends found jobs in factories because, as he said, the whites had gone to war. By 1918 he had earned enough to clear the debts he had incurred on emigration to Canada and to make a return trip to China. On his return to Canada the following year, he worked in a laundry shop in Regina, an employment which he kept until 1936. Then he returned to China with the thought of settling down for the rest of his life. However, he found that his native land was becoming poorer and poorer. Also, his eldest son and younger brothers had emigrated to Thailand a few years previously. When the Sino-Japanese War broke out in 1937, he concluded that the comfort of a family life and a kin circle was not for him, and once again he left his wife and ancestral land for Canada, perhaps for the last time. Back in Canada,

---

[3]   Two documents now possessed by the writer dated 15 April, 1940 and 20 October, 1940.

he worked as a kitchen helper in a Chinese restaurant in Winnipeg until his retirement in 1947. He could not take up the position of a waiter which had better pay because he could speak little English.

During his long years of retirement, he regularly sent a token sum of money to his son and brothers who were then his only surviving relatives. After his retirement he began to attend church service because he enjoyed the companionship there. Each day he spent hours sitting in an association, chatting and watching mahjong games. He died at the age of ninety-one, leaving one thousand and six hundred dollars in his bank account, more than sufficient to cover his funeral expenses. One important item in his will was: "Be sure that everybody who attends my funeral is treated to a sumptuous meal."

SOCIAL CHANGE AND CONCLUSION

By 1947, the Chinese communities in Canada had become communities of old men. On July 30, 1947, the *Winnipeg Free Press* painted a bleak picture which was both literally and metaphorically true of the Chinese communities in Canada:

It was a blistering night, and in every doorway were aged and wizened orientals, seeking a breath of air. Some were perched on chairs and stools, brought from rooms above Chinese stores and restaurants. Others huddled together beneath corner street lights, smoking their pipes and chatting in their native tongue. They looked old, very old. . . .

However, the Chinese communities did not disappear. Regulations for Chinese immigration were changed in 1947: new immigrants comprising the wives, husbands and children of Chinese residents of Canada were allowed to enter.

Under the 1947 immigration regulations, there were numerous cases of illegal entry by people from Hong Kong, which involved forgery, impersonation and international smuggling rings. In 1960 Chinese communities in the major cities across Canada were raided by the Royal Canadian Mounted Police. In response to the police action, Chinese voluntary associations presented their case through the mass media, asserting that the publicity of the problem of illegal entry was exaggerated. In the same year the federal government offered amnesty to the illegal entrants. Pamphlets in Chinese were distributed to Chinese residents, declaring that the illegal entrants, as long as they were not assisting the racketeers, would not be prosecuted and deported.

As a result of these events, the Immigration Department took stricter measures in admitting immigrants from Hong Kong, to make sure that they were authentic. Consequently, in 1960, the number of entrants of

Chinese origin dropped to about one-half of that in 1959; in 1961 and 1962, one-third; and in 1963, one-half. Only in 1964, did the number of entrants return to the main trend of increase (see Table 1). Invariably, in the early sixties, in the minds of many Canadians Chinese were associated with illicit entry into Canada.

Since 1962, a Chinese immigrant can enter the country as an independent immigrant on the basis of the "point system" of the 1962 Immigration Act. However, besides knowing the law, it is necessary to understand the way it is applied and consequently affects various people. The actual conditions of immigration into Canada reflect this country's traditional geographical preferences and are reminiscent of a passage from Prime Minister MacKenzie King's diary dated February 13, 1947:

There should be no exclusion of any particular race. That I think had really been wiped out against the Chinese but a country should surely have the right to determine what strains of blood it wishes to have in its population and how its people coming from outside have to be selected (as quoted by Pickersgill and Foster 1972:33).

While the great majority of the old immigrants were former peasants from rural China, most of the new immigrants are former residents of cosmopolitan Hong Kong. Many of them are thoroughly fluent in English before emigrating, and many are graduates of Canadian universities who were on student visas before applying for landed immigrant status. The average age of the community decreases with the increasing percentage of locally born Chinese and renewed immigration since 1947. The sex ratio is becoming more balanced; in 1961, it was 1.63 males to one female (*1961 census of Canada* 1964: I, 3–9, Table 114–2). Both the cultural and demographic factors contribute to forming a community which is more heterogeneous, and in certain ways more integrated into Canadian society.

Among the Chinese, the occupational distribution, while still oriented largely toward personal service, begins to ramify into other categories. According to the *1961 census of Canada* (1964: III, 1–15, Table 21), in service and recreational occupations, Asians[4] were still the most over-represented (24.5 percent compared to 8.5 percent of the total labor force in Canada). However, in professional and technical occupations also, Asians were slightly over-represented (9.6 percent compared to 7.5 percent of the total labor force in Canada).

Today for about a quarter of the Chinese population in Canada, restaurant work is their livelihood: waiters, cooks, kitchen helpers, cafe and restaurant owners. Some choose this occupation because of their kinship tie with the restaurant owners who may have sponsored their

[4] The Chinese constituted 47.7 percent of the Asian population in Canada in 1961.

immigration to Canada. Some of them are forced to do kitchen work because language is a problem. Some are paid at a wage below the minimal wage of the province; even in 1973, some workers in Chinese-operated restaurants in Winnipeg were paid at $1.35 per hour, despite a minimum wage of $1.75 per hour in Manitoba. For these people, some of the working conditions of old Chinatown remain unchanged.

Most of the people in personal service choose to settle in the larger cities where there is demand for their services; thus Vancouver and Toronto remain the focal points of Chinese settlement. However, some find employment in small towns where they may prefer to open cafes and restaurants. For example, in Manitoba, nearly all the towns with a population of 2,000 and over have one or two Chinese-operated restaurants or cafes.

In the 1940s, when the Chinese population was rapidly dwindling, it was thought that the number of Chinatowns in Canada would gradually disappear. However, this has not happened, even though some changes have occurred. Most of the new arrivals are dispersed throughout a city, and only a minority of the incoming Chinese population takes up residence in the Chinatown area. Moreover, land appropriation, urban renewal, and public work projects, such as the proposed fire hall at Pender Street and the Columbia-Quebec Connector in Vancouver, contribute to the decentralization of the Chinese population.

On the other hand, certain social factors are conducive to the continuation of Chinatowns. As reflected in the press, at least one section of the Canadian public favors the redevelopment of Chinatowns, as they serve as tourist attractions. Moreover, such development programs often receive the concrete support of government subsidies. For example, in Winnipeg, a sum of sixty-four thousand dollars has been allocated towards the cost of a feasibility study on the redevelopment of that city's Chinatown by the federal and provincial governments and the Winnipeg City Council. The redevelopment program calls for the construction of a senior-citizens' residence, clinic, high-rise apartment building, day-care center, shops, and restaurants.

Until redevelopment programs of this sort have been implemented, Chinatown at the present is functioning less and less as a residential area. In Winnipeg, for example, the principal residents consist of the old sojourners, resigned to spending their twilight years in Canada, and new immigrants employed in Chinatown or in the garment factories in the vicinity. The houses of such residents are among the poorest-lighted apartment blocks inhabited by poor white pensioners, Metis and Indians, and there were some old, probably substandard, frame houses along a couple of streets. To the new immigrants Chinatown is certainly not an attractive residential area; however, it is one place where foodstuffs and other commodities from the Far East can be purchased, where Chinese movies are shown periodically, and where festivals and social events are held. For the Chinese ethnic group, Chinatown is still functioning as a commercial and social center.

The traditional associations are declining. Most of the new immigrants do not adhere to the old concepts of surname, clan and territorial ties, and do not need to seek mutual aid and protection from the old associations, but are more concerned with governmental contributive welfare and government assistance programs. Among the old associations, the Chinese Freemasons is the one organization that maintains wide support from new immigrants as well as those born in Canada. This organization cuts across clan and territorial ties and sponsors popular recreational and athletic activities. With government subsidies, a few community centers serving the Chinese population are being formed. An organization such as this was formed recently in Toronto East; its function consists of English-language teaching, providing interpreters for new arrivals, and helping them to deal with governmental matters. In Vancouver a huge community center for the Chinese population is projected, again with the support of the government. Under the multicultural centers program started in 1972 by the federal government, more organizations of this nature will probably be established.

In terms of the cultural and demographic factors discussed previously, the new immigrants, in comparison with the old, are somewhat more integrated into Canadian society. However, as yet these immigrants have not had time to build up their circles of friends and networks of social relations. If an immigrant's social and kinship tie is predominantly outside Canada, he cannot find much meaning in Canadian society other than the fact that it is a place to earn a good living.

However, as shown by the increasing numbers of Chinese granted citizenship yearly (see Table 6), most of these immigrants are determined to make Canada their permanent home. Apparently, there is a growing acceptance of the Chinese in Canadian society. Still, they are far more conspicious than the size of the ethnic group (0.3 percent of the Canadian population in 1961) would suggest. In a survey of young people's impres-

Table 6. Citizenship certificates granted to persons born in China and Hong Kong, 1960–1970

Year	Certificates
1960	446
1962	1,117
1964	2,099
1966	1,913
1968	2,719
1970	2,902

Sources: Canada year book 1964: 217, 1967: 233, 1971: 282, 1972: 239.

sions regarding the visibility of the ethnic groups living in Canada, the listing corresponds moderately well to the size of various ethnic minorities in Canada. However, the Chinese were cited relatively more often than would have been predicted by their numbers in the actual population. Of the twenty-three ethnic minorities surveyed, the Chinese were third after the Italians and Germans in the ranking of relative visibility (Johnstone 1969:40–41).

In summary, the Chinese peasants emigrated in the last century as a result of poverty and overpopulation. In Canada they created occupations which were particularly adapted to the Canadian urban setting. The traditional associations, though established with various objectives, functioned largely as mutual-aid fraternal associations. A closely knit community was formed on the basis of both voluntary actions and the exclusion of the host society. Since 1947, the Chinese have become more heterogeneous, and in terms of their residential pattern, occupations, ability to speak English, and education are more integrated into Canadian society. The historical experience of the Chinese minority group is unique in many ways and well deserving of thorough study by social scientists.

REFERENCES

BALDWIN, S. L.
  1890   *Must the Chinese go? An examination of the Chinese question* (third edition). New York: Press of H. B. Elkins.
BERTON, PIERRE
  1971   *The last spike, the great railway, 1881–1885*. Toronto: McClelland and Stewart.
CAMPBELL, PERSIA CRAWFORD
  1923   *Chinese coolie emigration to countries within the British Empire*. London: P. S. King and Son.
Canada year book
  1912   *Canada year book 1912*. Canada: Dominion Bureau of Statistics.
  1923   *Canada year book 1922–1923*. Canada: Dominion Bureau of Statistics.
  1930   *Canada year book 1930*. Canada: Dominion Bureau of Statistics.
  1937   *Canada year book 1937*. Canada: Dominion Bureau of Statistics.
  1942   *Canada year book 1942*. Canada: Dominion Bureau of Statistics.
  1947   *Canada year book 1947*. Canada: Dominion Bureau of Statistics.
  1950   *Canada year book 1950*. Canada: Dominion Bureau of Statistics.
  1953   *Canada year book 1952–1953*. Canada: Dominion Bureau of Statistics.
  1961   *Canada year book 1961*. Canada: Dominion Bureau of Statistics.
  1964   *Canada year book 1964*. Canada: Dominion Bureau of Statistics.
  1965   *Canada year book 1965*. Canada: Dominion Bureau of Statistics.
  1967   *Canada year book 1967*. Canada: Dominion Bureau of Statistics.
  1968   *Canada year book 1968*. Canada: Dominion Bureau of Statistics.
  1971   *Canada year book 1971*. Canada: Dominion Bureau of Statistics.
  1972   *Canada year book 1972*. Canada: Dominion Bureau of Statistics.

Census of Canada
1936   *Seventh (1931) census of Canada*, volume VII. Canada: Dominion
       Bureau of Statistics.
1946   *Eighth (1941) census of Canada*, volume II. Canada: Dominion Bureau
       of Statistics.
1964   *1961 census of Canada*, volumes I and III. Canada: Dominion Bureau
       of Statistics.
CHENG, TIEN-FANG
1931   *Oriental immigration in Canada.* Shanghai, China: The Commercial
       Press.
CHUI, KUI-TSIANG
1965   *A history of Southeast Asia* (in Chinese). Singapore: Lien Yin Publica-
       tion.
HAMMOND, DOROTHY
1972   *Associations.* A McCaleb module in anthropology from the series
       Addison-Wesley modular publications. Reading: Addison-Wesley.
JOHNSTONE, JOHN C.
1969   *Young people's image of Canadian society: an opinion survey of Cana-
       dian youth 13 to 20 years of age.* Ottawa: Queen's Printer.
LEE, ROSE HUM
1949   The decline of Chinatowns in the United States. *The American Journal
       of Sociology* 54:422–432.
1960   *The Chinese in the United States of America.* Hong Kong: Hong Kong
       University Press.
OSTERHOUT, S. S.
1927   *Orientals in Canada. The story of the work of the United Church of
       Canada with Asiatics in Canada.* Toronto: Committee on Literature,
       General Publicity and Missionary Education.
PALMER, HOWARD
1972   *Land of the second chance. A history of ethnic groups in southern
       Alberta.* Lethbridge, Alberta: The Lethbridge Herald.
PICKERSGILL, J. W., D. F. FOSTER
1972   *The Mackenzie King record 1947–1948*, volume four. Toronto: Univer-
       sity of Toronto Press.
ROYAL COMMISSION OF CANADA
1885   *Report of the Royal Commission on Chinese immigration.* Ottawa:
       Queen's Printer.
1969   *Report of the Royal Commission on bilingualism and biculturalism*,
       book four: *The cultural contribution of the other ethnic groups.* Ottawa:
       Queen's Printer.
WRIGHT, J. F. C.
1955   *Saskatchewan. The history of a province.* Canada: McClelland and
       Stewart.

The Tuli–Chinese Balk Line: Minimal Group Self-Identity

COLIN E. TWEDDELL

> It is important to see that the self is in part a ceremonial thing, a sacred object which must be treated with proper ritual care and in turn must be presented in a proper light to others.
> ERVING GOFFMAN, "The nature of deference and demeanor."

BACKGROUND

It is the purpose of this paper to present and discuss the concept of the balk line of intergroup resistance and accommodation in the context of the relationship between the Tuli and the Chinese in Southwest China. The term balk line arises from the attitude of resistance within a general climate of accommodation (balkiness in contrast to insubordination and disorder), which is the psychocultural product of structured political, economic, and social relations between peoples and is manifested, of course, in these same sectors of pressure as well as in other cultural differences. Because the areas and aspects of resistance can be consistently anticipated in generally identifiable cultural situations I have used the word line, as in boundary line or line of deployment. Any such line implies two parties, and further implies that there may be consensus on, though not necessarily approval of, the existing arrangements. But since pressures to coerce, to resist, or merely to change are seldom equal, the weaker must needs be the more balky of the two.

I spent most of the years between 1924 and 1941 in East and Southeast

Sincere thanks are due to my colleagues at Western Washington State College, Professor Angelo Anastasio who read the first draft, and Professor John MacGregor whose many constructive suggestions greatly improved this revised presentation, and also to Professor Regina E. Holloman of Roosevelt University for editorial guidance.

China in contact with both Nationalist and Communist Chinese and with the Japanese. However, it was the three-and-one-half years between 1948 and 1951[1], which brought into focus the line of demarcation that often exists between adjacent cultures. "The Law of Absorption," which Spear (1967:63) said operated to assimilate Parthians, Sakas, Kushans, and others into the mainstream of Indian culture, also worked in Chinese society to incorporate their various Mongol and Manchu conquerors. But it did not operate among the mountains of Yunnan between the encompassing Chinese and the many tribal enclaves there, for neither group absorbed the other, although contact affected both.[2] It was the realization that Tuli acculturation was still stalemated after at least four or five centuries of increasing Chinese contact which triggered this study.Why did the Tuli balk at further change?

The portion of West Yunnan occupied by the Tuli is roughly and irregularly one degree square, viz. approximately 99.70 p°–101° east longitude by 24.4°–25.6° north latitude — the area surrounding the west-to-east bend of the Mekong river and the headwaters of the Red and Black rivers. In this region of mountains and forests the altitudes range from about 3,000 feet above sea level where the Mekong Gorge turns south again, to 8,500–foot ridges and 11,500–foot peaks. Our informants lived in the Kunglang district of southern Menghwa county, south of Tali.

---

[1] These periods of residence in China were while serving as a senior missionary with the China Inland Mission (since renamed the Overseas Missionary Fellowship), in Kiangsi, Anhui, and Yunnan provinces, and the opportunities for living amongst the friendly and gracious peoples there are hereby acknowledged. The explicit control of the People's Republic of China over West Yunnan began in late 1949, and we lived under that regime until leaving for the coast on May 5, 1951. It had initial impact upon Tuli–Chinese relationships in 1950. This paper deals with conditions prior and up to that period.

No attempt has been made to contact the Tuli since leaving the area, and no specific information is available beyond several generalizations. One, that the system of soviets (committees) extends from top to bottom of the governmental hierarchy, doubtless resulting in Tuli representatives on single and mixed ethnic committees. Two, the Tuli will needs be included in the organization of "national minorities" (see Liu 1967:26–29: "Yunnan . . . 6. Ta-li (Pai)", then referred to as "minority nationalities," quoted from Hu et al. 1960). Direct aim was taken in the Constitution to ensure ethnic equality: "Chapter One. General principles . . . Article 3. The People's Republic of China is a unitary multinational state. All the nationalities are equal. Discrimination against or oppression of any nationality, and acts which undermine the unity of the nationalities, is prohibited. All the nationalities have the freedom to use and develop their own spoken and written languages, and to preserve or reform their customs and ways. Regional autonomy applies in areas where a minority nationality live in a compact community. All the national autonomous areas are inseparable parts of the People's Republic of China" (Jan 1966:621). The confusion of the first year under the new regime did not see the fulfillment of this non-discrimination goal at that time.

[2] In this connection, the Social Science Research Council article on Acculturation notes that, "Cultural changes induced by contacts between ethnic enclaves and their encompassing societies would be definable as acculturation" (SSRC 1954:973–974).

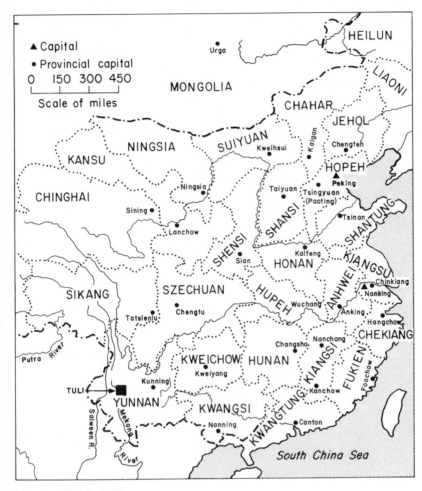

Map 1.   China in 1931

Chinese Infiltration and Suzerainty in Yunnan.[3]

The region of West Yunnan has been subjected to various dynastic controls under Indian and tribal kingdoms, with occasional Chinese interference,[4] until some time before A.D. 1253, when Kublai (Khan)

[3]   Rock's Introduction to vol. 1, part 1, is the principal source for the historical material in the sub-sections on Chinese infiltration and Tuli origins. Many other sources have been consulted, including Davies (1909), Goodrich (1963), Granet (1958), Li (1965), Tregear (1965), Tuan (1969), etc., and the present extremely abbreviated account appears to be consensual. See particularly Fitzgerald (1972:Chap. 3, 4 and 5) on the conquest of Yunnan.
[4]   The tentative nature of Chinese infiltration into and control of Southwest China for the more than 1,000 years between the first and thirteenth centuries A.D. (or perhaps the

annexed the area to the Mongol (Yuan) Empire. During these later years and at least until 1382, Sung, Mongol, and Ming emperors honored the various Southwest China tribal rulers with titles and insignia as Protectors of the Frontier, King of Yunnan, etc., and with gifts of silk, jewels, etc. That this region was not at that time an economic or manpower backwater was evidenced by the fact these rulers on occasion provided their imperial overlords with 10,000 silver taels (each one 1/3 oz. av.) and 20,000–40,000 armed fighting men. The emperors' honors maintained entrance for soldiers and officials, exiles, and merchants[5] who, with octopus-like tenacity, held fast the tentacles of domination — political, military, commercial, and cultural — and formed new lines and loci of communication. This expanding web of pulsating enclaves of Chinese immigrants shut the door behind the gradual southward Tai migrations of the previous 400 years. It also reversed the existing group-centered tribal orientations, causing these hinterlands to face eastward. All these factors have no doubt contributed to bringing to the conscious level the dichotomy between local tribal culture and autonomy and the authority imposed from outside.

Tuli Origins

The ancient peoples of Southwest China — P'u, Ch'iang, Pai, and others — were doubtless the progenitors of the P'u-man, Moso-Na-khi, Min-chia, Lolo, Miao, Lisu, Tai-Shan, etc., who presently occupy portions of West Yunnan. The old Chinese records[6] and illustrative woodcuts in provincial and county histories and family registers suggest considerable continuity amongst these peoples of basic architecture, and the use of cloth, furs, pleated hemp skirts, fiber rain-gear, tumpline, panpipes, and simple farming implements and weapons for many centuries past. One such group of about 250,000[7] people is called Tuli[8] by the Chinese but designate themselves La-Lo. Their completely indigenized and ack-

historian's use of sources, or the lack of data??) is exemplified by Li's statement that Han Wu-ti "pacified" the entire southwest region" by 109 B.C. and new administrative units were created which were the forerunners of modern Yunnan and Kweichow provinces" (Li 1965:110).

[5]   Goodrich points out that during the period of the Three Kingdoms, A.D. 220–280, "many Chinese married into the hitherto unassimilated non-Chinese peoples of the south and southwest" (Goodrich 1963:60). See also footnote 9.

[6]   The *Yunnan t'ung chih, Yunnan provincial encyclopedia*, vol. 182, provides ancient woodcuts of Lolo and Miao tribal peoples showing these things, also animals, hair styles, backpack baskets, tumplines, panpipes, crossbow and spears, etc., all items still found among them.

[7]   The population was estimated by counties by two well-travelled persons, a Chinese minor county official and Elder Brother, based upon the relative proportions of Chinese and Tuli households, and multiplied by five. Whether or not the Chinese gentleman distinguished between Tuli and other tribals is uncertain, but the two men agreed on the Tuli

nowledged position in the cultural mosaic of mountain tribes, their unique dialect of the regionally related Tibeto-Burmese Lolo languages, and their large population, all point to long residence in the area. Yet the only information the writer gleaned of the Tuli place of origin was the statement by the man herein designated simply as Elder Brother, who was both our gracious host and principal informant. He said their forebears arrived in the area from South Kiangsi province some thirteen or fourteen generations ago, which suggests a date between 1430 and 1530, the very period of massive transportations of people from East and Southeast China to Yunnan in Ming dynasty times. One such migration included troops from Kanhsien in South Kiangsi.[9] Partial Chinese origins could thus be indicated for at least the local group of Tuli to which our informants belonged. As of now anyway, Tuli speech is about 70 percent cognate with Upper Salween Lisu,[10] and my informants said the Tuli knew little Chinese a century ago. Tuli men are phenotypically similar to the indigenous Chinese population, except for a few typical features such as large, lustrous, chocolate brown eyes and a reddish tinge to the hair.[11] Their women are of better proportions and sturdier physique, and have a fuller bust development and a broader forehead than their Chinese sisters. In this paper "Chinese" are the Han Chinese who constitute the vast bulk of China's population.

Everything in the area points to a stable Tuli population. Few families were seen with more than three children and many with less. Elder Brother spoke of a low fertility rate for the Tuli when making up the vital statistics for his ward. Asked why he did not include his only child, an infant girl, he replied, "We never include children under two years; too many of them die, and we are required to account for them." The physical appearance of the local market town told the same story for the combined

---

figures. For comparison, the Lisu on northwestern Yunnan are estimated at 310,000, and the Pai or Min-chia of Tali and Chien-chuan counties at 560,000 (Hu et al. 1960:70).

[8]   The Chinese characters for Tuli are *t'u* [earth, soil] and *li* [profit], interpreted contentedly by the Tuli as "those able to gain benefit from the soil." The Chinese seemed unaware of the name "Lalo." They are the main one of the "Lolo 'tribes' such as the Meng-hua Lolo south of Tali" (Lebar, Hickey, Musgrave 1964:19).

[9]   The Ming histories name a famous statesman, philosopher and general, Wang Shou-jen or Wang Yang-ming, who conveyed troops from Kanhsien, South Kiangsi, to Kunming, Yunnan. Davies found Shans at Man-mu, 15 miles west of Sze-mao and 100 air miles south of the Tuli area, who said they came from Chiang-hsi (Kiangsi), and, he adds, so did the Chinese soldier husbands of Shan people in Kweichow, later known there as Chung-chia. All these cases probably point to local groups, not to Shan, Chung-chia and Tuli people in general (Davies 1909:95, fn.).

[10]   According to my manuscript fieldnotes, the Nurra dialect, spoken by a small group around T'u-u market, Lan-p'ing county, north of the Burma Road on the Mekong river, is also related to Tuli. The Tuli appear not to possess or use any Lolo script. Fraser (1922) gives the best account of the Lisu language.

[11]   The Tuli differed typically from the better-fed and square or oval-faced Chinese, the Miao with a heavy torso and short legs, the angular featured Puman, the taller, lithe and handsome Shan, and the Likiang Lolo and Tibetan of rugged frame and high cheekbone.

Chinese and tribal population. The contouring, width, and pebbling of the roads outside and of the streets inside the market, the trees around the periphery, the stone paving in the central "mall," the age and condition of the houses and their lean-to additions, all pointed to the same size population for at least the past sixty to eighty years.

THE THREE–FOLD NATURE OF THE TULI–CHINESE ETHNIC BOUNDARY: ECOLOGICAL NICHING, POWER RELATIONS, AND SOCIAL DISTANCE

Ethnic Boundaries

Tramping the open mountain trails in the clear sunshine and mild climate of the monsoon-blessed plateau of West Yunnan, with singing and whistling Tuli companions, it was difficult to remember that boundaries by definition are two-sided.[12] But, when a Chinese came into proximity or a Chinese market was approached, one could almost literally draw a line where Tuli language and custom ceased and Chinese began. The recognition of the situation was mutual, the line of demarcation was tacitly understood, and the adjustment of conduct was automatic.

It is probable that all ethnic boundaries include social distance as a minimal component: some are strengthened by power relations exercised by one or both groups; fewer cases are distinguished also by the separate ecological niches they occupy. These conditions are all present in the Tuli–Chinese case. Their ecological niching supplies a physical area for residence and livelihood for each group; the structures of Chinese society fix the sociopolitical bases for interaction; the social mores of both groups limit the closeness of intercultural contact between persons. But this is not the full explanation of cultural separation. Even with these factors as analytic givens, the directive facility that aligns and energizes these cultural norms and expectations is the psychocultural catalyst of purpose. That is, these peoples as individuals and as groups come to want or allow these diverse factors to function in this divisive manner. They actively maintain a boundary. The relationship between such structural factors and this psychocultural pattern of *accomodative resistance* is set out below.

Ecological Niching

Ecological niching refers to the situation wherein ethnic groups occupy separable physical environments, each utilizing its own resources to the

---

[12]   See Barth (1969:9–10, 132) on the "categories of inclusion/exclusion" which separate the Pathans from their neighbors.

general exclusion of other groups. Internal symbiosis is stimulated and external competition is minimized. In the Tuli–Chinese situation, altitudinal residence correlates considerably with ethnic identity (Lebar, Hickey, Musgrave 1964:26). The Chinese solidly occupy the Mitu and Menghwa

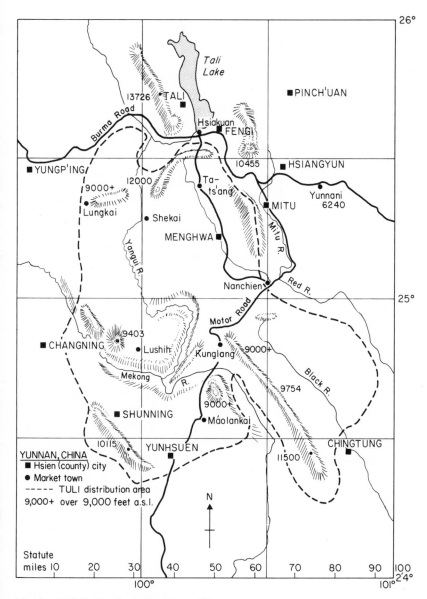

Map 2.   Tuli distribution in Southwest China

peneplains, and the river valleys and the easily terraced lower slopes support their irrigated rice culture. The (Mon-Khmer) P'u-man (or Puman)[13] cultivate rice in the bottom lands of the Mekong's southern bend, and the Tuli and some White and a few Black Lolo occupy the lower to upper mountainsides. At the highest levels of occupancy the Miao live in secluded slopes and hollows among their small fields of oats, barley, and rye. Throughout West China the general line of cleavage between Chinese and tribes-people is where wet rice ends and maize begins.

The Tuli practices of mixed agriculture are typical of mountainside cultivation. Terraced fields of corn (maize) and legumes, cultivated with plow and hoe, surround their villages on the lower or lower middle slopes. Above and below are occasional fields of sweet potatoes or tea or coffee bushes. Dry rice is not grown, and opium was forbidden about 1945. Vigorous forests of pines and deciduous trees clothe the middle slopes, wherein are small pockets of tea, coffee, or camellia shrubs (the latter yield prized oil nuts), or of bearded or other wheat or millet. The forest itself produces firewood, pine chips for illumination, grazing for live-stock, and water in clear rivulets. Cattle are grazed also on the grass and shrub uplands, where grass is cut for firewood and thatch and as binder in mud bricks. The rather barren upland fields, broadcast with sweet and bitter buckwheat, yield an uncertain reserve of food for the "hunger months" preceding harvest.

When we consider home people in their home environment, it can be assumed that the Chinese, with 2–3,000 years experience, were well aware they could preserve their *culture system* intact as long as they lived within familiar physical surroundings. Coming from Central and East China they indeed stayed within known environments and perpetuated their irrigated rice culture, their political sophistication and legal author-ity, their urban and rural technology, and their business acumen and organization. They presumably took for granted their capacity to win over, subdue, or bend to their ways other peoples, specifically tribal societies, with whom they had had contact for a millenium or two. Here was the rub that caused the itch. The Tuli, although they were acquainted with irrigated rice farming and used the plow, had mastered the art of mixed farming on the mountainsides. Their technical skills in bamboo, wood, stone, and simple metalwork sufficed to erect excellent housing and terracing and to produce their simpler tools and farm equipment when they wished. Their aboriginal political system of *t'u szu* [laird,

[13]   The Pu-man or P'u barbarians are variously named as P'u, P'u-jen or P'u people, and are doubtless the same as Major Davies' Shui P'u-yi or Water P'u aborigines. Speaking of a small group of Puman further south, Davies (1909:93) suggests the Puman are "apparently of the same family as the Las, Was, and Paluangs . . . (but) . . . have forgotten their own tongue and now talk the Wa, the Shan, or even the Chinese language" (Also Davies 1909:104–105, 147–147).

overlord] was probably similar to that of the Shan and the Salween Lisu. Technologically, culturally, linguistically, and psychologically the Tuli "belonged" to the mountains.

Concerning home people living in a different environment, Barth made a perceptive and often true statement that ". . . the same group of people, with unchanged values and ideas, would surely pursue different patterns of life and institutionalize different forms of behavior when faced with the different opportunities offered in different environments" (Barth 1969:12). However, the amazingly wise Chinese farmer seems to have a blind spot concerning unterraced slopes. He commonly applies to both sloping and flat ground his valued principle of deep cultivation, using an ecologically lethal weapon — a mattock with a 9 to 15 by 4-inch iron blade. With this mattock and method, he clears out stumps and roots and, without contouring or anchor strips of native growth, the rains are likely to slough his fields right off the mountainside within ten years. Tuan (1969:144) and Goodrich (1963:221) both refer to this early deforestation of the mountainsides, certainly from 1700 on, in South and Southwest China. They write that "the most elementary measures of soil conservation" were ignored, causing consequent erosion by heavy rainfall. This is not a tribal practice. These same Chinses farmers did not "pursue different patterns of life" in accord with this aspect of their new environment, but *perpetuated as clusters* their "values and ideas" *and* their "forms of behavior." The result was the initiation in Yunnan of the denudation so disastrously typical of many of China's mountains elsewhere. As to Tuli living *as Tuli* in another (Chinese or lowland) environment, we never met or heard of any except for a few who were for a time soldiers in the army.

But, when different people live temporarily in different environments, that is, when the persons or peoples concerned are in intercultural relationships with third parties elsewhere, the contacts are not permanent, no competition is engendered, and no balk line is likely to appear. Let us take four actual illustrations. First, Tuli men would spend the long summer months amongst Chinese or tribal groups one to two weeks' journey southwest, farming, housebuilding, and especially back-packing rock uphill and building retaining walls for terraces. Second, Chinese caravaneers with horse, mule, and donkey trains of general merchandise plodded regularly from Mitu and Menghwa south and southwest for two to three weeks' journey each way, contacting all manner of people. Likiang Lolo and Tibetan caravaneers occasionally stirred up fights. Third, Mr. X of Menghwa, a Chinese Christian businessman, twice took us several miles outside the city to introduce us to "my friends, the Tuli." At the first home we were all seated in honor on a beautiful white blanket of felted wool. At another home a special cake was steamed for us. Fourth, when two wet and exhausted foreign strangers tramped into

Tuliland to live, and arrived at Elder Brother's home on the mountain-side, the roaring fire of welcome was only surpassed by the silent grace of his Old Mother, as with work-scarred hands she gently removed the streaming raingear from my wife's drooping shoulders. Very different as these several environments were, none raised the balk line's shadow.

Power Relations

Tribal people *as such* had no standing, no dignity in a social system wherein, for instance, Chinese were officials, Chinese were merchants in all major markets, Chinese owned caravanserais, and Chinese controlled the school system. This was a clear case "where identity as a minority member gives no basis for action" as an equal participant (Barth 1969:31), for there were no "rank paths" (Culshaw 1967:235–236) for upward mobility open to the Tuli. Since the Chinese so overwhelmingly controlled access to authority, commerce, communications, education, rice, cloth, tools, manufactured goods, and registration of valley farm-land, competition for these privileges really did not exist.[14] This exemplifies an economic trait of majority-minority relationships that perpetuates dichotomies and generates stratified lines of friction, as implied in Barth's comment that "stratified poly-ethnic systems exist where groups are characterized by differential control of assets that are valued by all groups in the system" (Barth 1969:27). As long as the tribespeople operated within categories of assets not yet exploitable by the Chinese no friction arose. The Tuli, therefore, were vulnerable in their possession of certain cultivable lower slopes which the Chinese also were well able to dry farm. For the same reasons, silent and internalized friction was ever present in Tuli vigilance to avoid debt to the Chinese, and any confrontation which required the production of property deeds, for debt led to foreclosure, and deeds were never returned. The Chinese–Tuli situation provides a case study where ethnic identity, plus classes of tangible assets and types of subsistence patterns, constitute a decisive cluster of hierarchical characteristics upon which super- and subordination could be based.

   The economic part of the power relations included natural limitations on environmental resources and food surpluses, sociopolitical restrictions on occupations, and inability to freely use the potential services of the system of areal markets. These disabilities, together with the lack of a demand incentive for production, and a static array of tools, skills, and techniques, left the Tuli with a nonexpandable economy. The thesis

[14]   Note Barth's definition of an ethnic group: "Ethnic groups are categories of ascription and identification by the actors themselves, and thus have the characteristics of organizing interaction between people" (Barth 1969:10).

indicated here is that, for a given population within a given environment, the economy will develop to the limits of resources *plus* technology *plus* social values and structures *plus* political opportunity. Tuli economy developed within these limitations to the point delineated in this essay, and, seemingly for a very long time, has remained devoid of further developmental options. They saw no possibility of breaking out of this state of arrested development and accepted it as part of the price paid for being Tuli. While not all the above factors would be themselves individually responsible for slowing down or stopping economic advancement in a given society, if one or a conjunction of two or three became dominant this would be sufficient to do so. Two general conditions affecting development would be *de facto* isolation of the society (minority group, subculture, etc.) from other societies, and intervention from outside it. It is because of these effects that the above factors could be called *stoppage points* or *points of arrest*. For the Tuli and perhaps for others, the end result has been an equilibrium or *state of constancy* between all the possessions of and the possibilities available to a given people.

Social Distance

In view of the power relations described above, it can be readily seen that, as with the Maya of the Highland Chiapas of southern Mexico, where his "identity is shaped by the situation in which his Indianhood is the very basis of interaction" (Barth 1969:116), just so was it with a person's Tuli identity. Elder Brother unknowingly put his finger on a key distinction between the Tuli and other, dominant societies when he remarked that, "Some 300 years ago the Tuli were under a *t'u szu* family named Tso at Menghwa, which maybe was Tai because they used elephants in battle." The Tuli constituted an egalitarian society wherein relative affluence raised a family's rating but slightly, for there would be no tinge of authority mingled with added social respect or potential for making small loans. Dominance and its accompanying social distance were not Tuli characteristics. Even the phrase *t'u szu* was Chinese, and the Tai at the time of the story were probably the remnant elite of the then defunct Nan-chao kingdom. Also, nothing in the Tuli nomenclature, vocabularies, or kinship system, or in their observable behavioral relationships indicated any parallel to the stratified caste-type society of another Lolo-speaking people, the Independent Nosu of western Szechuan.[15] Chinese society, of course, was distinctly class conscious, and they applied

---

[15] The Nosu chieftains and their elite called Black Bones and the commonality called White Bones were sharply separated in the power and social structures, and never intermarried. Chinese officials normally dealt with the chieftain class. This was not possible with Tuli contacts.

this concept to themselves in contrast to all tribespeople so that class lines between the Chinese and such tribespeople remained rigid. There was no flow of personnel across local ethnic borders, (for the Chinese would lose face and no tribal person would gain face), because the distance aspect of stratification was imposed on such relations and borders. It can be said, then, that the Chinese-tribal relationship illustrates one of Barth's two factors in an overall polyethnic plural society, "the characteristic of which is the combination of *ethnic segmentation* and economic interdependence" (Barth 1969:10, emphasis added).

The Tuli Response

Responses to such structured intergroup relations may include, amongst others, positive sublimation and productive innovation, neutral acquiescence in the *fait accompli*, passive or active resistance, or some combination of these responses directed towards selective aspects of the contact pressures. As already indicated, the response chosen by the Tuli in the situation under investigation was accommodative resistance, or, resistance modified by accommodation. So in these circumstances, when acculturation drastically slows down or halts[16] and ethnic identities separately persist, the maintenance of ethnic boundaries may manifest one or more of three characteristics. For these I suggest the following emphasized captions: (1) the refusal of one or more parties to adjust any further develops *a balk line*; (2) to the party under pressure this balk line represents *the line of minimal uniqueness*, or, *the line of minimal self-identity*; (3) when the balk line becomes protracted or painful it may become *the line of friction*. At the time of my residence among the Tuli, the line of friction was covert and muted. The present discussion centers on the balk line and the line of minimal uniqueness. Just as cooperation with the dominant party represents the accommodative aspect of "accommodative resistance," so the balk line emphasizes the resistance aspect. The line of minimal uniqueness shows where accommodation has stopped. Both aspects are illustrated in the next section. The blend of the two aspects is the theme of the concluding section, culminating in the "state of constancy."

[16]   Barth comments on the structuring of interaction where stable interethnic relations exist, that some contact situations are prescribed and others are proscribed, "thus insulating parts of the cultures from confrontation and modification" (Barth 1969:16). Samples and similarities are observable in this paper.

THE SPECIFICS OF TULI–CHINESE ETHNIC SEPARATISM:
THE BALK LINE

The boundaries sketched above exist because overtly or covertly one or both parties to the contact situation want them there. The ethnographic details which follow illustrate the psychocultural facets of Tuli–Chinese separatism. Considerable emphasis is given to the resistance involved. But areas of accommodation made over the decades and centuries are mentioned when discussing the interchange of goods, the plow and carrying-pole, language, housing, family patterns and kinship terminology, religion, and dress. Similarly, a distinction has been made between resistance related to cultural habit and resistance arising from the conscious psychological stances adopted. The arrangement of the data parallels the threefold presentation in the preceding section.

Ecologic Perspective

Although as we have shown, the tribespeople of the area and the Chinese monopolize fairly distinct territories, provide some "important goods and services for each other ... and ... occupy reciprocal and therefore different niches" (Barth 1969:19–20), yet, with some wrenching adjustments, each could contrive to exist alone. As it is, the Tuli necessarily patronize Chinese markets or itinerant Chinese peddlers for items, such as salt, cloth, sugar, metal-ware, crockery, paper and pens (native brush or foreign styles), needles and threads, and rice. But the local Chinese themselves are fully dependent for the same items, except rice, as imports; the point being that the Chinese control all such import business. The local rice-rich Chinese are supplied, principally by the Tuli, with firewood, cereals (corn, millet, buck-wheat), live cattle and meat (beef, pork, goat meat), and oil (from walnuts, rape or mustard seed, camellia, and in past years opium seed). Additional lesser items supplied included: rattan, bamboo, basketry, mats, winnowing trays, walnuts, walnut oil-cakes for cattle feed, horse and soy beans, wheat, and a few fruits (pear, plum, and cherry). Services are minimal on both sides; no Chinese "served" a Tuli, and the Tuli avoided the Chinese as much as possible.

Manifest cultural forms related to ecology include dibble stick and tumpline, plow and carrying-pole. On their flatter terraced slopes the Tuli utilize the Chinese iron-tipped plow. Elsewhere they use the dibble stick, cultivate and weed with hoes, and broadcast their buckwheat. The Tuli backpack basket load of 40 *chin*[17] (50–55 lbs. av.) was supported by an

---

[17] Chin or catty. The sea-level carrying capacity is reduced by one third at 5–8,000 feet altitude.

encircling rope and a braided headband or tumpline, both attached to a shaped wooden shoulder-board — which no Chinese would be seen with. This outfit left both hands free, whereas the Chinese two-basket carrying-pole load of 60-plus *chin* (80-odd lbs. av.) had to be steadied with one hand, and was almost unmanageable if tipped out of horizontal balance on a steep slope. However, both Tuli and Chinese agreed on at least one common saying:

I-ko ren, liang t'ung shui; liang-ko ren, i t'ung shui!
(One person, two buckets of water; two persons, one bucket of water!)

So, the Tuli much prefer the carrying-pole and buckets for carrying water, but nothing else.

The ecologic use of domestic animals by lowland and upland peoples differs markedly. The Chinese keep water buffalo and cows for plowing (and occasional meat and milk), pigs for meat, ferocious dogs as guardians, and cats as ratters. A few wealthier Chinese and Tuli possessed each a pony for riding. Lacking irrigated ricefields and ponds the Tuli keep no water buffalo. Their cows, goats, and some sheep are their animated fertilizer factories, for the true word is, "No manure, no crops." Mulch is assiduously collected by the Tuli but seldom by the Chinese. The mulch was added to the surprisingly nonodorous layer of vegetation, straw, and manure two feet thick on the stable floor. Goatskins made valuable jacket-vests, and wool and kapok were potential wadding or blanket material. Sheepskins and hides were easily saleable on the market.

Power Perspective

"The stable, persisting ... social relations ... maintained across such (ethnic) boundaries ... are ... based precisely on the dichotomized ethnic statuses" (Barth 1969:10). In the public sector, the products and services, and the money and barter economy at the area's markets (excluding the tribal hill markets) were managed on a basis of ethnic divisions. Each tribal group by tacit agreement occupied a separate area alongside the road entrances to the market. They had the freedom of the market for purchases and, as long as they stood or kept moving, were permitted to sell their firewood, eggs and chickens, basketware, etc., on the main streets. Elder Brother once remarked, after being expelled from an inn where he came to keep an appointment with me, that, "We Tuli are not allowed to enter such places, or to sit down in a shop, or to spread a mat stall on the market street." Conversely, the only time that we knew the market Chinese willingly visited in Tuli homes was when a robber band threatened the district, and they came in droves with their valuables seeking shelter and safety up the mountain in tribal homes. They gave little thanks and less compensation for unrefused hospitality.

The public sector situation was characterized by the focus being one or more Chinese. Chinese was then spoken by all present except, usually, the Tuli women. Tuli was spoken regularly in all situations in the private sector of tribal intimacy. In overlapping situations there was switching of language but not switching of ethnic identity, i.e., "passing." The above discussion of power perspective illustrates where the dominant culture draws its balk line in order to maintain *a line of exclusion*.

Social Distance Perspective

"In the total social system, all sectors of activity are organized by statuses open to members of the majority group, while the status system of the minority has only relevance to relations within the minority." (Barth 1969:31). If ascribed status is regarded as an inherent matter of birth, and achieved status as an internal matter of intragroup performance, then imputed status is the external, cross-cultural assignment of relative rank and prestige.

Ethnic identity can be regarded as a status, and the accompanying limitations on roles may also include the person's partners in situations of contact. Barth points out that, " . . . regarded as a status, ethnic identity is *superordinate* to other statuses . . . which an individual with that identity may assume; (that) it is *imperative* . . . and in complex, polyethnic societies, quite comprehensive; (and occurs) . . . in *stereotyped clusters* . . . (with other) . . . moral and social conventions" (Barth 1969:17, emphasis added).

Anyone identified as a Tuli was automatically assigned a role of subservience in any situation involving a Chinese. When the market headman wanted road repairmen, his messengers to the Tuli village bawled and shouted for an immediate labor force. Money earmarked for wages never reached the Tuli. When the Tuli schoolteacher was summoned for (unpaid) duty and travel as census-taker, he hurriedly donned his long blue gown and went. (A literate Chinese would have been politely requested and paid.) An older Tuli peasant walking through the market was commandeered by a Chinese farmer for several days' forced labor; his reward? — a wornout T-shirt! One afternoon on the road we met a young Chinese acquaintance who politely pestered us into going several miles back to be his guests overnight. We were cheerfully shown our lodgings in the airy upstairs schoolroom in this extensive home. Somehow he found out that our carrier companions were Tuli. We were immediately turned out of the classroom and into a windowless outhouse room where we could sleep, supperless for all he now cared, on the damp earth floor. Very decidedly, their ethnic identity status as Tuli was "superordinate" over their status as our companions. It was "imperative" that this family's facilities not be desecrated by tribespeople. And, as partners with the Tuli in this situation, we also were summarily included as part of the "stereotyped cluster." Interestingly, the Tuli fumed at this studied indignity inflicted upon the whole party but never challenged their assigned inferior status.[18] They accepted this treatment as part of *their* cluster of friction line traits, part of the price they paid to preserve their minimal uniqueness. All of which underlies the fact that classifying by stereotype and value orientation tends to be self-fulfilling.

Achieved status for the Tuli was possible only through affluence and education. Such achievement produced mild prestige amongst themselves but only made the person more "useful" to the Chinese. The whole discussion of power relations and social distance has indicated the circumscription of potential achievement: that the achievement could only be within the established parameters of ecologic, power, and social restrictions, or, conversely, of limited options. For instance, a Tuli with a possible herd of sixty goats, thirty sheep, and twenty cattle would be rated "wealthy" by less well-endowed Tuli, and a visit to his larger and better furnished home would be for them "quite an occasion." But he did not thereby open for himself an expanding "export" business to the Chinese. To the Chinese officials, he would be primarily someone to be soaked for a higher tax. Again, Elder Brother was the single high school graduate in his village and was the village schoolteacher for some years. The market officials kept most of his salary, withheld books and equipment from the school, and gave him a "tea money" pittance for much extra official paperwork in the district. In Chinese eyes he had "achieved" nothing, for his third-class imputed status was the real one. A quasi-caste relationship was thus maintained by the dominant Chinese society.

The period of World War II when the Tuli grew opium illustrates the persistent character of established social relations between ethnic groups. Growing opium was widespread in the Tuli region and was their major crop and occupation at that time but, according to my informants, had been of very little importance previously. The harvesting of opium, then, was a crop, a technique, a minor "mass production" of sorts, and a major economic boom new to the Tuli. Now they had cash aplenty, and some expanded slightly their land holdings, improved their houses, and purchased additional silver jewelry — and also had to buy their food, especially the prestige food, rice. About 1945 the Nationalist government prohibited opium growing; the demand and traffic almost ceased, the boom died, the cash income was gone, and there was a food shortage in the area. By mid-1948 the previous state of constancy between resources

[18] An example of the rank concession syndrome or acceptance of social inferiority (Culshaw 1967:235–236).

and technology and the Chinese market system had been reinstated, albeit with some nostalgia for the times of cash surpluses. The specific point of interest here is that during this whole opium growing cycle no change at all had occurred in the relationships between the Tuli and the dominant Chinese culture.

Other Aspects of Cultural Separatism

The architecture of both single and two-storied houses were similar for both Tuli and Chinese, i.e., the floor plans and the materials used. The front door opened on to a public guest room with bedrooms on each side. The kitchen, washing place, firewood, farming equipment, and tools were variously located at the rear or at one or another end of the front veranda. The upstairs was reserved for storage of grain, bunched corn, and for the household shrine. But, unlike the Chinese who kept one or two head of cattle in a cleaned shed, the Tuli herd needed a permanent stable. This was provided by a stone-floored basement under the small house, built on the lower side of the paved or pebbled courtyard opposite the large main house. The ground floor of this lower house was for general purposes — to entertain guests, store grain bins, stack unprocessed corn and legumes, and maybe boast an empty, varnished coffin awaiting an aged parent. Sometimes salted pork was stowed in the coffin out of reach of the tree shrews, a use rather unthinkable to a Chinese.

The Chinese and the Tuli bedrooms differed typically in construction and radically in function. The Chinese bedroom contained separated beds commonly set on trestles, had no fireplace, and was off-limits to guests; the guest hall was for meals and entertainment of guests. The distinctively Tuli bedroom had several permanent sleeping places, set like a level, thirty-inch high platform, flush with and on three sides of a central square fireplace. Here, family and guests would gather for tea, meals, and conviviality. And, whereas the Chinese would pour boiling water from a kettle over tea leaves in the guest's cup, the Tuli would roast tea leaves in a tiny cup in the embers, and serve the guest a breath-stopping but miniscule potion, just as if he had been taught the art by a Bedouin sheik.

Kinship, adoption, and sex manifest areas of tenaciously separatist behavior. While Tuli family patterns, respect system, family surnames, and kinship terminology follow the general Chinese model, i.e., patrilineal, patrilocal, exogamous to the patrilineal surname (even though of different actual lineages), preferred extended family residence, etc., no parallel to the Chinese clan structure or concept was observed among the Tuli. Another distinction relates to lineage surnames. At least the following five surnames, quite common among the Tuli, are not included in the list of 438 commonest Chinese surnames:[19] Muh [wood, tree]; Tzu [written character or word]; Tzu [self, from]; Ch'a [tea]; A [interrogative particle]. They still preserved these surnames (among others, of course), even though their use immediately identified them as social inferiors.

Adoption, in the several cases investigated, was irrevocable. A Tzu boy adopted into the Li family used Li-Tzu as a double surname, and added a single personal name as identifier, e.g., Li-Tzu Shuen. He was entitled to operate under either surname, sell or work fields and claim inheritances thereunder, but cannot return to his original single membership in the Tzu family lineage. If two families without sons, e.g., Ch'a and Muh, jointly adopt a lad from a third family he takes their surnames as Ch'a-Muh. The first-named, as the senior adopter, claims one or both of the first two male sons born to the adoptee as Ch'a sons, the (second or) third will be a Muh boy; none go to the father's original family. Alternatively, the written agreement, which would be sealed into the house walls of the families concerned, may stipulate that all sons bear the double surname. These unusual and non-Chinese procedures appear to be Tuli mechanisms for preserving their separate identity through family structures.

Sex-related behavior differed from the Chinese custom as regards both young and old. The Chinese consistently separated the sexes to preserve female chastity. Tuli premarital assignations were expectable and usually covert, but a young fellow might cajolingly yodel at midday to a girl gardening in another village across the valley. He might also pay for his philandering with a bunch of cut fingers from his bolo-wielding spouse. We heard of no wife playing around, and a promiscuous girl must settle for a less desirable marriage. No Tuli flirts with a Chinese girl; and perhaps understandably the Tuli were pleased when the market fellows occasionally came up the mountain for a supposed rendezvous, for then they could be soundly thrashed. This was the only opportunity the Tuli had to physically vent their frictions and frustrations on the Chinese.

The conjugal bed is the Chinese rule, but was more or less deprecated throughout the Tuli areas visited, especially in the larger households, where men and women often slept separately in different parts of the house or veranda. Journeying couples, even though travelling light and advanced in years, may be refused hospitality if they insist upon sharing their coverlet together. Chinese hospitality was never refused on these grounds.

On the other hand, in religion the Tuli have manifested a considerable tolerance for borrowed items: *feng-shui* or geomancy, ancestor spirit shrines, a village temple to Kuan Yin (Goddess of Mercy) and satellite gods, a mountain earth-god shrine, door-god pictures and doorpost mottoes, the kitchen god, and the household worship shrine. If these were

---

[19]   See Fenn (1940:vii, xxxii), and the note on "S" on page viii. The Po Chia Hsing or Book of Surnames mentioned on page viii is the standard reference for Chinese surnames.

missing, the villagers felt somehow naked. More singularly Tuli were such items as: fear of the local sorceror, fertility rite of pouring rice water at roots of fruit trees, singeing of eyebrows and tail of a newly purchased pig, slips of red paper with the sorceror's spirit cipher writing pasted on to a freshly installed beehive, and so on. When comment was made concerning the purpose and utility of these latter matters, the reply was, this is our Tuli way to protect ourselves and to prosper. The Tuli, then, had obviously adapted their religious system by borrowing from the Chinese to make a new composite, and seemingly had tacitly decided to change no further. Thus we see once again that even in an area of relative tolerance there is still a threshold at which the balk line becomes salient.

Miscellaneous distinctions included language, which was the sharpest single distinction between all these peoples. Tuli, Chinese, Min-chia, Miao, Puman, and others spoke mutually unintelligible languages which would need to be separately learned for purpose of intercommunication. Tuli men and some women were fluent in at least market Chinese, but Chinese did not learn Tuli. Both Tuli men and women used local Chinese basic dress styles, except for occasional men's goatskin jackets, and the regular use by the women of colored edgings, silver jewelry, and large black cloth turbans. For carrying loads the Tuli used a shoulder packboard and tumpline. No Chinese woman would be seen wearing items of tribal dress, nor would a Tuli woman wear the Chinese woman's flat headband of embroidered black silk, and no Chinese man would dream of using the tribal packboard and tumpline basket.

Many other traits contributed to Tuli separateness, such as: habitual two-seed cropping, local work songs, cloth sold in squares, wooden "lock" for packboard rope, lighted pine chips on slate slab for nighttime illumination, wooden packsaddles for cows, use of panpipes and singular dances at unique hilltop festivals, dancing waiters at feasts, and the custom of the wife meeting her husband toward evening to carry home the plow for him. No confrontation was involved in these last-named items, for these belonged in the private sector of Tuli identity.

Values and goals

Values and goals are regarded as the formulations of the established psychological dynamics that form attitudes, guide decisions, and prompt actions. Within this definition the settled expectation that status and role will conform to certain criteria is considered a social value. The series of contrastive Tuli and Chinese values given below is suggestive rather than definitive and exhaustive. If there ever were any political innovators amongst the Tuli, we never heard of them, nor of nativistic movements, nor of records or tales of revolt. It is obvious from an inspection of the table, however, that two very distinctive group identities were being maintained, for values and goals are the essence of cultural separatism.

Table 1.   Tuli–Chinese values and goals

Tuli	Chinese
Independence: a conscious goal because its free enjoyment was curtailed.	Independence: unconscious because it was a present reality.
Equality not power: all normal adults assumed to be knowledgeable and responsible.	Authority: hierarchical control assumed to be normal.
Status: uniform.	Status: unequal.
Role: multiple and generalized.	Role: strong trend towards unitary and specialized.
Flexibility: to labor at own pace, to travel freely at own time.	Regularity: of labor by day and hour and job, under direction.
Economy: livelihood sufficiency.	Economy: financial affluence.
Security: based upon communal alertness.	Security: based upon national organization.
Self-identity: (a) pride in Tuli descent; (b) self-ascription as subordinate; (c) determination to remain distinct.	Self-identity: (a) pride in Han lineage; (b) self-assumption of superiority; (c) determination to maintain current ranking system.

TULI–CHINESE BOUNDARY MAINTENANCE: DISCUSSION AND CONCLUSIONS

I have shown in this paper that the Tuli response to cultural pressure was accommodative resistance and that the resistance aspect resulted in the balk line complex because of the threat seen to the people's uniqueness as a separately identifiable ethnic group. This resistance persisted, despite accommodation in various areas and items of borrowing from Chinese culture and adaptation to Chinese demands. To the Tuli and to other societies in the same dominated situation, boundary maintenance is simply boundary defense and self-preservation. This definition remains valid, whether the boundary is that seen by the majority group or the minority, or imposed upon the latter by the former. Pressure rather than symbiosis is the key factor. (If the response had been different, then of course boundary maintenance would need redefinition to suit the specific condition.)

In the Tuli–Chinese case, then, boundary maintenance is simply boundary defence and self-preservation. As with an individual, so with a society: the closer change approaches the peoples' central core of values and goals, of institutions, of treasured behavior patterns and of basic livelihood — threatening the separate identity and survival of the entity — the greater the resistance generated. A stage may come, the lines may be redrawn, and further changes may impinge upon or violate minimal criteria of uniqueness, until societal *raison d'être* is eroded or taken away and individuality is shattered. The fact of separate occupancy of definable territories had saved the Tuli from this latter danger, allowing their balk line and the line of minimal uniqueness to remain substantially unchallenged; hence, no overt line of friction developed. When Foster writes that "all societies are constantly in a state of relative tension" (Foster 1962:58), he is speaking of forces promoting change against forces maintaining the *status quo*. In the Tuli–Chinese situation change *per se* was not the issue, nor was resource competition; rather the main issue was Tuli wariness lest autonomy, a cardinal feature of their self-identity, be further eroded, in contrast to a Chinese fear that the ranking system be disturbed. Both parties were suspicious of change and saw therein only threats to the system of accommodation wherein each had trained itself to live. Tension, yes, but for a different reason.

Barth makes the pertinent observation that "... the persistence of the (ethnic) unit ... (and the) ... ethnic boundaries are maintained in each case by a limited set of cultural features ... (of) boundary-defining cultural differentiae" (Barth 1969:38), whereby their "separate identities are mirrored in the social landscape" (Eidheim, 1969:48). As the preceding data and discussion have shown, ethnic boundaries, which may be manifested as environmental, physical, or cultural differentiae, are primarily psychological and behavioral. Our focus has been primarily upon the Tuli balk line of identity maintenance. However, as we have pointed out, boundaries by definition are two-sided. These *parameters of separation*, which constitute the boundary between Tuli and Chinese can be viewed then as the Chinese *parameters of dominance* and the Tuli *parameters of identity maintenance*.

The Parameters of Dominance

Chinese cultural preeminence rested upon a multiple foundation.
1. Presence: Chinese culture was pervasive in the region.
2. Demography: the inertial mass of (then) 600-plus million Han Chinese.
3. Power: military, political, and legal authority was vested in Chinese hands.
4. Economy: markets, merchandising, and money were Chinese first choices.
5. Society: history, literature, philosophy, education, and technology, all proclaimed Chinese superiority, certainly over tribes south of the Yangtze and west of the Gorges.
6. Terminology: most literary and colloquial terms for tribespeople were casual or condescending in nature, even if used neutrally.

Without warfare or fanfare the Chinese had built here a massive wall of dominance parameters to preserve the prerogatives of *their* maximal uniqueness. Within those boundaries there was first-class citizenship for Han Chinese, but not for tribespeople.

The Parameters of Identity Maintenance

The supposed lure of first-class citizenship is consistently unappealing to many minority groups, and ineffectual for others, as Tucker, quoting from Walsh, points out: "We seem finally to have become aware of the universal unwillingness, among people who speak a minority language, to give up their mother tongues and the ways of life that these languages convey, as the price of first-class citizenship in the lands of their birth or their adoption" (Tucker 1972:237).[20] The Tuli realized that this citizenship was not an option for them, not even for bilinguals, so they acted long ago on the principle that "identities are signalled as well as embraced" (Barth 1969:18), and the balk line was born. The most obvious parameters of identity which signal the Tuli boundaries include the following items.

1. Physical: Tuli physical characteristics.
2. Ecologic: a cyclic interaction with environment and resources, rotation of crops, use of animals, blend of mixed agriculture and livelihood methods, etc., that borders on the symbiotic.
3. Demographic: about one quarter million people indigenized both into the environment and into the patterning of tribal interrelationships and history.
4. Cultural: distinctive (Lolo) dialect, dress, marriage and adoption patterns, household arrangements, and blend of religious practices.
5. Linguistic: retention of a Lolo dialect unique to themselves. Bi- or multi-lingualism meant nothing except a potential for wider intercommunication.
6. Value system: independence, equality, economic sufficiency, and self-ascription as to: (a) Tuli identity; and (b) interculturally assigned status.

---

[20]   If "universal" in this quotation be modified to "near universal" or "general" we can find abundant evidence for its substantial accuracy in the cases of very many minority peoples of Mexico, India, Soviet Asia, and the Philippines, as well as of today's black Americans and many of the Amerindian groups. It is true that some native/tribal/minority groups here and there are trending towards assimilation with the national majority and its language, particularly for many bilingual individuals who have switched to identity with the national group, and who seem to feel threatened by the slow or negative response of their own native group as a whole. This is the situation in a number of tribal minorities in Mexico, Russian Asia, and the Philippines. Nevertheless, since the condition delineated for the Tuli and the Chinese has existed for several hundred years and in both Mexico and the Philippines for 300 to 400 years, and Siberia for at least fifty years, the substantial (not "universal") truth of the Tucker-Walsh statement can be accepted.

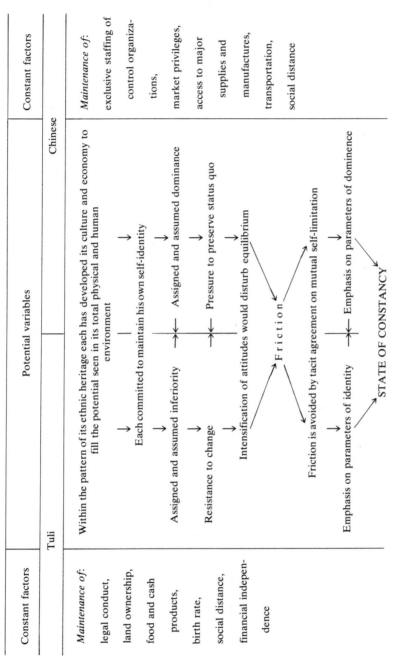

Figure 1. *Tuli–Chinese state of constancy*

Perhaps the two sets of parameters could have been strained to match at least the topics; but their very differences, after centuries of contact, emphasize the cohesion and permanence of the boundaries they represent. And, since the assumption of dominance was as unconscious to the Chinese as the possibilities of upward mobility were unrealistic to the Tuli, the boundaries, and the memberships of the peoples within them, have remained *in situ*.

The State of Constancy

The state of constancy chart (Figure 1 on p. 323) represents the Tuli-Chinese situation, and may also help to illuminate the processes of achieving equilibrium in other societies having balk line situations.

In conclusion, I would suggest that this balk line of minimal uniqueness is a human universal. That is, it is probably true that at some point or time or situation of incursion, every individual tapes his lips and draws a veil over some corner of his personality, each family and association maintains its distinctive name and character, every subculture retains some complex of habits, dress, or companionships, every society preserves its customs, values, and forms of organization, and every nation protects its language, sovereignty, and territory — lest he or it perish.

REFERENCES

BARTH, FREDRIK, *editor*
  1969   *Ethnic groups and boundaries: the organization of cultural difference.*
         Boston: Little, Brown.
CULSHAW, WESLEY J.
  1967   "Review of Martin Orans', *The Santals: a tribe in search of a great tradition.*" *Practical Anthropology* 14(5):235–236.
DAVIES, MAJOR H. R.
  1909   *Yun-nan: the link between India and the Yangtze.* Cambridge: Cambridge University.
EIDHEIM, HARALD
  1969   "When ethnic identity is a social stigma," in *Ethnic groups and boundaries: the social organization of culture difference.* Edited by Fredrik Barth. Boston: Little, Brown.
FENN, COURTENAY H.
  1940   *The five thousand dictionary: Chinese-English.* Peking. (Fenn's Chinese-English Pocket-Dictionary. Revised American edition 1944. Cambridge, Mass.: Harvard University Press.)
FITZGERALD, C. P.
  1972   *The southern expansion of the Chinese people.* New York: Praeger.
FOSTER, GEORGE M.
  1962   *Traditional cultures and the impact of technological change.* New York: Harper and Row.

FRASER, J. O.
  1922   *Handbook of Lisu (Yawyin) Language*. Rangoon.
GOFFMAN, ERVING
  1958   "The nature of deference and demeanor." *American Anthropologist* 50:497.
GOODRICH, L. CARRINGTON
  1963   *A short history of the Chinese people* (third edition). New York: Harper Torchbooks.
GRANET, MARCEL
  1958   *Chinese civilization*. New York: Meridian Books.
HU, CHANG-TU, *et al*.
  1960   *China: its people, its society, its culture*. New Haven, Conn.: Human Relations Area Files Press.
JAN, GEORGE P., *editor*
  1966   *Government of Communist China*. San Francisco: Chandler.
LEBAR, FRANK L., G. C. HICKEY, J. K. MUSGRAVE
  1964   *Ethnic groups of mainland Southeast Asia*. New Haven, Conn.: Human Relations Area Files Press.
LI, DUN J.
  1965   *The ageless Chinese: a history*. New York: Scribner's Sons.
LIU, WILLIAM T., *editor*
  1967   *Chinese society under communism: a reader*. New York: John Wiley.
ming ju hsueh an: wang yang-ming hsueh an
  1735   *Ming Scholars Literary Records: Wang Yang-ming Literary Records*.
ROCK, JOSEPH F.
  1947   *The ancient Na-khi Kingdom of Southwest China*, two volumes. Cambridge, Mass.: Harvard University Press.
SOCIAL SCIENCES SUMMER SEMINAR ON ACCULTURATION
  1954   Acculturation: an exploratory formulation. *American Anthropologist* 56(6):973–1002.
SPEAR, PERCIVAL
  1967   *India, Pakistan, and the West*, fourth edition. New York: Oxford University Press.
TREGEAR, T. R.
  1965   *A geography of China*. Chicago: Aldine.
TUAN, YI-FU
  1969   *China*. Chicago: Aldine.
TUCKER, A. RICHARD
  1972   "Review of *Language and Ethnic Religions in Canada* by Stanley Lieberson." *Language* 48 (1):236–237.
TWEDDELL, COLIN E.
  1948–51   Linguistic fieldnotes. Unpublished.
WALSH, D. D.
  1969   Bilingualism and bilingual education: a guest editorial. *Foreign Language Annals* 2:298–303.
Yun-nan T'ung Chih
  1835   *Yunnan Provincial Encyclopedia*, volume 182.

Jewish Communities as Cultural Units

WALTER P. ZENNER

The purpose of this article is to apply Naroll's operations for defining a cultural unit to Jewish groups, in order to stimulate the use of dispersed ethnic entities in cross-cultural comparative research and to examine certain questions about the relationship of culture to speech community and political boundaries.

In recent years, Naroll published several papers (1964, 1968, 1970) which have stressed the necessity to define the boundaries of a cultural unit in cross-cultural correlation. Naroll's definition of such a unit is observer-oriented. He is less concerned with the subjective definitions of group boundaries used by actors than with objective differences,[1] regardless of the views of the participants. Naroll's critics, especially Bessac (Naroll 1964:203–204; Bessac 1968), Leach (Naroll 1964:299), Hymes (1968), Moerman (1965), and Barth and his associates (1969) have stressed the actor's view of the situation.

Barth's distinction between ethnicity, which is a social structural boundary, and culture is implicit in the subtitle of his book on ethnic boundaries — "The social organization of cultural difference." One of the articles in that volume (Blom 1969), in fact, deals with a case where ecological and cultural variation did not result in a deep-rooted ethnic boundary. Barth's analysis parallels the distinction made by the Ameri-

This paper was prepared under a Faculty Research Grant (020-725A) from the Research Foundation of the State University of New York. Thanks are due to Stephen Childs, Craig Henrikson, Robert Carmack, John Mason, Werner Cohn, James L. Newman, G. de Rohan-Csermak, and others who read and criticized an earlier version. Sole responsibility for the contents is the author's.
[1] In saying that Naroll is concerned with objective differences does not mean that he is only concerned with observed behavior. He clearly states that the cultunit is a unit for analyzing "social and cultural patterns as they exist in the minds of culture bearers" (Naroll 1964:280).

can sociologist, Gordon (1964), between structural, behavioral, and identificational assimilation. A group may be separate in structure and identity, yet its members may come to closely resemble outsiders in their behavior. We have come to a point where not only is it necessary to view as separate aspects, race, language, and culture but ethnicity and culture as well. To the Boasian proposition that there is no necessary causal relationship between race, language, and culture, we may now add there is no one-to-one relationship between ethnicity and culture either. The connection between ethnic group and cultural unit is to be investigated rather than assumed. Naroll's original article was an effort to deal with cultural unit, even though he used the term, "ethnic unit." Since his goal is cross-cultural comparison of behavior and norms, rather than ethnic identification *per se*, he might consider separately characteristics such as the group's name for itself and similar aspects of group identification. A group's sense of sameness obviously influences its behavioral norms, but there is no one-to-one relationship between this sense and the norms.

For Naroll's purposes, the Jews as a group constitute an interesting problem. Naroll himself has referred to them as an "ex-tribe" or "ex-cult-unit." This is a named group whose members have a common history and sense of common destiny and who are quite conscious of boundaries between themselves and others. Nevertheless, modern Jews, such as those in America, are not distinguished by their speech, nor by political autonomy, which are among Naroll's most salient features. Naroll also (1970:731) writes concerning their religion: "Millions of people in the United States today call themselves Jews but neither believe in the truth of the Jewish holy books nor attend Jewish religious services. They all however claim descent from people who did believe and did attend. These in turn claim descent from members of the ancient Jewish states of Israel or Judah."

Naroll sees the Jews and other "ex-cultunits" (or "hyphenated" cult-units), as aggregates "whose bonds of unity are the conditions of their forebears rather than their own condition." While admitting the possible utility of defining such groups for certain studies, Naroll decides to ignore them for his studies.

Most authorities would agree that Naroll's definition of the cult-unit as "people who are domestic speakers of common distinct language and who belong either to the same state or the same contact group" does not apply to American Jews. After all, American Jews and other groups discussed by Naroll (e.g., non-Basque-speaking Basques, Maronites, or Moerman's Lue) are in an advanced stage of behavioral assimilation, even if there is some lag in their structural and identificational assimilation to their neighbors.[2] But what does one do with the middle category of

---

[2] The terms, structural, behavioral, and identificational assimilation are borrowed from Gordon (1964). It should also be pointed out that American Jews, by and large, speak the

Jews who "did believe in the Jewish holy books and did attend Jewish religious services," even though they did not live in a Jewish state. These communities constitute the bulk of Jewish history. Like other minorities and peasantries, the traditional Jewish groups represent sub-societies and part-cultures which deserve greater consideration in cross-cultural comparison than they have received. The cross-cultural samples of Murdock have either neglected this type or found it difficult to handle. Groups either are selected as if they were full cultures representing larger populations, such as the Lebanese (Orthodox Christians) or the (Israeli) Palestinian Druzes or they are not dealt with. In the former case, I have used parentheses to indicate what is unmarked in the Ethnographic Atlas (Murdock 1967:194–197). These labels are misleading in that the community used as a sample is specialized. Why should Arabic speaking peasants or post-peasants be representative of Lebanon as a whole, and can a Christian village represent all religions in Lebanon? Similarly, is an Israeli Druze community a good sample of all Druzes?

The classification of groups such as these involves consideration of complex societies (or social fields) in which one finds several cultures and sub-cultures, some dominating others. Naroll (1970:733) has proposed that culture-bearing units in such a field may be seen as belonging to either the Aztec-type or to the Aymaran type. The Aztec-type is defined as: "People who belong to a state in which unintertelligible dialects occur and who are domestic speakers of a dialect intelligible to speakers of the lingua franca of the state, that is, the dialect in which state officials usually transact their business"

The Aymaran type is defined as: "People who belong to a state in which unintertelligible dialects occur and who are domestic speakers of a dialect not intelligible to speakers of the lingua franca of the state" (Naroll 1970:733).

Most Jewish groups, it will be argued, can be considered either "Aymaran-type" groups or "ex-cultunits" within an Aymaran-type or Aztec-type unit.

NAROLL'S OPERATIONS FOR DEFINING CULTUNITS

In finding cultunits, Naroll proposes two strategies. One is to map all the cultunits in a given religion. In the case of stateless societies, linguistic and political boundaries should be defined, contact gaps based on the dates

---

same English dialects as their neighbors of similar class, with some minor differences and, in some cases, occasional use of Yiddish (or other languages) for foods, jokes, and the like. For structural distinctions between pre-modern and modern Jewish communities, see Zenner (1967, 1968). For a description of groups which maintain communal autonomy in the US, see Poll (1962).

when particular traits are present should be determined and mapped, and finally, actual cultural boundaries should be mapped. Because of Naroll's definitions, these boundaries will tend to coincide with political and linguistic ones. The other strategy (used in state-societies) is to find the cultunit affiliation of a given settlement. This procedure involves working from the individual community and mapping the linguistic and political boundaries from the small unit to the large (Naroll 1970:737–739). By showing how Naroll's operations may be applied to Jewish groups, we can illustrate the way cultunits are defined.

APPLICATION TO JEWISH GROUPS

In this section, Naroll's definition of the cultunit will be applied as given. Naroll's definition of the cultunit fits the Yiddish-speaking Jews prior to the eighteenth century Kingdom of Poland and later of Tsarist Russia and other states of Eastern Europe. One may question, in the case of those living under the rule of German-speakers, whether the Yiddish spoken was intelligible to those speaking standard German, although there are indications that this was the case (at least as much as the Tyrolean dialect). Two problems exist from Naroll's viewpoint. The Jews did not live together in contiguous area, a point emphasized in his 1964 paper, but played down in the 1970 version. Rather, they were dispersed in clusters among populations belonging to different language groups. The other problem is whether or not we are dealing with one cultunit or several.

Yiddish-speaking Jewry was dispersed throughout several East and Central European states, especially after the partitions of the Polish Kingdom. In the period preceding the First World War, one could find substantial numbers in the Tsarist, Austro-Hungarian, and German empires, as well as Rumania. Yiddish-speaking Jewry, which did not use standard Polish, Russian, German, or Rumanian, obviously fits the definition of an Aymaran-type unit. From Naroll's view, it is problematic whether this was one cultunit or several however, Naroll sees the political boundary as determining the unit. Mead in her introduction to Zborowski and Herzog deals with this issue by affirming that Yiddish-speaking Jewry was a single cultural entity, "whether they paid taxes and marketed in Polish or Ukrainian or Hungarian or were ruled by Czar or Emperor" (1952:13–14).

While this is, in essence, the position of Max Weinreich and his successors (M. Weinreich 1953, U. Weinreich 1954, 1963; Herzog, Ravid, U. Weinreich 1969; Lewis 1972), the use of extensive diffusion studies, both with regards to language and to other culture traits, leaves them an opening. Past and present political divisions are among the features that lead to the differentiation of both dialects and local customs. In the area of language, they could conceivably lead to a great enough differentiation to cause the loss of intertelligibility. This leads us to suggest that, rather than considering Aymaran-type units (and even the Aztecan type) as existing solely within the boundaries of one state, we should adopt concepts and procedures that Naroll has used in dealing with the stateless (Hopi type) units.

In such societies Naroll suggests the use of "contact boundaries" and "contact links." As defined by Naroll, a "contact link" is "two nuclear families . . . if every year one of the members of each speaks directly to one of the members of the other." In the case of non-literate "Hopi-type" units, Naroll specifies that we must assume that if the distance is more than 200 kilometers, no contact exists unless there is evidence to the contrary. This situation obviously is not the case in Jewish groups in Eastern Europe and elsewhere where we know that long-distance contacts took place at commercial fairs, pilgrimages to Hasidic rabbis, and attendance at schools.

The Weinreichs and their colleagues demonstrate and explain distributions of cultural and linguistic traits. For instance, M. L. Herzog (1964) relates the extinction of certain lexical and cultural features in northeastern Poland to the history of restrictions on Jewish settlement in certain regions, to the movement of settlers along certain trade routes as the restrictions eased, and to a tendency of settlers on a frontier to "lighten the cultural baggage which they bear with them."

While Herzog's study does not concentrate on the political aspect, it does provide much of the data needed to define contact boundaries. What we have written about the Yiddish-speaking Jews applies to Ladino-speaking Jews of the Balkans and Turkey. Again, we have an Aymaran-type unit in which the language spoken domestically is not intelligible to native speakers of the state's lingua franca. In this case, too, the speakers of Ladino (also known as Judeo-Spanish) were demarcated from local Jews speaking languages such as Greek and Arabic and from Gentiles who spoke other languages than Ottoman Turkish. The non-Jews constituted separate Aymaran-type units. Many of the non-Ladino-speaking Jews were, in fact, assimilated into the Ladino community (Bernadette 1952).

A more difficult case is where the Jews speak a dialect of either the state lingua franca or of a language spoken by other segments of the population. It is fairly easy to dismiss modern American Jews who are often non-practitioners of traditional Judaism as being members of an "ex-cultunit," but the same does not apply as easily to medieval German or Arabic Jewries. In these situations, these Jews apparently adhered to the dictates of Jewish law, both ideologically and practically. The degree of intertelligibility of the dialect spoken by Jews and Gentiles in such contexts must be treated in a case-by-case manner.

Using Blanc's summary of data on social dialects in the Arab world (1964), one would conclude that the Arabic spoken by Arabophone Jews was generally not unintelligible to other speakers of Arabic. In Baghdad, one found that there were distinctive dialects spoken by Jews, Christians, and Muslims. Jewish and Christian dialects belonged to one type of Mesopotamian Arabic, although they differed from one another while the Muslim dialect belonged to another type. Blanc (1964:170–171) explains these differences on the basis of migration to the city and similar historical developments.

Except for Hebrew loan-words, the Baghdadi Jewish dialect as recorded by Blanc (1964) is apparently intelligible to other speakers of Eastern Arabic. The words of Hebrew origin found exclusively in the Jewish dialect include the vocabulary of Jewish religious practice and some words which might be useful in the marketplace and other interethnic situations (including the words for danger, bribe, and thief). Since the Jewish community lacked war-making power, by Naroll's tests, the Arabophone Jews of Baghdad would be part of the same cultunit as their other Arabophone neighbors. Under the Ottoman Turks, this would be the Aymaran type, while under an independent Arab government, this would be of the Aztecan type.

If we follow Naroll's typology of culture-bearing units, we will find some traditional Jewish (and other minority) groups classed as separate "Aymaran-type" units, while some will be classed as segments (or "excult-units") of either "Aymaran-type" or "Aztecan-type" units. Since all of the Jewish groups are subordinate and lack sovereignty, the main criterion for classification becomes linguistic. In fact, the approach applied here raises questions regarding the relationship of language and political relations to other aspects of social and cultural life.

LANGUAGE AND THE MINORITY CULTUNIT

Hymes (1968) has suggested that Naroll's assumptions about the relationship of language to social units are problematical. Hymes points out that communication and mutual intelligibility depend on several factors, "of which sameness or similarity is but one." He suggests that different codes may be used for communication in different aspects of culture, such as with regard to "languages of religion."

This has particular relevance to Jewish units, since Hebrew constituted an important medium of communication within and between traditional Jewish communities. There are suggestions that even Jewish communities which shared mutually intelligible languages with their Gentile neighbors also made use of Hebrew for purposes of privacy, in religion or other areas.

There is some suggestion that Hebrew vocabulary was used, not only for areas of ritual, but other areas as well. As noted above, in Baghdad terms used in the marketplace or other interethnic situations were Hebrew. Denison (1971) points out that Jewish dialects and languages like "Jewish German" (or "Western Yiddish") and Eastern Yiddish served as concealment codes.[3] In non-Germanic Eastern Europe, the Germanically based Yiddish "went a long way towards meeting the need for concealment." In Germany, however, a special vocabulary was required. Thus among the cattle dealers and other Jewish tradesmen of Germany, a Hebrew vocabulary is found, including Hebrew numbers used for the discussion of prices and wares. Thus even within groups which Naroll would define as ex-cultunits one finds regions of activity in which mutual intelligibility is lacking.

The use of the concept of "domestic speakers" of a language also has complications in the Jewish case. In modern times, one can find Jewish families in which two or three languages are used in the household, sometimes over more than one generation (such as Hebrew and Yiddish, Hebrew and Arabic in Israel or Ladino, French, and Arabic in some Egyptian Sephardic households). Poll (1962:273–274) suggests a similar situation among the Hungarian Hasidim of the Williamsburg neighborhood of New York City, who simultaneously use English mixed with Hungarian and the Hungarian dialect of Yiddish.

POLITICAL BOUNDARIES OF THE CULTUNIT

As indicated above, there are problems with Naroll's use of political criteria in defining the cultunit. With regard to the Jews it seems advisable to use contact links, rather than the boundaries of a state in defining the limits of the unit. In fact, he appears to view the state as crucial in setting the blueprint for cultural and social patterns "Aztecan" and "Aymaran" cultunits. There are several problems in this. One is that many premodern states did not have the kind of power (and authority) assumed by Naroll. Second, states have differed widely in imposing a blueprint for behavior on those who live under their control.

On the first point, we must look at Naroll's definition of the state as a "territorially ramified territorial team occupying at least ten thousand square kilometers of land whose leaders assert and wield the exclusive right to declare and conduct warfare" (1970:731). The term "territorially ramified" allows for this fairly large unit to be made of component

---

[3] Western Yiddish and Eastern Yiddish are, of course, defined linguistically. Roughly speaking, the centers of Western Yiddish were in Germany and related areas, while Eastern Yiddish was spoken in Poland and other parts of Eastern Europe. See Herzog, Ravid, and Weinreich (1969) for further discussion.

334   WALTER P. ZENNER

"territorial teams," i.e., groups of "people whose membership is defined
in terms of occupancy of a common territory and who have an official with
the special function of announcing group decisions — a function exercised at least once a year."

While somewhat awkwardly stated, Naroll's definition fits others used
in anthropology. The use of arbitrary criteria, like the minimum of an
annual announcement of group decisions which assumes some sort of
collective leadership and of occupying at least 10,000 square kilometers,
is obviously a device needed for comparative purposes. The remainder of
the definition is compatible with the view that states, even primitive ones,
claim the right "to monopolize the use of force" (e.g., Adams 1966:44).

The monopolization of force by the state, however, is much less clear
with regard to such pre-modern governments as the Holy Roman
Empire, sixteenth-century Scotland, nineteenth-century Iran or
Morocco, than with regard to modern states (Vinogradov, Waterbury
1971). Keddie (1971), points out that the word "state" only attained its
modern meaning in European languages in the sixteenth century and that
it is somewhat absurd to speak of a monopoly on the legitimate use of
physical force for governments lacking significant standing armies. While
the combat between the nomadic tribes, urban factions, governors, and
other groups may not completely fit Naroll's definition of warfare as
"public lethal group combat between kin groups." Obviously if the
government of a state is unable to monopolize force within its boundaries,
it is likely to be permeable with regard to outside cultural influences as
well. Goitein (1971:1, 403–405) has demonstrated the degree to which
medieval Jewish communities maintained contact over often hostile political boundaries. They were allowed extensive autonomy, even in the
realm of law enforcement, as long as they paid their taxes and did not
overstep boundaries. The state did not use its power to impose the
dominant culture on them.

Naroll's model of the "Aztecan cultunit" is a centralized state which
not only controls violence within its boundaries but also imposes a common culture on its population. Examples of such imposition are certainly
found in pre-modern, as well as modern times. The Roman empire is
probably the most striking example. Nevertheless, even there one finds
that cultural diffusion did not stop at the boundaries of the empire, which,
in any case, were in flux. The Romans were influenced by alternative
"blueprints" from Iran, as well as from their own subject peoples, of
whom the Jews were one. Similarly communication links existed between
the Palestinian Jews within the Roman empire and the Babylonian Jews
within the Sassanian empire throughout the period prior to the Arab
conquests in the seventh century. The communication link cannot be
dispensed with in dealing with cultural units of this type.

An alternative to Naroll's effort to define territorially homogeneous cultunits is found in Anderson (1971). In dealing with medieval and early modern Europe, Anderson defines three "culture areas" (or co-traditions), those of the aristocrats, the burghers, and the peasants. The aristocrats had other aristocrats as their reference group, not burghers or peasants living in their own geographic region. Their cultural patterns were spread throughout Europe and moved independently of the others. If burghers or others sought to imitate them, then the aristocrats would modify the patterns to further differentiate them. The diffusion of the burgher culture was similarly not limited by locality. Although Anderson does not go into the communication links of the medieval Jews and Gypsies, they were similarly autonomous. Only the culture of the peasants was different. Their lack of mobility prevented the establishment of an independent communication network. Yet, in spite of this, we find similarities among peasants in different parts of Europe. Anderson suggests these similarities are explained by the fact that the aristocrats in different parts of Europe imposed similar patterns on their cultivators. Peasants are the type implicit in Naroll's Aztecan cultunit, while the other cases would require greater stress on communication links.

The use of contact links in analyzing cultural units does not negate political boundaries, but it does supplement them. Rather than assuming that political boundaries are the key, we could amplify the explanation of why particular divisions occur with trade routes, language, and ecological features. Another aspect — which we have neglected up to this point, should be part of the consideration of ethnic boundaries and cultural units.

RELIGION, ETHNICITY, AND THE CULTUNIT

In the preceding sections, religion was not used in defining the cultural unit because Naroll has explicitly omitted it. Naroll (1964:289, 1970:735) was obviously well aware of its role in determining group membership and cultural differences in Eurasia. His use of language and political boundaries and exclusion of religion, in fact, reflects both arbitrariness and reliance on modern nationalist criteria for the definition of the nation. The Jews, of course, are a classic example of an ethnic group whose identity has been determined by religious ideology, both Jewish and Gentile. In addition, the Jewish religious blueprint for society has played an important role in determining Jewish behavior.

In the Middle East, sectarian affiliation often determines the norms for cousin marriage, divorce, and inheritance patterns, as well as openness to acculturation from the outside (Zenner 1972). At the same time, even traditional Jewish societies during the Greco-Roman and medieval periods were faced with cultural patterns which rivaled those of their own religion. Works like Goitein's monumental study (1971) record how the actual behavior of Jews during various periods resolved the possible contradictions.

CONCLUSION

Naroll's attempt to define culture-bearing units has been useful in challenging anthropologists to deal with the relationship between the culture-bearing unit and the norms and behavioral practices to which they adhere. Traditional Jewish communities in many cases fit his categories, albeit with some minor modification. Nevertheless, Naroll's use of linguistic and political criteria and his neglect of other criteria, such as religion, have problems. In some measure, this is due to the fact that he and others who do cross-cultural correlations have tended to neglect groups like the Jews, the Gypsies, and other dispersed populations. There has been a tendency to think in terms of non-literate tribes and bands on the one hand and modern states on the other. With some exceptions (e.g., Ember, Ember 1972), such studies have also neglected processes of acculturation. It would be well for them to test this methodology on such problems.

REFERENCES

ADAMS, ROBERT McC.
1966   *The evolution of urban society*. Chicago: Aldine.
ANDERSON, ROBERT T.
1971   *Traditional Europe*. San Francisco: Wadsworth Publishing Co.
BERNADETTE, M. J.
1952   *Hispanic culture and character of the Sephardic Jew*. New York: Hispanic Institute in the United States.
BARTH, F., *editor*
1969   *Ethnic groups and boundaries: the social organization of culture difference*. Boston: Little, Brown.
BESSAC, F.
1968   "Cultunit and Ethnic Unit—Processes and Symbols," in *Essays in the problem of tribe*. Edited by June Helm. Proceedings of the annual spring meeting of the American Ethnological Society. Seattle: University of Washington Press.
BLANC, HAIM
1964   *Communal dialects in Baghdad*. Cambridge, Ma.: Harvard University, Center for Middle Eastern Studies.
BLOM, JAN-PETTER
1969   "Ethnic and cultural differentiation," in *Ethnic groups and boundaries: the social organization of culture difference*. Edited by Fredrik Barth. Boston: Little, Brown.

DENISON, N.
1971   Review of *Die Reste des Jeudisch-Deutschen. Jewish Journal of Sociology* 13(1):118–120.

EMBER, C. R., M. EMBER
1972   Conditions favoring multilocal residence. *Southwestern Journal of Anthropology* 28(4):382–400.

GOITEIN, S. D.
1971   *A Mediterranean society: volume II: the community*. Berkeley: University of California.

GORDON, M. M.
1964   *Assimilation in American life*. New York: Oxford University Press.

HELM, JUNE, *editor*
1968   *Essays on the problem of tribe*. Proceedings of the annual spring meeting of the American Ethnological Society. Seattle: University of Washington Press.

HERZOG, M. L.
1964   Channels for systematic extinction in Yiddish dialects. *For Max Weinreich on his Seventieth birthday*. The Hague: Mouton.

HERZOG, M. E., W. RAVID. U. WEINRICH, *editors*
1969   *The field of Yiddish: studies in Yiddish language, folklore, and literature* (third collection). The Hague: Mouton.

HYMES, DELL
1968   "Linguistic problems in defining the concept of tribe," in *Essays in the problem of tribe*. Edited by June Helm. Proceedings of the annual spring meeting of the American Ethnological Society. Seattle: Washington University Press.

KEDDIE, N. R.
1971   The Iranian power structure and social change, 1800–1969. *International Journal of Middle Eastern Studies* 2:3–20.

LEWIS, B.
1972   The emergence of modern Israel. *Middle Eastern Studies* 8:421–427.

MOERMAN, MICHAEL
1965   Ethnic identification in a complex civilization: who are the Lue? *American Anthropologist* 67:1215–1231.

MURDOCK, GEORGE P.
1963   *Outline of world cultures* (third edition). New Haven: Human Relations Area Files.
1967   Ethnographic atlas: a summary. *Ethnology* 6(2): passim.

NAROLL, RAOUL
1964   On ethnic unit classification. *Current Anthropology* 5:283–312.
1968   "Who are the Lue?" in *Essays in the problem of tribe*. Edited by June Helm. Proceedings of the annual spring meeting of the American Ethnological Society. Seattle: University of Washington Press.
1970   The culture-bearing unit in cross-cultural surveys, in *A handbook of method in cultural anthropology*. Edited by Raoul Naroll and Ronald Cohen. New York: Natural History Press.

PATAI, RAPHAEL
1971   *Tents of Jacob*. Englewood Cliffs, N.J.: Prentice-Hall.

POLL, SOLOMON
1962   *The Hasidic community of Williamsburg*. Glencoe: The Free Press.

VINOGRADOV, AMAL, JOHN WATERBURY
1971   Situations of contested legitimacy in Morocco: an alternative framework. *Comparative Studies in Society and History* 13:32–54.

WEINRICH, MAX
1953   Yiddish and Yiddishkayt. *Mordecai Kaplan Jubilee Volume*. New York: Jewish Theological Seminary.
WEINREICH, URIEL, *editor*
1954   *The field of Yiddish: studies in Yiddish language, folklore, and literature*. New York: Linguistic Circle of New York.
1963   *Culture geography at a distance: some of the problems in the study of East European Jewry*. Symposium on Language and Culture. Edited by V. Garfield and W. Chafe. Proceedings of the 1962 annual spring meeting of the American Ethnological Society. Seattle: University of Washington Press.
1965   *The field of Yiddish: studies in Yiddish language, folklore, and literature* (second collection). The Hague: Mouton.
ZBOROWSKI, M., E. HERZOG
1952   *Life is with people*. New York: International Universities Press.
ZENNER, W. P.
1967   Ethnic assimilation and corporate group. *Sociological Quarterly* 8:340–348.
1968   Syrian Jews in three social settings. *Jewish Journal of Sociology* 10:101–120.
1972   Some aspects of ethnic stereotype content in the Galilee. *Middle Eastern Studies* 8:405–416.

Rājasthān and Rājasthānī: Switching Over from Hindī to Rājasthānī

MOTĪ LĀL GUPTA

Immediately after India obtained independence in 1947, the task of legitimizing the statuses of various Indian languages arose. Sixteen languages were granted official status, but Rājasthānī, spoken in Rājasthān province, was omitted from the offical language hierarchy.*,1 One of the objections raised against Rājasthānī's candidacy was that it lacked a standard form. Attempts at standardization have as yet yielded no substantial results, but several scholars agree that Mārwāṛī, spoken in and around Jodhpur, may serve as the standard form for the Rājasthānī dialects.[2] For almost thirty years now, supporters have been advocating

*Two languages, Hindī and English, have national status. Concretely, this means that competitors for government jobs can qualify for employment under one or the other. The plan at Independence was to phase out the use of English. Attempts to do this in the early 1970s met with such strong resistance in southern India that the implementation was discontinued. As of 1977, Hindī was a required subject from the fifth standard in all states but Tamil Nadu, which follows a two-language policy (English and Tamil). The remainder of India follows a three-language policy (Hindī, English, and an official regional language, if different from Hindī). According to *India* (1976:10), the following fifteen [*sic*] languages have official status: Assamese, Bengali, Gujarātī, Hindī, Kanada, Kashmiri, Malayalam, Marāthī, Oriya, Panjābī, Sanskrit, Sindhī, Tamil, Telugu, and Urdu.—*Editor.*
[1]   Soon after Indian independence the question of one language for all of India engaged the attention of legislators. After due deliberation, it was provided in the Constitution of India that Hindī be the official language for the entire country. To facilitate work and allow time for Hindī to come up to the required standard in the various fields of activity, English was allowed to continue. Sometimes the question is asked if Hindī will have supremacy over other languages of the country and hinder their growth. But the policy of the central government is quite clear with regard to the provincial languages which have been recognized as the national languages on an appropriate schedule. Steps are taken to give support for the development and production of literature of these languages. They are to be used as the official languages and as media of instruction in their own areas. Hindī is to serve as the link language because of the number of speakers and the extent of the area in which it is used. The question of Hindī's supremacy does not arise, and the provincial languages have made good progress since.
[2]   The author of this paper is Rājasthānī and has experienced a peculiar combination of languages. I was born and raised in the area where Vraj, a dialect of Western Hindī, was

Rājasthānī, in place of Hindī, as the official regional language of the province. The Rājasthānī issue has been raised twice before the Indian Parliament, but for lack of popular support it was denied official recognition, and Hindī remains the sanctioned language of Rājasthān province.

In India the issue of language — which language will be used in the schools, in the courts, etc. — is a focal point for interethnic competition. Movements to elevate the status of various languages provide excellent opportunities for the observation of ethnic processes. This paper gives the background on one such struggle: the attempt to have Rājasthānī substituted for Hindī as the official language in the province of Rājasthān.

In the following section I examine the history of Rājasthānī as a term in linguistic usage, for the benefit of scholars. The general reader may wish to move directly to the next section, "Language Competition in Rājasthān."

LOCATING AND DEFINING RĀJASTHĀN AND RĀJASTHĀNĪ

The province of Rājasthān, a recent creation, followed independence. Earlier the area was known as Rājpūtānā and consisted of more than two

---

spoken. But all my higher education was done in places where Awadhī, a dialect of Eastern Hindī, is spoken. And the last twenty-five years of my academic life have been spent in the Rājasthānī-speaking area. I, therefore, feel quite at home with the problems delineated in this paper without being drawn toward any of the languages and am in a position to express frank and free views.

I can easily recall the days during 1948–1949, a couple of years after independence when the process of merging smaller units into greater Rājasthān was in progress. Those eastern states — Alwar, Bharatpur, Dholpur, and Karauli — were merged into one unit known as the United States of Matsya. (I carried out a survey of the manuscripts found in this area and published a book called *Contribution of Matsya to Hindī*). The United States of Matsya was also to be merged in the greater Rājasthān. Persons speaking Vrajbhāshā were opposed to this idea, and they petitioned the government of India with millions of signatures that they be merged with the Uttarpradesh where Hindī is spoken. There was, however, a counter move also, led by the chiefs of the states in which they opted for Rājasthān. After a great deal of hesitation and persuasion the linguistically heterogeneous elements were put together as Rājasthān. It is a happy thing to observe that after that period no such linguistic difficulty again appeared.

My study of the switchover process is based on three types of materials:

1. Experience in various parts of Rājasthān, where research opportunities were in the form of survey plans under University Grants Commission's assistance, and teaching assignments throughout the province.

2. Discussion with Rājasthānī and non-Rājasthānī scholars on several occasions.

3. Examination of available literature in the libraries of India and abroad. In the latter category, the India Office Library and the British Museum Oriental Library deserve special mention.

I have not treated the problem from the perspective of a political leader, many of whom promote Rājasthānī to serve such political ends as securing votes from Rājasthānī speakers. Neither have I dealt with the question purely on scholarly grounds, for that stand also lacks life realities and is often confined to theory alone. Rather, I have taken a more practical view of the problem and have tried to base my argument on issues and facts as they stand, or are likely to stand, with due consideration, of course, to general linguistic trends and the complicated workings of the human mind.

dozen independent princely states, subject to the dictates of the Agent General to the government and a network of political agencies under British officers. Each state followed its own particular linguistic form, but in many of the western states, official work was conducted in Rājasthānī.

Rājasthānī is a very broad linguistic term, and it is worth analyzing its geographic boundaries and varied linguistic forms. The greatest work in this area has been done by Sir George Abraham Grierson, whose monumental work *Linguistic Survey of India* (1961) is the main basis of linguistic investigations and research into Indian languages. In Volume X, Part II of this work Grierson deals with the central group of the Indo-Aryan family, namely Rājasthānī and Gujarātī. The two blended together for a number of centuries. Only in the last 500–600 years were distinct demarcation lines drawn and definite areas and linguistic forms designated.

Grierson claims that he invented the term "Rājasthānī" to distinguish the language group from Hindī and Gujarātī. While old Indian literary documents show that the term existed much earlier, the concept of Rājasthānī (in the sense of a group of dialects spoken in Rājasthān) may have begun with Grierson's publication (1961). Previously, the dialects were known by their respective names, and there may have been no single term to encompass all the Rājasthān dialects. Grierson delineates Rājasthānī as the language of fifteen million people residing over 1,800 square miles. The number of speakers has now swelled to twenty-five million inside Rājasthān and some two to three million outside the province.

Map 1 (p. 343) shows how Rājasthānī is bordered in the east by Vrajbhāshā and Bundeli of Western Hindī, in the south by Bundeli, Marāṭhī, Bhīlī, Khāndeshī, and Gujarātī. Toward the west Sindhī and Lahandā are found. Bāgrū, Lahandā, and Panjābī are spoken in the north. Rājasthānī itself has several forms. Around A.D. 1000, Old Rājasthānī branched off into three directions:

Table 1. Old Rājasthānī around A.D. 1000

West		East		South	
Far West	West	East	Far East	Far South	South
Gujarātī	Mārwaṛī	Jaipurī	Mewātī	Nemāṛī	Mālvī
	Mewāṛī	Torāwāṭī	Ahirwāṭī		
	Shekhāwāṭī	Hāṛautī			

Rājasthānī dialects form a group which is differentiated both from Western Hindī and Gujarātī. They constitute a distinctive linguistic group and differ much more from Hindī than does, for example, Panjābī. Under no circumstances should they be classified as dialects of Western Hindī. The Rājasthānī group is different in both inflexion and declension.

Analyses of statistical data have established that the number of speakers of the Mārwāṛī dialect and the area they inhabit are greater than those of all the other Rājasthānī dialects combined. Mārwāṛī is classified into six different forms:

1. Standard Mārwāṛī: spoken in and around Jodhpur;
2. Eastern Mārwāṛī: Gorāwāṭī, Merwāṛī, Ḍhūḍhāṇī, Mārwāṛī;
3. Southern Mārwāṛī: Godwāṛī, Sirohī, Deorawāṭī, Mārwāṛī-Gujarātī;
4. Western Mārwāṛī: Thalī, Jaisalmerī;
5. Northern Mārwāṛī: Bīkānerī, Shekhāwāṭī, Bāgṛī;
6. Mixed Mārwāṛī: several dialects.

Many scholars, including some Europeans, mistakenly include the dialects of Rājasthān under Hindī. However, I must emphasize that Rājasthānī refers to a distinct linguistic group spoken in Rājasthān province.

The Mārwāṛī dialect is spoken extensively outside Rājasthān as well. As far back as 1891 it was estimated that 451,115 speakers lived outside the main area. They resided in Bengāl, Mahārāshtra, Assam, and other far off regions. Further, Mārwāṛī has a considerable recognized literature. A number of poems in old Mārwāṛī, or Ḍingal, as it is more often referred to, are in existence. Many of these have now been published, but a large number of the poems remain in manuscript form. Besides chāraṇ poetry, there is an enormous body of literature in various other forms. Besides bardic chronicles and historical documents, there is a large body of religious literature, mostly attributed to the saints. There are also prose collections, and if retrieval efforts are made, much more historical and scientific literature awaits recognition.

Overall, Mārwāṛī and Jaipurī have been of widest importance, and it is a happy phenomenon that the two share many similarities. For example, the genitive form in Jaipurī is "ko" whereas in Mārwāṛī it is "ro." This difference is the primary means of distinguishing between the two forms. During a recent symposium on the Rājasthānī dialects, an important point in the discussion concerned the present tense singular first person (I am). In Jaipurī it is "chhū̃," whereas in Mārwāṛī it is "hū̃." The past forms are: Jaipurī "chho" (I was) and Mārwāṛī "ho." So also in the future first person: Jaipurī "mārsyū," alternative form "mārūlo." In Mārwāṛī there are three forms: "mārnū̃," "mārūlā" and "mārūgo." The differences are not markedly distinct.

LANGUAGE COMPETITION IN RĀJASTHĀN

In several parts of India there has been trouble over the question of linguistic priorities. In the Panjāb as well as in Mahārāshtra, it created a serious problem of law and order. In Assam the disputes were an issue of governmental concern. Rājasthān is a laudable exception in this respect, in spite of the fact that the west and the east speak dialects belonging to two different languages. The absence of conflict is attributed to the fact that the official language has been Hindī since independence. Of course there have been some linguistic demands in other parts of the "Hindī Province" as it was sometimes called (Map 1 shows the boundaries of this province). In Uttarpradesh there has sometimes been a demand that the larger province be divided into two parts, Vraj Pradesh and Awadh Pradesh, on the basis of western and eastern types of Hindī. This causes occasional conflict, but the demands have never actually gained momentum.

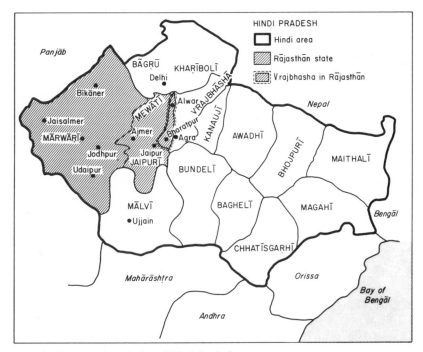

Map 1. Language boundaries of Hindi Pradesh.

Indian national leaders, including Mrs. Indirā Ghāndī, have often remarked that such tendencies of linguistic bifurcation might lead to unscientific and uneconomic fragmentation of the country, and as far as possible, these demands should be ignored. One argument advanced against Rājasthānī was that if the language is granted national status, then several other language areas will claim a similar status, and there may be no end to these demands.

The language question is a very sensitive one. Even for Hindī, the path of acceptance has not been easy. When the Indian constitution was framed, it was provided that by 1965 Hindī would replace English as the national language. A commission was appointed in 1957 to facilitate the transistion as constitutionally prescribed, but when it came to actualizing the provision the South threatened that it would rather have a separate Dravidistān than accept Hindī as the language of the land. Similarly in Bengāl, the response to linguistic nationalization was unfavorable.

As previously noted, in a number of the former princely states of Rājasthān official work was conducted in the dialects of each region. Records found in the Archives of Rājasthān and in some libraries abroad prove very conclusively that in Jodhpur, for example, Mārwārī was used for all official purposes. In schools to the level of upper primary, Mārwārī was the medium of instruction; above this level only English was used. Formerly in almost all of India's upper primary classes and above, all subjects including Indian languages were taught in English. The situation was changed in Jodhpur due to the influence of Swāmī Dayānand Saraswatī, the founder of the Āryasamāj.[3] Although he was a Gujarātī, he was also an orthodox supporter of Hindī. As a result of his influence, Hindī gained prominence over Mārwārī in Jodhpur. Therefore, even for several decades during the British regime, the importance of Hindī was becoming increasingly evident.

Presently, Hindī is the state-sanctioned language inside Rājasthān. But the actual situation is not as clear as it may appear. Although there are governmental resolutions and orders supporting Hindī as the official language for all purposes, most of the work is conducted in English. The government circulars and orders are most often in English; in the higher courts English is used extensively. In higher education, save several subjects in the arts and social sciences, English is the language of instruction. Even in day-to-day correspondence, the elite think it more appropriate to use English. This is the case in almost all the states where Hindī or a regional language is normally in use.

Efforts are being made in Rājasthān to insure that Hindī is used consistently, and it is hoped in certain circles that in the next decade Hindī, in fact, will be the official language. At a transitional state such as this the question of Rājasthānī's status is not palatable to many. It appears they would prefer to ignore the issue, at least for the time being, until Hindī is credited its proper position. But the fact remains that Hindī is not the language of a rather large area of Rājasthān.

I had occasions to visit several interior regions of Rājasthān, and my

---

[3] The Āryasamāj is a socioreligious organization founded by Swāmī Dayānand Saraswatī to uplift the position of the weaker sections of the Hindī society. It placed special emphasis on female education, widow remarriage, and removal of outdated customs. It aimed at believing in the doctrine of the Vedas and decried worship of several purānic deities. Most of the aims of the Samāj have since been achieved, also because of the spread of education and Western influence. At present the Āryasamāj continues as a subreligion and a political force in Hindū society.

experience is that both in the interior and in the villages, Hindī is not used. The people there remarked, "Let alone your Angrezī,[4] speak in Mārwāṛī." However, the situation is changing quickly in the towns, where even at the family level Hindī is displacing Rājasthānī. My impression is that the younger generation speaks Hindī far more frequently. In well-to-do families, children are put in public or mission schools where English plays an important part, next in importance to Hindī. Rājasthānī has no place at all. The situation seems to be that: English is being replaced slowly and reluctantly by Hindī. At another level, Rājasthānī is being displaced by Hindī, a process that is opposed by many people.

To an involved observer, the push for a change in Rājasthānī's status may seem a little out of tune. "Why Rājasthānī?" one may ask. It must be admitted on historical grounds that Rājasthānī has a claim to regional status. Thus, the question cannot be put off so lightly. The needs and aspirations of the Rājasthān people also must be respected.

Let us see what the main difficulties are in switching over from Hindī to Rājasthānī. The question has to be placed in a broad perspective. By switching over we mean:
1. Rājasthānī is to be used in all governmental offices.
2. It is to be the medium of teaching and instruction in as many subjects as possible, especially in those subjects where Hindī is presently employed.
3. Commercial business is to be carried on in Rājasthānī.
4. Public meetings or get-togethers are to be conducted in Rājasthānī.
5. The entire atmosphere need be suited to the spirit of the language.

To some, the changeover may seem a simple process, given that the two languages are so very similar. Not only are the general morphological patterns the same, the script employed is the same as well. Hindī and Rājasthānī are sometimes called "two sisters of the same stock." They owe their origins to the same form of Apabhransh through which Shorsenī became Hindī and Gujarātī became Rājasthānī. Moreover, the two languages are so closely associated that there are a number of people who consider Rājasthānī a sublanguage of Hindī. They believe Rājasthānī's status is only a bit above that of a Hindī dialect. They confine Rājasthānī only to domestic use. They are obviously mistaken, for such notable linguists as Grierson are of the firm conviction that Rājasthānī should not be regarded as a sublanguage of Hindī.

Regarding matters of affinity, Grierson and others believe that Panjābī and Hindī are more closely allied than Hindī and Rājasthānī. Gujarātī can claim greater affinity with Rājasthānī, for they share the same origin

---

[4] Angrezī is the Indian equivalent of English. The English people were called Angrez and their language Angrezī. But in the rural areas any language not intelligible to the common people was called Angrezī. If a particular form of language, Indian or foreign, was not intelligible to the village people it was termed "Angrezī" by them.

and were one language for hundreds of years. Somehow, the mix between Hindī and Rājasthānī has been so intimate that the two seem very close. Thus a change over may appear rather simple, involving no difficulties for the linguistic communities concerned. The actual situation is a bit different, however.

On closer analysis, the problems of transition are many and varied, the most important being the deep-rooted Hindī atmosphere maintained by the educated class in the Rājasthānī area. This has been the case for a number of years. In recent years, the spread of Hindī has been emphasized by governmental and other channels. The teaching community has been a major factor. Most of the teachers have been imported from Hindī-speaking Uttarpradesh. Even now the number of teachers in the Rājasthānī universities from Uttarpradesh is very large, as is also the case with judiciary and the secretariat. These sectors are very important, for they are in close touch with the general public and the young generation.

The influx of Sindhīs to Rājasthān province is regarded as another setback in the propagation of Rājasthānī. My own feeling is that the Sindhīs are not at all problematic. They are closer to Rājasthānī than the Hindī-speaking population and they have always tried to learn the language of the common man rather than that of the elite. They speak Rājasthānī much more frequently than Hindī. The major difficulty remains in overcoming the pervasive atmosphere of Hindī.

Another problem in the transition is the training of personnel to work in Rājasthānī. A switch to Rājasthānī as the language of instruction is necessary. Rājasthānī is used up to the middle grades, but it must be extended to higher and college education. Today, even after so many years of Hindī, there are complaints from students, on one hand, and teachers, on the other, that the language used in higher grades is either English or some curious mixture with English. It is very well known that teachers of the upper grades have been taught in English and very naturally want to continue the same. The students' demands for a transition are very rarely attended to, for it would involve much hard work on the part of the teaching community. The complaints of the students stem from genuine difficulties, for they prefer to study and write in their mother tongue. Although English is nearly compulsory in almost all parts of India, language acquisition is poor and does not suffice to meet students' needs.

Connected with these issues is the question of textbooks. Even now there are complaints that the textbooks in Hindī are inadequate and that serious learning difficulties stem from using these instructional materials. The government of India is spending large sums of money, and the scholars, great amounts of time and energy, to publish books of university standard, both by way of translating foreign texts and in writing original texts. There are some adequate materials in language and social science, but materials are scarce in the sciences and technology and much work remains to be done in these areas. Rājasthānī, too, has been lagging behind in this sphere. There is a government-run institution, the Rājasthānī Hindī Granth Academy, for the production of University standard books. If Rājasthānī replaces Hindī, all this activity has to be redirected. Undoubtedly, translation from Hindī to Rājasthānī will not be difficult. But much time and money would be required for that purpose, and the results are expected to be unsatisfactory. Of course, with the availability of standard textbooks much of the difficulty can be overcome for both the teacher and the student. However, one more hitch remains. Persons who can be expected to translate are not trained in Rājasthānī; they know either English or Standard Hindī. Therefore, the Rājasthānī versions will be inexpressive and variable. Truly, the switch is an arduous process requiring great devotion.

The spread of Hindī through various channels, both governmental and otherwise, has created an unfavorable atmosphere for the transition to Rājasthānī. The educational community, those in the courts and other public realms, politicians and social reformers; all oppose Rājasthānī because the higher strata of the population do not speak Rājasthānī. Although they live in Rājasthān, and try to converse with the natives (mostly for their own ends), they are not likely to align themselves with the Rājasthānī-speaking community.

To grant a language official status, it is essential that linguistic ambiguities be cleared up. This end is achieved only when grammar and semantics are standardized. This process seems to be in the final stages in the case of Hindī, where the Kharibolī dialect has been formalized. An ideal stage, of course, can never be reached. New linguistic forms and words will always appear, for language is not a static entity, and there is an ever-present need for new expressions. It takes time for innovations to blend into standard linguistic usage. This fluidity need be tolerated for a language to develop and grow. In Hindī, it may be said that a more or less fixed and standardized state has been achieved.

Standardizing Rājasthānī necessitates the same process. Mārwāṛī is certainly the most extensively used Rājasthānī language, but dialects such as Jaipurī and Hāṛautī are equally demanding on the standardization process. Even in Mārwāṛī, the dialectal variations both in pronunciation and grammatical forms are numerous. This problem is not peculiar to Rājasthānī. It has been thus everywhere in the initial stages of standardization. In England, Russia, China, in fact almost everywhere linguistic forms have been standardized, some dialects have had to be sacrificed. Standardization requires a sense of altruism for the sake of the country, or the province, as the case may be. One form of one Rājasthānī dialect must be standardized just as the Kharibolī form was in Hindī. To introduce fresh forms, thus creating an artificial dialect, would only increase the difficulty. This alternative has been avoided everywhere; we must follow suit. This issue of standardizing a particular form of a dialect need not be problematic. But the process does require a concerted effort in the same way other national problems do.

Mārwāṛī occupies a unique position in Rājasthān. Estimates hold that Mārwāṛī has influence over 50 percent of both the area and the population of the province. It, therefore, is analogous to Hindī as a language selected from among all the tongues spoken to India. Due to the number of Hindī speakers and the area occupied by these speakers, it was the most suited to be the official language of India and the lingua franca of India. The same argument and statistics apply also in Rājasthān, and we can very easily single out Mārwāṛī as the dominant dialect of Rājasthān.

When we come to the question of deciding upon a definite dialect for standardizing grammatical forms and syntactical bases, the Mārwāṛī used in Jodhpur is most suitable. In the state of Mārwāṛ, this dialect has successfully played the role of the official language in the past. Mārwāṛī has a standard grammar, and the forms used in the area are not very variable.

There is yet another point in favor of Mārwāṛī. The dialect selected to occupy such an important position should have a firm base in acknowledged literature and a renowned past. Of all the Rājasthānī dialects, Mārwāṛī alone has a literature of recognized merit. It is considered one of the richest languages of India. We can boast of Rājasthānī literature only because of Mārwāṛī's body of poetry, drama, stories, and political, economic, ethical and religious literature. The bardic literature and the devotional songs are known all over India. It is necessary to bring this vast treasure to the attention of the scholarly world.

On the basis of both published and unpublished works, the Indian Sāhitya Academy conferred on Rājasthānī the status of an Indian literary language,[5] along with the other developed languages of the country. In fact, it is only because of Mārwāṛī that Rājasthānī has been recognized as a developed language, and it will only be through Mārwāṛī that progress can be made toward standardization. Surely this recognition is a step toward elevating Rājasthānī to one of the national languages of the country. Literary status can easily be followed by granting Rājasthānī the position of the official language of the province.

Standardizing Rājasthānī through Mārwāṛī is the first step of the transition. Thereafter, massive amounts of information and books will be

---

[5]   A literary language is not necessarily an official language. It should have a rich literature in the past with a tradition of its own which the scholars constantly enrich by their contributions in various fields. In India Maithilī and Rājasthānī provide good examples. They are not official languages but they are recognized languages in literature and they have a place under the Sahitya Academy of India. Literary language, as in all places, is a little different from the language of the common people.

needed, but once standard forms are determined, the efforts of competent scholars and the government can proceed. Government participation is of paramount importance. The process of nationalizing a language is instituted by the Indian parliament, and it is the responsibility of the provincial government to make the Center decision effective. As far as I know, the position of the Rājasthān government is not very favorable to Rājasthānī at this point. Following Independence, they showed a "willingness" to institute Hindī only due to pressures from different quarters, including the Center. They had to undertake substantial work to facilitate the transition to Hindī. Replacing Hindī with Rājasthānī would mean much more work and, in some ways, a step back. All sorts of additional difficulties can be pointed out, such as funds, personnel, feasibility, and the like. Influence must be exerted to convince the government to accept the wishes of the people and to support them on this issue.

There is one more point to be considered. Thus far, the inhabitants of Rājasthānī can carry on with two languages: Hindī and English. If Rājasthānī is recognized, they will need to know three languages. Actually, people should not begrudge this situation. They should keep in mind the other provinces where regional languages exist along with Hindī and English. The residents of Rājasthān will need to learn Hindī sooner or later because it is the official language of the country, and they will need to know English because it is the international language. In sum:

1. They should agree to have one dialect and one form for the whole state.

2. They should devote selfless efforts to produce standard literature rapidly, covering all branches of knowledge.

3. Funds are to be provided not only by the government, but by all those people of Rājasthān whose benevolence is open to such good causes.

4. The teachers in the educational institutions should work a little harder not only to use Rājasthānī in instruction, but also to produce books for teachers and students at all levels.

5. A helping attitude of the governmental representatives is necessary. They should realize the responsibility which they owe to the voters. The government machinery is to be of a similar mind and should not attempt to block the transition.

In these days of democracy, we cannot afford to neglect the people, especially those in the remote regions. We have to promote educational opportunity and political consciousness. We have to insure that all Indian citizens feel that they occupy a responsible position in society. In Rājasthān this can be done most successfully if the people are educated through their own dialect or, at best, in the form of Rājasthānī selected for state use. Mārwāṛ and Rājasthān are large areas, and the question of fragmentation can be avoided if we carry out our plans thoughtfully.

There may be demands from persons speaking Mewātī and perhaps even more pressure from those speaking Vrajbhāshā. But, they should pose no serious problems. Although there are many persons who promote bilingualism for India, it has been concluded by many others that the "three language formula" alone can solve the several linguistic problems of this vast country. Trilingualism can solve the difficulties experienced in Rājasthān as well. We can tabulate it below as:

Table 2.

Area	International language	National language	Regional language
Tamil Nadu	English	Hindī *	Tamil
Vrajdesh	English	Hindī	Rājasthānī (replacing Hindī)
Rājasthān	English	Hindī	Rājasthānī

* Tamil Nadin does not, in fact, accept the three-language policy (*Editor*).

REFERENCES

GRIERSON, G. A.
   1961   "Note on the principal Rajasthani dialects." *Linguistic Survey of India*, volume IX(II)

INDIA
   1976   *India: 1976*. Government of India, Ministry of Information and Broadcasting.

When Brokers Go Broke: Implications of Role Failure in Cultural Brokerage

MICHAEL SALOVESH

> The position of [cultural] "brokers" is an "exposed" one, since, Janus-like, they face in two directions at once. They must serve some of the interests of groups operating on both the community and national level, and they must cope with the conflicts raised by the collision of these interests. They cannot settle them, since by doing so they would abolish their own usefulness to others. Thus they often act as buffers between groups, maintaining the tensions which provide the dynamic of their actions.
>
> ERIC WOLF[1]

This paper is a study of cultural brokers in action. Ultimately, it is aimed at the same kinds of questions that Wolf asks in his pioneering article (1956). Wolf, however, chose to look at cultural brokers as part of an attempt to understand complex societies at the national level. I will examine the effects of cultural brokers in a local community. If the cultural broker is Janus, then the anthropologist, too, must look both ways to grasp the import of cultural brokerage. Because I share with Wolf an interest in learning how the larger society operates, I am examining the interface between local community and the national-level society. Wolf's later works (1959, 1969) have pointed the way to national-level interpretations — a lead that has been followed by many others (cf., e.g. Banton

Fieldwork on which this paper is based took place in 1958–1959, 1960–1961, 1962, 1963, 1968, and 1972. The support of the Social Science Research Council, the Department of Anthropology of the University of Chicago, and the Purdue Research Foundation is gratefully acknowledged.
[1]   In: *Aspects of group relations in a complex society: Mexico*, page 1076.

1966; Adams 1970). Studies of cultural brokerage from the local viewpoint are a necessary complement to those which concentrate on the
national scene. This paper is such a study.

I begin with a brief overview of the relations between ethnic groups in
Venustiano Carranza, Chiapas, Mexico, the town which provides a setting for the brokerage activities examined here. Then follows a detailed
examination of the roles played by both an indigenous local leader and an
outsider (whose role as conscious agent of directed culture change also
involved cultural brokerage). The interplay between these two strong
brokers is the center of specific empirical data examined here. Finally, the
conflict of brokers and the ultimate "failure" of both of them provide
entry into a discussion of the structural implications of role performance
and role failure in cultural brokerage.

The cases studied here took place around forty years ago. Why have I
not chosen more contemporary cases? The first reason has already been
stated by Wolf: "group relationships involve conflict and accommodation, integration and disintegration, processes which take place over
time" (1956:1066). The consequences of the activities examined here,
parts of a series of processes in which the local community went through
dramatic readjustments in its relationships with outsiders, have had the
necessary time to work themselves out. In recent years, culture change
has been so dynamic in this community, and so many brokers have arisen
and fallen, that it would be difficult to pick up the threads of a single series
of events without writing several books of explanation. Even then, the
explanation would be as incomplete as the processes themselves. Finally,
I have had to face serious ethical problems in examining, for public
presentation, the activities of contemporary figures on the local scene.[2]
What I write here will shortly become available to officials of national and
state government, and to at least some members of the community itself.
Although I have closely followed the activities of many cultural brokers in
the community during the last fifteen years, I cannot allow myself the
luxury of publishing the details of their activities now. There is too much
danger that they will suffer from my indiscretions. Nonetheless, I cannot
wipe out what I know; some of the conclusions presented in the final

---

[2] Three cases from my notes will illustrate the possible drastic consequences, on both
brokers and the community, of public knowledge of details of brokerage activities. An
Indian who turned cultural brokerage to his own financial profit was repeatedly accused of
witchcraft, and eventually killed by other Indians — "coincidentally" at the time when some
of the extent of his profit became known. A self-styled "mestizo" go-between was shot from
ambush when a powerful rancher learned of the broker's nearly successful attempt to
reclaim illegally-expropriated Indian communal lands. A priest who established a school in
which Indian and poor Ladino children had a chance to make up for discrimination against
them in the official Escuela Federal was "exiled" to a remote, isolated community when his
superiors learned about the school. (I hasten to add that this was because church-connected
schools are forbidden by law, not because the priest's superiors were opposed to education
as such, nor because they favored discrimination.)

section of this paper have been shaped in part by my knowledge of recent brokerage relationships.

THE TWO COMMUNITIES OF VENUSTIANO CARRANZA[3]

Venustiano Carranza (formerly called San Bartolomé de los Llanos) has been an important agricultural community in Chiapas, Mexico, since the sixteenth century (see, for example, Gage 1946:143; Thompson 1958:139). Cotton was a major cash/trade crop in the sixteenth through eighteenth centuries, and there have been several periods of cattle ranching as a major source of income during the present century, but the products of milpa agriculture have been the prime economic base throughout recorded history. Large surpluses of maize and beans grown in the fertile lands near the Río Grijalva (Río Grande de Chiapa) are exported annually, except in years of severe drought.

Censuses taken in the town at various times from the sixteenth through the eighteenth centuries show a steady growth in population to an apparent peak, in 1778, of at least 4,800 (Trens 1957:222). The population in the 1930s was something on the order of 7,000; between 1960 and the present, the town has grown from about 10,000 inhabitants to perhaps 15,000 today. (Censuses in the Colonial epoch are notoriously undependable in their precision; my own investigations suggest that there are also gross errors in the reported population of V. Carranza in the decennial censuses of 1960 and 1970. I prefer to avoid the specious accuracy that would be implied by citing the exact figures that appear in published censuses.)

More interesting than the basic population figures is the fact that V. Carranza has been a mixed community, part Indian, part "Ladino," at least since the early 1600s. "Ladino" is the local term for Spanish-speaking individuals oriented to supra-local norms. The term "Indian" is used here to mean individuals whose first language is a native American one — in this community, Tzotzil Maya — and who participate in the affairs of some local, closed corporate peasant community (cf. Colby and van den Berghe 1961; Wolf 1957). Census figures suggest that Ladinos constituted at least 10 percent of the local population by 1712; at the turn of the present century, they made up about a third (or less) of the inhabitants of a temporarily reduced town center. In the early 1930s, Ladinos were a rapidly rising segment of the population, slightly less than 40 percent of the total; by 1960, Ladinos made up about half the popula-

---

[3]   In the remainder of this paper, I shall use Venustiano Carranza to refer to the town as a whole. When I speak of the Indian community within the town, I follow the practice of Mexico's Instituto Nacional Indigenista and the Museo Nacional de Antropología by calling the Indian community San Bartolomé.

tion; today, as many as two out of three inhabitants of the town may be
Ladinos. (The recent rise in Ladino population, in both absolute and
relative terms, is due more to in-migration from other parts of the state
than to any differential in reproductivity or mortality rates within the
town.)

In this century, settlement patterns in V. Carranza have gone through
three major stages. Prior to the Mexican Revolution, the bulk of the
population came into the town center only for ceremonial occasions.
(Most of the Indians were bound in debt peonage to owners of outlying
fincas, and many of the Ladinos resided on cattle ranches or plantations
well away from the town.) Military campaigns in the surrounding countryside around 1917 made a move to some densely settled center a
practical necessity (see, e.g. Moscoso 1960). At about the same time, the
Revolution ended the system of debt peonage, freeing the Indians to
return to their old town-center. Finally, heavy Ladino in-migration in the
late 1920s and early 1930s, together with the seizure of much Indian land
within convenient walking distance of the town, led the Indians (but not
the Ladinos) to a divided settlement pattern which continues to this day.
In this pattern, women and children reside in the town all year long.
Indian men, however, follow a typical pattern of leaving the town on
Mondays, sleeping in their distant fields during the week, and returning
to their families on Friday evening. (In Salovesh [1965] I comment on the
effects of this "periodic manlessness" on patterns of acculturation among
the Indians of this town. In that article, I suggest that the same pattern
occurs elsewhere, albeit rarely; and that the effects of the pattern where it
occurs are so important that they justify adding this category to those
established in Tax [1937]. The other patterns I have described here are
what Tax would call a "vacant town" and a "town nucleus" type of
settlement pattern.)

From 1917 to 1934, there were two kinds of formal governmental
structures which reigned in V. Carranza. The first, the Ayuntamiento
Constitucional, was established under the provisions of the 1917 Constitution of Mexico and the dependent provisions of Chiapas state law.
Under the law, this Ayuntamiento (like its predecessors in prior centuries) was recognized as the legitimate governing body of both the town
and a large territory (now called a *municipio*) surrounding it. V. Carranza
was, and is, the *cabecera* [head town or administrative center] of both the
municipio and an even larger judicial district, governing both the rural
periphery and several subsidiary towns. (Among the administrative
dependencies of the *cabecera* are the Indian community of
Aguacatenango and the Ladino town of Socoltenango.) Until 1934 or
1935, neither the Presidente Municipal nor any members of the Ayuntamiento (the *regidores*, or "councilmen") were Indians. Since 1936, it
has become the custom for one of the *regidores* to be selected from among

the Indians of the town center. (The Tzeltal-speaking Indians of Aguacatenango remain unrepresented on, but subordinate to, the municipal Ayuntamiento.)

In parallel to the council and officers recognized as legitimate by state and national law, V. Carranza had a separate Indian Ayuntamiento until 1934. Legally, this Ayuntamiento had no binding jurisdiction as a general governing body, although it could and did control access and title to lands owned communally by the Indians (see *Constitución* 1962: Article 115; *Leyes* 1959: Article 64 et seq.). But the Indian Ayuntamiento functioned extralegally as the basic organ of Indian government. (I use the term "government" in the sense defined in Smith 1956.) This group also served as one of the central foci of the traditional politico-religious hierarchy through which the Indians organized their public life. (Structure of this hierarchy in San Bartolomé is described and analyzed in Salovesh [1971]; for an overview of similar hierarchies in Mesoamerica in general, see Carrasco [1961]).

Two kinds of divisions within the Indian community of San Bartolomé will become relevant later in this paper. First, the community was and is organized into five partially independent groups based on territorial divisions within the town. These groups, (*barrios*) were traditionally in control of separate segments of the communally owned agricultural lands. Each *barrio* was led by its own "council of elders" (the *principales*, "principal men," those who had risen to the top of the hierarchy through service in temporary civil and religious offices). A second kind of internal division within the Indian community was the lingering aftermath of an ancient moiety division. *Barrios* were wholly included subdivisions of the moieties. In some unspecifiable past, strict moiety endogamy had been practised, but this custom had pretty much disappeared by the 1920s. (Still, those who wished to marry across the lines of the old moiety division are said to have been required to seek permission of the *principales* of the *barrios* concerned; no such permission was needed for inter-*barrio* marriage within a moiety.) Men from one *barrio* found it easy to use lands traditionally assigned to another *barrio* within their own former moiety, but it was extremely rare for a man to make his *milpa* on lands assigned to the opposite moiety, and a complicated process of seeking formal permission was a prerequisite. Since the 1920s, the last vestiges of formal moiety organization, as such, have disappeared. But the old *barrio* allegiances to the former moieties have provided the nucleus for continuing factional alliances in the political structure of the community.

The existence of two separate formal organs of government within V. Carranza was but a reflection of a larger social reality. I have shown elsewhere (Salovesh 1971: especially Chapter 3) that the physical commingling of Indian and Ladino residents within the town does not conceal the fact that for all practical purposes there were two socially separate communities within the town during the time period with which this paper is concerned.[4] Here and elsewhere, when I speak of the Indian community within V. Carranza, I refer to it as the community of San Bartolomé. In many ways, the lives of the Indians of San Bartolomé are very much like those of their Tzotzil-speaking cousins in such better-known communities as Zinacatan (Vogt 1969) or Chamula (Pozas 1959). But the immediate physical presence of such a large proportion of Ladinos within the same town, and the imbedding of the Indian community within a surrounding and superordinate Ladino community in virtually the same physical space, has led San Bartolomé to a series of unique adjustments to the Ladino world.

Within a period of about five years before and after 1930, the community of San Bartolomé underwent drastic shifts in its relationships with the surrounding Ladino community. The activities of two men, who are called "Bartolo" and "El Maestro" in this report, were central to these developments. Both were cultural brokers; both had careers marked by temporary success, but ultimate "failure" in their brokerage roles. Let us now examine what they did, and how.

A *CACIQUE* AS CULTURAL BROKER

Bartolo was born an Indian of San Bartolomé. Unlike nearly all of his contemporaries, however, Bartolo was sent to a school for Indians in another town at an early age, and he remained there at least until his late teenage years. At school, Bartolo gained an excellent command of Spanish, and he became comfortably literate. At the same time, he became fluent in his understandings of how Ladino culture worked — particularly in the political sphere. Later in life, Bartolo's command of spoken and written Spanish and his knowledge of Ladino culture made him unique among the Indians of San Bartolomé.

When Bartolo returned to V. Carranza and San Bartolomé, he was well past the age for service in the bottom level of the politico-religious hierarchy. He did serve, once or twice, as a lower-level *mayordomo* in those groups within the hierarchy that were responsible for the celebration of annual fiestas, but he never rose very high in the ladder of offices and never was a *principal*, in the traditional sense. Instead his literacy in

---

[4]   I have come to speak of the community of San Bartolomé as if it were totally, rather than partially, separate from the Ladino community with which it shares the town of V. Carranza. I thus take the position that relations between San Bartoleños and Ladinos within the town reflect, in microcosm, the relations between isolated peasant communities and the larger national community. (Treating the Indian segment of a mixed community as if it were an independent, isolated community of its own is hardly an innovation in Mesoamerican studies; see, for example, Tax [1953], Gillin [1951], Tumin [1952], etc.)

Spanish and familiarity with Ladino ways soon led to Bartolo's appointment as the Secretary of the Indian Ayuntamiento.

The post of Secretary carried no authority in the traditional Indian
system. It was customarily held by younger men, who were temporarily
excused from service in the fiesta hierarchy during their service as quasi-
official scribes. The post was regarded as an onerous burden, which took a
great deal of the incumbent's time but yielded no increment of prestige
and little other reward save a token salary.

But Bartolo's knowledge of the Ladino world, and his comfort in
handling the written record, was far superior to that of his predecessors in
the office of Secretary. As broker between the Indian community and the
surrounding Ladino world, he was able to use the written record to
recover some Indian land rights, and he was an effective representative of
Indian viewpoints when minor conflicts between Indians and Ladinos
arose. On this base, Bartolo began to build a series of interlocking
networks with many of the leaders of the Indian community. Eventually,
he forged alliances of mutual obligation and particularly close ties of
compadrazgo [affinal relationship or work-group association] with major
leaders from all five *barrio* territories within the community.

At the same time that Bartolo was building a power base out of his
position as Secretary of the Indian Ayuntamiento, he made himself a vital
link in communications between the Indian community and agencies of
Ladino government and powerful individuals in the Ladino community.
Drawing on his connections within all five Indian *barrios*, Bartolo could
deliver labor levies or cash contributions in the quantities requested by
Ladino authorities. And, having delivered Indian goods and services in
response to the demands of outside authorities, he could later call on
those authorities to cut corners in granting permission to the Indians to
conduct activities they considered vital. (Law or custom, according to the
specific case, called for Ladino authorities to grant or withhold permission for Indians to celebrate a public fiesta, to bring crops into or through
town, to send delegations to state or national authorities, to clear trees
from *milpas* being prepared for new planting, *ad infinitum, ad nauseam*.)
Eventually, Bartolo was able to convert his control of the written record
and of access to outside authorities into power that made him the *cacique*
(political boss) of the entire Indian community. He exacted a toll of
power and prestige from both sender and receiver whenever communication took place between the Indian community and the outside, Ladino
world.

Bartolo's position of power ultimately depended on the unique command of communication channels he had taken into his own hands. True,
the *principales* of the five *barrios* usually forged interlocking alliances
that resulted in a unitary power structure within each *barrio* — but
Bartolo's alliances entered into all five *barrios*. Many *principales* were

able to join their counterparts in neighboring *barrios* to form larger units of political control by the manipulation of kinship and *compadrazgo* links across *barrio* lines, but the lingering aftermath of the old moiety system stood in the way of expansion of these links to the community as a whole. No *principal* had close solidary links outside the two or three *barrios* of his own moiety, and Bartolo used his own connections to keep such links from forming. A constant struggle over diminishing land resources led the *principales* of the two opposing groups to a strong desire to maintain exclusively in rights of usufruct on communal lands to their own followers, and Bartolo used his control of the land records to keep the two groups apart.

Another part of Bartolo's control of communication channels came from his personal network of dyadic relationships with powerful authorities in the Ladino world. The most notable of these was his unique relationship with the Secretary-General of the Department of Agrarian Affairs of the national government. This major leader had political ambitions centering on his native state of Chiapas; he later was to move from the Department of Agrarian Affairs to become manager of the National Bank of Ejido Credit, and finally gained election as Governor of Chiapas. In all of these posts, this leader was in a position which could be used either for or against the Indians of San Bartolomé. And whenever an Indian delegation from the community went to see him, in one or another of his official capacities, Bartolo served as spokesman for the group. It was Bartolo who wrote to ask for appointments, Bartolo who controlled the written records, and Bartolo who had the greatest confidence in speaking Spanish with such an important figure. And, whether or not the community could get the actions it sought from the head of such powerful outside organizations, the community under Bartolo's leadership could provide a strong base of apparent popular support for the future of the man who might use his government offices to help them. Bartolo also used his position within the Indian community to form similar relationships with other outside leaders on the local and state levels. In each case, Bartolo's access to those outside leaders was far different qualitatively and quantitatively from that available to any other Indian leader.

Eventually, Bartolo's power within the Indian community was to be sorely tried by events originating outside that community. The ways he moved to meet those challenges, and the effects of his actions on the community as a whole, can only be examined after we have looked at the position of a Ladino cultural broker whose activities complemented Bartolo's for many years.

A TEACHER AS A CULTURAL BROKER

El Maestro was born and raised in Veracruz. He first came to Chiapas as a major in the Constitutionalist forces during the latter part of the Mexican Revolution. Late in the 1920s, he was appointed head of the federally supported primary school in V. Carranza; soon afterwards, he set up evening and Sunday adult education classes for Indians and Ladinos alike. His classes, particularly those for adults, were El Maestro's platform for the advocacy of political, economic, and social change throughout his residence in V. Carranza.

El Maestro was soon appointed as a local organizer for the "official" political party — called, in its early days, the Partido Nacional' Revolucionario, or PNR. In the early 1930s, it was the conscious policy of the PNR to beat swords into plowshares by making teachers out of former Army officers. But the civilian function of these ex-officers was, in a sense, a continuation of their old military missions: as party organizers, their primary duty was to mobilize support for both the PNR and the national government and its programs (see Bosques 1937:10, 59–61).

Today, San Bartoleños recall that El Maestro's teachings began with a call for unity and solidarity. Many of them quote him as repeatedly saying "now we are a single pueblo, united in the interests of all." From El Maestro's viewpoint (and that of the PNR), the "we" of this statement meant the people of Mexico — but to the Indians of San Bartolomé, the words were taken as a call for cross-*barrio* and cross-moiety unity. Later, when he preached a message of class solidarity for all members of "the agricultural sector" — i.e., *milperos* and agricultural laborers — he was interpreted as supporting the possibility that poor, landless Ladinos be allowed to use Indian communal lands.

In fact, El Maestro's activities took on just such a local flavor. As he built the *campesino* section of the local PNR apparatus, and tried to build local support for the land reform programs of the central government, El Maestro had to break down old allegiances and avoidances. To consolidate his power on the local front, he eventually had to mount a three-pronged attack on the forces of leadership in the Indian community by initiating or promoting changes in labor relationships, in religious participation, and in access to land. In all of these programs, he was at the same time taking power away from the old *principales*, the Indian Ayuntamiento (and Bartolo, its Secretary), and the exclusively-Indian Comité Agrario (the land-holding alter ego of the Ayuntamiento).

For centuries, Indians in San Bartolomé had been subject to service in unpaid labor levies at the beck and call of Ladino authorities. Allegedly, this service was supposed to be *pro bono publico*, and limited to such work as road-clearing, cleaning streets and public areas, and the like. But it was customary for rich Ladinos to use the system as a means of obtaining free labor on their ranches and plantations. The Indians were not unaware that similar practices had been among the causes of the Revolution, and they had begun to resist Ladino calls for labor levies even before El Maestro's arrival. (Bartolo's rising power, in that initial period of resistance, came from the fact that his community-wide ties with leaders in all *barrios* made him uniquely able to deliver workers in the desired numbers, while *principales* limited to a base of followers in only one or two *barrios* often could not get together an adequate work force when asked to do so.) But it took El Maestro's constant reiteration of the labor articles of the 1917 Constitution to make a convincing case. In 1932, El Maestro — acting on behalf of some members of his adult-education classes, who had been threatened by the Indian Ayuntamiento with jailing for their repeated refusal to contribute labor to public projects — got legal support through his PNR connections. As a result, the labor levy system was officially ended, and future work on public projects became a matter of paid labor.

Prior to El Maestro's arrival, and for some years afterwards, Indians also contributed both labor, goods, and money to the fiesta-celebrating wings of their politico-religious hierarchy. From the beginning (which, after all, coincided with a militant phase of anticlerical activities at the national level) El Maestro fought against this. Again, many informants today impute the same words to him, suggesting that he taught the following as a kind of litany: "A man who gives to the fiestas carries a load like a pack animal." (This was an obvious play on the word *cargo*, meaning both "burden" and "fiesta office.") "When he has money, he burns it up in skyrockets and liquor in the fiestas. When you get money, you should save it to buy a burro. Then the animal can do the work of an animal, and you can walk upright like a man. But when you give money or work to the fiesta, then you will remain like an animal, nothing more."

Finally, El Maestro sought to promote class solidarity by opening access to all sections of the Indian communal lands to any member of the community, regardless of *barrio* affiliation, and to poor Ladinos as well. The Indian Ayuntamiento resisted this proposal with all the force it could muster, under the particular urging of Bartolo as *cacique*. At the same time, Indians in general resisted any move to cut down on, or away from, the celebration of fiestas in the traditional way. If San Bartolomé had been isolated from outside forces in these matters, El Maestro's programs would have been an utter failure; but outside forces did operate, dramatically.

In August, 1933, the Governor of Chiapas ordered that all churches in the state were to be closed and locked permanently (Lópes Gutiérrez 1957: III, 449–450). Federal troops acting under his orders came to V. Carranza on November 1 to insure that these orders were carried out. (At the same time, they seized and burned church records, images of the saints, and altar decorations, both from the churches and from attempted refuges in private homes. The day is locally called "the burning of the saints.") The troops remained in the town for several years, serving as the local police force. There was no public celebration of fiestas for the next six years; traditional recruitment to office in the politico-religious hierarchy came to a permanent end.

In February, 1934, Lázaro Cárdenas, President-elect of Mexico, made an unprecedented tour of Chiapas, fulfilling his campaign pledge to visit every part of the country. Cárdenas received a San Bartolomé delegation led by El Maestro, the only local leader to be received individually by the President-elect. It is my impression that Cárdenas, himself a general, undertook a private visit with El Maestro as part of his program to unite and continue his hold on former as well as present officers in the military as Cárdenas maneuvered for control of the emerging official party. But back in V. Carranza, local Ladinos took El Maestro's visit with Cárdenas as a signal that he enjoyed the direct support of the President-elect.

On his return to V. Carranza, El Maestro, at the head of a squad of locally garrisoned Federal troops, released the prisoners who had been jailed by the authority of the Indian Ayuntamiento. He then marched the troops over to the building which had been occupied by the offices of the Indian Ayuntamiento, padlocked the Indian offices, and posted a military guard to insure that the Indian Ayuntamiento could no longer exercise quasi-legal power. He was supported in these actions by the town's Ladino authorities and by most of the Indian pupils of his adult-education classes. The way was now clear for a direct confrontation between El Maestro's followers and those Indians linked to Bartolo, the *cacique*. The arena for this confrontation was to be provided by questions relating to access to the communal lands.

Before examining the most dramatic episodes of confrontation between El Maestro and Bartolo, let us stop to consider whether, and in what ways, El Maestro can properly be considered as a cultural broker rather than a politician, a teacher, or an agent of directed culture change. To a certain extent, anyone occupying one of the latter three roles must often act through means that are indistinguishable from those of the cultural broker. Generally speaking, however, each of these three roles is directed at ends quite different from those of the cultural broker, and brokerage activities are simply one set of means out of many that might be used to achieve the ends implicit in these other roles. The cultural broker, on the other hand, exists — or, rather, persists in his role — only so long as he can keep the cultures he bridges dependent on his services as intermediary. El Maestro's activities as politican were based on his attempts to unite a single segment within the Indian community (and, to a lesser extent, the lower levels of the Ladino community as well), not really to advance the avowed aims of the PNR he nominally served. He took two different attitudes toward teaching: when teaching Ladino children, the occupation from which he derived primary support, he taught to national standards by traditional schoolroom methods, with the end result that at least some of his pupils were able to go on to further schooling on their own. But he did little more for the Indian children in his classes than to keep them in the classroom; he made little or no effort to help them learn Spanish, and did not lead more than half a dozen to even rudimentary literacy in all his years of teaching in the town. His adult education classes, insofar as they served as something more than a pulpit for message preaching, served to increase the dependence rather than the independence of the students. The new programs and techniques he introduced called for more sophisticated knowledge than he was willing (or able?) to impart for their continuation without the intervention of a cultural broker as intermediary. (I am convinced, but do not have the space to demonstrate here, that this was deliberate policy on El Maestro's part, designed to consolidate his own position.) Finally, the major effect of the cultural changes El Maestro introduced was to cut down on the independent avenues to power and communication formerly available to the Indian community while increasing the community's dependence on his own power through his control of intercultural communication. All of these activities are much more consonant with the classic role of cultural broker, who must struggle to maintain the separation between the groups he bridges, than they are with the other roles El Maestro played.

BULLS AND BEARS: BROKERS IN CONFLICT

The two brokers we have been examining had often taken opposite sides in their approaches to power through control of the gates of intercultural communication. Bartolo had obtained his power through manipulation of the traditional system; El Maestro worked to undercut the traditional system through ending labor levies, fiesta participation, and the authority of the Indian Ayuntamiento. Their struggles came to a head in a continuing conflict over land control.

Until April, 1934, title to the extensive communal lands owned by the Indian community was formally held by a group called the Comité Agrario. Service as a member of the Comité Agrario was coterminous with formal membership in the Indian Ayuntamiento. When El Maestro, aided by Federal troops and Ladino authorities, closed down the Indian Ayuntamiento, its former members continued to serve as the Comité Agrario for a short time. As in the past, the committee members were only nominally in control of that organization; their actions were totally controlled by the body of *principales*. The *principales*, acting through the Comité Agrario, controlled the allocation of use-rights on communal lands and the rental of those lands to outsiders; they adjudicated land disputes between Indians, and represented the Indian community before legal authorities when land disputes arose between Indians and Ladinos. But when the Mexican government adopted a new Agrarian Code in April, 1934, and that Code was implemented by Chiapas law a short time later (*Código Agrario* 1934), the Comité Agrario of San Bartolomé was formally dissolved by law. Its titles and functions were transferred to a new landholding organization called Bienes Comunales.

The first crisis over disputed lands under the Bienes Comunales organization came as that organization was being formed. The old Comité Agrario had rented some fallow lands to a group of Ladino cattlemen, who used the lands for grazing. Bartolo had been instrumental in gaining the approval of the *principales* in this arrangement. Now some Indians wanted to return those lands to cultivation, only to be rocked by the cattlemen's claim that they had purchased, not rented, the land. El Maestro, fully familiar with the legal provisions of post-Revolutionary land acts, knew that it was legally impossible to alienate communally owned lands. Capitalizing on the impression of power gained through his visit with President-elect Cárdenas, El Maestro sought the intervention of local authorities. At that time, the Ladino Presidente Municipal (roughly equivalent to a combination of town mayor and chairman of a country board) was a man who had several relatives who were landless milpa farmers. The Presidente agreed to recognize the Indian claims to return of their lands, on condition that some of his poorer relatives be allowed to farm on Indian communal land. El Maestro formalized this arrangement by agreeing to use his influence to open full participation in Bienes Comunales to any landless Ladino *milpero*; Bartolo, anxious to bring the rented lands back to Indian control so that he would not be blamed for their loss, joined El Maestro in this commitment. The Presidente then obtained court orders restoring the disputed lands to the control of Bienes Comunales.

In the first elections of Bienes Comunales officers, newly admitted poor Ladinos joined El Maestro's followers among the Indians in electing an Indian who was fully sympathetic to El Maestro's views as head of the new organization. But several other officers chosen in the same election were *principales* firmly linked to Bartolo, and Bartolo's old job of secretary meant that he still retained physical possession of the land titles, basic documents, and records of the Indian community. The initial phases of internal struggle within Bienes Comunales, then, resulted in no clear advantage for either cultural broker.

Events on the national scene brought strong outside pressure on the newly formed Bienes Comunales organization. The accelerating pace of land reform under President Cárdenas was pushing Bienes Comunales toward a legal reorganization of its land titles, even though those titles were recognized as valid under the new Agrarian Code.[5] Under Cárdenas' program of land reform, the *campesinos* of V. Carranza were asked to reconstitute themselves as an *ejido*, a form of cooperative landholding group. If a majority of the members of Bienes Comunales agreed to take this step, the former landholding organization would be disbanded and its lands transferred to the *ejido* (cf. Simpson 1937). I will not review here all the ins and outs of arguments favoring or opposing the formation of an *ejido*, in V. Carranza or elsewhere, but a very abbreviated summary may prove helpful to those unfamiliar with the history of this institution in Mexico. (Both Simpson [1937] and Tannenbaum [1964] provide good overviews of the problem from a national viewpoint.)

If Bienes Comunales were to be completely supplanted by an *ejido* under the national program of agrarian reform, the law provided that title to enough land to support the new organization would be guaranteed. Much of the land would, of course, come out of lands to which Bienes Comunales already held uncontested title; but many areas of highly productive land had been alienated from Bienes Comunales control, particularly in areas close to the town. Formation of an *ejido* held the promise of regaining these alienated lands for use by *milperos*. An *ejido*, furthermore, would have access to credit from the National Bank of Ejido Credit, from which Bienes Comunales was effectively precluded. An *ejido* would also be entitled to technical assistance, aid in forming a marketing cooperative, and wholesale buying privileges for a consumer cooperative if the members of the *ejido* decided to form one (*Plan Sexenal* 1934: par. 52, 53; *Código Agrario* 1934: Article 148, 153). For *milpero* Ladinos newly given access to communal lands, there was the further advantage that they would be guaranteed legal protection for continued access to *ejido* land, while the original land grants on which Bienes Comunales based its successful struggle for recognition of title to the communal lands had been made "a los Indios nativos de San Bartolomé de los Llanos . . ." (to the *Indians* native to San Bartolomé and their descendants).

There would also have been many disadvantages resulting from the replacement of Bienes Comunales by an *ejido*. The promise of restoration of lands close to town carried with it the threat of losing some of the most fertile land in the area, bottom lands along the Río Grijalva that were too far from the town center to be legally assigned to an *ejido* based in V. Carranza. Agricultural land would have to be divided into individually held plots, a method of landholding inappropriate to the *milpero*'s tech-

---

[5]   Somehow, against the overwhelming tide of Mexican history between 1847 and the 1911 Revolution, most of the Indian communal lands had remained in the community's control (cf. Simpson 1937:15–55). In 1934 and early 1935, Bienes Comunales sought and received legal recertification of its land titles (see *Código Agrario* [1934: Art. 27 et seq.] for a statement of the legal grounds for this recertification).

niques of shifting cultivation. Furthermore, each member would have to give 5 percent of his crops to the *ejido* for the formation of a general fund (see *Código Agrario* [1934: Article 139, 153] for the legal provisions underlying these disadvantages). Most Indians of San Bartolomé viewed the legal formalization of poor Ladino access to Indian lands with suspicion, if not alarm. Finally, in general it could be argued that the Bienes Comunales way of holding the land was closer to tradition, more secure in its operation, and more likely to survive any new shifts which might occur in the national laws than the ways of an untested and unfamiliar *ejido*.

There was no way for Bartolo and El Maestro to remain aloof from this struggle over the landholding organization if they were to maintain their positions as cultural brokers. Whatever was done would require recourse to outside authorities, and if the two cultural brokers did not take part, they ran great danger of losing their previous control of communication between the community and the outside world. In the ensuing events, El Maestro (true to his role as supporter of President Cárdenas) pushed hard for the formation of an *ejido*. Bartolo, seeing a chance to regain some of the power he had lost with the closing of the Indian Ayuntamiento, urged his associates among the *principales* to oppose the *ejido*. Within the Indian community and in Bienes Comunales, Bartolo's views eventually held the field — but most of the Ladino *milperos* and a sizeable minority of the Indians hived off from the community. They petitioned for recognition as a new *ejido*, establishing the town of La Vega del Paso in the fertile bottom lands near the Río Grijalva (see *Código Agrario* 1934: Articles 99–108). By establishing their *ejido* center near the river, the *ejidatarios* obtained title to the best available land base; most of their land was located outside the former territories of Bienes Comunales, but they took a large chunk of the best portion of Bienes Comunales land as well.

El Maestro's partial success in aiding the foundation of an *ejido* contained the seeds of his downfall as a cultural broker. The new community was located some twenty miles away from V. Carranza, and his school duties kept him from close contact with the *ejido*, which contained nearly all his close supporters and those who had been most dependent on his brokerage activities. Eventually, El Maestro's position as a Federal employee got him embroiled in the struggle over the Chiapas gubernatorial elections of 1936. The outgoing Governor's chosen candidate was generally opposed by Federal employees, and Governor Grajales took strong measures against many of them while he still held office. Nonetheless, the candidate supported by Grajales lost the election, and the incoming Governor — Gutiérrez Rincón, Bartolo's old contact in the Department of Agrarian Affairs and later in the National Bank of Ejido Credit — was highly suspicious of those who had retained Federal employment during Grajales' program of persecuting his opponents (see López Gutiérrez [1957: III, especially 457] for an insider's view of this struggle over the

1936 Chiapas gubernatorial succession). For a short time, El Maestro was put in jail by officials of one side or the other. This made the weakness of his alleged support from President Cárdenas apparent on the local scene. Even worse for El Maestro, most of his strongest local supporters now no longer lived in V. Carranza, and their *ejido* was not as successful as they had been led to hope. (The problems of the La Vega *ejido* were of a piece with those making problems for new *ejidos* all over Mexico; see, for example, Whetten [1948:216–224], Simpson [1937:335–353]). As a result, El Maestro was unable to prevent his discharge from the Federal school in V. Carranza; he was forced to leave the town to seek further employment elsewhere.

For a time, Bartolo paradoxically gained new power after his failure to block the formation of the new *ejido*. Many of his most vocal opponents among the Indians were drained out of the community for all practical purposes. Ladino *milperos*, with whom Bartolo had not developed either relationships of control or mutual dependence, were reduced to a very small proportion of those who remained with Bienes Comunales. Furthermore, while the *ejido* had great difficulties in its early years, those who stayed with Bienes Comunales had several comparatively good crop years in a row. Finally, Bartolo's old political patron in Mexico City was now the Governor of Chiapas, and willing to listen sympathetically to requests for assistance from the Indians of San Bartolomé — provided those requests were channelled through Bartolo's intervention. (Symbolically, Bartolo's apparent position of power was reinforced when his daughter received gifts and a congratulatory semipublic telegram from the Governor on the occasion of her marriage.)

But Bartolo's reaccession to power as the acknowledged *cacique* of the San Bartolomé Indians was to prove much more limited than his old powers as Secretario of the Indian Ayuntamiento. One series of events, among many, will serve to show how these limits were made clear. In 1938–1939, public legal pressure against the celebration of religious fiestas was considerably lightened. By accident, a majority of the ritual specialists needed for the customary Indian celebrations happened to be inhabitants of Bartolo's *barrio*, and because of his particularly close relationship with the *barrio principales* Bartolo was able to exercise a major measure of control over how and where the ritual specialists would perform. As the fiesta cycle was re-established, Bartolo tried to use this control to dictate the conditions under which fiestas would be celebrated. He asked that the Indians return to the old system of obligatory labor service within the fiesta groups. In 1939, Bartolo became the elected Indian representative on the municipal Ayuntamiento; he used the power of that office to cause the jailing of Indians who would not obey him or the *principales* when labor levies were being assembled. These extralegal attempts to impose control were ended permanently in March, 1940. At that time, outgoing President Cárdenas made a second tour of Chiapas. A delegation of Indian leaders, mostly young men but including a few *principales*, went to a pan-Indian conference called by Cárdenas, and while there they complained that their followers were being forced into labor levies without compensation. On his return, one of the dissident leaders advised the men of his *barrio* to refuse unpaid service in the fiesta organization. Bartolo jailed that leader, but the leader's friends went to the state capital for the assistance Cárdenas had promised. Bartolo's old champion was no longer Governor, and the new Governor issued official orders freeing the dissident leader and jailing Bartolo in his turn. (In the subsequent legal hearing before the Ladino municipal judge, all charges were dropped on both sides, contigent on future good conduct.) After that series of events, Bartolo was replaced by another Indian on the municipal council. From that time until his death in the mid-1940s, the old *cacique* was largely limited to expressing his public position through participation in ritual affairs. Even there, he was reduced to the role of one leader among many. (For example, his name is painted on the doorway of a small church that was rebuilt in 1945 as one of those who contributed to the reconstruction. That is more recognition than was given to most of the participants, who are acknowledged by a collective "y demás otros socio" [and other participants in addition]: but his name is not first on the list of four, and one of the others listed specifically is the same "dissident leader" Bartolo had put in jail in 1940.)

DISCUSSION: "FAILURE" AND "SUCCESS" IN BROKERAGE

The events I have described here, and other similar sequences I have observed in San Bartolomé in more recent times, raise serious questions about how we are to define "failure" and "success" as we examine cultural brokerage in the context of goal-oriented activities. It is clear that much of the literature on cultural brokerage has had a consistent eufunctional bias, despite Wolf's caution that brokers often have to act to "maintain . . . the tensions which provide the dynamic of their actions" (1956:1076). My knowledge of cultural brokerage in San Bartolomé inclines me to believe that those outcomes which are functional in maintaining cultural brokerage as a means of coping with boundary problems at the interface of two cultures may very well be dysfunctional in their effects on at least one of the cultures involved in the contact situation: conversely, it may be that the community's "success" depends on the broker's ultimate "failure." Let us briefly reexamine the two cases cited here to expand on possible applications of these ideas.

El Maestro's role with regard to the Indians of San Bartolomé can be seen from three viewpoints: (1) that of the political party at the national level; (2) of the community; (3) as an example of the interests of a cultural broker. Whichever of these viewpoints one adopts, his activities ultimately resulted in failure. As promoter of the programs of the PNR, El Maestro did succeed in establishing an *ejido*, and in linking *ejido* members firmly to national institutions. But most San Bartoleños remained firmly committed to the traditional forms of community organization by staying with Bienes Comunales. As soon as external pressure was lifted, they returned to the celebration of the old fiesta cycle — modified, it is true, by the removal of such "official" sanctions as the jailing of those who were reluctant to serve, but still a pattern closely similar to that of the old days. The PNR, on the other hand, was firmly anti-Church in its programs. Agricultural productivity remained essentially unchanged despite El Maestro's attempts to introduce technological innovations. Finally, San Bartoleños remained uninvolved in and uncommitted to the idea of participation in the national, state, or municipal communities. From the viewpoint of the local community, El Maestro's activities resulted in a reduction of local autonomy when he closed the Indian Ayuntamiento. The ending of labor levies, viewed by the Indians as a good in itself, nonetheless had the result of removing one bargaining counter which had been an effective means of gaining some concessions from Ladino authorities. As one result, Indians lost the support of formerly sympathetic Ladinos in later land struggles. Finally, the fact that El Maestro was forced to leave the community constitutes sufficient demonstration of his failure to protect his own interests.

Bartolo's career, in the period examined here, was one of a type that could be called a holding action against external forces constantly militating against each position of power he was able to develop. First, the Ayuntamiento which had provided him a base through his post as secretary was dissolved. Indian labor levies, which he was uniquely able to deliver and in exchange for which he was able to gain support from Ladinos to his own advantage, were ended. He was forced to participate in opening Bienes Comunales to Ladino participation — even though he knew full well that these new participants were entirely capable of communicating with outside authorities by themselves, and would have little or no use for his services as intermediary. His later attempts to consolidate control through his election to the Ayuntamiento Constitucional were likewise blocked, ultimately by his removal from that council.

We are not concerned here, however, with the question of whether a particular individual manages to make a success of his chosen activities. In all cultures, some people do better, some do worse, in achieving their own ends. Here, I have been interested in the balance between the personal ends of a cultural broker and the effects of his activities on the communities he bridges. Both brokers we have watched in action here (and their successors in the same community) had ambivalent vested interests. Full promotion of the best interests of the community would have led to the elimination of any need for the services of a cultural broker. If El Maestro had been completely successful, within the framework of the ideas he was supposed to promote for the PNR, San Bartolomé would have become an integrated part of the national community — and the local community of V. Carranza as well. If Bartolo had been completely successful in promoting the ideals of his own natal community (ideals which were obviously impossible of accomplishment), the Indians would have become completely independent of outside, Ladino interference. Every move toward partial accomplishment of these ultimate goals was a move away from the community's dependence on the services of either of the cultural brokers. But if they had been unable to deliver some kind of progress toward *both* integration and independence, they would have been unable to continue in their roles as brokers through failure to serve the interests of their "clients."

The cases I have examined here, then, are more than detailed examples of how two individuals operated in the context of an ethnically divided town. They suggest that the cultural broker is both more and less than a Janus-like figure, facing in two directions at once. Unlike Janus, who was a keeper of the gates, cultural brokers have their deepest interests in keeping the gates of communication between cultures or between ethnic groups closed. For the broker to succeed *as a broker*, he must try to control those gates so as to guarantee that only the broker himself may pass them freely. To maintain that sort of control, the broker can only afford to give a surface impression of serving some of the interests of groups operating on both the community and national level. While doing so, the broker who would continue to maintain himself in his brokerage role must ultimately work against the interests of both communities while appearing to serve them.

REFERENCES

ADAMS, RICHARD
  1970   *Crucifixion by power.* Austin: University of Texas Press.
BANTON, MICHAEL, *editor*
  1966   *The social anthropology of complex societies.* A.S.A. Monograph 4. London: Tavistock Publications.
BOSQUES, GILBERTO
  1937   *The National Revolutionary Party of Mexico and the six-year plan.* México, D.F.: Bureau of Foreign Information, National Revolutionary Party.
CARRASCO, PEDRO
  1961   The civil-religious hierarchy in Mesoamerican communities: pre-Spanish background and colonial development. *American Anthropologist* 63:483–497.

Código Agrario
1934 *Código Agrario de los Estados Unidos Mexicanos.* México, D.F.: Departamento Agrario.

COLBY, BENJAMIN N., PIERRE L. VAN DEN BERGHE
1961 Ethnic relations in Southeastern Mexico. *American Anthropologist* 63:772–792.

Constitución
1962 *Constitución política de los Estados Unidos Mexicanos.* México, D.F.: Librería Porrua. (This document available in many editions, from several publishers; the edition cited is reprinted and redated annually whether or not there have been intervening amendments. No special significance of the particular edition is implied by its citation here.)

GAGE, THOMAS
1946 *Nueva relacion que contiene los viajes de Tomas Gage en la Nueva España.* Guatemala, C.A.: Biblioteca "Goathemala."

GILLIN, JOHN
1951 *The culture of security in San Carlos.* Middle American Research Institute Publication 16. New Orleans: Tulane University.

Leyes
1959 *Leyes des Estado de Chiapas*, tomo I: *Constitución política del estado y leyes.* México, D.F.: Galeza.

LÓPEZ GUTIÉRREZ, GUSTAVO
1957 *Chiapas y sus epopayas libertarias* (third edition, revised and enlarged). Tuxtla de (*sic*) Gutiérrez, Chiapas, Mexico.

MOSCOSO, PRUDENCIO
1960 *El Pinedismo en Chiapas.* México, D.F.

Plan Sexenal
1934 *Plan sexenal del P.N.R.* México: Partido Nacional Revolucionario.

POZAS A., RICARDO
1959 *Chamula: un pueblo indígena de los altos de Chiapas.* Memorias del Instituto Nacional Indigenista 8. México, D.F.: Instituto Nacional Indigenista.

SALOVESH, MICHAEL
1965 Pautus de residencia y estratificacíon entre los Mayas: algunas perspectivas de Son Bartolome, Chiapas. *Estudios de Cultura Maya* 5:318–338.
1971 "The political system of a Highland Maya community: a study in the methodology of political analysis." Unpublished doctoral dissertation, Department of Anthropology, The University of Chicago.

SIMPSON, EYLER N.
1937 *The ejido: Mexico's way out.* Chapel Hill: University of North Carolina Press.

SMITH, M. G.
1956 On segmentary lineage systems. Curl Bequest Prize Essay for 1955. *Journal of the Royal Anthropological Institute* 86:39–80.

TANNENBAUM, FRANK
1964 *Mexico: the struggle for peace and bread.* New York: Alfred A. Knopf.

TAX, SOL
1937 The *municipios* of the midwestern highlands of Guatemala. *American Anthropologist* 39:423–444.
1953 *Penny capitalism: a Guatemalan Indian economy.* Institute of Social Anthropology Publication 16. Washington, D.C.: Smithsonian Institution.

THOMPSON, J. ERIC S., *editor*
  1958 *Thomas Gage's travels in the New World*. Norman: University of Oklahoma Press.

TRENS, MANUEL B.
  1957 *Historia de Chiapas*. México, D.F.

TUMIN, MELVIN
  1952 *Caste in a peasant society: a case study in the dynamics of caste*. Princeton, New Jersey: Princeton University Press.

VOGT, EVON Z.
  1969 *Zinacantan: a Maya community in the highlands of Chiapas*. Cambridge, Massachusetts: Belknap Press (Harvard University Press).

WHETTEN, NATHAN L.
  1948 *Rural Mexico*. Chicago: University of Chicago Press.

WOLF, ERIC R.
  1956 Aspects of group relations in a complex society: Mexico. *American Anthropologist* 58:1065–1078.
  1957 Closed corporate peasant communities in Mesoamerica and Java. *Southwestern Journal of Anthropology* 13:1–18.
  1959 *Sons of the shaking earth*. Chicago: University of Chicago Press.
  1969 *Peasant wars of the twentieth century*. New York: Harper and Row.

SECTION FOUR

Ethnicity and the Future

Class and Ethnic Consciousness: The Case of the Mapuche Indians of Chile

BERNARDO BERDICHEWSKY

INTRODUCTION

Since the time that the hacienda system was initiated, the fundamental problem of indigenous peasantry in Latin America has been the economic and social super-exploitation of their agricultural labor force by the landholding class. Furthermore, racial discrimination — a mask for socioeconomic exploitation and an ideological superstructure — always accompanied the system and facilitated its reproduction. Thus, it is not sufficient for a social analysis of indigenous peasantry to deal exclusively with socioeconomic and class variables while neglecting related ethnic aspects.

Our interest in this paper is not only to see the infrastructural relation between social class and ethnic group, but also, and above all, to examine the ideological superstructural relationship between them. It is manifested especially in the appearance of social consciousness and the further development of a double ethnic and class consciousness. We will examine this situation through the historical case of the Mapuche Indians of Chile.

A DEFINITION OF THE MAPUCHE GROUP

The most recent Indian law (number 17.729) passed in Chile in September, 1972, defines the Indian in the following manner: "The person who is found in one of the following situations will, for all legal purposes, be taken as Indian: (1) invoking the right emanating directly or immediately from a government granted property title (*titulo de Merced*) or a free property title (*titulo gratuito de dominio*) issued in conformity with the law; (2) invoking a declared right recognized by a decision in a trial dividing an Indian community with titles conferred in accordance with legal dispositions; (3) living in any part of the national territory and forming a part of a group which habitually expresses itself in an aboriginal language and which is distinguished from the generality of the inhabitants of the Republic by conservation of patterns of living, norms of interacting, customs, forms of labour and religion coming from the autochtonous ethnic groups of the country" (IDI 1972). "The classification of Indian will be accredited by a certificate from the Institute of Indigenous Development (Instituto de Desarrollo Indigena)" (IDI 1972:3).

We can summarize this paragraph by saying that the *land* element (indicated in points 1 and 2), which had been the only one that legally defined the Indian in the original draft proposal of the law, has had added to it, by the legislators, a second element: *autochtonous ethnic culture* (point 3). There is a third element missing which is even more important than the others. It is the recognition of an *ethnic identity* which cannot be enacted simply by a *certificate of identity* (point 3, at the end). When the three previous factors exist, certification can do no more than legalize the fact. The desire to belong or to have an identity is fundamental and cannot be overlooked.

Since the legislation does not recognize this individual *sentiment of self-determination* in defining an Indian, it carries an implicit discrimination since it forcibly defines both those who have assimilated and those who, although not legally recognized as Indian, find themselves identified as such.

We will now attempt to define the Chilean Indian not so much from the legal point of view as from the social standpoint. It is still possible to discover some biological characteristics in the Chilean Indians, especially among the northern Aymara, but generally the Indians are mestizos. This is especially true for the Mapuche. For this reason, biological or racial variables no longer adequately define the Indians of Chile. For example, to refer to an Araucanian race is, scientifically speaking, a complete error, unless it is meant only in a figurative or literary sense.

Trying to define the Indians of Chile requires that we establish the kind of social aggregate to which they belong in order to understand a social definition of them (Berdichewsky 1972). It is obvious that a definition limited to considerations of class is insufficient in spite of the fact that the great majority of the Indians of Chile have integrated into the peasant sector. More than 10 percent however are urban and belong primarily to the working class and secondarily to the urban petite bourgeoisie — small businessmen and professionals, especially schoolteachers.

The peasantry is a heterogeneous conglomerate that transcends the boundary of any single social class. This is true also for the indigenous peasantry among whom are found a majority of minifundists, a few other small and medium-sized landholders, a significant percentage of hacienda laborers (*inquilinos*), and a group of peons and agricultural day laborers. Also, in more recent times, there are a number of Mapuche peasants in the reformed agrarian structure — in settlements (*asentamientos*), Centres of Agrarian Reform (CERAS) and cooperatives (Berdichewsky 1971).

Among the Mapuche peasantry, the majority is composed of the members of reservations or Indian communities. Their attachment to the land, recent or ancestral, still plays the dominant role. Divided reservations are generally formal minifundios, and the undivided ones, still the majority, are formally held by communal land tenure. But in fact, the latter also are broken up into familial minifundios.

In brief, although the direct or indirect link with the indigenous agrarian community, as heir to the old collective tribal community, predominates among the Indian population of the country, it is no longer the only affiliation. Consequently it is difficult to speak of an "Indian class." Our definition must be extended to include the concept of ethnic group.

The definition of an ethnic group lies not so much in its racial characteristics, as in its social and cultural features and idiosyncracies. It is a certain social group with material and spiritual creations, customs, norms of behavior, its own language, its belief systems and values, etc. Therefore, we should consider as Indian any person who has been enculturated or socialized (to any extent) to the cultural pattern of his indigenous ethnic group, especially by way of language. This positive process of enculturation, combined with other sometimes negative ones such as racial discrimination or conflict, produce in the individual a feeling of identification with his ethnic group.

It is important to note here that ethnic groups and communities exist and have existed in all kinds of socioeconomic forms. This is true regardless of the dominant mode of production, whether it be primitive or class societies — slave, asiatic, feudal, capitalist, or socialist.

We believe that the correct designation for Indian social aggregates should be "ethnic community," typified by common characteristics of a *cultural* (including language), *psychological* (including the feeling of identity), and *socioeconomic* (workers, agrarian subsistence communities, minifundios, exploited classes) order. Other factors, such as biological ones, are much less important.

The ethnic structure and character of ethnicity arise from and are determined by a social and economic base typified by the socioeconomic stratum occupied within the overall stratification of the nation. A social and institutional superstructure, cultural and ideological, from which ethnic symbols and other aspects of an ethnic identity are developed is an expression of the material base and of the group's attempts to survive, accommodate, and adapt. Ethnic identity, placed on the superstructural summit, comes from and is determined by the previous structures. As a reflection and a dialectic, it is converted into a dominant and diagnostic factor of ethnicity. Yet, in the final instance, it is determined by the material base which generated such an ethnic community.

Whether for purposes of integration or differentiation, the ethnic community develops a series of mechanisms of interrelation with the larger society which do not depend on the ethnic community itself, but rather on the character of the larger society. Such mechanisms tend to assure subsistence, defense, and adaptation of the community and can be of ideological, institutional, or material character. These are the things that somehow preserve ethnic boundaries.

In summary, *we should consider as Indians all those who possess, incorporated in their personality, the culture of their ethnic group, feel identified with it, and share with it certain social and economic characteristics as well.*

A material base, expressed in economic structures and social organization, ethnic culture and ethnic identity, consequently, are the key elements. Other elements, such as juridical or biological ones, may be added to these, but if the three key ones do not exist, the others will have no meaning.

A Mapuche is a person who lives in or outside the community and possesses the Mapuche language (to a greater or lesser extent), belongs to its social structures (such as indigenous kinship groups and exploited social strata), shares some customs, values, and beliefs, and, above all, feels that he is identified with the Mapuche people. These aspects may be found to varying degrees among distinct groups or individuals. Also, enculturation and identification can be more or less intense. The important thing is that they exist to some extent. All of this is not an absolute and definitive state of existence at one time but, rather, it corresponds to a dynamic process which can intensify the identification. If it is lacking, it can tend to negate that identification and give a push towards assimilation. Both tendencies occur to different degrees and with different force according to distinct historical conditions. Nevertheless, the community will continue to exist independent of the individuals who can separate themselves from it by assimilating.

Thus, the Indian problem is a social and not a racial or biological one. Moreover, racial prejudice against Indians is no more than a form of social discrimination that is a product of indirect and direct economic exploitation to which the Indians of Chile and of Latin America have always been subjected. The indigenous social problem is then made up of two aspects: one is of class character, common to the exploited and working classes; the other is of ethnic character. The former can be resolved with the liberation of workers both in the country and in the city, and the latter by the liberation of the most oppressed ethnic communities, such as the indigenous ones. These communities have, in fact, been considered and treated as unprotected castes of pariahs on many historical occasions. Undoubtedly, the liberation of the oppressed ethnic community of a class society such as the Chilean, is inseparable from the social and economic liberation of the exploited working classes.

The indigenous ethnic communities of Chile (at least the Mapuche and the Aymara) constitute, in fact, true *national minorities* within the Chilean nation. And if we refer to the Chilean national culture as a global one (with all the variations and differences that such a large unit implies), we can consider the cultural expressions of the indigenous communities as subcultural. This is not stated pejoratively, but simply to designate it as a specific sector of that culture (Bunster 1964; Saavedra 1971).

The majority of Mapuche are, as we have said, minifundists who live principally on reservations and belong to the exploited peasant strata. At the same time, they can be defined as an *indigenous ethnic community* that evolved from a tribal society and changed into a national minority within the Chilean nation (Lipschutz 1968, 1973).

Forcibly incorporated into Chilean society, the Mapuche people, as an ethnic community, changed socially and economically, as well as culturally, as they became a subculture. The traditional Mapuche culture was modified in both its form and content. But, above all, its function was changed as it became a culture of resistance — that is, as a mechanism acting in defense against discrimination (Berdichewsky 1973).

Like all cultures, it fulfills the social function of preserving the group, but it also functions in rejecting racial discrimination and reinforcing cohesion and identity, thereby playing an ideological role (Berdichewsky 1973). This change in function brings with it the danger of perpetuating the form of subsistence economy and of socioeconomic backwardness which are also forms of class exploitation. Thus, this change may serve as an obstacle to the formation of class consciousness among the Mapuche if it promotes a petit bourgeois ethnic "nationalism" among them.

The positive way to focus on this problem would be for the state to offer the means for overcoming the subsistence economy and its backwardness by including the ethnic community in agrarian reform. Access to the market economy and commercialization, technical preparation, including training for artisans and others, would be made possible by such reform. It is here that the Mapuche school could play an important role.

Such changes would be necessary to preserve Mapuche spiritual culture by recognizing their history, by transforming their oral literature into written, and by developing their forms of artistic expression. In this way, education would play an important role, particularly by promoting bilingualism in the schools.

But these changes are aspirations and not yet reality. The organization and struggle of the Mapuches to obtain these goals, and the closing of ranks for a permanent resistance against any kind of aggression and abuse, has led to the development from a passive identity to a militant and even aggressive one. Once this kind of identity has developed, we can speak of a true ethnic consciousness.

INTEGRATION OF THE MAPUCHE COMMUNITY INTO THE CHILEAN PEASANTRY

To consider the ethnogenesis of the Mapuche community, we should go back to the beginning of the present millennium when the tribal agricultural communities were developing in the central-south of Chile. During the fifteenth century, the time of the Inca Conquest, and, even more so, during the sixteenth century, the time of the Spanish Conquest of a great part of the region, the three principal local ethnic groups, all very closely related, formed themselves into one people. They were, from north to south, the Picunche, the Mapuche, and the Huilliche. While conserving certain differences, they did identify themselves as one people and are known in the literature from that point on as the Araucanian people. The Picunche were the only ones to be conquered, first by the Incas and soon after by the Spanish. After several uprisings during the sixteenth century, they were finally totally dominated and subjugated during the seventeenth century. Miscegenation with the Spanish rural population took place, creating the principal base for the Chilean peasantry which grew and multiplied in the "Kingdom of Chile." By the end of the colonial period at the beginning of the nineteenth century, the Picunche ethnos had totally disappeared. They had become diluted in the new mestizo Chilean peasantry, constituting the labor base of the agrarian system of the hacienda. They were more deeply rooted in the Hispanic than the indigenous tradition and were totally monolingual in Spanish.

On the other hand, the Mapuche and Huilliche succeeded in maintaining their independence in the southern region because of a prolonged guerrilla war lasting 400 years, first against the Incas, then against the Spanish, and finally against the Chileans themselves. This war is known as the Araucanian War. In the prolonged vicissitudes of this almost permanent warring state which could often be described as a "cold war," they were not only able to reintegrate themselves under the hegemony of the Mapuche, but were also able to expand toward the east, toward the Andean mountain range, and even beyond into the Argentine pampas, transculturated and became integrated with the Araucanian people.

In the 1870s and 1880s, the Araucanian people were finally militarily defeated. Two modern armies, well equipped with repeating rifles, were able, almost simultaneously, to conquer them on both sides of the mountain range and, consequently, to divide them into two groups — one conquered by the Argentine army, the other by the Chilean army. Both were forcibly incorporated into their larger societies. In this way we have, one hundred years later, two relatively different Araucanian ethnic groups, respectively called the Argentine Araucanians and the Chilean Mapuches.

The Mapuche community was integrated into the Chilean agrarian system when it was forcibly concentrated in the so-called Indian reservations.[1] This measure freed a large part of the best agricultural land to be given to the latifundios which were expanding rapidly and aggressively towards the southern region of the country. By the beginning of the twentieth century, the hacienda system — called "fundos" in Chile — had been implanted in practically all of the Chilean Araucanian zone, successfully incorporating, by one means or another, the Indian reservations established some decades before. By the middle of this century, the system had totally crystallized. The Indian reservations were incorporated firstly, by the expansion into this area of latifundios at the cost of the reservation lands which were taken either by direct and forcible appropriation, by legalistic trickery, or by legal or fraudulent purchase. The reservations lost much of their land in this way and, at the same time, experienced demographic growth which reduced the man-land ratio to a very low minimum — a pair of hectares. This produced a situation of potential unemployment on the reservations, which lead to total or partial emigration outside the reservations. Most of the emigrants from the reservations became members of the labor force of the fundos, as inquilinos within the haciendas under semi-servile conditions, or as sharecroppers required to divide the produce in half, or to raise animals and divide the newborn evenly. Many became semi-wage laborers on the haciendas. This situation increasingly led to the conversion and transformation of the Indian reservations into real minifundios. Although their land tenure system continued to be communal, production was changed almost entirely into one of familial character. This resulted in a further reduction of available hectares. In short, the reservations, legally had communal land ownership but, in fact, functioned as minifundios. In addition, many reservations were pushed towards the legal division of their lands and thus eventually established the minifundios both in fact and in law.

To sum up, we can state that after the military conquest and domination of the Mapuche and the establishment of the system of reservations, the latifundio expanded even more at the expense of reservation lands. The reservations were transformed into true minifundios, the necessary counterpart of the latifundio. Then the hacienda system converted the

---

[1] Although the first law on Indian reservations was passed in 1866, it was implemented only from 1884 after the Mapuche were defeated.

pauperized indigenous minifundists into a super-exploitable reserve force of cheap labor for the haciendas in addition to the inquilinos or peons on the haciendas and sharecroppers on minifundios. In this way the latifundist hacienda system succeeded in absorbing the Mapuches of the Indian reservations into the diverse strata of Chilean peasantry.

DEVELOPMENT OF SOCIAL CONSCIOUSNESS

We clearly indicated in the previous sections how and why the great mass of the Mapuche became an integral part of the Chilean peasantry and, at the same time, constitute a differentiated ethnic community. In their two social categories — peasants and Indians — they are equally a constituent part of the Chilean agrarian system of the latifundist hacienda in the central-south region of Chile.

Both the traditional mestizo peasants and the indigenous peasants (to a larger extent) have sporadically revealed their opposition to the land-holders of the fundos in one form or another. But these rebellions and protests were broken up and isolated, never coordinated, and they always ended in failure and still greater subjugation. Although on a very elementary level, a peasant movement was initiated at the end of the 1920s when the first law for peasant unionization was passed in Chile. During this period and in the 1930s and 1940s considerable industrialization of Chile occurred. The basic industries remained the extractive ones — copper, saltpeter, and iron — which provided 70 percent of the Gross National Product (GNP) of the country. On the other hand, agriculture at the end of the decade of the 1960s provided only 8 percent of the GNP in spite of the fact that 27 percent of the population earned its living in agricultural activity (Baytelman 1971:7). Nevertheless, though Chile is not one of the most typically agrarian countries of Latin America, nearly one-third of its active population is thus employed, placing it in the category of an underdeveloped country. Within this agrarian structure the hacienda system predominated, following much the same pattern as the great majority of Latin American countries. Studies carried out by the Comite Internacional de Desarrollo Agrícola (CIDA 1966) show that more than 80 percent of the agricultural land was concentrated in the hands of only 3 percent of the active agricultural population — the latifundists who possessed less than 7 percent of the total agricultural units. Yet the minifundists held a miserable 0.2 percent of the total agricultural land and 37 percent of the total agricultural units while constituting 23 percent of the active population in the agrarian sector.[2] If we add to them the salaried agricultural laborers who make up more than 47 percent of the

[2]   This figure includes the minifundists of the indigenous communities.

active agricultural population and who own no land (most of them being members of the same families as the minifundists), these two poorest strata of the peasantry make up more than 70 percent of the active agricultural population. To these two sectors of the Chilean peasantry, we should add the small landowners who possess small agricultural units, a bit larger than the minifundios which, unlike them, permit the maintenance of a peasant family. This sector of family units reaches 40 percent of all the agricultural units, but occupies little more than 7 percent of the agricultural land and makes up 15 percent of the active agricultural population. Three percent more may be added to this total if the inquilinos and sharecroppers who live and work with them are added. This would raise the total peasant population in its three basic strata (small landowners, minifundists, and agricultural peons) to 88 percent of the active agricultural population who, as a whole, did not possess even 8 percent of the total agricultural lands. The rest of the active agricultural population (some 9 percent) would be made up of two-thirds of rural bourgeoisie — that of the administrators of haciendas or farms (Barraclough and Domike 1970:47–51).

In the 1930s and 1940s, after the depression and the great crisis of international capitalism and, especially during World War II and the immediate postwar period, the relative industrial growth of Chile brought parallel urban development, plus that of the great mining centers, and the growth of a politically powerful middle class. This, together with the rapid development of an industrial and mining working class — to a great extent at the expense of the migration of the pauperized peasantry — sharpened the contradictions within agriculture even more. In the middle of the century, Chile, which had been a food exporting country for the past century and a half, became a food importing country.

The latifundist structure of the hacienda system showed itself to be even less effective. For the first time, peasant opposition was manifested, not only by rebellious acts and uncoordinated uprisings, but also in organizations such as the first agricultural unions which developed, especially in the central zone during these two decades. These unions were still few in number and only semi-legal, since the famous peasant unionization law of 1924 was practically moribund. It was obstructed by representatives of the landholding oligarchy who were powerful enough to pressure the progressive, democratic government of the Popular Front led by presidents from the middle class parties (Radical Party and others) which was supported by the workers from 1938 to 1948. Both President Pedro Aguirre Cerda in 1939 and Gabriel Gonzalez Videla in 1946 issued and maintained decrees which set up obstacles to the application of the unionization law (Affonso 1971:8, 10).

In any case, the peasant unions and the organization of the peasant class grew, to a small extent, aided by the mining and industrial workers

unions (Petras and Zeitlin 1968:235). This peasant unionization movement developed principally in the central zone among the salaried
agricultural workers of the great vineyards (Petras, Zeitlin 1970:503). In
the 1950s a peasant strike movement of some importance grew with the
aid of the working class political parties (Communist and Socialist) and
the progressive parties of the middle class, such as the Christian Demo-
crats. As a result of this, a new level of peasant organization, clearly of a
class nature, was reached by the formation of peasant federations. This
time the movement took in the southern zone peasants as well, including
the Indians. In this way, diverse peasant sectors began to organize themselves with the help of the urban political parties of the center and the left
and succeeded in freeing themselves from the political control of the
owners of the fundos. Important sectors of the rural proletariat and
minifundists, including the indigenous sectors, were organized into
peasant unions, principally under the tutelage of the workers' parties.
Other important peasant sectors (inquilinos) were organized primarily by
the Christian Democratic Party into Christian peasant federations.
Naturally, the political differentiation of these strata is not clearly
defined. Nevertheless, it does demonstrate a tendency. There were still
no genuine mass movements which could mobilize a large part of the
peasantry. But with all their deficiencies and insecurities, these groups
were an important beginning to the class organization of the peasantry
and, consequently, to the appearance and development of class consciousness.

The first class organization of the peasants was The National League of
Defense of Poor Peasants founded in 1935 in Santiago with the support,
at the beginning, of the Chilean workers union organization (Liga
Nacional de Defensa de los Campesinos Pobres). In 1939, popular front
government organized the first peasant conference with an attendance of
over 300 delegates from all over the country (Affonso 1971:8). The
National Peasant Federation grew from this congress. At this same time,
the Chilean workers' union organization or CTCH, the Confederation of
Workers of Chile (Confederación de Trabajadores de Chile) made up the
Provincial Union of Agricultural Unions of Chile (Unión Provincial de
Sindicatos Agricolas de Santiago), formed by almost forty unions. Also at
this time, the first Christian organization of peasants, called Peasant
Unity (Unión de Campesinos), was formed. It was made up of inquilinos
on twelve haciendas but was forced to dissolve by the Church in 1941
because of pressure from Catholic landholders.

In 1944 another Christian peasant organization was formed, the
National Association of Chilean Agriculturalists (Asociación Nacional
de Agricultores de Chile), which grouped small landholders, renters,
sharecroppers, communal landowners, and squatters (Affonso 1971:9).

In 1946, at the Second Peasant Congress of the National Peasant

Federation, then called the Industrial[3] Federation of Agricultural Workers and supported by the CTCH, the peasant organization, for the first time formally presented the problem of agrarian reform. The following year there was a large march of peasants in Santiago and a Third Peasant Congress.

The remaining years of the government of Gonzalez Videla (1948–1952) were ones of repression of the union and workers' movements in general. But in the period of the populist government of General Ibañez (1952–1958), the peasant union movements and peasant organizations returned with new vigor. In 1952, the Christian Union Federation of the Land (Federación Sindical Cristiana de la Tierra) was formed, and the following year it convened its first congress and organized a series of peasant strikes.

At this time, the first indigenous peasant organizations made their appearance. Near the end of 1953, the first Mapuche Indian National Congress of Chile (Congreso Nacional Mapuche Indigena de Chile) was held in the city of Temuco, the capital of the Araucanian region. It differed from the other peasant congresses in that it resolved to fight for the return of the usurped land which had belonged to the Indian communities as its central task, and to fight for the creation of a Mapuche peasant federation.

The period from the middle of the 1950s to the middle 1960s was a decade of great mobilization of the peasant and Indian masses. At this time, the Christian peasant movements reached a peak, and were made up of two large Christian Federations and one smaller one. They are the following:

1. the Unity of Christian Peasants (UCC, La Unión de Campesinos Cristianos);
2. the National Association of Peasant Organizations (ANOC, La Asociación Nacional de Organizaciones Campesinas); and
3. the Independent Peasant Movement (Movimiento Campesino Independiente).

Later, they were coordinated into the Peasant National Confederation (Confederacion Nacional Campesina). The Christian peasant movement now presented, as one of its principal goals, agrarian reform and also a detailed program for its achievement. This Christian peasant movement was protected, backed, and controlled by the Christian Democratic Party. The peasants played a relatively important role in the electoral triumph of that party's candidate for president of the Republic in 1964, President Frei.

The Communist, Socialist, and Workers' parties continued to help the poorest sectors of the peasantry, including the Indians, through their

---

[3] The word *industrial* was added because the unionization law of 1924, still in effect, made reference only to industrial workers.

General Confederation of Workers (Confederación General de Trabajadores). They united the four peasant organizations which they protected
into the National Peasant and Indian Federation (Federación Nacional
Campesina e Indigena). This was a union of the former Industrial Federation of Agricultural Workers, the National Association of Agriculturalists, the National Indian Association of Chile, and the Front of the
Workers of the Land. This federation supported the presidential candidacy of Dr. Salvador Allende of FRAP, the Popular Action Front (Frente
de Acción Popular), who was defeated by Frei in the 1964 election. This
peasant federation also promoted a program of agrarian reform as a
principal platform of its struggle.

In the mid-1960s, at the end of the period we have been discussing, the
progress of mass struggle and the organization of the peasant class was
impressive. It was undoubtedly the beginning of the mass peasant movement and the appearance of class consciousness that impelled them to
clear and definite positions in defense of their class against the landholding class. Fundamentally, this was rooted in the struggle for agrarian
reform and in the political action taken to bring it into effect. The growing
politicization of important sectors of the peasantry clearly indicates the
presence of such a class consciousness. It is true that in the Chilean case —
different from the Mexican Revolution of the 1910s and 1930s and the
Bolivian Revolution of the 1950s which were basically agrarian — peasant consciousness and class and political organization would not have
been possible without the help and intervention of the urban parties of
the petite and middle bourgeoisie and of the working class.

The last decade of the social history of Chile (1964–1974) was a
turbulent one in which a mass peasant movement crystallized for the first
time in Chilean history, as did its political and union organization.[4] But,
more importantly, this decade brought great revolutionary changes which
profoundly modified the socioeconomic structure of the country and
profoundly affected the national peasantry. The populist government of
President Frei began this process from 1964 to 1970, and the socialist
government of President Allende continued it until the last part of 1973
when he was brutally removed by a rightist military coup. Among all the
great changes this decade produced, two are of such a permanent character that it will be difficult for the new military government, however
reactionary, to overturn. They are the nationalization of the great mines,
especially copper, and agrarian reform. The latter produced, irreversibly,
the destruction of the hacienda system. It is obvious that neo-latifundism
will grow with the military coup, but it will be of different character than
the former great haciendas. Probably it will be capitalist agriculture based
on salaried labor rather than the system of "inquilinaje."

---

[4] There were more than 100,000 peasants organized in the three existing federations.

Another social fact in the agricultural sector which appeared for the first time in that decade was class consciousness among a large part of the peasantry. It will not be easily destroyed, even by the repressive practices of the new government.

This social process succeeded, more than anything else, in integrating the Mapuche Indians into the social struggles of the national peasantry. In the development of their social consciousness, the appearance of both peasant class and consciousness and indigenous ethnic consciousness can be observed. Although the Mapuches also fought for peasant unionization and were incorporated into existing peasant organizations, they formed their own Indian organizations, creating local committees, regional federations, and even a national federation. They also fought for agrarian reform, together with the inquilinos, rural wage laborers, small landowners, etc. But, at the same time, their struggle for land manifested itself in the proliferation of land-grabbing movements against the latifundists and even the small and medium-sized landholders with the object of recouping lands usurped by the latifundio. In the last two decades the Mapuche have held several regional conferences, seminars, and two national congresses. They established their goal of getting back their lands and freedoms through the class struggle, and they presented their cultural ethnic goals.

We can conclude that growth of the peasant social movement in the last four or five decades, but especially in the last decade, permitted the increasing development of social and class consciousness among indigenous peasantry. At the same time that this phenomenon integrated the Mapuche with their class, it did not eliminate, but rather increased, the parallel development of their ethnic consciousness as well. To what degree these two processes will combine in the future is difficult to predict, but one thing is clear — class consciousness and ethnic consciousness are not necessarily mutually exclusive, but when both exist their destiny is to combine.

Naturally, any social consciousness, and particularly class consciousness, is not an absolute or static feature, but rather it is a dynamic process which depends on the conditions of the class struggle in a given society. It is obvious that after the military coup in Chile this process suffered a vast retrogression. But during the previous decade, a first level of this process was attained and it is qualitatively irreversible; that is, it attained the initial phase of class consciousness. This is the equivalent of saying that the Chilean peasantry, at least the poorest and most exploited layers of it, entered a stage of conversion from a "class in itself" to a "class for itself."

388　BERNARDO BERDICHEWSKY

REFERENCES

AFFONSO, ALMINO
1971　*Trayectoria del movimiento Campesino Chileno*. Santiago: ICIRA.
BARRACLOUGH, SOLON L., ARTHUR L. DOMIKE
1970　"Agrarian structures in seven Latin American countries," in *Agrarian problems and peasant movements in Latin America*. Edited by R. Stavenhagen, 41–94. New York: Anchor books.
BAYTELMAN, DAVID
1971　*Planificación y reform agrarian*. Santiago: Impr. RR. PP.
BERDICHEWSKY, BERNARDO
1971　*Antropologia aplicada e indigenismo en los Mapuches de Cautin*. Santiago: CORA.
1972　*En torno a los origenes del hombre americano*. Santiago: Editorial Universitaria, University de Chile.
1973　"Agrarian reform in Chile and its impact on Araucanian Indian communities." Paper presented at the IX International Congress of Anthropological and Ethnological Sciences, Chicago.
BUNSTER, XIMENA
1964　Una experiencia de antropología aplicada entre los Araucanos. *Anales de la Universidad de Chile* 130:96ss.
CANTONI, WILSON
1969　*Legislación Indigena e Intergración del Mapuche*. Santiago: Centro de estudios sobre la tenencia de la tierra.
CIDA
1966　*Chile, Tenencia de la Tierra y Desarrollo Socioeconomico del sector agrícola*. Santiago: Comite Internacional de Desarrollo Agrícola (CIDA).
IDI
1972　Ley de Indigenas nr. 17.729. Santiago: Instituto de Desarrollo Indigena (IDI), Ministerio de Agricultura.
LIPSCHUTZ, ALEJANDRO
1968　*Perfil de Indoamerica de Nuestro Tiempo. Antología 1937—1962*. Santiago: Andres Bello.
1973　The "Law of the Tribe," the "Law of the Nation" and the "Law of Double Patriotism," in Latin America. Paper presented at the IX International Congress of Anthropological and Ethnological Sciences, 1973, Chicago.
PETRAS, JAMES, MAURICE ZEITLIN
1968　"Miners and Agrarian Radicalism," in *Latin America: Reform or Revolution*? Edited by J. Petras and M. Zeitlin, 235–248. Greenwich, Conn.: Fawcett.
1970　"Agrarian Radicalism in Chile," in *Agrarian Problems and Peasant Movements in Latin America*. Edited by R. Stavenhagen, 503–532. New York: Anchor Books.
SAAVEDRA, ALEJANDRO
1971　*La Cuestion Mapuche*. Santiago: ICIRA.

Problems of Identifying Ethnic Processes

V. I. KOZLOV

In a constantly changing world individual human communities are also subject to change. Some of them suffer substantial transformation and may even become extinct, while others in their turn may emerge. The contemporary ethnic map of Europe, for example, differs in content from the map showing the settlements of European ethnic groups at the beginning of the Christian era.

In many of their cultural and everyday habits Russians today differ essentially from Russians living at the outset of the century and the more so from those of the seventeenth century. The Russian ethnos did not exist as such in the thirteenth century: it had not yet emerged from the eastern Slavic community. Some peoples of the Soviet Union, such as the Turkmen and the Altaians, emerged only in the twentieth century. The formation of many African ethnic communities can be observed in our day.

In its development, ethnography gradually went over from the description of general and specific features characterizing the culture, everyday life, and other peculiarities of a group, to studying the changes taking place and analyzing ethnic processes. In the Soviet Union the study of ethnic processes developed chiefly in the 1960s. At present this subject commands the attention of ethnographers and sociologists of many countries but the basic trends of these studies and their methodology do not always coincide. This calls for an explanation of the trends and methods followed by Soviet scholars.

In Soviet literature one differentiates between ethnic processes taken in both broad and narrow meanings of the term. Ethnic processes taken in a broad sense are those which are manifested in a substantial change of any one of the basic features of an ethnos and, first of all, of the language and culture, although these changes may not influence directly the existence of the group. Hence, substantial changes in the material and spiritual culture and in everyday traditions, considerable language borrowings, the development of bilingualism, radical changes in the social pattern of the ethnic community, and other diverse phenomena may be regarded as ethnic processes.

In this sense the distinctions, for example, between the contemporary Russian or Ukrainian ethnos, on the one hand, and the Russian or Ukrainian ethnos of the beginning of the twentieth century, on the other, are conditioned to a considerable extent by ethnic processes. Although ethnic processes taken in their broad sense embrace a wide range of phenomena which have long been the subject of ethnographic study, the methodology of studying these processes is not yet adequately developed. In some cases a clearcut distinction between ethnic processes proper and other types of processes is lacking. Language changes, for example, are included in the sphere of language processes studied by linguists, while changes in the social pattern are among social processes studied by sociologists and other social scientists.

Ethnic processes taken in a more precise meaning of the term are processes leading in the final analysis to changes in ethnic self-consciousness which reflects existing ethnic ties. Changes in self-consciousness mean that one or another person or group of people has gone over from one ethnic community to another one. In the USSR and in other countries where the people's affiliations are determined in censuses and other statistical data on the basis of their nationality, ethnic processes may directly influence the results of the census.

Thus, the USSR censuses of 1959 and 1970 showed that the number of Karelians and Mordvinians had somewhat diminished: a part of them had become affiliated with the Russian community. Ethnic processes in the narrow sense do not embrace all the radical changes that take place in the language, culture, and other elements of ethnos, but only those that influence the ethnic identification of people.

Inasmuch as Russians, for example, still consider themselves Russians despite the sweeping changes that have taken place in their material and spiritual culture since the beginning of the twentieth century, these changes cannot be regarded as true ethnic processes. Ethnic processes taken in the narrow sense are easier to separate from language, social, economic, and other types of processes, and their study is important both from the point of theory and practice. It is on these processes, consequently, that we shall concentrate our attention.

In classifying ethnic processes I propose to distinguish between two main types: processes of ethnic division and processes of ethnic unification. The first includes processes under which a formerly unified people is divided into several independent ethnic groups or when parts of the ethnos break away to form independent units.

Ethnic division may be the result of more-or-less extensive migrations of parts of a group — such processes were particularly widespread under the primitive communal systems — or the result of the different social organization of the separate parts of a group which is growing numerically and expanding in territory, for example, the emergence of Germanic tribes and tribal groups.

In class society, with the emergence of states, political state borders began to play an important role in the division of social groups. Today processes of such ethnic division are a characteristic feature of African peoples, parts of which became confined territorially within different states, with attendant distinctions in their national development. However, here too, the processes of ethnic division are manifested not in their "pure" form but are combined with other processes, namely those of ethnic unification.

The merging of several previously independent ethnic groups (or their ethnically heterogeneous parts) into a single large ethnic community with an entirely new name or one borrowed from one of its ethnic components is a process of ethnic unification. It is these processes that are the most typical of our time and are the most widespread. They lead to a historically natural reduction of the total number of entities due to their merging with each other.

Processes of ethnic unity may be divided into three subtypes: those of ethnic consolidation, ethnic assimilation, and interethnic integration.

Ethnic consolidation includes processes when several ethnic communities (or parts of them), usually of kindred origin and having cognate languages, merge into a single one. The merging of the Western Slavic tribes (Polyane, Mazowszane, Slenzhane, etc.) into the Polish nation; the merging of the Eastern Slavic tribes (Vyatichi, Krivichi, Ilmen Slovenes, etc.) into the Russian ethnic group, and that of the Yomud, Teke, Goklen, and other tribal groups into the Turkmen people, can be mentioned here as examples.

Inasmuch as kindred ethnic components usually carry their origin from a once-united ethnic and language community, the development of ethnic consolidation in many cases can be regarded as a kind of dialectical negation of the processes of ethnic division.

Their development is highly influenced by a political factor — the uniting of components of a group within the bounds of an independent state, or those of a territorial autonomy within a multinational state. Thus the national-territorial demarcation that took place in Central Asia in the 1920s and the founding of Soviet republics there, accelerated and facilitated the consolidation of the Turkmen, Kirghiz, and other nations.

Ethnic assimilation is the ethnic absorption of alien ethnic groups living within a bigger ethnic community or one that prevails numerically in a given territory. It can embrace groups of national (ethnic) minorities of a specific state, for example, the assimilation of the Welsh by the English, or the Bretons by the French, etc., or immigrants who have settled permanently in other countries such as Italians in France, America, and elsewhere, which is a most frequent case.

One must, however, distinguish between natural and forced assimilation. Natural assimilation is brought about by direct contact of ethnically heterogeneous groups of people and is the result of the demands of their common social, economic and cultural life, such as ethnically mixed marriages. Forced assimilation chiefly occurs in countries where different nations do not enjoy equal rights; there it is the result of government policy or the policy of local authorities in education, administration, and other aspects of social life aimed at accelerating this process.

As for interethnic integration, it is understood as the process of interaction between groups with different languages, cultures, and other characteristics, within the bounds of multinational states. At present the processes of interethnic integration, as distinct from ethnic consolidation and assimilation, do not yet have a clearcut character; even in regard to Switzerland, where a number of factors (absence of national-territorial autonomies, wide-spread bilingualism and trilingualism, etc.) have stimulated this process to a considerable extent, the term "Swiss" carries mostly a political and not an ethnic meaning.

The chief aim of this paper is to give an analysis of problems dealing with the identification of ethnic processes at their intermediary and final stages. The first stage involves the emergence of the so-called ethnically transitional groups of people, i.e., groups gradually drawing away from their ethnic community.

Particular attention will be devoted to the mapping of ethnic processes. There are several peculiarities distinguishing the map as a means and method of studying the regularities of the territorial distribution of different phenomena, in our instance ethnic groups, from the text. As opposed to presentations in a text which may contain multilateral descriptions of the phenomena, or mention the conditionality or inadequacy of one or another characteristic and even contain debatable conceptions, the possibilities of the map are more limited. In most cases, the map can reflect only the basic aspects of the phenomena. At the same time, however, it offers a more precise method of identification, one that calls for a detailed elaboration of the terminology and conceptual apparatus and a clearcut definition not only of the substance of the mapped units and phenomena, but also of the indicators employed to this effect. It was while drawing up ethnic maps of the peoples of the USSR, the peoples of Europe, etc., that the majority of problems dealt with below came up.

The principal units dealt with in mapping ethnic phenomena are the ethnic groups. The concept of ethnic communities, which is the chief subject of ethnography, has of late received a more precise definition in

Soviet publications. However, a thorough elaboration of the scientific theory of ethnic processes remains a task for the future. It is important to note the expediency of making a detailed comparative analysis of this concept with concepts accepted among scholars of other countries. As for ethnic process giving rise to ethnically transitional groups of people, these have still not been mapped. Until now ethnic maps have shown only the end results of these processes but not their transitional stages. On the map of European peoples, for example, all ethnic units regardless of whether these are nations having statehood and characterized by a stable ethnic integrity or ethnic minorities which have become considerably assimilated are defined by the same methods and symbols.

In order to overcome the somewhat static character of cartographic depiction and to show particular phenomena in their development, one must single out certain major and easily observed states in this process. Their depiction on the map would give an idea of the development of this process both from the point of view of time and space. Limiting ourselves to assimilation processes which are at present most widespread in Europe and other advanced countries, it should be noted that their key stages include economic and social absorption, cultural assimilation, and as a final stage, ethnic transformation, which influences changes in ethnic consciousness.

Language transformation, i.e., transition to another language not only in external communications but also in family relations, is an important if not the key stage of ethnic transformation. Special note should also be taken of the distribution of ethnically mixed marriages, each of them usually disrupting the ethnic line of either husband or wife (children resulting from these marriages are usually incorporated in the prevailing ethnic group); the total number of such marriages may reflect the intensity of either processes under way.

This paper does not envisage a detailed analysis of each of the stages of ethnic processes. I should like to mention, however, that in concrete conditions some of these stages can be omitted. In Britain, for example, the Welsh who are assimilated by the English pass over the stage of naturalization; and the assimilation of immigrants from Ireland, for whom English has long since become a native language, does not include the stage of bilingualism and language assimilation. At the same time, other stages may appear, such as those connected with overcoming different religious and racial distinctions between the groups in contact. It is sufficiently clear that in Britain the assimilation of "colored" immigrants, particularly of Negroes from the West Indies and Africa, may develop only provided there is a sharp increase in the number of interracial marriages. Finally, the sequence of stages in ethnic development introduced in this paper may change in each concrete situation.

The identification and mapping of the different stages of ethnic processes or the "ethnically transitional" groups involved in these processes, may be achieved by observing two basic conditions. The first is to work out the ethnic nomenclature and define the criteria which may be employed in singling out the types of ethnic processes and the stages of their development. To what I have already said on the subject of this condition, I can add that in those instances when interaction takes place between groups of kindred origin, languages, and culture, but having considerable distinctions in numerical size and other parameters (Italians and Friulians in Italy, the Dutch and Frisians in the Netherlands, etc.) it is difficult to draw a line between consolidation and assimilation or consolidation and interethnic integration. Consequently, the ethnic classification which is being worked out now must in all probability envisage the existence of undifferentiated phenomena.

I refer once again to the fact that agreement has not yet been reached on the terminology and concepts used by the ethnographers and ethnosociologists of different countries. This concerns not only specific concepts (cultural adaptation and assimilation) but even the more general ones. A good example of this is the term "nation" which in some countries, including the USSR, is used first of all in the ethnic sense, and in others, implies a political meaning. Most certainly the time has come for ethnographers to turn their minds to the compiling of a multilingual dictionary of terminology.

The second major condition is to obtain detailed materials and, first of all, statistical data, which, on the one hand, would characterize ethnic processes according to the adopted system of classification and, on the other, would be localized from the point of view of territory. Of foremost importance in this respect are population censuses taking into account the people's ethnic (national) affiliation.

By comparing these materials with the results of language statistics, it is possible to define the different stages of language changes, from bilingualism to complete language assimilation, by comparing them with the data on citizenship, the stage of naturalization, etc. Unfortunately none of the world's censuses can boast of a sufficient number of indicators which could be used in determining the different stages of ethnic processes. Only a comparatively few censuses employ more than two indicators. In Yugoslavia, for example, censuses take stock of the people's ethnic belonging, native language, and religion; in Canada they show their ethnic origin, native and official language, religion, and citizenship. The 1970 census in the USSR took account of the people's nationality, native language, and knowledge of other languages of the USSR.

The inadequacy of census materials in regard to ethnic and language indicators, and even more, to ethnocultural indicators, which are usually not considered at all, can be considerably made up for by selective ethnosociological investigations. Of late, investigations of this kind were started in many regions of the country that were ethnologically interesting. In several areas (the Tatar Republic, for example) they have already yielded valuable materials for the study of ethnic processes. Similar ethnosociological investigations are carried out in other countries. Suffice it to recall in this connection the extensive work carried out by the London Institute of Race Relations in studying the position of "colored" immigrants in Britain. One can recommend once again that the content of the basic ethnic concepts and indicators used in such investigations by ethnographers and sociologists of different countries, and sometimes within one and the same country, be more or less identical.

With the fulfillment of the aforementioned conditions, other obstacles in the way of determining ethnic processes, particularly the mapping of "ethnically transitional" groups, would be overcome easily. For example, it is not so difficult to find cartographic means of depicting such groups, developing special symbols which enable to distinguish "ethnically transitional" groups from stable ethnic communities.

If necessary, special maps may be drawn up, showing ethnic processes; the standard ethnolinguistic classification may be replaced in this case by a classification according to types and stages of ethnic processes. It would be expedient to draw up maps showing the distribution of bilingualism and population groups which have gone over to the languages of other groups. One can hope that such maps will be compiled in the nearest future.

Detailed analysis of concrete materials on the development of ethnic processes in different countries calls for monographic investigations and consequently cannot be dealt with in this paper. My aim has been to draw attention to certain important but insufficiently developed problems, and to promote cooperation between ethnographers of different countries in the study of problems dealing with the identification of ethnic processes.

The Peculiarities of Ethnonational Development in the Polyethnic Liberated Countries

IU. V. MARETIN

The consideration of the liberated countries from the standpoint of their ethnic and national development presupposes answers to three main issues: (1) the ethnic structure of these countries; (2) conditions of development (factors of integration and disintegration); and (3) present-day trends of their ethnonational processes.

I. The overwhelming majority of the liberated (Third World) countries are ethnically (and frequently also racially) rather heterogeneous. This is mainly due to the peculiarities of their historical development, as well as the fact that building statehood in the Third World (a process which itself is in many cases far from being accomplished), as a rule, occurs before the establishment within a state of separate nations and even more so before the establishment of a single nation.

Each of these states incorporates anywhere from a few to several dozen or even hundreds of peoples (ethnoses). These states, according to the data of ethnolinguistic classification, are inhabited by a total of over 1,500 ethnoses. The complete record, taking into consideration all dialect and tribal groups, would be even more complicated (*Chislennost' i rasselenie* 1962). In this case, the African states south of the Sahara alone account for about 2,000 languages (*Voprosy sotsial'noi lingvistiki* 1969:136); South America, according to the calculations of the eminent linguist C. Loukotka, numbers some 588 languages (*Chislennost' i rasselenie* 1962:41), and thorough research into Indonesia alone proves over 350 ethnic units and more than 1,000 dialects (*Voprosy sotsial'noi lingvistiki* 1969:184–185).

In these countries, there coexist ethnic entities representing diverse stages of development and different levels of ethnic consciousness.

Included is almost the whole ethnic scale with its many nuances: tribes; groups of tribes; nationalities (*narodnost*) and groups of nationalities; nations, both homogeneous and heterogeneous. There occur also ethnic formations that are at an intermediary stage of transition from one level to another. These unities mostly are involved in the process of development of the entire state ("nation"). Various specific unities — ethnolinguistic, ethnocultural, ethnoeconomic and ethnoconfessional — are also represented.

Lastly, in recent years within the frameworks of independent states, one could observe the formation of new ethnoses popularly called "nations," for instance, "Indian," "Indonesian," "Nigerian," and others. Exceeding the boundaries of an ethnos (or kindred ethnoses), these units claim to be supranational formations. On the basis of the Marxist statement that nation (not merely a state-political unity) is the highest stage of development of an ethnos for the present time, the formations under investigation could likewise be regarded as supranational ones. Thus, these countries are characterized by ethnic pluralism.

The problems of ethnonational development, including those dealing with the Third World countries, have been intensively tackled by Soviet scholars (*K itogam diskussii* . . . 1970; *Etnicheskaia istoria Afriki* 1977; *Natsional'nye problemy sovremennogo Vostoka* 1977; *Iugo-Vostochnaia Aziia* 1977). An increased interest in these problems is also in evidence in American and European literature (Naroll 1964; Shibutani, Kwan 1965; Barth 1969; Schermerhorn 1970).

An analysis of these problems is of utmost importance to specify more precisely the concepts of "ethnos" and "nation," to establish accurate terminology, to more clearly display the types of ethnic unities, to build up a typology of ethnic processes, and to illuminate the influence of the national liberation struggle on speeding up the process of ethnonational development. The example of the liberated countries makes it crystal clear that ethnic unities are not static with sharply demarcated stages, but rather dynamic systems related to the whole complex of historical, ecological, and other developments and conditions (*Etnogenez i etnosfera* 1971).

The term "nation" can be confusing, since the various scholarly traditions use it in different ways. In our literature as applied to these states, it has one of two meanings: ethnosocial and state-political. The concept of "ethnos" also demands, as Iu. V. Bromley (1971) has shown, a dual approach: as ethnos proper (or ethnikos) and as an ethnosocial organism (ESO) representing an ethnos existing within the framework of a particular social organism. (One social organism can contain a number of ethnoses.) The ESOs at a certain stage of their development generate a sociocultural, historical and, as a rule, economic unity of peoples, i.e., nation in its Marxist interpretation (Bromley 1971, 1972, 1973).

The terms "ethnic development" and "national development" are not identical.[1] The first one is related to the evolution of ethnos proper and its attributes and can be applied equally to tribal and national levels. It is linked to the concept of ethnic identity. The second term is not only an index of the higher level of development of an ethnos (or of several closely related ethnoses) at the capitalist or socialist stage, but also has a state-political aspect of numerous component ethnoses that make up the present state and are within the range of its general development. In the course of this twofold process, some common ethnic features pertaining to the whole state can be formed, and it is but natural that these features and their intensity are somewhat diversified in various concrete cases.

Special terms have been advanced in Soviet science to delineate such ethnically complicated units: "national-political unity" (Bruk and Cheboksarov 1961), "ethnopolitical unity" (Bruk, Cheboksarov, Chesnov 1969), "regional," "ethnoterritorial complex," etc. In our opinion, the terms "polyethnic state unity" and "polyethnic state" are most appropriate (Maretin 1969; Ismagilova 1971; Barth 1969).

The suggested terms reflect the structural side of a unity with heterogeneous ethnic composition. If the dynamic characteristics are to be specified, they represent, in our opinion, a community of a specific type. Such a unit need not remain a mechanical combination of different peoples, but may result in the formation of a true single nation.

Such a nation, rather conventionally, may be called a polyethnic nation in a state of formation. In the present period the state-political content of the term prevails, but gradually, we may expect the consolidation of common ethnic traits.

II. There are, however, peculiarities and complications of ethnonational development of the liberated countries, apart from polyethnicity. A multistaged structure of ethnic unities is inevitably combined with a multiplicity of forms of economic and social life and is based on the latter, i.e., ethnic pluralism is supported by economic pluralism.

The whole socioeconomic structure of these countries is transitory. Most of them are characterized by economic backwardness, regional isolation, inadequate development of communication. Their economy, with several economic-cultural types within one country, is multiple in its

---

[1] The ethnogenetic process of the emergence of "several . . . independent ethnoses" as a result of migrations and assimilation including those occurring nowadays, is revealed by Bruk, Cheboksarov and Chesnov (1969:98–99). The formation of a "new nation" due to "merging of several heterogeneous groups of different nationalities-ethnikoses" is stated by Bromley (1972:78). An ethnogenetic aspect of the processes which nowadays take place in Africa is discussed in *Kratkoe Soderzhanie* . . . (1972:40–42, 1972–1973:60–61; *Ethnicheskaia istoria Afriki* 1977:3–17) and by Ismagilova (1971, *Sotsial'nye sdvigi* . . . 1977:87–121).

forms and frequently represents a series of branches that do not make an integrated system, a single economic organism. There are usually numerous local markets, whereas their common internal market is either very limited or has not yet been built up at all (*Natsii Latinskoi Ameriki* . . . 1964:139ff.; Maretin 1971:47–90; El'ïanov 1976).

The formation of a national state, as V. I. Lenin has shown, is specified by the economic necessity and is based "on common roles in the economy" of the country (Lenin vol. 24:385, vol. 2:207). As to the intensification of economic ties within the country, it is not only a means of uniting all the modes of economic life of the country, but also the basis for advance in the delivery of information, such a delivery being one of the supporting processes of the ethnosocial group (Arutiunov and Cheboksarov 1972:27).

Under these conditions, ideology plays a specific part in the cohesion of the society. The idea of development becomes a prevalent one, and "state power is proclaimed to be the main source and guiding instrument of progress" (Lukin 1969:38). Social consciousness under conditions of the low level of development of the Third World countries and their complicated social and class differentiation for the most part is refracted through the prism of interests of non-proletarian classes and strata. Ideology, (mainly bourgeois and petit bourgeois) has no clear outlines; a great role is played by the subjective factors.

The emerging bourgeoisie strives to turn the ideology of nationalism into its monopolistic weapon, neglecting class contradictions within the state ("nation"), treating national ties antihistorically, frequently shifting to reactionary nationalism. At the same time, because of the polyethnic character of their states, local nationalisms are growing more and more manifest (Simoniia 1972; Lukin 1969; Ul'yanovsky 1970:3–25; 1972:410ff.; *Zarubezhnyi Vostok i sovremennost'* 1974:v.2:95; Gafurov 1976:171–185; Emerson 1960; Silvert 1963).

After independence is gained, the state becomes a powerful guiding force of the process of ethnonational development. In the bulk of such countries (which are nowadays on the capitalist road) the existence of a single nation is officially proclaimed, though practically speaking state unity and single citizenship are implied. Parties and organizations common for the entire nation are officially encouraged. The degree of detribalization is exaggerated. National consolidation implies education in feelings of loyalty to the state. Thus an ideology of "state nationalism" is being developed. This approach reflects the objective necessity to preserve maximum cohesion in front of external and internal reactionary forces which often choose this time to stir up interethnic enmity. At the same time the danger of this approach lies in voluntarism, since the state is declared to be a primary condition and prerequisite of the formation of a nation. While the nation is believed to be formed by merging individual wills in common activity, what actually happens is that the state decree often replaces the quest for real ways of solving the ethnic problems (Starushenko 1967; Erasov 1971; Maretin 1976:91ff.).

Of great importance is the problem of the state (all-national) language and literature developed with every possible aid of the state. If the common language is not that of an ethnic majority, it spreads painlessly (the Indonesian, Swahili, etc.). In other cases serious opposition arises from the population using the other languages, not ranked as state ones. In a number of the states the question of preserving the language of a former metropoly, as well as the problem of the development of numerous local languages and literature, has not been quite solved.

The latter is especially complicated in the case of the countries possessing multiple languages with developed literature, where the interest of development of the whole state, however, demands a common language (India, Indonesia, a number of African states). The use of local languages, as a rule, for primary education and for the elimination of illiteracy of the adult population, brings about new and very complicated practical problems (development of written language, normalization of grammar, phonetics, etc.), still failing to accomplish the main task of uniting peoples of the country with the help of a common language. That is why one can observe a general push to reduce the number of languages taught (Le Page 1964; *Voprosy sotsial'noi lingvistiki* 1969; Ismagilova 1971:92ff.).

As far as culture as a whole is concerned, there is a need to eliminate colonial heritage from the spiritual life of society, to form a public ("national") self-consciousness, to struggle against imperialist propaganda, which encourages a "positive nationalism" (i.e., a nationalism collaborating with imperialism), to develop a feeling of cohesion and friendship among peoples of the country, to form a sense of unity of cultural values, and to struggle against tribalistic and separatistic tendencies and religious intolerance. The solution of this series of problems is closely related to a reorganization of the public education system, higher learning, and sciences (Dreier 1972; Agosti 1959, 1971).

The centers of the struggle for new, common national culture are the capitals and large cities; which often are industrial centers as well. They also serve as penetration grounds for influences that internationalize the sphere of material and spiritual culture. The results of migration also play a substantial part in ethnocultural development. However, it is in the cities again that interethnic differences which lead to the formation of associations of countrymen and to the display of ethnic patriotism (viz., the appearance of "tribal unions" in some African cities) are most apparent.

The religious factor is likewise rather important. If a population professes a single religion, that is an additional uniting force, but it serves as a divisive factor when representatives of an ethnos profess different religions (the case of Batakland, Indonesia, etc.). On the other hand, in countries where one or another religion is adopted as the state's religion, those who profess it are considered to belong to this "nation," while others are declared national minorities. Usually contradictions between groups of the bourgeoisie underlie religious conflicts.

At the same time, the bourgoisie employs a religion for sowing discord in order to strengthen their influence on the masses. In the case of the confrontation of interests of ethnically different bourgeois groups who, also differ with respect to religion, ethnic factors not infrequently play the leading part, pushing other factors into the background. The inter-bourgeois contradictions and religious differences grow into national enmity (Gordon-Polonskaia 1963; Ionova 1972).

The most important factor in provoking interethnic and interstate conflicts is the fact that the borders of the majority of the developing countries do not correspond to ethnic, historical, and economic groupings of peoples. This is in fact characteristic of the bulk of the polyethnic liberated countries, especially in Africa.

This factor, combined with contradictions among bourgeois groups and with ethnic prejudices has brought up armed conflicts between countries (Ethiopia and Somalia, Somalia and Kenya, Morocco and Algeria, etc.), as well as collisions within these countries. Some of such "inner" conflicts had an obvious character of national liberation movements and thus acquired an international significance (for example, the struggle of the former Eastern Pakistan's people for independence and the establishment of the Republic of Bangladesh).

The aggravation of interethnic contradictions is also promoted by non-Marxist scientific and popular literature. Psychological peculiarities of nations are given an absolute character: the nation is described as a "psychocultural unity," the implementation of a "national spirit," a "national idea," etc. On the other hand, the restoration of traditional values in a country built on a bourgeois-nationalistic basis brings about the hyperbolization of peculiar features in the history and culture of these peoples. As a result, declarations are not so much of cultural originality as of "cultural exclusiveness" are transformed into a cultural chauvinism.

A cultural-nationalistic strategy sometimes takes the form of promulgation of general concepts of unity and superiority of entire regions, continents, and races — from Maphilindo (the idea of unity of Malaysia, the Philippines and Indonesia) and Pan-Arabism to the theory of unity of the Latin American countries ("Latinidad"), pan-African "Nègritude" and "Africanité," etc. (Zubritskii 1960; Erasov 1971, 1972; Sagadeev 1964; Senghor, 1964).

This approach is antihistorical. Moreover, the fact that in each class society there exists the culture of the exploited and the culture of the exploiters is quite obvious. Furthermore, objective processes of ethnic development in localities frequently are neglected and the principle of national equality is not always carried on.

There are other ethnopsychological factors. For instance, the masses of society do not always consider the state to be a required social institution, both because of their corporative attachments to their own ethnos and because of their application to the present-day situation of notions formed about the state during colonial rule. A great hindrance are negative elements in the development of political superstructure, primarily those related to elitism on the part of groups exercising state power (*Tretii mir* . . . 1971; Erasov 1971, 1972; *Zarubezhniyi Vostok i sovremennost'* 1974).

A marked peculiarity is the presence in many Third World countries of nonindigenous populations, (the Chinese, particularly in the countries of Southeast Asia and the Indians in the same region, in Africa, Oceania, etc.). As a rule, the economic position of the nonindigenous population is very strong, with the "trade bourgeoisie" emerging principally from them. This fact arouses discontent in the aboriginal population, sometimes resulting in national enmity. Processes of natural integration (or assimilation) with the indigenous population are developing slowly and often involve merely a formal acquiescence of the nonindigenous population to the national identity promoted by the government.

All these circumstances hinder the transformation of the national idea into a factor in political and economic development; moreover, as Tiul'panov states: "National idea not infrequently becomes an instrument of exploitation and even suppression of some peoples by others, representatives of which have occupied a leading position in the organs of new power" (*Tretii mir* . . . 1971:7–8).

The above-enumerated intricacies and contradictions, which remained in the background during the periods of the national liberation movement and the all-national front, have interwoven and complicated the process of post-independence ethnonational development by aggravating the instability of new states. These issues have provided some foreign authors (including writers from the very liberated countries) the opportunity to describe them as only "feelings" or "necessities" of national existence in these countries (Emerson 1960). Meanwhile, the processes of ethnonational development, including those favoring the consolidation of a nation (or nations), occur in the liberated countries on a large scale, much more intensively than earlier in the countries of developed capitalism.

III. Ethnonational developments in the polyethnic liberated countries take two directions. First, the further consolidation of already existing nations and other ethnic units takes place within the framework of boundaries of the present-day states and the shift of units of a lower stage to a higher level of ethnic hierarchy (sometimes even avoiding certain stages). This is a natural process which contributes to the further objective of accelerating socioeconomic progress of the peoples and their ethnic development. Its free manifestation only promotes the rise of the anti-imperialist and democratic struggle unless there are influences of local nationalistic groups and pro-imperialist forces.

Second, the integration of all peoples inhabiting a country into a kind of macro-unity of supraethnic and supranational nature. Such a unit has not yet become a nation, since it possesses a polyethnic (frequently even multinational) structure. But a nation eventually will emerge only if interethnic centripetal processes are not interrupted, but, on the contrary, are increased through the accumulation of common features. Perhaps, the most exact definition of this process would be the term "intrastate national integration" (Ismagilova 1971:20–21).

Both processes described above essentially can be regarded as a single flood of ethnonational development moving in parallel but dual directions or streams: a centrifugal one leading to the formation of numerous equal unities (nations, etc.) within a multinational state, and a centripetal stream directed toward the more or less distant prospect of the formation of a single nation (heterogenous or polyethnic in its origin) (Maretin 1972; *Kolonializm i natsional'no-osvoboditel'noe dvizhenie* ... 1972:23–54).

Considering the liberated countries from the standpoint of the degree of ethnonational integration (or disintegration), one can define a number of types varying from countries with a single leading nation and numerous minorities retarded in socioeconomic respect (Cambodia) to countries with several large, developed nations and multiple ethnic unities with a different level of development (India). A specific type of ethnonational development is represented by the peoples that have no state of their own (the Baluchis, Kwids, etc., in Asia; the Ewe, Bakongo, Ashanti, Tuaregs, etc., in Africa; the Quechua, etc., in Latin America).

The emerging nations tend to become centers of ethnic attachment for kindred ethnoses which are either assimilated (the smallest ones) or gradually incorporated in them. These nations act, therefore, as cores (focuses, centers) of national consolidation (Maretin 1969: 21–27).

As concerns the state structure of polyethnic countries, it is evident that the proclamation that all peoples of a polyethnic country are a "single nation" does not solve essential problems of the development of the whole country and each of its peoples. Moreover, this declaration, which is of enormous mobilizing significance in the period of the national liberation struggle, neglects a series of most complicated ethnic problems, thus frequently aggravating them (Simoniia 1972: No. 1:10–101; No. 2: 89–100).

The declaration of self-determination demands a very careful approach, because inherent in its nature is the likelihood for abuse by local nationalistic forces, backed by interested imperialist countries. Eventually, the solution of the ethnonational problems depends on the socioeconomic basis of the country and the character of its political development. But the forms of a state system may favor or hinder ethnonational development. The experience of the Soviet Union in this respect is of great significance. The optimal solution seems to be not a number of microstates, nor the neglect of ethnic diversity, but a single state with a due consideration of interests of various ethnics (Bagramov 1966).

The most important factor in overcoming the above-enumerated complications is socioeconomic. As V. I. Lenin indicated, economic liberation is the very essence of the liberation. Hence, there follows the necessity of measures to serve as the basis of the further struggle for economic and social liberation of peoples of a country (elimination of the dominance of foreign monopolies, radical agrarian reforms, industrialization, etc.), encouraging the ethnonational progress of its peoples. In the end the complex problem of ethnonational development stands out as a part of the general question of socioeconomic changes.

The tendencies of ethnonational integration are, no doubt, progressive and inevitable (on a large, universal-historical scale) because they reflect the continuous course of ethnic history of these peoples under conditions of the middle and second half of the twentieth century.

Nowadays something like a beginning of a new circle of ethnogenetic process can be observed, since the recently started formation of the "Indonesians" on the basis of the Javanese, Sundanese, Madurese, Minangkabau and dozens of other large and small ethnoses of the "country of 333 dialects;" or the "Tanzanians," "Kenyans," "Ugandans," and representatives of other amalgamating nations in Africa; or the "Peruvians," "Colombians," etc., in Latin America. All these examples show elements of common culture are formed: national self-consciousness emerges; new ethnonyms (usually after the name of the state) arise under independent state status; on the basis of spreading common language, the increase in population migration, condensation of information networks, and mixed marriages begin to increase, etc. In other words, the elements of a new ethnos are growing, the ethnos being on a national level.

As to the speed of centripetal and centrifugal developments, in particular cases, it depends on a large number of factors. It can be stated that today the quest for integration does *not* predominate in the Third World. Where such integration processes are found, they may rightfully be called progressive only when they take a democratic form and represent the interests both of peoples inhabiting the state and of a universal democratic movement in which the polyethnic countries of the Third World have played a great part and will play an even greater one.

REFERENCES

AGOSTI, H. P.
1959   *Nación y cultura* [Nation and culture]. Moscow.
1971   *Problemy kul'turnogo stroitel'stva v nezavisimykh stranakh Afriki* [The problem of cultural construction in the independent countries of Africa]. Moscow

ARUTIUNOV, S. A., N. N. CHEBOKSAROV
1972   "Peredacha informatsii kak mekhanizm sushchestvovaniia etnosotsial'nykh i biologicheskikh grupp chelovechestva" [The transfer of information as a mechanism for the existence of ethnosocial and biological groups of mankind] in *Rassy i narody* 2. Moscow.

BAGRAMOV, E. M.
1966   *Natsional'nyi vopros i burzhuaznaia ideologiia* [The national question and bourgeois ideology]. Moscow.

BARTH, F., *editor*
1969   *Ethnic groups and boundaries: the social organization of culture difference*. Boston: Little, Brown.

BROMLEY, IU. V.
1971   "K kharakteristike poniatiia 'etnos'" [Toward a definition of the concept of "ethnos"], in *Rasy i narody* 1. Moscow.
1972   Opyt tipologizatsii etnicheskikh obshchnostei [An attempted typology of ethnic communities]. *Sovetskaia etnografiia* 5.
1973   *Etnos i etnografiia* [Ethnos and ethnography]. Moscow.

BRUK, S. I., N. N. CHEBOKSAROV
1961   Sovremennyi etap natsional'nogo razvitiia narodov Azii i Afriki [The contemporary stage of the national development of the peoples of Asia and Africa]. *Sovetskaia etnografiia* 4.

BRUK, S. I., N. N. CHEBOKSAROV, IA. V. CHESNOV
1969   Problemy etnicheskogo razvitiia stran zarubezhnoi Azii [Problems in the ethnic development of the foreign countries of Asia]. *Voprosy Istorii* 1.

Chislennost' i rasselenie
1962   "Chislennost' i rasselenie narodov mira" [Numerical strength and distribution of the peoples of the world], in *Narody mira. Etnograficheskie ocherki*. Moscow.

DREIER, O. K.
1972   *Kul'turnye preobrazovaniia v razvivaiushchikhsia stranakh* [Cultural transformations in the developing countries]. Moscow.

EL'IANOV, A. IA.
1976   *Razvivaiushchiesia strany: problemy ekonomicheskogo rosta i rynok* [Developing countries: problems of economic growth and the market]. Moscow.

EMERSON, R.
1960   *From empire to nation*. Cambridge.

ERASOV, B. S.
1971 Kontseptsii "kul'turnoi samobytnosti" v stranakh "tret'ego mira" [Conceptions of cultural distinctiveness in the countries of "The Third World"]. *Voprosy filosofii* 1.
1972 *Tropicheskaia Afrika. Ideologiia i problemy kul'tury* [Tropical Africa. Ideology and problems of culture]. Moscow.
Etnicheskaia istoria Afriki
1977 *Etnicheskaia istoria Afriki* [Ethnic history of Africa]. Moscow.
Etnicheskie protsessy v stranakh
1974 *Etnicheskie protsessy v stranakh Iugo-Vostochnoi Azii* [Ethnic processes in the Southeast Asian countries]. Moscow.
Etnogenez i etnosfera (diskussiia)
1971 *Etnogenez i etnosfera* (diskussiia) [Ethnogenesis and ethnosphere (a discussion)]. *Priroda* 2.

GAFUROV, B. G.
1976 *Aktual'nye problemy sovremennogo natsional'no-osvoboditel'nogo dvizhenia* [Actual problems of the contemporary national-liberation movement]. Moscow.

GORDON-POLONSKAIA, L. R.
1963 *Musul'manskie techeniia y obshchestvennoi mysli Indii i Pakistana (kritika "musul'manskogo natsionalizma")* [Islamic currents in the social thought of India and Pakistan (a critique of "Islamic nationalism")]. Moscow.

IONOVA, A. I.
1972 *"Musul'manskii natsionalizm" v sovremennoi Indonezii* ["Islamic nationalism" in contemporary Indonesia]. Moscow.

ISMAGILOVA, R. N.
1971 *Etnicheskie problemy sovremennoi Tropicheskoi Afriki* [Ethnic problems of contemporary tropical Africa]. Special report. Moscow.
Iugo-Vostochnaia Aziia
1977 *Iugo-Vostochnaia Aziia: problemy regional'noi obshchnosti* [Southeast Asia: problems of regional community]. Moscow.
K itogam diskussi
1970 *K itogam diskussii po nekotorym problemam teorii natsii* [On the results of the discussion of some problems of the theory of nationhood]. *Voprosy istorii* 8.
Kolonializm i natsional'no-osvoboditel'noe dvizhenie
1972 *Kolonializm i natsional'no-osvoboditel'noe dvizhenie v stranakh Iugo-Vostochnoi Azii* [Colonialism and the national liberation movement in the countries of Southeast Asia]. Moscow.
Kratkoe soderzhanie
1972 *Kratkoe soderzhanie dokladov godichnoi nauchnoi sessii Instituta etnografii AN SSR* [Abstract of the reports of the yearly session of the Institute of Ethnography of the USSR Academy of Sciences]. Leningrad. (Also 1972–1973, 1974.)

LENIN, V. I.
Polnoe sobranie sochinenii [Complete collected works] 2, 22, 24.

LE PAGE, R. B.
1964 *The national language question: linguistic problems of newly independent states.* London-New York.

LUKIN, V.
1969   "Ideologiia razvitiia" i massovoe soznanie v stranakh "tret'ego mira" ["Ideology of development" and mass consciousness in the countries of "The Third World"]. *Voprosy filosofii* 6.

MARETIN, IU. V.
1969   Ochagi natsional'nogo formirovania v usloviiakh bor'by za obshchein-doneziiskoe edistvo [Hotbeds of national formation in Indonesia in conditions of a struggle for all-Indonesian unity]. *Tezisy konferentsii po istorii, iazykam i kul'ture Iugo-Vostochnoi Azii*. Leningrad.

1971   Znachenie vnutrennego rynka dlia Indonezii i trudnosti ego for-mirovaniia [The significance of the internal market for Indonesia and difficulties in its formation]. *"Tretii mir": strategiia razvitiia i uprav-leniia ekonomikoi*. Moscow.

1976   Etno-natsional'noe razvitie Indonezii i problema tsentralizatsii i avtonomii [The ethno-national development of Indonesia and the prob-lems of centralization and autonomy] in *Strany i narody Vostoka*, vol-ume 18. Moscow.

NAROLL, R.
1964   On ethnic unit classification. *Current Anthropology* 5(4).

Natsii Latinskoi Ameriki
1964   *Natsii Latinskoi Ameriki. Formirovanie. Razvitie*. [The nations of Latin America. Formation. Development]. Moscow.

Natsional'nye problemy sovremennogo Vostoka
1977   *Natsional'nye problemy sovremennogo Vostoka* [National problems in the contemporary East]. Moscow.

Problemy kul'turnogo stroitel'stva
1971   *Problemy kul'turnogo stroitel'stva v nezavisimykh stranakh Afriki* [Problems of cultural building in the independent countries of Africa]. Moscow.

SAGADEEV, A. V.
1964   Problema "natsional'noi filosofii" v ideologii arabskogo natsionalizma [The problem of "national philosophy" in the ideology of Arab nation-alism]. *Sovremennye ideologicheskie problemy*. Paris: Humanisme.

SCHERMERHORN, R.
1970   *Comparative ethnic relations: a framework for theory and research*. New York.

SENGHOR, L. S.
1964   Negritude et humanisme. Paris.

SHIBUTANI, T., K. M. KWAN
1965   *Ethnic stratification: a comparative approach*. New York-London.

SILVERT, K.
1963   *Expectant peoples: nationalism and development*. New York.

SIMONIIA, N. A.
1972   Natsionalizm i politicheskaia bor'ba v osvobodivshikhsia stranakh [Nationalism and the political struggle in liberated countries]. *Mirovaia ekonomika i mezhdunarodnye otnosheniia* 1, 2.

Sotsial'nye sdvigi
1977   *Sotsial'nye sdvigi v nezavisimykh stranakh Afriki* [Social changes in independent African countries]. Moscow.

STARUSHENKO, G. B.
1967   *Natsiia i gosudarstvo v razvivaiushchikhsia stranakh* [Nation and state in the developing countries]. Moscow.

Strany i narody Voroka
1976 *Strany i narody Vostoka* [Countries and peoples of the East], volume 18. Moscow.
"Tretii mir"
1971 *"Tretii mir": strategiia razvitiia i upravleniia ekonomikoi* ["The Third World": a strategy for development and direction of the economy]. Moscow (Collaboration of S. I. Tiul'panov and V. L. Sheinis.)
UL'YANOVSKY, R. A.
1970 *Sovremennye ideologicheskie problemy stran Azii i Afriki* [Contemporary ideological problems of the countries of Asia and Africa]. Moscow.
1972 *Sotsializm i osvobodivshiesia strany* [Socialism and the liberated countries]. Moscow.
1974 *Socialism and the newly independent nations.* Moscow.
Voprosy sotsial'noi linguistiki
1969 *Voprosy sotsial'noi lingvistiki* [Questions of social linguistics]. Leningrad.
Zarubezhnyi Vostok i sovremennost'
1974 *Zarubezhnyi Vostok i sovremennost'* [Foreign East and contemporaneity], volumes 1, 2. Moscow.
ZUBRITSKII, IU. A.
1960 Latinidad i ego sushchnost' [Latinidad and its essence]. *Vestnik istorii mirovoi kul'tury* 1.

Contemporary Ethnic Processes in Siberia

I. S. GURVICH

Over the past ten or fifteen years, Soviet scholars have accumulated a substantial amount of material on the contemporary ethnic development of the aboriginal nations of Siberia, including the small ethnic groups of the Far North and the Far East of the Soviet Union.

An analysis of different ethnic processes in Siberia promotes the solution of the problem of the ethnic evolution of the nations of this vast region and, naturally, is of great theoretical and practical significance.

For most Soviet ethnographers, ethnic processes mean changes in specific elements and traits (the language, culture, family structure, everyday life, identity) which tend to modify these communities. Of all the factors influencing ethnic processes, researchers generally study changes in the territory of the habitat, population trends, the numerical strength of the population and of interacting groups of other nationalities, socioeconomic, political and juridical conditions, mixed marriages, etc.

In recent years all the nations of Siberia have made gigantic strides in their political, economic, and cultural development. However, due to differences in the natural and geographical conditions, levels of social and economic development, economic orientation, numerical strength, and the population distribution, ethnic processes of the nations of southern and northern Siberia differ in many respects. This calls for a special investigation of ethnic changes among the nations of southern Siberia, formerly engaged in farming and cattle breeding, and among the small ethnic groups of the north whose chief occupations include trapping, fishing, reindeer breeding, and hunting sea animals.

The nations of southern Siberia include the Burjats numbering 315,000, the Jakuts numbering 296,000, the Tuvinians numbering 139,000, and the Altaians who are 56,000 in number (*Itogi Vsesojuznoj perepisi* 1973:10, 11). Drawn to varying degrees into Russia's Market system prior to the Socialist Revolution of 1917, these nations did not experience the stage of industrial capitalism. Up to the Revolution, the dominant structure here was semi-feudal, with strong survivals of the tribal system. The development of these nations was hampered by the nomadic and seminomadic economy, primitive methods and implements in agriculture, and harsh exploitation by the tsarist government and the local rich. These factors tended to perpetuate the backwardness of these nations. As a result, individual tribal, local, and ethnographical subsystems were to a great extent isolated and thus have retained their unique cultures.

The October Revolution eliminated all forms of national oppression and ushered in an era of national statehood for the peoples of Siberia and the North. In 1922, autonomy was given to the Jakuts and, in 1923, to the Burjats. The year 1922 saw the formation of the Gorno-Altai Autonomous Region and 1930, the formation of the Khakass Autonomous Region. In 1921, the Tuvinian People's Republic was formed, and in 1944 it joined the Soviet Union as an autonomous region; in 1961 it acquired the status of an autonomous republic.

The selfless aid from more advanced Soviet nations to these national republics and regions brought about dramatic changes in their economy. Socialist industrialization, reconstruction of agriculture, and cultural upsurge resulted in substantial and complicated ethnic changes. At the outset of the socialist transformations, the Burjat language included a number of dialects differing in their vocabularies and phonetics (the Khorin, Selenga, Tsongal, Tunkin, and others). The Mongolian written language with its vertical script was the prerogative of the Lamaists and was inaccessible to broad masses of the people. In fact, the Burjats had no written language.

In the 1920s, the Burjat written language evolved, first on the basis of the Latin and then the Russian alphabet. That was followed by the development, on the basis of the Khorin dialect, of the literary language close to the spoken language of the Burjat. These were significant factors that largely influenced the consolidation of the Burjat people. The introduction of the Burjat language in the schools and the advent of newspapers, magazines, and radio broadcasting in that language helped to eliminate the dialect differences. The socialist reconstruction of agriculture and the setting up of large-scale collective farms allowed the former nomads to settle down.

The continuous expansion of the sowing area, the development of virgin lands, the transfer, in a number of districts, from primitive pasture cattle breeding to indoor maintenance of cattle and the large-scale industrial construction on the territory of the republic were all conducive to improving the condition of the Burjat people. These factors and, in particular, the appearance of large Burjat settlements that attracted the population of smaller ones undermined the archaic tribal structure of the Burjats. The former division of the Burjats into endogamous tribes that the tsarist government had tried to perpetuate for fiscal reasons lost its significance in the new economic and social conditions. This promoted the national consciousness of the entire Burjat people. It was further promoted by the national autonomy of the Burjats, the general growth of their cultural level, the development of national literature, and the appearance of professionalism in the performing arts and music.

Ethnically, the consolidation of the Burjat nation took place not only through overcoming the former isolation of individual ethnographic groups, but also through the merging with the Burjats of the so-called "equestrian" Tunguses who had long spoken the Burjat language. According to the Census of 1959, most equestrian Tunguses identify themselves with the Burjats. Thus, recent years have seen a substantial consolidation of the Burjat ethnos (*Istorija Burjat-Mongolskoj* ASSR 1948; *Narody Sibiri* 1956: 217–266; Zateev 1961; Vjatkina 1969).

The Jakuts have also made great strides in their ethnic development in this period. Formerly a backward outlying region of tsarist Russia, Jakutia has turned into a republic with a developed mining industry and agriculture. The abandonment of the seminomadic mode of life, the primitive natural economy, the shift of the population from separated homesteads and small villages to bigger settlements, and overcoming the isolation in family life have undermined the tribal forms of identity of the Jakuts and put an end to their archaic division into separate tribes. At present, young Jakuts usually have no idea of their parents' tribe of origin. All kinds of exogamous taboos have disappeared.

The socialist construction has smoothed away the differences that formerly existed between the Jakuts inhabiting the territory between the Lena and Amga Rivers and those inhabiting the Viluy, Upper Yana, Kolyma, and Olekma basins. This is also the case with the northern Jakut reindeer breeders whose mode of life in the past was closer to that of the nomadic Evenks than of the seminomadic Jakut cattle breeders. At present, the northern Jakuts are rapidly merging with the majority of the Jakut nation in their everyday life and culture, materially and spiritually.

Groups of Jakut-speaking Evenks and Evens in areas with a prevailing Jakut population are also coming closer together and in some cases merging with the Jakuts. The ethnic consolidation of the Jakut nation has, doubtless, been facilitated by the monolithic nature of the Jakut language. Following the evolution of the Jakut written language in 1922, teaching in the Jakut language was introduced not only in primary but also in secondary schools. The uniformity of the language accelerated the development of Jakut literature and stage art. At present, the Jakut have a well-developed culture which is enjoyed by the entire nation

(*Narody Sibiri* 1956 267–328; *Istorija Jakutskoj ASSR* 1956–1963; Gurvich 1960).

Consolidation processes have also been under way in Tuva. Prior to the socialist transformations, the country suffered from the feudal isolation of separate administrative areas, *khoshuns*, which were divided into equally isolated districts, *sumons*. That was accompanied by the survival of tribal divisions. The socioeconomic transformations carried out in the Tuvinian People's Republic (1921–1944) liquidated the feudal system. After Tuva joined the Soviet Union, the republic entered a period of stormy industrial growth. The setting up of large-scale collective farms and the great changes in cattle breeding — the basic branch of Tuva's agriculture — allowed the nomads to adopt the settled mode of life. This also provided for close economic ties, so that the former economic isolation of such ethnic groups as the Tuvinians-Tojins has been eliminated. According to investigations carried out in the republic, there has been a territorial mixing of different tribal groups of Tuvinians over the past decades, which is a graphic demonstration of the national consolidation process.

In 1930 the Tuvinian written language evolved. The subsequent evolution of norms in the Tuvinian literary language gave a powerful impetus to the liquidation of illiteracy and the development of Tuvinian literature and also was instrumental in doing away with linguistic and cultural isolation of some ethnographic groups.

Other factors promoting the consolidation of the Tuvinian nation include the establishment of the modern school system in the Tuvinian language and of a network of educational and cultural institutions and the development of professional art forms (Dulov 1952:420–472; Vajnshtejn 1961; Serdobov 1971).

In general, the ethnic processes under way in the socialist nations of southern Siberia that have emerged in recent times are expressed in the following ways: (1) the transformation of the traditional forms of culture; (2) dramatic changes in the languages accompanied by the disappearance of the dialects; (3) the liquidation of the outdated tribal structure; (4) the overcoming of the isolation of separate ethnographic and local groups; (5) the supplanting of tribal and local forms of identification by national forms; and (6) the incorporation of small, separate ethnic groups into the bulk of the nation.

To understand better the nature of the ethnic development of the nations of southern Siberia, it is worthwhile to follow the ethnic development of the Altaians and Khakasses which have recently emerged as nations. Prior to the October Revolution, the population of the Altai Highlands was divided into tribes and territorial groups largely isolated from one another. These tribes and groups had no common name or common ethnic identity. The collective term "Altaians" was used only in scientific literature, but the tribes — the cattle breeding tribes of the southern Altai; the Altai-Kizhi, Telengites, Teless and Teleuts, and the Taiga tribes of the Northern Altai; and the Tubalar, Chelkan and Khumandin tribes — differed in their languages and culture. In turn, the tribes were divided into exogamous families that existed as separate units.

The regional autonomy, the development of the economy and ways of communication, and the liquidation of the former cultural backwardness brought closer together separate territorial and tribal groups of the Altaians. Since 1920, ethnographic literature has referred to the population of the Altai Highlands as the Oirats, after the name of the folklore hero Oirot-khan. Subsequently, as a result of the consolidation of national identity, the tribal names were replaced by the general term, the Altaians.

Profound transformations in the economy and everyday life have largely smoothed away ethnographic differences among separate Altaian tribes. The ethnic and linguistic unity of the Altaians has been promoted by a literary language that evolved on the basis of the southern dialects. That has made it possible to introduce primary education in the Altaian language. Fiction also has been written in this language. However, the northern dialects have not yet fallen out of use. In view of the small number of the Altaians and of the limited vocabulary of their literary language which has emerged only recently, the Russian language plays a prominent role in the social life of the Altaians. Today the Altaians have consolidated into a single ethnic group whose culture combines unique elements of the traditional culture of the Altaian tribes and their age-old labor experience with the general Soviet culture (Potapov 1952, 1969).

The past decades have seen the rise of the single Khakass nationality. It incorporates five Tiurk-speaking tribes of the Minusinsk Depression: the Kachin, Koibal, Sagai, Beltir, and Kyzyl (*Narody Sibiri* 1956 376–420), whose economy and culture differ in many respects.

The most striking peculiarites have been observed in the ethnic development of the twenty-six nationalities referred to as "the small nationalities of the North and the Far East of the Soviet Union" which, taken together, number close to 151,000. Eighteen nationalities of this group inhabit territories north and south of the Arctic Circle. These are the Chukchee and Chuvins (14,000 in 1970), the Koryaks (7,500), the Asian Eskimos (about 1,300), the Itelmens (1,300), the Aleutians (about 500), the Yukaghirs (600), the Evens (12,000), the Evenks (25,000), the Dolgans (4,900), the Nganasans (1,000), the Nenetz and the Entz (29,000), the Selkups (4,800), the Kets (1,200), the Khanty (21,000), the Mansi (7,700), and the Saami (1,900). Eight nationalities of this group inhabit the Far East. These include the Nivkhs (4,400), the Nanais (10,000), the Ulchis (2,400), the Udeghe (1,500), the Neghidals (about

400), the Oroch and the Orok (1,100), and the Tofalars (about 400). The latter inhabit the Sayan Mountains (*Itogi vsesojuznoj perepisi* 1973:10).

In pre-revolutionary Russia these nationalities were the most backward. The remoteness of the homeland of these hunters and reindeer breeders from the country's cultural centers, the severe climate, the specific nature of seasonal hunting and fishing, and the entire nomadic mode of life resulted in the extreme isolation and separation of these nationalities throughout the ages. The socialist reconstruction of the economy of these peoples, profound changes in their culture and the entire mode of life, and their ability to overcome their former isolation have had a tremendous impact upon their ethnic development. The Koryaks provide a good illustration of these processes.

According to the Census of 1926–1927, the Koryaks were divided into two groups: the nomadic reindeer breeders (55 percent) and the settled fishermen and hunters of sea animals (45 percent). Although they maintained regular barter contacts, the seaside and the nomadic Koryaks did not regard themselves as a single nationality, as expressed in different names they called themselves.

The seaside Koryaks were subdivided into eight separate local dialectal groups. In 1930, the Koryaks were given national autonomy and the Koryak Autonomous Region was formed. The subsequent reconstruction of their economy and the setting up of large-scale fishing and reindeer breeding cooperatives helped to bring closer together the two basic groups of the Koryak people.

The appearance of the Koryak written language and of the local press and radio broadcasting smoothed away the dialectal differences of the past. Some minor dialects of the Koryak language (Itkan, Kerek) have disappeared completely. The settled mode of life of a substantial portion of the population and its concentration in bigger settlements have brought about frequent marriages between different groups of the Koryaks. As a result, national identity has overcome local identity. It must be noted that the consolidation of separate segments of the Koryak nationality is only part of the ethnic development of the Koryaks. Past decades have seen the combining of a small group of Evens with the Koryaks, in areas inhabited by the Koryak. Following socialist changes in the economy of Kamchatka, the local Evens have in many respects assimilated with the Koryaks. They have changed over from hunting to more profitable reindeer breeding of the Koryak type and have adopted the clothing of the Koryak reindeer breeders. Marriages among the Evens and the Koryaks have become quite common (Gurvich 1970:195–225). Similar ethnic changes are typical of the Chukchee, Khanty, Evenks, Nenetz, and other peoples in the north.

I shall not dwell in detail upon the numerous specific ethnic changes in the course of the development of the socialist nations of the Soviet Far

North and Far East. In general, the changes consist in overcoming tribal differences, in the merger of small ethnic groups, or in their incorporation with neighboring nations. These changes result in dramatic linguistic changes and bring about an essentially new ethnic structure of the peoples of the Far North and the Far East, eliminating the local and tribal forms of identity.

This review of ethnic processes in the nations of Siberia and the north would be incomplete unless we touched upon the growing ties between these nations with all the nations of the Soviet Union and primarily with the neighboring Russian population.

The development of industry and agriculture, large-scale housing construction, and sociocultural transformations in Siberia and the north attracted a great number of migrants to these territories in the 1930s and 1940s. At present, industrial development unprecedented in its rate and scope is taking place in the north of the Soviet Union. The Chukchee National Region in the north east is developing rich deposits of gold and nonferrous metals; the mining industry in the north of Jakutia brings in tin, gold, and diamonds; oil-and gas-processing industries are being built on the basis of the Soviet Union's biggest deposits of oil and natural gas in the Khanty-Mansi and Yamal-Nenetz National Regions. The Taimyr National Region boasts the gigantic nonferrous metal works in Norilsk and is carrying out a large-scale development of newly discovered deposits. (Slavin 1961; *Sever Dal'nego Vostoka* 1970). Industrial growth and expansion of modern ways of communication attract a mass of migrants to these areas.

According to the Census of 1959, the aborigines accounted for 46.4 percent of the population of Jakutia; 20.2 percent of the population of Burjatia;24.2 percent of the population of the Gorno-Altai Autonomous Region; 18.5 percent of the Koryak National Region; and 21.4 percent of the Chukchee National Region.

Although the migrants, chiefly Russians, normally settle in towns and industrial areas, the population of most villages in these parts is mixed in composition of nationalities. As a result, the nations of Siberia and the north have adopted a number of elements of Russian culture and everyday life over the past decades. In recent years, due to the spread of secondary and higher education and frequent contacts with the Russians, a substantial portion of the aboriginal population of Siberia and the Far North has become bilingual i.e., in addition to their native languages, the aborigines also speak Russian. This is of utmost importance for the nations of Siberia and the north, for it brings within their reach the entire spiritual wealth produced by mankind and contemporary art forms.

According to the Census of 1970, 66.7 percent of the Burjats, 41.7 percent of the Jakuts, 38.9 percent of the Tuvinians, 54.9 percent of the Altaians and 52.5 percent of other nations of the Far North and East were fluent in Russian. For some part of these nations, Russian has become the native tongue. Over the period between the censuses of 1959 and 1970, the number of such persons has increased in Burjatia from 5.1 percent to 7.4 percent, in Jakutia from 2.4 percent to 3.7 percent, in the Altai Region from 11.5 percent to 12.8 percent, and with the nations of the Far North and Far East, from 24 percent to 32.6 percent (*Itogi vsesojuznoj perepisi* 1973:10).

Marriages between the nationalities of Siberia and the North and migrants, chiefly Russian, have become more common. Special investigations carried out in a number of different places have shown that with the Nenetz, mixed families number some twenty percent (Khomich 1970:28–61). The Altaians also account for a substantial portion of mixed families. Nonetheless, the numerical, dynamic growth of all nations of Siberia and the north between the censuses of 1959 and 1970 is indicative of the stability of these ethnic communities. The closely linked processes of the internal consolidation of the nations of Siberia and the north and their growing ties with all the nations and ethnic groups of the Soviet Union are an indication of the profound progressive transformations currently under way in the vast territory of the Soviet Union.

REFERENCES

DULOV, V. I.
1952   Perezhitki obshchino-rodovogo stroja i rodovogo byta u tuvinstev v XIX – nachale XX vv [Vestiges of the communal tribal system and tribal way of life among the Tuvinians in the nineteenth to the beginning of the twentieth century]. *Sovetskaia ethnographia 4.*

GURVICH I. S.
1960   Sovremennye etnicheskie protsessy, protekajushchie na Severe Jakutii [Contemporary ethnic processes taking place in Northern Jakutia].
1970   Etnicheskie protsessy na krajnem Severo-Vostoke Sibiri [Ethnic processes in extreme Northeast Siberia]. *Preobrazovanie v khozjajstve, kul'ture i etnicheskie protsessy u narodov Severa*, 195–225, Moscow.

Istorija Burjat-Mongolskoj ASSR
1948   *Istorija Burjat-Mongolskoj ASSR* [History of the Burjat-Mongol ASSR]. Ulan-Ude.

Istorija Jakutskoj ASSR
1956–1963   *Istorija Jakutskoj ASSR* [History of the Jakutsk ASSR], parts two and three. Moscow.

Itogi Vsesojuznoj perepisi
1973   *Itogi Vsesojuznoj perepisi naselenija 1970 goda* [The Soviet population according to the 1970 census]. Moscow.

KHOMICH, L. V.
1970   Sovremennye etnicheskie protsessy na Severe evropejskoi chasti SSSR i zapadnoj Sibiri [Contemporary ethnic processes in the Northern

European part of the USSR and western Siberia]. *Preobrazovanie v khozjajstve, kul'ture i etnicheskie protsessy u narodov Severa*, 28–61. Moscow.
Narody Sibiri
1956   *Narody Sibiri* [Peoples of Siberia]. (Serija Narody Mira, *Etnograficheskie ocherki*), pages 217–266, 267–328, 376–420, 420–472. Moscow, Leningrad.
POTAPOV, L. P.
1952   K voprosu o natsional'noj konsolidatsii altajtsev [On the question of the national consolidation of the Altaians]. *Sovetskaia etnografia* 1.
1969   *Etnicheskij sostav i proiskhozhdenie altajtsev* [The ethnic composition and origin of the Altaians]. Leningrad.
SERDOBOV, N. A.
1971   *Istorija formirovanija tuvinskoj natsii* [The history of the formation of Tuvinian nation]. Kyzyl.
Sever Dal'nego Vostoka.
1970   *Sever Dal'nego Vostoka* [The Northern Far East]. Moscow.
SLAVIN, S. V.
1961   *Promyshlennoe i transportnoe osvoenie Sovetskogo Severa* [The assimilation of industry and transport in the Soviet north]. Moscow.
VAJNSHTEJN, S. I.
1961   *Tuvintsy-todzhintsy* [The Tuvinians-Tojins]. Moscow.
VJATKINA, K. V.
1969   *Ocherki kul'tury i byta burjat* [Essays on the culture and daily life of the Burjats]. Leningrad.
ZATEEV, V. I.
1961   Formirovanie i rastsvet Burjatskoj sotsialisticheskoj natsii [The formation and flowering of the Burjat socialistic nation]. Ulan-Ude.

Socialism and Ethnic Features of Nations: The Example of the Peoples of the Union of Soviet Socialist Republics

M. I. KULICHENKO

The proletarian revolution and the building of socialism bring new life to each nation. Socialism, by its very essence, causes profound changes in all spheres of the life of nations and nationalities. The liquidation of social and national oppression; abolition of private property and the substitution of public property, complete equality, and volunteerism in mutual relationships; close cooperation between the advanced and the formerly backward nations; the assistance of the former to the latter and the growing desire for unity with bigger and more developed nations on the part of more backward ones; as well as an increased concern of the Soviet Union for the national interests of big and small peoples — all this has ensured the rapid advancement of all peoples in the Soviet Union.

The liquidation of private property and establishment of national ownership of land, mineral wealth, water, forests, and so forth, have facilitated national consolidation. This has lifted the obstacles that used to hinder national ties between various parts of the nation and even individuals. It is under conditions of socialism that all Ukrainian, Belorussian, Latvian and Moldavian lands were reunited, and national delimitation of the peoples in Central Asia and Kazakhstan took place. In this connection one may recall that before the October Revolution, czarism and capitalism arbitrarily divided many peoples: the Turkmen and the Tajiks were divided into two groups; the Kazakhs and the Uzbeks into three; the Kirghiz into four; the Tatars into five; and the Chuvash into six.

The unification, more than half a century ago, of big and small peoples in a single Soviet multinational state on the basis of a socialist type of national relations ensured a qualitatively new character of universal internationalization of their economic, political, and cultural life. The common territory of each nation or nationality, in conjunction with the common territory of the entire Soviet people as a new internationalist community, has become an important factor in their coming closer together for the purpose of helping each people to solve common problems.

The social role of such an important ethnic feature of nations and nationalities as national culture has become a qualitatively new factor in the conditions prevailing in the Soviet Union. Based on Marxist-Leninist ideology and incorporating mankind's achievements of the past, national culture has become a major factor in the progress of nations and nationalities and of their contribution to the treasure house of world culture.

Illiteracy, which was considered a major indication of people's backwardness before the October Revolution, was virtually abolished before World War II. All peoples in the Soviet Union are now completing the transfer to universal, full secondary schooling.

School in the Soviet Union functions primarily as a national institution. For instance, in the Moldavian republic, where by the late sixties the Moldavians accounted for 64.6 percent of the entire population, instruction in 65 percent of all schools was in Moldavian; in Turkmenia, where the Turkmen comprised 65.6 percent of the republic's population, 76 percent of schools were Turkmen in the late sixties. The needs of people of other nationalities living in the given republic are also taken into consideration. In Turkmenia, for example, 8.3 percent of all schools were Russian, 4.9 percent Uzbek, 2.9 percent Kazakh, and about 8 percent were mixed Turkmen-Russian, Turkmen-Kazakh, Russian-Uzbek, and others. In 1971 textbooks and other aids for general schools were published in fifty-two languages of the peoples inhabiting the Soviet Union.

During the years of Soviet power, skilled personnel with higher and secondary education have been trained in the union and autonomous republics of the Soviet Union. A higher rate of growth of the number of national personnel was registered in the republics of Central Asia and Kazakhstan, the Transcaucasus, and the autonomous republics along the Volga and in the North Caucasus. At present, the rate of training specialists in nine of the fifteen union republics and in seventeen of the twenty autonomous republics is higher than the average rate for the Soviet Union as a whole. With a total growth in the number of secondary school students amounting to 55 percent during the period 1962–1963 and 1969–1970 for the entire country, the number of students — Kazakhs, Moldavians, Turkmen — increased by almost 100 percent, and Uzbeks, Azerbaijanians, Kirghiz, Tajiks, and others by over 100 percent.

An enormous growth in the number of books and magazines published in the native language is an important factor in the life of socialist nations and nationalities. In 1913 not a single book or pamphlet was published in the Turkmen, Tajik, and Kirghiz languages, whereas in 1971, 3.95 million copies of 275 books and pamphlets in Turkmen were published, 3.85 million copies of 397 books and pamphlets in Tajik, and 3.79 million copies of 446 of the same in Kirghiz.

If we take national languages in which literature was published in pre-revolutionary times, the picture is no less striking. Book publication in 1970 compared with 1913 was 20.4 times greater in Armenian, 28.6 times in Georgian, 79 times in Kazakh, 134 times in Ukrainian and 268 times in Uzbek.

Newspaper and magazine circulation is very wide. In 1971 there were 66 books and magazines per 100 persons in Usbekistan. The comparable figures per 100 persons were: 67 in the Ukraine, 89 in Georgia, 92 in Moldavia, 119 in Lithuania, 135 in Latvia and 159 in Estonia. Out of a total of 3.2 thousand million copies of books and pamphlets printed in the Ukraine during the years of Soviet power, 2.4 thousand million were in the Ukrainian language. At present almost two-thirds of all newspapers and magazines are published in Ukrainian in that republic.

Many peoples have reached heights of art and culture only in Soviet times, a fact testifying to great changes in the development of national cultures under the impact of socialism. Dozens of nations and nationalities have for the first time created their symphony and jazz music, opera, ballet, and fine arts.

Culture has virtually become part and parcel of people's lives. In Kazakhstan, for instance, there were twenty-four professional theaters and sixty people's (amateur) theaters, fifteen philharmonic societies, 7,164 clubs and Houses of Culture, and 7,650 libraries by the end of 1970. Amateur art activities are widespread. In the Ukraine alone more than 3.5 million people participate in various forms of amateur art. All in all, there are 23 million amateur art enthusiasts in the Soviet Union.

Literature and arts of nations and nationalities reflect processes of their national development. And they also reflect international processes. In the Soviet Union national cultures influence and enrich one another, thus forming one Soviet culture. A single whole in its national multiformity, Soviet culture is not merely a sum total of national cultures but is the highest synthesis of the best achievements of each one of them, exerting an enormous influence on the intellectual life of each people.

The growing role and popularity of foreign literature in translation is an important factor in the coming closer together, mutual influence, and mutual enrichment of national cultures. In 1971 books and pamphlets were translated from sixty-four languages of the Soviet peoples and forty-five languages of peoples of other countries; all in all, more than 159.3 million copies of 7,417 titles have been translated into eighty-nine languages of the peoples of the Soviet Union this year.

In the Ukraine, more than 230 million copies of 9,000 book titles of classical and modern Russian literature were published in the fifty-odd years of Soviet power, as well as 2,000 titles of Belorussian, Georgian, Armenian, Latvian, and other literatures. At the same time works by Oles Gonchar have been translated into twenty-three languages of the Soviet peoples, and works by Alexander Korneichuk into twenty languages, to mention but a few. As many as 700 books by Estonian authors have been translated into thirty-seven Soviet languages and appeared in 77 million copies. The novel *Abai* by the Kazakh writer, Mukhtar Auezov, has appeared in twenty-nine languages. More than 200 works by Tatar writers and poets alone have been translated in the Chuvach language. Works by Udmurt writers have been translated into fifteen languages of the Soviet peoples.

The community of language plays a qualitatively new role in people's lives under socialism.

In Lenin's view, the development of nationalities into nations already under capitalism leads to a re-creation of language. However, under the power of the bourgeoisie, some nations often develop at the expense of others, and therefore the development of national languages cannot be universal and free. On the other hand, socialism greatly accelerates this process and involves all peoples, big and small, in it.

The formation of language community under socialism is ensured above all, by a genuine freedom of development of each language. This is prompted not by people's will but the objective necessity of the development of language, for without it the national advancement of the peoples (their economic and cultural progress and their sociopolitical activity) is out of the question.

During the years of socialist construction more than forty languages acquired a written form; this fact testifies to the growing role of language community in people's life. Even "the lowest of the low," the formerly oppressed peoples who, before socialism, were merely an object of history, often doomed to extinction, have become the creators of history and their languages have become literary ones. Before the October Revolution literature was created in only thirteen languages of the Russian peoples, whereas now there are seventy-five such languages.

The consolidating and merging of dialects has created a language community for the nationalities involved, and vocabularies have been enriched. The social function of language has grown immeasurably; within a short period of time, national languages have become the medium of instruction and of state office procedure and a means of developing science and technology, the press and radio, literature and art.

Along with the development of national languages and in view of the requirements of the economic and political life and the peoples' cultural advancement in Soviet society, the significance of the Russian language is steadily growing. Russian, not being a state language, has become, on a voluntary basis, a means of intercourse between nations. According to the 1926 Census, 6.5 million non-Russian people named Russian their native language, and in 1970 the number of such people grew to 13 million. The number of people who know Russian as well as their native tongue has almost doubled.

It is important to emphasize that the growing role of the Russian language as a means of communication between nations, far from weakening the development of national languages, accelerates it. This is due, first, to enriching the vocabulary and expressiveness of national languages with the help of Russian. Second, the use of the Russian language, along with the native tongue contributes to the national literature and the arts. Third, Russian provides an outlet to cultural treasures of all other peoples of the Soviet Union and to world culture.

The socialist system has also changed radically the way of life, customs, and traditions of nations and nationalities.

The improved living standards of the population ensured by socialism, abolition of distinctions between town and countryside and between mental and manual labor, industrialization of production and introduction of scientific and technological achievements are exerting a profound influence on people's lives. Fifty-seven percent of the Soviet population live in towns, and the peasant way of life is no longer very different from that of town and city dwellers. At present one can hardly find a village that does not have electricity and radio.

In all republics, reconstruction of villages has now been launched on a broad scale with a view to turning them into urban-style settlements with central heating, running water, sewage systems, and cultural and public catering facilities in each settlement. This will transform the life of each nation and nationality to a still greater extent.

Considerable change has occurred in customs and traditions. Those leading to national isolation, fostering national identity, and those connected with violations of freedom of the individual or disrespect for women have gradually withered away. Many customs and traditions have been transformed. In bourgeois Latvia, for example, the *Ligo* festival used to have a nationalist flavor, which it not longer has. Many new customs have come into being, reflecting the present life of the peoples. They often consist of elements borrowed from other fraternal nations and nationalities. Song and dance festivals whose birthplace is the Baltic country are widespread among many peoples; the harvest festival in the Ukraine now includes elements from traditional Belorussian *obzhinki*. The seeing-off winter festival in the Ukraine, Belorussia, and the Baltic republic has borrowed much from Russian traditions.

Mixed marriages also show the Soviet peoples' attitudes toward old customs and traditions and point to the new in ethnic self-consciousness. Soviet scholars note that in Latvia, Ukranian cities, Baku, and Tashkent, mixed marriages account for about one-quarter of all marriages, and in the Belorussian city of Vitebsk, about one-half.

The natural growth of uniformity of clothes in both towns and villages and the borrowing of certain customs and national traditions of other peoples do not at all mean the loss by a nation or a nationality of its own national "make-up," but only reflect internationalization of all spheres of their life. And under socialism, internationalization does not retard the national development of the peoples, on the contrary, it facilitates it, opening up new possibilities and prospects.

Changes in the distinctive ethnic characteristics of nations and nationalities cannot be regarded as purely quantitative. They have been radically changed and their role in the various peoples' social advancement has grown.

Erroneous views sometimes expressed in foreign literature state that socialism leads to a weakening of national consciousness and national feelings. On the contrary, great achievements of each people in developing their economy, culture, and Soviet national state have ensured a considerable growth of national consciousness and feelings, national pride in their progress, for their contribution to the common cause of all peoples of the Soviet Union building socialism and communism, and to the treasures of world civilization.

It should also be noted that the leap forward from the patriarchal-feudal and, in some cases, from the patriarchal-communal system to developed socialism, from the Middle Ages to the summits of civilization, has been accomplished within several decades by small groups who, before the October Revolution, were doomed to extinction. The turning of tribes and nationalities into socialist nations has been accompanied by a mighty upsurge of national consciousness and feelings. However, their essence has undergone profound qualitative changes. The liquidation of private property and exploitation and oppression connected with it destroyed the basis for nationalism and the former alienation of peoples, and engendered fraternal feelings and community of aims and ideals. National consciousness, national feelings of Soviet working people of any nationality, are permeated with proletarian internationalism and friendship for workers and peasants of other nations and nationalities. These feelings have consolidated especially in connection with the great mutual assistance which has played an enormous role in the relations between the peoples during the years of Soviet power.

Soviet patriotism, which has become a most profound feeling of working people of all nations and nationalities, is based on a combination of love for the native land, national pride for Soviet achievements, socialist internationalism, and devotion to the Soviet homeland and the ideals of socialism and communism. In the grim years of the war against Hitler's fascism, the Soviet warrior defended not just the native land of his people but the entire Soviet nation: "socialism as the homeland." In peacetime, each man's labor for the sake of the further advancement of his nation or nationality means also a contribution to the common cause of progress of the entire mighty family of fraternal peoples. Therefore national consciousness and national feelings do not oppose Soviet patriotism and socialist internationalism and come out in an indissoluble unity and merge in a single socialist consciousness.

These transformations in the ethnic features of nations and nationalities are due to the great advantages of socialism over capitalism. This should be mentioned particularly because views are sometimes expressed in foreign literature that the progress of nations and nationalities achieved in the Soviet Union should be ascribed to the general advancement of humanity, and not the specific advantages of socialism. Of course, the progress of humanity does influence the development of each nation and nationality in the Soviet Union. But never, at any presocialist stage of historical development have the people achieved such unprecedented progress during only one generation; nowhere has any other social system ensured such an active and genuine mass participation of all people in their national development and such comprehensive character of this development. It is common knowledge that dozens of small nations and nationalities saved by socialism from extinction have willingly joined the national historical activity and together with big nations formed a long time ago, are making a worthy contribution to the progress of humanity. Their contribution to implementing, for the first time in history, the theory of advancing to socialism while bypassing capitalism is invaluable.

If one compares the successes scored by the peoples in the Soviet republics with those in capitalist countries one will see the inaccuracy of the claims that the Soviet peoples have achieved such great success due only to the general progress of humanity and not the advantages of socialism.

In the late sixties there were more than 3.25 million Tajiks and over 1.5 million Uzbeks in Afghanistan; therefore it would be interesting to compare the development of Afghanistan with that of the Uzbek and Tajik Soviet Socialist Republics. At a time when the Tajiks and Uzbeks in Afghanistan are still at the patriarchal-feudal stage, the people of the Tajik and Uzbek Soviet Republics live under developed socialism and have become advanced socialist nations. One of the indices of progress is the per capita production of electricity: by the 1970s, 1,101 kilowatt-hours were produced in Tajikistan and 1,511 in Uzbekistan, whereas the figure in Afghanistan was 20, in Pakistan 47, and so on.

The number of students of higher educational establishments is also indicative. The latest data is shown in Table 1.

The number of doctors per 10,000 population in the Central Asian republics in 1965 reached eighteen (in 1970 the figure was 19.5), while in neighboring India it was 2.2, in Iran 3.3, and in Pakistan 1.7.

Such are the transformations in the ethnic features of nations and nationalities under the impact of socialism; such is their significance for the social advancement of the peoples of the Soviet Union.

Table 1. Number of university students per 10,000 population

Foreign countries			Soviet republics		
Country	School year	Number of students	Republic	School year	Number of students
Japan	1968/1969	119	Russian Federation	1970/1971	199
France	1966/1967	96	Estonia	1970/1971	175
Britain	1968/1969	83	Kazakhstan	1970/1971	165
Italy	1967/1968	70	Moldavia	1970/1971	143
FRG	1967/1968	48	Kirghizia	1970/1971	139
India	1964/1965	35	Azerbaijan	1970/1971	136
Turkey	1967/1968	36	Uzbekistan	1970/1971	134
Pakistan	1966/1967	27	Turkmenia	1970/1971	129
Iran	1967/1968	15	Tajikistan	1970/1971	118

The Development of Interethnic Relations in the Ukraine

V. I. NAULKO

The ethnic composition of the Ukrainian Republic today presents a rather complex picture. Apart from the Ukrainians, who form a socialist nation numerically second only to the Russians, and who account for some three-quarters of the Republic's population, there are considerable sections of other East Slavonic peoples (Russians, Belorussians) as well as Western and Southern Slavs (Poles, Czechs, Slovaks, and Bulgarians). From among other language groups, numerically strongest are Greeks, Romanic-speaking peoples (Moldavians, Rumanians), ethnics of the Urals and Altai language families (respectively, Hungarians and Estonians; Tartars and Gagauz), and finally Jews, who by and large speak Russian or Ukrainian.[1]

The non-Ukrainian ethnic groups living in the territory of the Republic are subjects of thorough investigation that parallel studies of the culture and daily life of the Ukrainians. Early in the 1920s this task was undertaken by the Ethnographic Commission at the Ukrainian Academy of Sciences as well as by a number of national scientific institutions. Currently a project is under way to compile a regional historico-geographical atlas of the Ukraine, Belorussia and Moldavia which marks a new stage in the studies of Ukrainian culture and daily life.

Considerable attention is given to ethnodemographic and ethnosocial processes. With this in view, several rural zones in the Ukrainian Republic have been analyzed for their ethnic composition and geographical arrangement of the various ethnic groups, as well as for the specific

---

[1] According to the 1970 All-Union Population Census, the total population of the Ukrainian Republic was 47.1 million, of whom 74.9 percent were Ukrainians, 19.4 percent Russians, 1.6 percent Jews, 0.8 percent Belorussians, 0.6 percent Poles, 0.6 percent Moldavians, 0.5 percent Bulgarians, and 1.6 percent other ethnic groups ("The population of our country," in *Pravda*, April 17, 1971).

features in their socioeconomic and historical development (Naulko 1971:9–10). The material for this study was collected with the use of a questionnaire (*Oprosnyi list* ... 1968) worked out in the N. N. Miklukho-Maklai Institute of Ethnography. It contained questions on ethnic identity and language, interethnic mixed marriages, sex and age structure, natural and mechanical mobility, and international traits in the culture and daily life.

During the years of Soviet rule, the unification of all the Ukrainian lands under a single socialist state resulted in an increase in the number of Ukrainians in the Republic. Significant changes have also been registered in the numerical strength of other peoples of the Republic (Naulko 1965:68–85).

The dynamics of the national composition of the Ukraine's population and the present geographical map of distribution of the various ethnic groups throughout the territory of the Republic depend on three processes: (1) the natural dynamics of the population (birth rate, death rate, and natural increase); (2) migration processes; and (3) ethnic processes. The dynamic picture of the Ukraine's population immediately reveals the tragic consequences of World War II, particularly of the policy of genocide pursued by the Nazi occupation authorities in the territory that temporarily fell under their rule.

One of the factors behind the marked upheavals in the ethnic composition of the Republic's population and in the geographical distribution of the various ethnic groups was socialist industrialization with its attendant urbanization. Thus, while before the Revolution over four-fifths of the Ukraine's population lived in rural areas (a reflection of the agrarian nature of the whole country) nowadays over half the population (60 percent in 1977) lives in urban communities.

The migration processes, greatly increased under Soviet rule, have contributed to the growing complexity of the ethnic composition of the Ukraine's population and have broadened the geographic distribution of Ukrainians throughout the Soviet Union. The planned socioeconomic changes and, above all, the shifts in the distribution of productive forces, have drastically modified the migration flows and changed their directions. On the one hand, the development of local personnel, particularly factory workers (Kim, Siniavskii 1963:58) and intellectuals, has minimized the need to attract migrants from other Soviet Republics. On the other hand, rapid industrialization of some areas, as for example, Western Ukraine, has turned "traditional" population outflow centers into focal points of population inflow.

The replacement of the Ukraine's population is considerably affected by the natural increase. A dramatic reduction in the mortality rate, resulting from the improved living standards of the Soviet people, is a typical feature in the Ukraine. Thus, as compared with the prewar period, the total death rate has been reduced by almost 1.7 times, while infant mortality has decreased ninefold (*O predvaritelnykh itogakh* 1970). At the same time, the Republic's population as a whole, as well as its separate peoples, show a tendency toward a lower birth rate, with a resulting decline in the average annual natural increase. Thus, in 1969, the natural population increase in the Ukraine was 6.0 per 1,000, while in Tadzhikistan the corresponding figure was 28.6; in Turkmenia, 27.3; and so forth (Bruk 1971:15).

The recent birth rate decline in the Ukraine is primarily a consequence of abnormalities caused by the war in the population age structure and in the relative proportions of men and women, which in turn adversely affected the marriage index (Bondarenko 1966:6). At the same time, it is difficult to find any death rate variations from one ethnic group to another, as justly noted by Bruk (1971:16).

The present-day ethnic processes in the Ukraine go in the direction of consolidation of the Ukrainian Soviet Socialist nation and promote further cohesion of peoples both on the republican and on the all-union scale.

The processes of ethnic consolidation of the Ukrainian people are closely linked with other trends in the development of that nation. Yet the growth of national consciousness, manifested in an emphasis on Ukrainian culture, and the growing cohesiveness of the Ukrainians with other peoples, has not led to the disappearance of various ethnographic groups (Gutsuls, Lemki, Boiki, etc.) which had established themselves within the Ukraine under specific historical, socioeconomic, and natural conditions.

The zones of ethnic mixing, particularly among heterogeneous groups, are characterized by natural ethnic assimilation shaped by a number of factors, such as the numerical strength and geographical distribution of the peoples, degree of kinship of their languages, social structure of the population, etc.

The majority of peoples making up the population of the Ukrainian Republic, along with their native languages, widely use Ukrainian and Russian. This constitutes an important medium of interethnic communication, instrumental in bringing the peoples closer to one another. Speaking about the functional distribution of languages in the Ukraine, it must be noted that most of the Ukrainian peoples are trilingual (i.e., they speak Ukrainian, Russian, and their native tongue), the native tongue being used mostly in the family and in daily life.

According to the 1970 National Population Census, 32.7 million people in the Ukraine gave Ukrainian as their native tongue; of these 32.3 million were Ukrainians and over 400,000 represented other ethnic groups (*O predvaritel'nyth itogakh* . . . 1970). The extent of usage of a language largely depends on how long the contacting peoples have lived together in a given locality. For example, the considerable proportion of

Ukrainian Belorussians who named Belorussian as their native tongue can be accounted for, in all probability, by a noticeable increase in their number in the Ukraine just in the past several decades.

The degree of distribution of a language and its functioning directly depend on the social structure, the ethnic composition of the population, and the geographical distribution of a given people. Among the Ukrainians, numerically the strongest people of the republic, and also in villages of uniform ethnic composition, such discrepancies are minimal.

The various peoples of the Ukraine from year to year grow ever closer to one another, manifestations of national isolationism or exclusiveness gradually disappear, as is evidenced by a steep rise in the number of mixed marriages under Soviet rule. A comparison of the marriage indices for 1969 with those of the mid-1920s,[2] calculated by soviet Ukrainian demographers, shows the unmixed marriage indices to have diminished by more than two times among the Ukrainians (from 80.3 percent to 34.3 percent) and the Russians (from 67.8 percent to 30.4 percent); by one and one-half times among the Jews (from 95 percent to 66.3 percent); by three times among the Poles, etc. (Naulko, Chuiko, 1970:50–53).

Social relations had been a powerful factor in the development of interethnic relations in the Ukraine of the past. Even within a single ethnic group, contacts among representatives of different social layers had been a problem. Thus, the Bulgarians who belonged to the social category of colonists and thereby enjoyed substantial privileges, were reluctant to intermarry with the Bulgarians who belonged to the so-called Boog Cossacks, for the latter, like their Ukrainian neighbors, were denied these privileges.

Today, national development is accompanied by a growing trend toward social homogeneity of ethnic communities. Unskilled laborers diminish in number among all ethnic groups making up the republic's population, which is a mark of scientific-technological revolution and indicates a leveling off of the socioeconomic standards of the urban and rural population (Arutiunian 1971:75).

Educational standards are an important indicator reflecting the level of a people's socioeconomic development and determining their social mobility. Soviet achievements are particularly impressive in the field of eradication of illiteracy. Suffice it to say that in the first years after the Revolution (according to the 1926 Population Census) only 44 percent of the Ukraine's population could read and write: among them 41.2 percent of Ukrainians; 55.5 percent of Russians; 48 percent of Poles; 27.1 percent of Moldavians, etc. (*Korotki Pidsumky* 1928:62).

The cohesion processes developing in the Republic on the basis of

[2]   The idea of marriage indices is to find theoretically substantiated measures of influence of certain personal traits (race, sex, age, social standing, etc.) on the choice of a prospective spouse.

ideological unity, social consolidation, and gradual obliteration of the differences between the working class and peasantry do not interfere with original national traits, but manifest themselves in the interaction and mutual enrichment of the cultures of different peoples, in the internationalization of their mode of life.

The current ethnocultural relationships in the Ukraine depend to a considerable degree on the historically evolved relations among the peoples, the levels of their socioeconomic development, natural-geographical factors and so forth. Thus, when the Greeks who lived around the Azov Sea switched from cattle-breeding to agriculture in the past century, it caused an upheaval in their culture and daily life.

Ethnocultural interaction is particularly noticeable where several ethnic groups are linked by a long history of living together in the same locality (for instance, the Ukrainians and Belorussians of Polessye, the Ukrainians and Moldavians of the Chernovtsy region). As often as not, this factor is no less serious than common ancestors. It is interesting to note that ethnic traditions persist most strongly at the periphery of ethnic territories.

Common terminology in various spheres of cultural and daily activities is one of the manifestations of interethnic relations and, to an extent, reflects the complex nature of the ethnoformation process. This feature is also most pronounced where different peoples have long lived side by side on a common territory. For instance, the Ukrainians and Moldavians in the Chernovtsy region use terms taken from both languages.

Some elements of the culture and daily life of the Ukraine's population have retained rather strong traditional features, particularly those which are of aesthetic importance or which have to do with some spheres of spiritual and social activities (interior decoration of the dwelling, elements of the national dress, dialects, folklore, etc.). Certain cultural phenomena exhibit clear ethnic specificity (popular use of Russian baths, preservation by the Bulgarians and Greeks of some elements of a South-European dwelling, traditional wedding rites, song festivals of the Ukrainian Estonians, and the like).

In the sphere of material culture, the viability of traditional elements is determined by their economic expedience and efficiency and only to a minor extent by the traditional notions, tastes, and national psychology. In densely populated areas, the various population groups, formerly heterogeneous in the ethnographic sense, have undergone a process of unification of their culture and mode of life. Thus, the Bulgarians who live in the region between the Proot and Dniestr rivers had come from different parts of Bulgaria, where they had been noted for marked differences in terms of culture and daily life. At the first stage in the development of Bessarabia they adhered to a type of dwelling most adapted to the new conditions: two rooms divided by a third one having an *aiyat* [open hearth]. The traditional Bulgarian garb has also been unified to a large extent; in most villages (even where different types of dress had been worn at first, a modified type, *rockley*, has become widely popular (Markova 1966:8–9).

The process of formation of new territorial communities marked by cultural homogeneity, which had begun in the capitalist phase, depended to a great extent on the national "traditions" and on the place of a given region in the social and economic life of the country. At first, the people's culture, particularly the dress and the dwelling, retained features reminiscent of their former homeland, innovation being introduced only minimally. Subsequently, socialist industrialization, increased mobility of the population and improvement of the socioeconomic standards, all gave rise to numerous common features characteristic of given cultural-economic regions of the Ukraine.

With the broadening of contacts among the various peoples living in the Ukrainian republic, the cultural-domestic homogeneity became progressively more pronounced. Thus, the Greeks, Bulgarians, and Gagauzes had long preserved the types of South European dwellings best adapted to the new conditions of their life. But by the turn of the century their dwellings already bore some likeness to the typical Ukrainian homes. At present, there are more elements in common than there are differences — in construction methods, floor plan, typology, decoration, etc., — between the dwellings of the peoples mentioned above and the Ukrainians.

The natural-geographical zones of the Ukrainian Republic partially coincide with the historical-ethnographical regions. In the past they played a more important role in the formation of cultural-domestic peculiarities of different localities. Even today, however, geographical factors still determine to a certain extent the lines of economic activity and the cultural-domestic peculiarities of the population. As an example, it is enough to compare the modern dwellings of the Russians living at the mouth of the Danube (Vilkovo) and in the neighboring steppe areas of the Odessa region.

In the years of Soviet rule, as an aftermath of collectivization of agriculture, and particularly in consequence of the consumer goods industry advances, urban elements in clothing rapidly spread in the countryside. The artistic concepts, imagery, designs, and forms, however, remained relatively stable, with only those alterations being introduced that are most in keeping with the people's idea of expedience and convenience and with some traditional elements being preserved (Mironov 1972:19–21). Modern garments, designed on a traditional popular basis, sometimes display elements of century-old ethnocultural interaction. Thus, it is easy to find characteristic traits of Moldavian garments in the *voloshka* shirt popular among the Ukrainians of the Transcarpathian region (Mironov 1972:24–25).

The elements of traditional folk culture, to a greater or lesser extent preserved by the Ukrainian population, constitute an important source for a student of ethnogenetic processes and ethnic history. For instance, for all the homogeneity of the traditional garb of the Russians living in some regions of the Ukraine (a bell-shaped silhouette of the unfastened upper garment, various kinds of peasant dress), it still exhibits some distinctions which link the Russians with their original homeland and which is indicative of their lack of ethnographical homogeneity.

The Ukrainian peoples' domestic culture is closely associated with the peculiarities of their family and social life. Thus, the open hearth of the Greeks and Bulgarians is associated with specific rites, family, and public festivities; it is prominent in the folk poetry of these peoples. The specificity of the family and social way of life is reflected in the interior of the dwellings, in the functional use of the rooms, etc.

There are many common features in the wedding rites of different peoples, related to the major stages of the wedding ceremony, its structure, the composition of the participants, rites, terminology. For instance, in some Hungarian villages of the Transcarpathian region, ethnically and adjoining the Ukrainian massif, the wedding rites contain elements in common with their Ukrainian analogs: the rites symbolizing the "purchase" of the bride; the custom of barring the bridesgroom's way (*pereymy*); the gathering of the youth of the day preceding the wedding (*gooski*); the "substitution" of the bride; the strewing of the path of the newlyweds; the act of admission of the bride into the group of married women, and so forth. This fact is all the more remarkable since in the past intermarriage between Ukrainians and Hungarians had been rare because of their different religious creeds.

Studying wedding rites, one should take into account the factor of ethnocultural interaction of peoples living in adjacent geographical territories. Thus, the present-day Ukrainian wedding in the part of the Ukraine bordering on the Moldavian Republic features a number of customs and rites typical of the Moldavians. These are manifest in the common terminology (the main treat is called *messamari*; the best men, *kunakariyi*) and in some customs (invitation to the wedding by treating to wine from a special ritual vessel, *plosky*, and so forth). In areas adjoining the Belorussian Republic, elements of the Belorussian wedding are visible (unbraiding of the bride's hair outside of the house, the custom of *zapoyiny*, etc.). Some elements of the Polish wedding are encountered in the Volyn region, in villages bordering on Polish settlements (Kravets 1958:70–71).

Modern wedding rites of most peoples living in the Ukraine acquire new forms and become infused with new contents, though they are all based on the century-old traditions handed down from generation to generation. Some of the archaic customs, particularly those connected with religious ritual and shot through with superstitions, are gradually disappearing; some elements are losing their magic import and remain only in their aesthetic capacity. Many of the once popular adverse cultural and domestic elements associated with the patriarchal and backward forms of life have vanished altogether (for example, the custom of hiding their face behind a red cape, *bulo*, required of Bulgarian brides at their weddings).

The ethnocultural processes currently developing in the Republic in the direction of further progress of the peoples and their cohesion take most diverse forms. The development of the culture and daily life of the peoples making up the population of the Ukraine is not an isolated process, but one unfolding against the background of interaction with all Soviet peoples, with new elements absorbing the best, most progressive traditions of the past and enriching all the peoples of the country.

REFERENCES

ARUTIUNIAN, IU. V.
  1971   *Sotsialnaia struktura selskogo naseleniia SSSR* [Social structure of the rural population of the USSR]. Moscow.
BONDARENKO, V. V.
  1966   *Problemy narodonaseleniia Ukrainskoi SSR i zadachi demografiches-kikh issledovanii v respublike* [Problems of the population of the Ukrainian SSR and the tasks of demographic investigations in the republic]. Kiev.
BRUK, S. I.
  1971   Etnodemograficheskie Protsessy v SSSR [Ethnodemographic processes in the USSR]. *Sovetskaia etnografiia* 4:15–16.
KIM, M. P., S. L. SINIAVSKII
  1963   Rost rabochego Klassa v 1953–1961 gg. [The growth of the working class in the years 1953–1961]. *Voprosy istorii* 3:58.
Korotki pidsumky perepysu
  1928   Korotki pidsumky perepysu naselenyia Ukrainy 17 grudnia 1926 r. [Short summaries of the Ukrainian population's correspondence of December 17, 1926]. *Statystyka Ukrainy* 5(124) Seriia I, vyp. 2. Kharkiv.
KRAVETS, O. M.
  1958   Suchasne kolhospne vesillia, zh. [The contemporary Kolkhoz wedding]. *Narodna tvorchist ta ethnographia* 2:70–71.
MARKOVA, L. V.
  1966   Nekotorye tendentsii razvitiia kul'tury i byta bolgar Iugo-Zapadnykh raionov SSSR [Certain tendencies of the development of culture and daily life of the Bulgarians of the Southwestern areas of the USSR]. *Pervyi kongress balkanskikh issledovatelei.* Moscow.

MIRONOV, V. V.
1972 Rozvytok ukrainskoho narodnoho kostiuma za radianskoho chacu, zh. [Development of the Ukrainian folk costume during Soviet times]. *Narodna tvorchist' ta ethnographiia* 2:19–21, 24–25.

NAULKO, V. I.
1965 *Etnichnyi sklad naselennia Ukrainskoi* RSR [The ethnic composition of the population of the Ukrainian SSR] Kiev, pp. 68–85.

1966 *Karta suchasnoho etnichnoho skladu naselennia Ukrains'koi RSR* [Ukr. Map of the ethnic composition of the Ukrainian SSR's population] Kiev.

1971 K voprosu metodiki etno-sotsiologicheskikh issledovanii v rayonakh etnicheskogo smesheniia [On the question of the methodology of ethnosociological investigations in areas of ethnic mixing]. *Vsesoiuznaia nauchnaia sessiia, posviashchennaia itogam polevykh arkheologicheskikh i etnograficheskikh issledovanii 1970 g. Tezisy dokladov.* Tbilisi.

NAULKO, V. I., L. V. CHUIKO
1970 Mezhnatsional'nye braki v Ukrainskoi SSR [Inter-nationality marriage in the Ukrainian SSR]. *Materialy ko II Vsesoiuznoi konferentsii po probleme 'Izmenenie sotsial'noi struktury sovetskogo obshchestva, vyp, 6.* Moscow.

O predvaritel'nykh itogakh
1970 O predvaritel'nykh itogakh Vsesoiuznoi perepisi naseleniia 1970 goda po Ukrainskoi SSR [On the preliminary results of the All-Union population census of 1970 for the Ukrainian SSR]. *Pravda Ukrainy* 4(30).

Oprosnyi list po
1968 *Oprosnyi list po izuchneiiu sovremennykh etnicheskikh protsessov v SSR* [Questionnaire on the study of contemporary ethnic processes in the USSR]. Moscow: Institut etnografii im N. N. Miklukho-Maklaia. A. N. USSR.

PTUKHA, M. V.
1971 *Vybrani tvory* [Selected works]. Kiev.

Biographical Notes

BERTALAN ANDRÁSFALVY. No biographical data available.

MAHADEV L. APTE (1931–   ) received his M.A.s from Bombay and London Universities and Ph.D. in linguistics and anthropology from the University of Wisconsin, Madison. He taught at the University of Wisconsin, University of Poona, India, and has been in the department of anthropology at Duke University since 1965. His major research interests are sociolinguistics; South Asian languages, societies, and cultures; ethnography of humor; and acculturation and ethnicity. His publications include numerous articles on various aspects of linguistic diversity in India and on the society and culture in Maharashtra, India.

WILLIAM ARENS (1940–   ) was born in New York. He received his Ph.D. from the University of Virginia. Presently, he is Associate Professor in the Anthropology Department of the State University of New York at Stony Brook and author of various articles and essays on ethnicity and change in Africa.

SERGHEI A. ARUTIUNOV (1932–   ) did his postgraduate work in the Institute of Ethnography, Moscow. He has worked in the same institution since 1954. He received his Candidat of History (equivalent to a Ph.D.) in 1962 and a doctor of history (equivalent to full professor) in 1970. He did fieldwork in Japan (Ainu and Japanese) in 1960 and 1963, in Vietnam (hill tribes of Haut-Tonkin) in 1958, and in the USSR among Eskimos of the Bering Strait (1959, 1962, 1963, 1965, 1970), the latter combined with archeological excavations. His areas of emphasis include ethnic anthropology, traditional culture of the Far East, and Eskimology.

BERNARDO BERDICHEWSKY (1924–   ) was born in Santiago. He graduated in 1956 from the University of Chile and did postgraduate studies at the universities of La Plata, Argentina; of Saarland, Germany; and of Madrid, Spain (where he received his Ph.D. in 1961). During the early seventies, he did research for the Agrarian Reform Corporation on the situation of the Mapuche Indians in the Agrarian Reform process in Chile. He was Professor of Anthropology at the University of Chile until the military coup of September, 1973, when he left the country and was teaching at CUNY, in New York, and at the University of Texas in Austin, Texas. He is presently Visiting Professor of Anthropology and Sociology at the University of Victoria, B.C. Canada. He has published extensively on the ethnology and archeology of South America, and also on ethnic problems.

VASILY K. BONDARCHIK (1920–   ) is a corresponding member of the Academy of Sciences of the Belorussian SSR. In 1952 he graduated from the Belorussian State university, then from the postgraduate courses of the Academy of Sciences; his thesis for a candidate's degree was "E. R. Romanov as an ethnographer" (1958), then the thesis for a doctor's degree "History of the Belorussian ethnography of the XIXth — the beginning of the XXth century" (1965); he is the author of the monographs on the historiography of Belorussian ethnography, on the activities of the prominent Belorussian ethnographers, of a number of works on modern ethnocultural processes, family mode of life, atheism, and folklore. He is the editor of a many-volumed code of Belorussian folklore, and of a number of monographs on ethnography and culture of Belorussians. At present he is the Chief of the Department of Ethnography at the Institute of Art, Ethnography and Folklore of the Academy of Sciences of BSSR.

YU. V. BROMLEY (1921–   ) received his B.A. in 1950 from Moscow University and his Ph.D. in 1958 from the Institute of Slavic Studies. He has been Director of the Institute of Ethnography in Moscow since 1966. In 1976 he was awarded the title of Academician of the USSR and, in the same year, became Vice-Secretary of the Academy of Sciences. Areas of interest include cultural and social anthropology of Slavic peoples, and problems of ethnicity in general. Among his publications (written in Russian) are: *Establishment of feudalism in Croatia* (1964); *Ethnos and ethnography* (1973); and *Main trends in Soviet ethnography* 1976).

EUGENIY PROKOPIEVICH BUSYGIN (1914–   ) Doctor of History, Professor at the Kazan University. After 1946 he started ethnographical studies of the peoples of Central Volga Region. He is the author of many articles and books on the culture and life of the Russian population of the Central Volga historical and ethnographical region.

W. S. CHOW. No biographical data available.

O. A. GANTSKAJA works in the Institute of Ethnography, Moscow, and she is a specialist on the ethnography of Slavic peoples, especially of Poland.

MOTĪ LĀL GUPTA (1910–   ) studied at the Universities of Allāhābād, Vārāṇasī and London and received M.A. degrees in Hindī, Sanskrit and English. He received his Ph.D. in manuscript literature of Eastern Rājasthān and D. Litt in applied linguistics. He taught Hindī, Sanskrit and Linguistics at the University of Rājasthān in the capacity of a lecturer and an associate professor, and later as reader and head of the department of Hindī at the University of Jodhpur. He guided research in linguistics, Hindī and Rājasthānī to about a dozen candidates, obtaining the degrees of Ph.D. and D. Litt. His main fields of study, at present, are dialectology, semiotics, manuscriptology and instrumental phonetics. He has attended several international congresses; vice-president 2nd World Congress of Phoneticians, Tokyo and co-chairman plenary session Montreal Congress of Phonetics. His publications include *Contribution of Matsya to Hindī, Linguistic analysis, Modern linguistics* and many others together with several research papers published in India and elsewhere. He has received awards from the UGC (India), and DAAD (Germany) and British Council (GB).

ILIA S. GURVICH (1919–   ) received his B.A. in History from Moscow University. In 1949, he received his Ph.D. and has been a Full Professor since 1966. He has worked as an anthropologist in the north of the Yakutsk SSR, and has also done fieldwork in the Kamchatka and Chukotka peninsulas. His main areas of interest are the cultural anthropology of northeastern Siberia (Yakuts, Evens, Yukaghirs, Chikchu, Koriaks), as well as general problems of modern ethnic developments among the peoples of the USSR. Since 1965 he has been the head of the Northern and Siberian Department of the Institute of Ethnography, Moscow. His publications include (all in Russian): *Ethnic history of the northeast of Siberia* (1966); *Culture of the northern reindeer breeding Yakuts* (1977); and numerous articles on related topics.

REGINA E. HOLLOMAN (1931–   ) did her undergraduate work at Ohio State University and holds three degrees from Northwestern University, an M.A. in Sociology (1956) and both M.A. (1967) and Ph.D. (1969) in anthropology. She did fieldwork among the Sän Blas Cuna of Panama in

1966 and 1967; among Latins and Appalachians in Chicago (1974); and in India (1977). She has also done postdoctoral work in computer simulation. She is Professor of Anthropology at Roosevelt University, where she has been since 1970. Her areas of emphasis are cognitive anthropology, and community development.

V. I. KOZLOV works in the Institute of Ethnography, Moscow. He is author of several monographs on demography and ethnostatistics.

M. I. KULICHENKO. No biographical data available.

IURI VASIL'EVICH MARETIN (1931–   ) graduated from Leningrad University in 1955 and completed a research studentship, at the University of Ethnography in Leningrad, in 1958. He has worked at the Institute since that time and is a Senior Research Fellow and Head of the Museum. His main interests are ethnonational processes, social structures, and the ethnology and history of Indonesia. He has published extensively on these subjects.

MAGOROH MARUYAMA (1929–   ) was born in Japan. He received his B.A. from the University of California at Berkeley and Ph.D. from the University of Lund, Sweden. He has been on the faculty at University of California Berkeley, Stanford University, Brandeis University, Antioch College and University of Illinois. He has been a consultant to government agencies including the Canadian Federal Ministry of State for Urban Affairs, U.S. Office of Economic Opportunity, National Bureau of Standards and NASA. His interests are the application of anthropology to community development, urban and regional planning, future cultural alternatives, and extraterrestrial community design.

VSEVOLOD I. NAULKO (1933–   ), Professor of Kiev State University (Ukrainian SSR), Doctor of History was educated at the University of Kiev. His basic research interests include modern ethnic processes, problems of ethnic demography and ethnocultural relations. He participated in the VIIth, VIIIth, and IXth International Congresses of Anthropology and Ethnology in Moscow, Tokyo, and Chicago and is the author of a number of monographs and teaching aids: "Etnichniy sklad naselennia Ukrainskoyi RSR" (1965); "Karta suchasnogo etnichnogo skladu naselennia Ukrayinskoyi RSR" (1966); "Razvitiye mezhetnicheskih svyasei na Ukraine" (1975), "Kultura i bit ukrainskogo naroda" (1977).

BORIS F. PORSHNEV (1905–1973) was born in Leningrad and received his B.A. in 1925 from Moscow State University. In 1943 he became Professor at the Institute of History in Moscow. Major publications (written in

Russian) include: *People's uprisings in France before the Fronde* (1948); *Essays on political economy of feudalism* (1956); *Social psychology and history* (1966); and *On the beginning of human history* (1974).

ROBERT E. T. ROBERTS (1915–   ) is Professor of Anthropology and Sociology at Roosevelt University (Chicago). A native of Chicago, he earned his B.A. (1936) in Sociology and Anthropology at Central Y.M.C.A. College (Chicago), and M. A. (1940) and Ph.D. (1956) in Anthropology at the University of Chicago. He has taught at Roosevelt University since 1951, with the exception of two years as Visiting Professor of Anthropology at the University of Liberia and two years as Visiting Professor of Anthropology at the American University in Cairo. His research interests and publications have centered on the fields of race and ethnic relations, interracial and interethnic marriage, social stratification, and social and cultural change. Since 1937 he has conducted research on interracial marriage, particularly in Chicago.

MICHAEL SALOVESH (1931–   ) studied anthropology at the University of Chicago (A.B. and Ph.B., 1956; A.M., 1959; Ph.D., 1971) and at the University of California (Berkeley). He has taught at the Chicago City Colleges, the University of Minnesota, and Purdue University; he is now a member of the Department of Anthropology of Northern Illinois University. His special interests include social and political organization, stratification, and interethnic relations; his continuing research in Chiapas, Mexico began in 1958.

HENNING SIVERTS, received his doctorate in 1959 at the University of Oslo and is now Senior Curator at the University of Bergen. In 1953–1954, 1961–1962, and 1964, he did fieldwork in Tzeltal and Tzotzil of the Highland Chiapas, Mexico, and in 1970–1971 worked among the Jívaro (Aguaruna) of the Montaña in North Peru. His other research interests include political systems, ethnicity, ecology and human adaptability in tropical forest regions, and language in society (cognitive systems and ethnographic procedures). Publications on the above topics include "The Aguaruna Jívaro of Peru: a preliminary report" and *Tribal survival in the Alto Marañon: the Auguruna case*.

ELLA R. SOBOLENKO (1936–   ) is a Belorussian, she was born in Gomel (Belorussian SSR). She graduated from the Belorussian State University (1959), then from the postgraduate courses of Academy of Sciences of BSSR, her thesis for a candidate's degree was "Life of Belorussians in the creative work of Jakub Kolas" (1967), she is the author of the monograph "Ethnological heritage of Jakub Kolas (1969), of sections in monographs "Belorussian people's dwelling" (1973),

"Changes in mode of life and culture of agricultural inhabitants of Belorussia" (1976), of articles on modern economical processes, family mode of life, and ethnical situation. At present she is the Head Instructor of the Department of Philosophy of the Institute of Culture in Minsk.

L. N. TERENT'EVA is Deputy Director of the Institute of Ethnography, Moscow. Her main interests are in the ethnography of Baltic peoples.

COLIN E. TWEDDELL (1899–   ) after basic education in Melbourne, Australia, completed his degree work successively in Far Eastern languages and civilizations (B.A., 1945, summa cum laude and Phi Beta Kappa), anthropology (M.A., 1948), and linguistics (Ph.D., 1958) at the University of Washington, Seattle. In between terms as a senior missionary with the Overseas Missionary Fellowship in China and the Philippines, he taught Chinese language at the University of Washington (1942–1945), and phonetics at Simpson Bible College (1951–1952); and since 1965 has been teaching anthropology and linguistics at Western Washington University. His main interests and publications are in Southwest Chinese and Philippine ethnology, linguistics, and religions, also in Oceania and amongst the Pacific Northwest Coast Indians; Bible translation; and intercultural confrontation. Present activities include preparation of a textbook on Peoples of Asia and a linguistic chapter for a Handbook of Indians of Washington State. He was elected an Outstanding Educator of America (1972; and is listed in American Men and Women of Science, 13th edition, and A.M.W.S.: Consultants (1977), and in international directories of scholars, linguists, and anthropologists.

WALTER P. ZENNER received his Ph.D. (1965) from Columbia University. His fieldwork includes Syrian Jews in Jerusalem and New York City, Arabs in the Galilee, and New York State government employees. He has taught at Lake Forest College and Haifa University and has been on the faculty of the State University of New York at Albany since 1966. He is currently working on a book comparing Jews with other economically specialized minorities.

NIKOLAY VLADIMIROVICH ZORIN (1923–   ) candidate of history, assistant professor at the Kazan University. He started ethnographical studies in 1955. He is the author of many articles and books on the ethnography of the Russian population of the autonomous republics of the Central Volga region.

Index of Names

Index of Subjects